THE COMPREHENSIBILITY OF THE UNIVERSE

The Comprehensibility of the Universe

A NEW CONCEPTION OF SCIENCE

NICHOLAS MAXWELL

CLARENDON PRESS · OXFORD
1998

Oxford University Press, Great Clarendon Street, Oxford OX2 6DP
Oxford New York
Athens Auckland Bangkok Bogota Bombay Buenos Aires
Calcutta Cape Town Dar es Salaam Delhi Florence Hong Kong Istanbul
Karachi Kuala Lumpur Madras Madrid Melbourne Mexico City
Nairobi Paris Singapore Taipei Tokyo Toronto Warsaw
and associated companies in
Berlin Ibadan

Oxford is a registered trade mark of Oxford University Press

Published in the United States
by Oxford University Press Inc., New York

British Library Cataloguing in Publication Data
Data available

Library of Congress Cataloging in Publication Data
Maxwell, Nicholas, 1937–
The comprehensibility of the universe : a new conception of
science / Nicholas Maxwell.
Includes bibliographical references.
1. Science—Philosophy. 2. Metaphysics. 3. Science—Methodology.
I. Title.
Q175.M4116   1998   501—dc21   98-7550
ISBN 0–19–823776–6

1 3 5 7 9 10 8 6 4 2

Typeset by Best-set Typesetter Ltd, Hong Kong
Printed in Great Britain
on acid-free paper by
Bookcraft (Bath) Ltd,
Midsomer Norton, Somerset

To
Clare Venables

PREFACE

The aim of this book is to change the nature of science. At present science is shaped by the orthodox view that scientific theories are accepted and rejected impartially with respect to evidence, no permanent assumption being made about the world independently of the evidence. This view is untenable. We need a new orthodoxy, which sees science as making a hierarchy of increasingly attenuated metaphysical assumptions concerning the comprehensibility and knowability of the universe. This is the new conception of science that I argue for in this book.

This new conception has a number of implications for the nature of science. One is that it is part of current scientific knowledge that the universe is comprehensible, even physically comprehensible (something not recognized at present). Another is that metaphysics and philosophy, instead of being excluded from science, are actually central to scientific knowledge.[1] Another is that science possesses a rational, if fallible and non-mechanical method of discovery (not at present adequately understood). And yet another implication is that the whole picture of scientific method and rationality needs to be changed. Instead of theories being assessed impartially with respect to evidence, they are assessed with respect to two considerations: (1) evidence, and (2) compatibility with the thesis that the universe is physically comprehensible. As we pursue the problematic aim of discovering in what precise way the universe is comprehensible, our knowledge and understanding improve; our aim improves, and with it the methods we employ to assess theories. There is positive feedback, in other words, between improving knowledge and improving knowledge-about-how-to-improve-knowledge. Science adapts its nature to what it finds out about the nature of the universe—a vital feature of scientific method which helps explain the explosive growth of scientific knowledge.

This new conception of scientific method has implications, not only for science, but for any human endeavour whose aim is problematic. It leads to a new general conception of rationality according to which, whenever our aims are problematic, we should try to improve aims and methods as we proceed, in the light of success and failure. This has implications for the gigantic task of creating a genuinely civilized world. And it has revolutionary implications for academic inquiry as a whole, the overall aim of which becomes to promote not just knowledge but rather wisdom.[2]

The subtitle of this book is, I must confess, in some respects misleading. The conception of science that I defend is not entirely new. It has its roots in the thought of the Presocratic philosophers, over 2,000 years ago. It is similar, in some respects, to 'natural philosophy' as created and pursued in the sixteenth and seventeenth centuries by such figures as Kepler, Galileo, and Newton, for whom scientific questions were inextricably intermingled with questions of metaphysics, philosophy, epistemology, and even theology. And in any case the view I defend has been inherent in the scientific enterprise from its inception; what is new is that I make explicit what has hitherto been implicit (but even this has implications for the nature of science, as I have indicated).

Aspects of the view I defend were explicitly used by Einstein in creating special and general relativity. Subsequently, Einstein advocated a view that resembles, in some respects, the one defended here.

There is another way in which the view defended here is not altogether new. I have been expounding a version of it, in and out of print, for over a quarter of a century. It arose from my realization that Popper's conception of science is untenable (Maxwell 1972*a*). My first account of the view was in a lecture I had been invited to give by Larry Laudan at Pittsburgh University in 1972.[3] The lecture was grandly called a 'Colloquium' and was, for me at least, a memorable occasion. I had a lot to say; half way through, we had to move to another room. Afterwards I discovered my watch had stopped; I had been lecturing non-stop for three hours! During my stay at Pittsburgh I had a long debate with Larry Laudan: he defended his 'problem-solving' conception of science while I defended my then new 'evolving-aims-and-methods' view.[4]

Despite all this, the subtitle of the book is not entirely misleading. In the first place, for most readers the view defended here *will* be new: my efforts to communicate the idea for over a quarter of a century have not met with overwhelming success.[5] In the second place, the view expounded in this book is such a radical improvement over earlier versions as almost to constitute a 'new' conception of science. Whereas before there were five levels to scientific knowledge, there are now ten. My earlier efforts at solving the key problems of simplicity and induction have, I believe, been improved to such an extent that they may be held to be new: see Chapters 4 and 5. I have tried to make the book the definitive defence of the view it expounds. I am entirely serious in my aim to change (for the better) the nature of science, and that of academic inquiry more generally.

I would like to thank Larry Briskman, David Crowell, Brian Easlea, and Katherine Crawley for their enthusiastic, critical support for ideas expounded in this book. I am especially grateful to Robert Seymour, Gordon Fleming, Chris Isham, Colin Howson, and Harvey Brown for helpful discussion and critical comments. I am grateful to Margaret Morrison, Donald Gillies, Marcus Appleby, and John Watkins for their comments on parts of the manuscript that they have read. Thanks, too, to Elliot Leader for constant encouragement. Above all, I would like to thank those students who reacted enthusiastically and/or critically to my lectures over the years at University College London on the themes of the book. I would like to thank the Philosophy Department at the London School of Economics for providing me with an intellectually congenial base after my departure from University College. Finally, I would like to thank my dear partner in life, Christine van Meeteren, for her help, encouragement, and love during the course of the writing of this book.

N.M.

London, 1998

CONTENTS

FIGURES

TABLES

ABBREVIATIONS

AOE	aim-oriented empiricism
B	blueprint
C	comprehensibility thesis
CP	classical physics
GL	Galileo's laws of terrestrial motion
GR	general relativity
KL	Kepler's laws of planetary motion
MQT	macro-quantum theory
MT	classical electrodynamics
NT	Newtonian theory
OQT	orthodox QT
PK	partial knowability of the universe
QCD	quantum chromodynamics
QED	quantum electrodynamics
QEWD	quantum electroweak dynamics
QFT	quantum field theory
QP	quantum postulates
QT	quantum theory
SE	standard empiricism
SM	standard model
SR	special relativity
U	unified something that determines all change in the universe
V	that which varies in the universe, determined by U

1

A New Conception of Science

1. HOW DOES SCIENCE MAKE PROGRESS?

During the last century or so, natural science has met with astonishing success in increasing our knowledge and understanding of the natural world. Science has, it seems, made progress at an ever-accelerating rate.

The question arises: What has been responsible for this progressive success of science? Before the birth of modern science, with the work of Galileo, Kepler, and others in the sixteenth and seventeenth centuries, knowledge grew in a rather slow, faltering way, an advance here being offset by a step backwards there. After Galileo and Kepler, the scene is transformed: scientific knowledge begins to grow apparently with ever-increasing rapidity, confidently embracing wider and wider ranges of phenomena. What has made this possible? Assuming that it is above all the exploitation in practice of so-called *scientific method* that makes this dramatic progress in knowledge possible,[1] what precisely *is* scientific method, and how does it make scientific progress possible? What is the methodological *key* to the unprecedented progressive success of modern science?

These questions are thrown into especially sharp relief by the long-standing failure of scientists, and historians and philosophers of science, to provide an acceptable account of how scientific method does make the growth of scientific knowledge possible. Most strikingly and dramatically, there is the problem of induction—the problem of how it is possible at all to verify scientific theories by means of evidence. Ever since David Hume (1959) first posed the problem in something like its modern form in 1739, a succession of scientists and philosophers have struggled with the problem: Kant (1961); Mill (1973–4); Peirce (1934); Duhem (1954); Poincaré (1952); Russell (1948); Hempel (1965); Carnap (1950); Reichenbach (1938); Ayer (1956); Popper (1959); Lakatos (1970); and many others.[2] Even though there are a few thinkers who claim to have solved the problem—most notably Popper (1972: 1) in recent times—nevertheless the consensus is, in my view correctly, that none of the widely known attempts at solving the problem succeeds. As science has gone from strength to strength, attempts to *understand* how and why science has achieved such astonishing progress have not met with comparable success. Science makes progress, but philosophy of science, it seems, does not.[3]

In this book I put forward a view of science, similar to Einstein's in some respects, according to which science makes a hierarchy of increasingly contentless cosmological assumptions concerning the comprehensibility and knowability of the universe. Corresponding to these cosmological assumptions there are methodological rules which, together with empirical considerations, govern acceptance and rejection of scientific theories. The more contentful of these assumptions (and the methods that correspond to them) evolve with evolving scientific knowledge; the more contentless are permanent items of scientific knowledge, upheld independently of empirical considerations.

This view, I shall argue, solves the central problems of what scientific method *is*, and how and why it is so astonishingly successful in enabling science to increase our knowledge of Nature. The view, which I call *aim-oriented empiricism* (for a reason which will emerge below), at the same time contains a diagnosis as to why other approaches to solving these key problems concerning the nature and rationality of scientific inquiry have failed. Aim-oriented empiricism, furthermore, has implications not just for the philosophy of science—not just for our understanding of science—but for science too. Not surprisingly, as a result of improving our understanding of science, we are able to improve science itself.[4] Indeed, as I have argued elsewhere, when the view is generalized there are fruitful implications not just for science, but for all of inquiry and, in a sense, for all of life.[5]

2. THE ORTHODOX CONCEPTION OF SCIENCE IS UNTENABLE

Aim-oriented empiricism differs from the orthodox view of science, upheld by most scientists, and many philosophers, according to which *the* distinctive feature of science is that laws and theories ought, ideally, in the end, to be accepted and rejected solely with respect to the justice that they do to the evidence, *no substantial thesis about the world being permanently upheld as a part of scientific knowledge independently of empirical considerations*. As Max Planck once put it, 'Experiments are the *only* means of knowledge at our disposal. The rest is poetry, imagination' (Atkins 1983, p. xiv). Or, as Poincaré (1952: 140) put it,

'Experiment is the sole source of truth. It alone can teach us something new; it alone can give us certainty.' Or, again, as Popper (1963: 54) has put it, 'in science, *only* observation and experiment may decide upon the *acceptance and rejection* of scientific statements, including laws and theories'.

Despite being widely accepted and immensely influential, this *standard empiricist* conception of science (as I shall call it) is untenable, as we shall see in more detail in Chapter 2. The basic objection is simply this. In physics, any theory, *T*, however well established empirically, will apply to a vast range of phenomena never observed, most of which, indeed, will never occur at all. It is thus easy to concoct endlessly many rivals to *T* which agree precisely with *T* as far as all observed phenomena are concerned but disagree with *T*, in arbitrary ways, for different specific unobserved phenomena. There will always be infinitely many such grossly *ad hoc* rivals to *T*, all as successful empirically as *T* itself. It is easy, indeed, to concoct endlessly many *ad hoc* rivals to *T* that are empirically more successful than *T* is. If empirical considerations alone govern choice of theory in science, on what grounds are these infinitely many rivals to accepted theories rejected, independently of, or even against empirical considerations?

There is a reply to this objection. Most of those who defend versions of the orthodox view recognize that considerations that have to do with the simplicity, explanatoriness, or unity of theories play an important role in science in determining what theories are accepted and rejected *in addition* to empirical considerations. This is true, for example, of Planck, Poincaré, and Popper. The reason, then, that empirically successful, *ad hoc* rivals to accepted theories are rejected is that these theories, being *ad hoc*, violate requirements of simplicity.[6]

But this reply fails (as we shall see in more detail in Chapter 2). It has at least two fatal defects. First, in persistently rejecting theories that violate requirements of simplicity, however empirically successful they may be, science in effect makes a persistent, substantial assumption about the world independently of empirical considerations, to the effect, at the very least, that the phenomena occur as if exhibiting simplicity (so that all *ad hoc* theories are false). This violates the central tenet of standard empiricism that no such assumption must be permanently upheld in science as a part of knowledge. Secondly, attempts to explain what the simplicity of a theory *is*, within the framework of standard empiricism, all fail. In Chapter 2 we shall see that there are further objections to standard empiricism, in all ten problems which the doctrine cannot solve.

3. THE FUNDAMENTAL EPISTEMOLOGICAL DILEMMA OF SCIENCE

The collapse of standard empiricism means that it is impossible to do science without some permanent assumption about the nature of the universe being made independently of empirical considerations. If no such assumption is made, the empirical method breaks down. Science becomes drowned in an ocean of empirically successful *ad hoc* theories.

But what ought this assumption to be? And on what grounds can it be made?

It might seem that this assumption ought to be the least contentful that can be made that makes theoretical physics possible. This idea will be considered and rejected in Chapter 3; further arguments against it will be given in Chapter 6. A basic objection to the idea is that it turns out to be impossible to formulate an assumption which is *both* (1) sufficiently precise and contentful to be incompatible with all empirically successful *ad hoc* theories, *and* (2) sufficiently imprecise and contentless for its acceptance to be justified on the grounds that, unless this assumption is made, science and the acquisition of factual knowledge more generally become impossible. An additional objection is that an assumption which merely excludes *ad hoc* theories is insufficiently scientifically fruitful; what we really require is an assumption that promotes the growth of theoretical knowledge, which guides us to the development of good new theories.

It is important to appreciate just how unavoidable and fundamental is the dilemma[7] confronting the entire scientific endeavour that we are considering here—a dilemma whose very existence is obscured by the acceptance of standard empiricism. If science is to be possible at all, some kind of assumption must be made about that of which we are most ignorant: the ultimate nature of the universe.[8] But even worse, it is above all here, where we are most ignorant, that it is vital, for the success of science, that we make as good an assumption as possible, one which does the best possible justice to the real nature of things. For it is this basic cosmological assumption that will determine our methodology, what kinds of theory we are prepared to consider. If, for example, we believe that a society of gods governs the natural world then, in seeking to improve knowledge of and control over natural processes, it will be entirely rational (relative to this belief) to adopt such methods as prayer, sacrifice, consultation of prophets, oracles, omens, and dreams. But if we believe that a pattern of physical law governs natural processes, quite different methods will need to be adopted, namely those of putting forward precise hypotheses concerning possible laws governing phenomena, to be tested against observation and experiment. Metaphysics determines methodology. This makes it of paramount importance that a good basic metaphysical conjecture is adopted, one which corresponds near enough to how the universe actually is. A bad basic metaphysical conjecture, hopelessly at odds with the actual nature of the universe, will lead to the adoption of an entirely inappropriate set of *methods*, and the result will be failure—failure, possibly, of a peculiarly persistent kind. The wrong kind of hypotheses will persistently be put forward, which will be assessed in the wrong kind of way. Thus, if the world is in reality governed by a society of gods but we are convinced it is governed by a fixed, unified pattern of physical law, our whole approach to improving knowledge and control of Nature will be misguided. Instead of trying to find out what it is that pleases and angers the gods, so that we may encourage the former and avoid the latter, we will put forward and test hypothetical laws governing natural processes. Our efforts in this direction will succeed only in so far as the gods choose to behave in a precisely regular fashion. But if the gods are anything like gods traditionally have been believed to be (wilful, vain, childish), our attempt to reduce them to patterns of lawful regularity is likely to provoke them into behaving with unpredictable outrage. Our specific laws will be refuted but, convinced that laws of some kind must govern phenomena, we will try to discover more successful laws; we will not conclude that our whole approach is wrong. Equally, of course, if things are the other way round, and we are convinced phenomena are controlled by gods in a world that is actually governed by some utterly impersonal pattern of physical law, our whole approach to improving our knowledge of and influence over natural processes will be inappropriate. There will be some apparent successes, as when the tribal witch-doctor or shaman apparently succeeds in curing disease or causing rainfall by calling upon the gods; these successes will help to keep alive the basic creed. Many failures need not at all, however, cast doubt on the basic creed, for the creed will contain explanations as to why such failures should occur: anger of the gods at undisclosed crime, or evil thoughts, within the tribe, for example. Indeed, if the creed determines the methodology whereby beliefs are developed and assessed, beliefs that clash with, or cast doubt on, the basic creed will be excluded a priori as it were. In this way, it may be very difficult indeed to escape from a bad choice of basic metaphysics, even though it leads to a programme of improving knowledge and control of natural processes that meets with only very limited success.[9] (It is in part for this reason that it took so long for humanity to create modern science.[10])

The dilemma, in short, amounts to this. In order to proceed at all we must make some assumption about the ultimate nature of the universe; in order to proceed successfully we must make an assumption that is near enough correct; if our assumption is badly wrong, not only will progress in knowledge be seriously impeded but, in addition, it may be very difficult for us to discover our basic mistake: and yet it is above all here, concerning the ultimate nature of the universe, that we are horribly ignorant, and are almost bound to get things hopelessly wrong.

Aim-oriented empiricism, the view defended in this book, emerges as the solution to this dilemma. It can be summarized like this. We need, first, to make explicit that cosmological assumption that may be regarded as being implicit in our current methodology, and then extract from this a hierarchy of increasingly attenuated metaphysical[11] cosmological assumptions concerning the comprehensibility and knowability of the universe, until we arrive at assumptions which are such that doubting them cannot help the growth of knowledge, whatever the nature of the universe may be. At each level in the hierarchy of assumptions we adopt that one which holds out the greatest hope for the growth of knowledge, and which seems best to support the growth of knowledge. If currently adopted cosmological assumptions, and associated methods, fail to support the growth of empirical knowledge, or fail to do so as apparently successfully as rival assumptions and methods, then assumptions and associated methods are changed, at whatever level appears to be required. In this way we give ourselves the best hope of making progress, of acquiring authentic knowledge, while at the same time minimizing the chances of being taken up the garden path, or being stuck in a cul-de-sac. The hope is that, as we increase our knowledge about the world, we improve the cosmological assumptions implicit in our methods, and thus in turn improve our methods. As a result of improving our knowledge, we improve our knowledge about how to improve knowledge. Science adapts its own nature to what it learns about the nature of the universe, thus increasing its capacity to make progress in knowledge about the world.

4. AIM-ORIENTED EMPIRICISM

In a little more detail, aim-oriented empiricism holds that scientific knowledge, at the most fundamental level, needs to be represented at the following ten levels at least:[12] see Figure 1. (P_1, P_2, ..., P_{10} represent propositions accepted as embodying scientific knowledge at each level.)

Level 1: P_1. *Evidence.* Empirical data (low-level observational and experimental laws).[13]

Level 2: P_2. *Theory.* All accepted fundamental dynamical theories, or accepted laws governing the way physical phenomena occur if no dynamical theory has been developed that applies to the phenomena in question. In terms of current scientific knowledge, this level consists of the so-called standard model plus general relativity.

Level 3: P_3. *Blueprint.* The best available more or less specific metaphysical view as to how the universe is physically comprehensible, a view which asserts that everything is composed of some more or less specific kind of physical entity, all change and diversity being, in principle, explicable in terms of this kind of entity. Examples, taken from the history of physics are: the corpuscular hypothesis of the seventeenth century, according to which the universe consists of minute, infinitely rigid corpuscles that interact only by contact; the view, associated with Newton and Boscovich, according to which the universe consists of point-atoms that possess mass and interact at a distance by means of rigid, spherically symmetrical, centrally directed forces; the unified field view, associated with Faraday and Einstein, according to which everything is made up of one self-interacting field, particles of matter being especially intense regions of the field. Some might argue that the best blueprint available today is the basic metaphysical idea of superstring theory: the universe consists of minute quantum strings that move in ten or twenty-six dimensions of space-time, all but four of which are curled up into a minute size, thus escaping detection. I shall argue in Chapter 3, however, that the best available blueprint is a somewhat more general thesis that I shall call *Lagrangianism*.

Level 4: P_4. *Physical Comprehensibility.* The more imprecise thesis that the universe is physically comprehensible in some way or other, everything being made up of just one kind of physical entity (or perhaps just one entity), all change and diversity being in principle explicable in terms of this one kind of entity. This thesis asserts that the universe is such that some as-yet-to-be-discovered unified physical 'theory of everything' (in the current jargon of theoretical physicists) is true.

In what follows I will use the term 'physicalism' to refer to this level 4 thesis that the universe is physically comprehensible.

There are a number of ways, other than physicalism, in which the universe might be comprehensible (if it is). It might be that God exists,

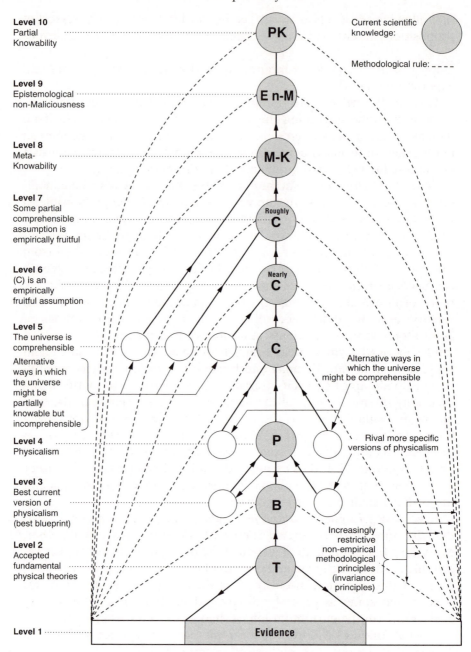

Level 10
Partial
Knowability

PK

Current scientific
knowledge:

Methodological rule: _ _ _ _

Level 9
Epistemological
non-Maliciousness

E n-M

Level 8
Meta-
Knowability

M-K

Level 7
Some partial
comprehensible
assumption is
empirically fruitful

Roughly
C

Level 6
(C) is an
empirically
fruitful assumption

Nearly
C

Level 5
The universe is
comprehensible

C

Alternative
ways in which
the universe
might be
partially
knowable but
incomprehensible

Alternative ways in
which the universe
might be comprehensible

Level 4
Physicalism

P

Rival more specific
versions of physicalism

Level 3
Best current
version of
physicalism
(best blueprint)

B

Level 2
Accepted
fundamental
physical theories

T

Increasingly
restrictive
non-empirical
methodological
principles
(invariance
principles)

Level 1

Evidence

FIG. 1. Aim-oriented empiricism

all natural phenomena being explicable in terms of the will of God. It might be that a society of gods exists, natural phenomena being the outcome of (and being explicable in terms of) the diverse, and sometimes conflicting, desires of the gods. It might be that, even though there is no God, there is some sort of overall cosmic goal, everything being explicable in terms of this cosmic goal (being required to fulfil the goal). Or it might be that there is some kind of cosmic programme, somewhat like a computer programme, which determines how events unfold; in this case events would be explicable in terms of the basic cosmic programme.

These conflicting views as to how the universe is comprehensible, together with physicalism, despite their diversity, all have something in common. They all hold that the universe is such that there is *something* (some kind of physical entity, God, tribe of gods, cosmic goal, cosmic programme, or whatever) which does not itself change but which, in some sense, determines or is responsible for everything that does change (all change and diversity in the world in principle being explicable and understandable in terms of the underlying unchanging *something*). This is the thesis at the next level.

Level 5: P_5. *Comprehensibility*. The thesis (even more imprecise than physicalism) that the universe is comprehensible in some way or other, there being *something*, or an aspect of something (some kind of physical entity, God, society of gods, cosmic purpose, cosmic programme, or whatever) that runs through all phenomena, and in terms of which all phenomena can, in principle, be explained and understood. The thesis that the universe is comprehensible pushes to the limit the thesis that the universe is such that some phenomena can be explained and understood, to some extent at least: it asserts that the universe is such that *all* phenomena can, in principle, be fully explained and understood (in so far as this is logically possible), all phenomena being explicable in terms of the one, unchanging *something*, present everywhere, at all times and places, throughout all phenomena, in an invariant form.[14]

Level 6: P_6. *Near Comprehensibility*. The even more imprecise thesis that the universe is 'nearly comprehensible'. This means that the universe is sufficiently nearly comprehensible for the hypothesis that it is perfectly comprehensible to be more fruitful to adopt than any comparable assumption from the standpoint of the growth of knowledge.

Level 7: P_7. *Rough Comprehensibility*. The even more imprecise thesis that the universe is 'roughly comprehensible' in the sense that the universe is such that there is some assumption of approximate comprehensibility (including the possibility of perfect comprehensibility as a special case) which is the most fruitful rationally discoverable[15] assumption to adopt from the standpoint of the growth of knowledge.

Level 8: P_8. *Meta-Knowability*. The still more imprecise thesis that the universe is 'meta-knowable', which means that the universe is such that there is some rationally discoverable assumption about it which leads to improved methods for the improvement of knowledge.

Level 9: P_9. *Epistemological non-Maliciousness*. The universe is such that it does not exhibit comprehensibility, meta-knowability, or even mere partial knowability more generally, in our immediate environment only. However drastically phenomena at other times and places may differ from local phenomena, nevertheless the general nature of all such phenomena is such that it can in principle be discovered by us by developing knowledge acquired in our immediate environment. If inexplicable, arbitrary phenomena occur (phenomena specifiable only by some grossly *ad hoc* theory of the kind indicated in Section 2 above), their occurrence is discoverable by us in our immediate environment.

Level 10: P_{10}. *Partial Knowability*. The universe is such that we possess and can acquire some knowledge of our immediate environment as a basis for action.

Corresponding to each metaphysical assumption, at level r, where r runs from 3 to 9, there is a methodological rule (represented by sloping dotted lines in Figure 1) which asserts: accept that level $r - 1$ assumption (or collection of fundamental dynamical theories if $r = 3$) which best exemplifies the level r assumption, and which best promotes the growth of empirical knowledge (at levels 1 and 2), or at least holds out the greatest hope of doing this.

A few words of clarification concerning the principles at levels 3 to 10. They all assert, in different degrees, that the cosmos is more or less comprehensible or knowable.[16] As we ascend from level 3 to level 10, the theses become increasingly imprecise and contentless and thus, other things being equal, increasingly likely to be true. Theories at level 2 are burdened with massive precision and content; aim-oriented empiricism predicts that, however empirically successful they may be, if, taken together, they clash with physicalism (as at present), then they are false. They are, in this case, fragmentary, imperfect glimpses of an underlying unity. The best blueprint at level 3 is the best current attempt to do justice both (*a*) to theoretical knowledge at level 2, and (*b*) to physicalism at level 4. Ideally, it exemplifies physicalism in the sense that, what the blueprint postulates to exist that determines the way events occur must be (like what physicalism postulates) invariant throughout all phenomena. (If a blueprint is to exemplify physicalism perfectly, in other words, it must not add to physicalism in a patchwork way, for some, but not for all possible phenomena.) Level 3 blueprints have vastly less precision and content than current level 2 theory (standard model plus general relativity); it is nevertheless reasonable to hold that all blueprints proposed so far are false, even if physicalism is true.

Each assumption, from level 3 to level 6, asserts that the universe is comprehensible (to some degree at least), but with decreasing precision and content as we ascend from 3 to 6. At level 7, P_7 asserts, still more modestly, that the universe is such that some assumption of partial comprehensibility is more fruitful than any rival, comparable assumption. It might be the case, for example, that the universe is such that there are *three* fundamental forces, theoretical revolutions involving the development of theories that progressively specify the nature of these three forces more and more precisely. In this case, the assumption that there are three distinct forces would be more helpful than that there is just *one* fundamental force (required if the universe is to be perfectly comprehensible physically). Alternatively, it might be the case that the universe is such that progress in theoretical physics requires there to be a series of theoretical revolutions, there being, after each revolution, one more force: in this case, the assumption that the universe is such that the number of distinct forces goes up by one after each revolution would be more helpful for the growth of knowledge than the assumption that there is just one fundamental force. P_8, even more modestly, asserts merely that the universe is such that existing methods for improving knowledge can be improved. These methods might involve consulting oracles, prophets or dreams; they need not involve developing explanatory theories and testing them against experience. P_9 asserts, still more modestly, that the universe is such that local knowledge can be developed so that it applies non-locally;[17] and P_{10} asserts, even more modestly, that the universe is such that some factual knowledge of our immediate environment exists and can be acquired.

It is important to appreciate that these assumptions are to be understood in such a way that they presuppose some existing body of empirical knowledge (at levels 1 and 2) and existing methods for improving knowledge implicit in current practice. What is being asserted is that the universe is comprehensible, or meta-knowable, to *us*, with our current factual knowledge and implicit methods for improving knowledge. (This point will be amplified in Chapters 4 and 5.)

The logical relationship between the propositions at the various levels is as follows. Let us suppose, initially, that the universe really is physically comprehensible, and the true theory of everything, T, at level 2, has been discovered. In this case, ideally, P_2 would entail P_1, and P_r would entail P_{r+1} for $r = 2 \ldots 8$. (P_9 does not entail P_{10}, as we shall see below.) For $2 \leq r \leq 8$, we may think of P_{r+1} as consisting of a statement of the form 'P_r or $P_r{}^*$ or $P_r{}^{**}$ or . . .', where $P_r{}^*$, $P_r{}^{**}$, etc. are rival cosmological theses to P_r. In moving down from level $r + 1$ to level r we adopt the factual conjecture that $P_r{}^*$, $P_r{}^{**}$, etc. are all false, and P_r is true.

For $5 \leq r \leq 8$, the above does not represent an idealization; in our present state of knowledge, P_r entails P_{r+1}. But for $r < 5$ the above is an idealization in many ways.

To begin with, even if we had discovered the true, unified theory of everything, T, this P_2 proposition at most entails P_1 propositions in so far as they are couched in the form: if such-and-such a state of affairs, S_1, exists at time t_1, then such-and-such a state of affairs, S_2, exists at time t_2. If T is comprehensive and true then it entails all true conditional statements of this type. However, our ability to extract detailed implications from T is bound to be severely restricted: the equations of T are likely to be solvable only for a few, extremely simple states of affairs; they may, indeed, not be solvable precisely at all, it being necessary to use approximation methods to extract predictions from T. This may involve making dubious additional assumptions, or simplifying assumptions known to be false. As theoretical physics has advanced, from Newtonian theory to general relativity and the standard model, so equations have become immensely more difficult to solve; it is reasonable to suppose that this trend will continue into the future.

Granted that we have discovered T (the true, unified theory of everything), no problem should arise in connection with P_2 implying P_3, P_3 in turn implying P_4, and P_4 implying P_5. But of course we have not discovered T (and may never do so, physicalism, perhaps, being false). Instead, we have at present at least two very different, even clashing, fundamental physical theories—the so-called standard model and general relativity. This means P_2 conflicts with P_3. Even taken individually, currently accepted theories belonging to P_2 may clash with P_3 (as when Newtonian theory clashes with the corpuscular blueprint, or Maxwellian electrodynamics clashes with the Boscovichian blueprint). Furthermore, in trying to formulate P_3 in such a way that it does as much justice as possible to the theories of P_2, P_3 may conflict with P_4.

Although a theory, *T*, at level 2, may clash with a blueprint, *B*, it may also be a *B*-type theory, in the sense that it is a more or less disunified exemplification of *B*. Thus *B* might assert that the universe is made up of one kind of point-particle that interacts by means of one kind of force, and a theory, T, might postulate two (or more) kinds of point-particle, with different masses, perhaps, or charges. In this case, even though T is incompatible with B, it is nevertheless a B-type theory, a more or less disunified exemplification of B. (Only theories which exemplify B perfectly imply B; theories which are more or less B-disunified are incompatible with B.[18]) Analogous remarks concern the ways in which T may be related to physicalism, or B may be related to physicalism. In fact, quite generally, given theses P_r and P_s at levels r and s with $2 \leq r < s \leq 9$, P_r may be a more or less unified or adequate exemplification of P_s, even though P_r contradicts P_s.

An important non-empirical methodological rule of aim-oriented empiricism asserts, in effect, that, given two rival level r theses, P_r and Q_r, that one is to be preferred (other things being equal) which exemplifies the accepted level $r + 1$ thesis, P_{r+1}, in the more unified, more adequate way.

The clashes (or disunities) between levels for $r < 5$, and clashes within levels, especially within P_2, serve to drive theoretical physics forward. These pose the problems that physicists try to solve. They are symptomatic of our ignorance. Progress in theoretical physics is to be assessed in terms of the extent to which a contribution promises to bring physics closer to the ideal state of affairs in which P_2 implies both P_1, and P_3 and P_4, P_2 being a candidate for the true, unified theory of everything.

Given these metaphysical principles about the nature of the universe, we can also consider infinitely many further such principles, $\{Q_3\} \ldots \{Q_8\}$, such that, for $r = 4 \ldots 8$:

(1) Q_r implies P_{r+1} or exemplifies P_{r+1} more or less adequately, but is not implied by P_{r+1};
(2) Q_r is incompatible with P_r.

Given (1) and (2), we can regard each Q_r as a possible rival to P_r. Solving the justificational problem of induction involves, in part, justifying preference for P_r over rivals $\{Q_r\}$ that satisfy (1) and (2), for $2 \leq r \leq 8$.

5. HOW AIM-ORIENTED EMPIRICISM SOLVES THE FUNDAMENTAL DILEMMA

How does accepting these eight metaphysical theses, at levels 3 to 10, as a part of scientific knowledge, solve the above fundamental epistemological dilemma of science?

To begin with, empirically successful *ad hoc* theories are excluded from science (something which standard empiricism cannot achieve, as we have seen, without becoming inconsistent[19]). In order to be accepted as a part of theoretical knowledge, a fundamental dynamic theory must be (1) such that it is sufficiently empirically successful, and (2) such that it, together with all other fundamental dynamic theories, exemplifies the best available level 3 metaphysical thesis sufficiently well (which in turn must exemplify the best level 4 metaphysical thesis sufficiently well, and so on). Empirically successful *ad hoc* theories satisfy (1) but are rejected because they fail to satisfy (2)—just as many beautifully unified theories satisfy (2) but are rejected because they fail to satisfy (1).

Furthermore, as a result of accepting eight increasingly contentless metaphysical assumptions as a part of scientific knowledge, it becomes possible to give different justifications for accepting these assumptions, at different levels.

Thus, acceptance of the assumptions at levels 9 and 10 is justified on the grounds that accepting these assumptions can only help, and can never hinder, attempts to improve our knowledge of the world around us, whatever the world may be like. As I shall argue in Chapter 5, we are justified in holding that these assumptions are a part of scientific knowledge because circumstances can never arise in which improving our knowledge of factual truth would be better served by excluding either or both of these assumptions from the domain of knowledge. These two assumptions are permanent components of knowledge.

Acceptance of assumptions at levels 3 to 8 is justified on the grounds that these assumptions are the most fruitful that are available from the standpoint of generating (apparent) empirical knowledge at levels 1 and 2. At any level from 3 to 8, that assumption is accepted which (*a*) best exemplifies the assumption at the level above it, (*b*) leads to the most empirically progressive research programme[20] when assumptions and theories at lower levels are chosen which best exemplify the assumption in question. Choice of assumption at levels 3 to 8, in other words, is governed by the empirical fruitfulness of the research programmes that these assumptions sustain, or at least by the promise of such empirical fruitfulness.

The common factor governing choice and acceptance of metaphysical theses at levels 3 to 10 is the role that these assumptions have in promoting the growth of empirical knowledge. The assumptions at levels 10 and 9 are accepted for this reason but, in these cases, acceptance does not depend on any kind of empirical support. Making these assumptions can help, but cannot impede, the growth of knowledge; these assumptions do not require revision in any circumstances whatsoever. As we descend from level 8 to level 3, the corresponding assumptions become less and less vague, more and more substantial in what they assert about the world, and thus increasingly likely to be false, and to stand in need of revision; when level 3 is reached we arrive at a thesis that is almost certain to require revision. These assumptions are increasingly chosen on the basis of the empirical fruitfulness of the scientific research programmes to which they lead.

All this solves the above dilemma by providing science with a framework of fixed metaphysical assumptions and associated methods, which does not require revision in any circumstances whatsoever, within which increasingly specific metaphysical assumptions, increasingly fruitful heuristically and methodologically if correct, but increasingly likely to be incorrect, may be developed and assessed from the standpoint of their actual capacity to promote the growth of empirical knowledge. Precisely because of the profoundly problematic character of metaphysical assumptions about the ultimate nature of the universe which science is required to make, the near inevitability of any such assumption being so false as to stultify progress, aim-oriented empiricism provides a framework within which science can progressively *improve* such assumptions as it proceeds, in the light of the empirical success or lack of it that they sustain. Science can accept metaphysical assumptions sufficiently specific to be highly fruitful heuristically and methodologically if correct, but all too likely to be incorrect, without risking being stuck with a false assumption that blocks progress, because of the aim-oriented empiricist framework which facilitates the development of alternatives and their assessment with respect to the empirical fruitfulness of the research programmes they generate.

It follows from what I have said so far that as one descends from level 8 to level 3, the corresponding assumptions and associated methods are increasingly dependent on history, on the way the pursuit of knowledge has developed in the past up to the present. In a different universe, science having a different past and different present content, the metaphysical assumptions and associated methods would be increasingly different as one descends from level 8 to level 3. If Nature had been controlled by a society of gods, for example, then, as I have already indicated, the whole character of science and technology, its assumptions and methods, would, if successful, differ dramatically from what we possess today.

It is of course conceivable that, in the future, we may discover (or appear to discover) that the universe is very different from the way we suppose it to be today, on the basis of our current scientific knowledge and understanding. Almost certainly we will need to revise current ideas at level 3; we may need to revise ideas at level 4. It seems unlikely, however, that we will need to revise assumptions at level 5 or 6; but this is a possibility. Just conceivably, there could be such a dramatic revolution in our knowledge of the universe that we discover a rival to the level 5 comprehensibility thesis, which is compatible with the level 9 thesis, and which sustains an empirical research programme even more successful than that of modern science.[21] What makes this seem implausible is the generality and immense fruitfulness of the current level 5 assumption that the universe is comprehensible, in that the search for explanatory theories has met with immense (apparent) success. It seems implausible that there could be a rival assumption, at this level, capable of being even more fruitful. There are, of course, infinitely many rival assumptions, all equally fruitful so far, which assert that the universe is only comprehensible locally, so that, for example, at some time in the future it becomes more or less incomprehensible in some way or other. These assumptions are excluded on the grounds that they clash with the assumption at level 9.[22] It is interesting to note, nevertheless, that most people throughout history appear to have believed that Nature is comprehensible but ultimately unknowable, in that God (or a society of gods) is believed to provide an ultimate explanation as to why things happen as they do, but this is believed to be unknowable in that God (or the gods) cannot be known by us.[23]

On the other hand, almost all sustained attempts to improve knowledge and understanding of Nature, scientific and pre-scientific, throughout history, have sought to develop explanatory theories of some kind of other, or have assumed that explanations of some kind exist as to why things happen as they do. Viewed from the standpoint of aim-oriented empiricism, the human endeavour to improve knowledge has, implicitly at least, accepted the level 5 thesis that the universe is comprehensible, or at least the level 6 thesis that the universe is such that comprehensibility is the most fruitful assumption to make at this level (even if, in more recent times, misguided allegiance to standard empiricism has led to this being denied[24]).

But even though the efforts of humanity throughout history to improve knowledge have not seriously challenged the idea that the universe is comprehensible (or at least 'nearly' comprehensible), nevertheless, within the framework of this very general assumption, there has been the difficult task of discovering in what kind of way the universe is comprehensible—the task of discovering what level 4 assumption needs to be accepted. As I have already indicated, there are a number of different possibilities, each leading to its own highly distinctive methodology.[25]

6. AIM-ORIENTED EMPIRICISM AS THE KEY TO SCIENTIFIC PROGRESS

Modern science arose when a particular level 4 view about the sort of way in which the universe is comprehensible, and its associated set of methods, were adopted by a few thinkers *and the resulting research programme began to exhibit signs of great empirical success*. The view of Nature was that some kind of pattern of physical law (specifiable with mathematical precision) governs natural processes or, as Galileo put it, that 'the book of Nature is written in the language of mathematics' (Burtt 1932: 75). The set of associated methods involved putting forward mathematically precise (level 2) hypotheses about laws or regularities governing natural processes, such as planetary and terrestrial motion, and subjecting these to the scrutiny of precise observation and experimentation. The empirical success of this whole approach became manifest after the publication of Newton's *Principia*, with its wealth of accurate predictions concerning both astronomical and terrestrial motion. The outcome is modern science. The immense success of modern science is due, then, first to the adoption of a metaphysical view of the universe which appears to do much better justice to the actual nature of the universe than rival views and, secondly, to the adoption of a set of methods, appropriate to the metaphysics, in the pursuit of knowledge, understanding, and technological know-how. We see here, at what may be termed the *metamethodological* level, selection of *metaphysics plus associated methods* in the light of the empirical success or failure that the associated research programmes encounter.

Subsequent science continues this process. As scientific knowledge has improved it has been possible (it seems) to improve the basic metaphysical view of the universe upon which science is based. This in turn has made it possible to improve the associated methods of science. This means that methods for improving knowledge themselves improve. As scientific knowledge improves, in short, knowledge about how to improve knowledge improves as well. There is a kind of positive feedback between improving knowledge and improving knowledge about how to improve knowledge—a vital feature of scientific rationality, which helps to explain the explosive growth of scientific knowledge.

This key feature of scientific rationality can be expressed slightly differently in terms of positive feedback between improving knowledge and improving *aims* and methods. A basic fixed aim of science (fixed for the time being at least) is to discover in what precise way the universe is comprehensible, it being presumed that it is comprehensible in some way or other. At any given stage in the development of science, a much more specific, and much more problematic, aim is pursued: to discover in what precise way the universe is comprehensible, it being presumed that it is comprehensible in such-and-such more or less specific, level 3 way (i.e. in terms of atoms interacting by contact, say, or in terms of some unified, self-interacting field). The basic aim, formulated in this rather more specific way, has associated with it rather more specific (and therefore, potentially, more helpful) methods (such as accept theories that posit atoms that interact by contact, or that posit self-interacting fields). The price that must be paid for this advantage is that the *aim* itself becomes much more problematic; even if the universe is comprehensible in some way or other, almost certainly it is not comprehensible in the more specific way it is presumed to be (there being, ultimately, no atoms that interact only by contact, or no unified, self-interacting field). Thus, in order to make progress, science must seek to *improve* its more or less specific basic *aim* and associated *methods*. As scientific knowledge improves, it becomes possible to improve the basic more or less specific *aim* of science and associated *methods*, which in turn makes possible the further improvement of knowledge. The more or less specific (and highly problematic) aim and methods of science evolve with evolving knowledge within the framework of a (more or less) fixed aim for science and fixed metamethodological methods. It is this feature of science, vital to the success of science according to the view being advocated here, that accounts for the name: *aim*-oriented empiricism.

This, then, in outline, is the view of science to be defended in this book—a view which, I maintain, both depicts and justifies the methodological *key* to the unprecedented success of modern science. Furthermore, as I shall argue in Chapters 4 to 6, aim-oriented empiricism succeeds in solving the ten fundamental problems which standard empiricism cannot solve.

The vital role that aim-oriented empiricism has played in promoting scientific progress has been obscured by the fact that standard empiricism has long been the official conception of science. But with Einstein's discovery of special and general relativity, something close to aim-oriented empiricism came to be put explicitly into practice. In his search for underlying unity, Einstein put forward physical principles, which could also be interpreted as methodological principles, such as the principle of relativity and the principle of equivalence, which then guided him towards his great discoveries. Subsequently, Einstein came close to advocating aim-oriented empiricism (Maxwell 1993c: III). Einstein's new way of doing physics has had an immense impact on theoretical physics, as the subsequent importance given to symmetry principles, and to the search for theoretical unification, attests; despite this, standard empiricism still lingers on as the official view. The time is long overdue for the false, stultifying orthodox view of standard empiricism to be swept away, and for aim-oriented empiricism to be accepted instead—a conception of science necessary for and all but explicit in Einstein's profound discoveries.

7. TRADITIONAL RATIONALISM AND EMPIRICISM

Aim-oriented and standard empiricism are incompatible. Aim-oriented empiricism holds that there are two substantial theses about the nature of the universe that are upheld as a permanent part of scientific knowledge, independently of evidence. These are the level 10 thesis that the universe is such that it is at least partially knowable locally, and the level 9 thesis that there is something that makes the universe partially knowable locally that prevails throughout the universe. Standard empiricism, by contrast, asserts that no substantial thesis about the universe can be permanently upheld as a part of scientific knowledge independently of the evidence. Aim-oriented empiricism even holds that the very much more substantial level 5 thesis that the universe is comprehensible is an almost permanent item of scientific knowledge, being upheld independently of empirical considerations in the short term, and only capable of being rejected in the long term if a rival thesis seems better able to support long-term empirical growth. Indeed, according to aim-oriented empiricism, the even more substantial level 4 thesis of physicalism is an item of scientific knowledge more securely established than the most empirically successful of physical theories, such as quantum theory. Existing fundamental physical theories, the so-called standard model and general relativity, clash with physicalism (since these theories lack overall unity). This means, according to aim-oriented empiricism, that it is current fundamental physical theories that are false (despite their immense empirical success); it does not mean that physicalism is false. Physicalism is, according to aim-oriented empiricism, a very much more secure and permanent item of scientific knowledge than the 'paradigms' of Kuhn's version of standard empiricism.

The distinction just drawn between aim-oriented and standard empiricism corresponds, very roughly, to the distinction between traditional *rationalism* and *empiricism*. Traditional rationalism, versions of which were defended by Descartes (1949), Spinoza (1955: *The Ethics*, part I), Leibniz (1956), and Kant (1961), holds that a priori knowledge about the nature of the world is possible and does exist—knowledge that is established by an appeal to reason rather than experience. Traditional empiricism, versions of which were defended by Locke (1961), Berkeley (1957), and Hume (1959), holds that all our knowledge about the world is based on experience, there being no a priori knowledge at all.

The main differences between these traditional doctrines, and the doctrines being considered here are the following. Traditional rationalism and empiricism both hold that scientific knowledge, in so far as it exists, consists of propositions that are all but conclusively *verified* or *justified*. Aim-oriented and standard empiricism make no such claim: both allow that all scientific knowledge is every bit as conjectural as Popper, let us say, has persistently maintained. In particular, then, whereas traditional rationalism holds a priori knowledge to consist of substantial propositions about the world *which have been decisively established and proven by reason alone*, for aim-oriented empiricism (as understood here) such knowledge is entirely impossible. For aim-oriented empiricism, a priori knowledge is irredeemably *conjectural* in character (even though we have good reasons for accepting such knowledge, as indicated above). A second important difference between traditional rationalism and aim-oriented empiricism has to do with the *content* of a priori knowledge (rather than its epistemological status). Whereas traditional rationalists tried to stock a priori knowledge with quite precise and detailed propositions about the nature of the universe (even if they disagreed sharply with each other about what these propositions ought to be, a feature of the situation which does not inspire confidence), aim-oriented empiricism holds that there are just *two* highly *imprecise* items of (conjectural) a priori knowledge, namely (roughly): the universe is such that it is partially knowable locally, and such that what makes this possible locally exists everywhere.

These differences have a crucial bearing on the acceptability of the various doctrines. Lethal arguments against traditional rationalism (having to do with the impossibility of proving by argument alone factual propositions about the world) no longer apply to aim-oriented empiricism. Whereas traditional empiricism is, perhaps, a more acceptable doctrine than traditional rationalism, standard empiricism is very much less acceptable than aim-oriented empiricism.

8. CLASHING PRINCIPLES

A rather more illuminating way of comparing and contrasting standard and aim-oriented empiricism is to see these two doctrines as being based on the following two principles.

(I) *The Principle of Empiricism.* In science, *only* observation and experiment may decide upon the *acceptance or rejection* of scientific statements, including laws and theories (Popper 1963: 54).

(II) *The Principle of Intellectual Integrity.* Assumptions that are substantial, influential, problematic, and implicit need to be made explicit, so that they can be critically assessed and so that alternatives may be put forward and considered, in the hope that such assumptions can be improved (see Maxwell 1984*a*: 224).

The basic idea behind (II) is that this principle needs to be put into practice if we are to give ourselves the best chances of making progress. Substantial problematic assumptions are likely to stand in need of improvement; if also influential, failure to improve such assumptions is likely to block progress. As a result of making such implicit assumptions explicit we put ourselves in a much better position to discover improved versions of such assumptions. We are much greater victims of unacknowledged, implicit false assumptions than we are of assumptions that are openly acknowledged as fallible conjectures. I will argue, in Chapters 4 and 7, that scientific progress has indeed been impeded by the failure of scientists to make explicit, and explore alternatives to, influential implicit metaphysical assumptions—due, in part, to allegiance to (I) rather than (II).

For standard empiricism, (I) represents a sort of ideal of scientific integrity (although most proponents of standard empiricism, in acknowledging that simplicity considerations play an important role in science, recognize that (I) does not quite work). Aim-oriented empiricism, by contrast, emerges as a result of taking (II) seriously.

(II) is more fundamental than (I). If the two clash, then it is (I) rather than (II) that must be abandoned. In the first place, what is of value in (I) is, in effect, implicit in (II). The process of unravelling empirical consequences of scientific theories so that they may be tested against observation and experiment is, in effect, a process of making explicit what is implicit in theories, so that the theories may be critically assessed. But in the second place, (II) is of universal applicability; whatever the intellectual context, it must always be necessary to intellectual integrity and rigour, to rationality, to make explicit what is substantial, influential, problematic, and implicit. (II) is closely associated with the idea of a valid inference. If, in deriving *B* from *A*, it is necessary to smuggle in substantial additional assumptions during the process of deduction, the inference is invalid. The claim that such an inference is valid involves a kind of deception: we are being told that if we hold *A* to be true then we *must* hold *B* to be true as well, when this is not the case. In order to make such an inference valid, (II) must be implemented; the substantial implicit assumptions smuggled in during the deduction must be made explicit and added to *A* as additional premises. In short, (II) is essential to rigour, to intellectual integrity, and if it clashes with (I) then it is the latter that must give way.

But (I) and (II) do clash in the following sense. Doing science in accordance with (II) violates (I) quite straightforwardly, in that (II) demands that the permanent, substantial, influential, and problematic assumption about the universe that is implicit in the persistent rejection of empirically successful *ad hoc* theories needs to be made explicit within science, as an assumption upheld independently of evidence. This violates (I). On the other hand, the *attempt* to do science in accordance with (I) leads either to scientific sterility, or to intellectual dishonesty and the violation of (II). If (I) is implemented honestly, so that empirical success or failure *alone* really does determine what theories are accepted and rejected, then science will be swamped by infinitely many empirically successful *ad hoc* theories: scientific progress will cease. If science is to make progress, it must be the case that non-*ad hoc* theories are persistently preferred to empirically more successful *ad hoc* theories. This commits science to a substantial, influential, and problematic assumption about the nature of the phenomena, to the effect that the phenomena occur (locally at least, to a high degree of approximation) as if governed by non-*ad hoc* laws. But this assumption is upheld independently of, or even in violation of, empirical considerations. Scientific allegiance to (I) will make it impossible to make such implicit assumptions explicit, in direct violation of (II).

We need, in short, to adopt (II), and reject (I); this is tantamount to adopting aim-oriented empiricism and rejecting standard empiricism. The hierarchy of levels of aim-oriented empiricism, discussed above, can be regarded as emerging as a result of successive applications of (II), this process only stopping when it can no longer help the growth of knowledge.

9. FROM STANDARD TO AIM-ORIENTED EMPIRICISM

The chief purpose of this book is to establish that standard empiricism is untenable and deserves to be rejected, whereas aim-oriented empiricism is a rigorous and fruitful conception of science that deserves to be accepted and put explicitly into scientific practice. In a little more detail, there are eight points to be established:

1. Standard empiricism is untenable. If honestly implemented in scientific practice, it would bring scientific progress to a standstill. Only the *dishonest* implementation of standard empiricism makes scientific progress possible.

2. Aim-oriented empiricism, by contrast, is the methodological *key* to the astonishing progress of modern science. It provides us with an intellectually rigorous and rational conception of science, and a conception of method specifically designed to facilitate scientific progress (as I shall argue in more detail in Chapters 3 to 7). It is because aim-oriented empiricism has been put into scientific practice, at least approximately (despite standard empiricism being proclaimed as the official view), that it has been possible for modern science to be so extraordinarily successful.

3. Scientists and philosophers of science recognize that there are a number of baffling unsolved problems about the nature of scientific inquiry. There is the problem of induction, the problem of how theories can be verified by evidence. There are the following two problems of simplicity. Granted that, in science, preference is given to theories that are simple (or unified or explanatory), we are at once confronted by the problems: What is simplicity? How is giving preference to simple theories to be justified? There is a problem concerning scientific discovery: how is it possible for theoretical physicists to come up with new theories which subsequently turn out to yield astonishingly accurate empirical predictions, often predictions of entirely new, unsuspected phenomena? Especially notable in this respect are: Newtonian theory, Maxwellian electrodynamics, Einstein's special and general theories of relativity, Bohr's quantum theory of the atom, Heisenberg's and Schrödinger's non-relativistic quantum theory, Dirac's relativistic quantum theory of the electron, quantum electrodynamics of Tomonaga, Schwinger,

Feynman, and Dyson, and quantum electroweak dynamics and quantum chromodynamics developed by Yang, Mills, Salam, Weinberg, Gell-Mann, and others. How is all this possible? There is the mystery of the applicability of mathematics to the physical world. Mathematicians on occasions develop new mathematical ideas in a context apparently remote from physics which subsequently turn out to be applicable to the physical world in a way no one initially anticipated. (Examples are given towards the end of Chapter 2.) Again, how is this possible? There is a serious problem about what it can possibly *mean* to say that physics is making progress granted that it staggers from one false theory to another (the problem of verisimilitude).

In Chapter 2 I argue that these and related problems in the philosophy of science cannot be solved granted standard empiricism. In Chapters 4 to 6 I set out to solve these problems within the framework of aim-oriented empiricism. This is the core of the book. If the argument succeeds it provides decisive grounds for rejecting standard empiricism and accepting aim-oriented empiricism in its stead. As the argument develops it will, I hope, become apparent that the failure of standard empiricism to solve the above problems is closely related to its harmful consequences for science, while the success of aim-oriented empiricism in solving these problems is linked to the fruitfulness of this view for science.

4. Aim-oriented empiricism is built into the bones of modern science. It is inherent in the intellectual and institutional realities of the scientific enterprise. So far, however, it has not been put into scientific practice in a fully explicit and thoroughgoing way. This is because the scientific community officially believes in and attempts to implement standard empiricism. Belief in (versions of) standard empiricism goes back to the downfall of Cartesian physics and its associated rationalist methodology (a precursor of aim-oriented empiricism), and the triumph of Newtonian physics and its associated empiricist methodology (a version of standard empiricism), in the late seventeenth and early eighteenth centuries.[26] Since then, despite the intellectual superiority of aim-oriented empiricism, the scientific community has believed that the central tenet of standard empiricism (namely that theories must be assessed impartially with respect to evidence, no proposition about the world being upheld in science independently of evidence) is of the essence of scientific integrity and rectitude. It is this, so it is believed, which distinguishes science from religion, philosophy, and ideology: nothing in science must be accepted permanently on grounds that are independent of evidence. Fortunately, standard empiricism has been

put into scientific practice in a sufficiently *hypocritical* fashion to permit scientific progress to take place. Belief in (versions of) standard empiricism has not prevented scientists from acting sufficiently in accordance with aim-oriented empiricism to make scientific progress possible.[27]

5. In order to understand science as it has actually been pursued, from Newton's time down to our own, it is necessary to do so in terms of both aim-oriented and standard empiricism. Aim-oriented empiricism is needed in order to understand those features of science—intellectual, institutional, personal, and social—which are associated with the growth of scientific knowledge and understanding. Standard empiricism is needed in order to do justice to the official, public face of science, those aspects of science which have been influenced by the belief of scientists that science ought to proceed in accordance with standard empiricism. Actual science is in part the outcome of a tension between the instinctive feeling of creative scientists to proceed in accordance with aim-oriented empiricism and the official view that science ought to proceed in accordance with standard empiricism.

6. As I have already indicated, aim-oriented empiricism was first put explicitly into scientific practice by Einstein in developing special and general relativity. In creating these theories Einstein made essential use of aim-oriented empiricism; without it, the discovery of the theories would not have been possible. We have here dramatic confirmation of the extraordinary scientific fruitfulness of aim-oriented empiricism when put explicitly into practice.[28]

7. We need to bring about a scientific revolution—or at least a scientific *reformation*. Standard empiricism needs to be repudiated by the scientific community, and aim-oriented empiricism needs to be adopted instead as the new orthodoxy. More importantly, aim-oriented empiricism needs to be put into scientific practice in a thoroughgoing fashion, unconstrained by belief in standard empiricism. The outcome would be fruitful, not only for our *understanding* of science, but for *science* itself, for the way it is pursued, developed, taught, and related to the rest of society and culture. The whole character of science would change somewhat, in beneficial ways. Science would become more like natural philosophy—a vitally important part of a more general philosophical quest for greater understanding. Science would become an integral part of thought and culture quite generally, instead of being somewhat split off from it.[29]

8. This reformation of science would have fruitful consequences, not just for science, but for all inquiry and, in a sense, for life. What is at issue here is how in general we ought to go about trying to learn, to

make progress, taking science as one strikingly successful exemplar of learning, of making progress. An improvement in our understanding of how scientific learning or progress comes about, not surprisingly, has implications for attempts at learning and making progress in all sorts of other contexts: personal, social, cultural, global. (See Maxwell 1984*a*, forthcoming, *b*.)

10. IMPLICATIONS OF ADOPTING THE NEW CONCEPTION OF SCIENCE

I now summarize, in the following eleven points, some consequences that flow from abandoning the attempt (or the pretence) to do science in accordance with standard empiricism, so that instead science is both understood and pursued, explicitly, in accordance with aim-oriented empiricism.

(i) There is a substantial increase in the scope of what we can legitimately take to *be* scientific knowledge. From the standpoint of standard empiricism, we do not (yet) possess scientific knowledge about the ultimate nature of the universe. From the standpoint of aim-oriented empiricism, we do. Implicit in existing scientific knowledge there is the thesis that the universe is comprehensible in some way or other; indeed, there is the more specific thesis that the universe is *physically* comprehensible. These theses are more secure items of scientific knowledge than any physical theory, such as quantum theory, however well verified empirically.

(ii) In making explicit, in this way, knowledge that is at present only implicit in science, we gain an item of scientific knowledge that is of profound significance, namely that the universe is comprehensible. From a general intellectual and cultural standpoint, many detailed, technical, theoretical, and observational discoveries of science are *not* of general significance—though of course some are (such as Darwin's theory of evolution). The scientific discovery (as we may choose to call it) that the universe is comprehensible in some way or other and, more specifically, that it is *physically* comprehensible is, like the theory of evolution, one of those discoveries that has implications for the whole of thought, and for all of our culture. It means, for example, that our whole human world, imbued with such things as colour, sounds, feelings, thoughts, consciousness, free will, meaning, and value, must somehow be accommodated within the general framework of a physically comprehensible universe. Very general constraints are imposed on the way we can think about human life, its meaning, nature, and value.[30]

(iii) According to standard empiricism, scientific knowledge consists of essentially just *two* domains: (*a*) observational and experimental data, and (*b*) empirically testable laws and theories. According to aim-oriented empiricism, it consists of at least five domains: (*a*) observational and experimental data, (*b*) testable laws and theories, (*c*) untestable metaphysical blueprints, (*d*) the thesis that the universe is physically comprehensible (physicalism), and (*e*) the untestable metaphysical thesis that the universe is comprehensible in some way or other.[31] There is indeed, according to aim-oriented empiricism, vital additional scientific knowledge to this, namely *knowledge-about-how-to-improve-knowledge* which takes at least two forms: (*f*) observational and experimental *methods* or *techniques* (empirical know-how), and (*g*) theoretical *methods* or *techniques* (theoretical know-how). These two forms of know-how, vital for further scientific progress, are embodied in the evolving aims and methods of science, which are such an essential feature of aim-oriented empiricist science (see Figure 1).

(iv) According to standard empiricism, ideas in science are to be assessed in terms of their empirical success and failure. This means that ideas in science must at least be open to being assessed in this fashion. They must be empirically testable. Metaphysical and philosophical ideas, which are not empirically testable, must be excluded from science (in accordance with Popper's famous principle of demarcation[32]). Aim-oriented empiricism, by contrast, insists that untestable, metaphysical ideas—rival conjectures as to how the universe may be comprehensible—form a vital, integral part of the intellectual domain of science. In addition, untestable ideas about possible aims-and-methods for science—ideas that belong to the *philosophy of science*—form an integral part of the intellectual domain of science.

(v) In some respects, standard and aim-oriented empiricism uphold diametrically opposed intellectual standards for science—diametrically opposed conceptions of scientific integrity and rigour. According to standard empiricism, it is of the essence of scientific integrity and rationality that untestable metaphysical and philosophical ideas are excluded from the intellectual domain of science. According to aim-oriented empiricism, by contrast, scientific integrity and rigour demand that untestable metaphysical and philosophical ideas, implicit in scientific knowledge and methods at any given stage, be made *explicit* within science, so that these ideas can be critically assessed and improved.

Whereas standard empiricism demands that science *shields* itself from untestable metaphysical and philosophical ideas in order to preserve its scientific integrity, aim-oriented empiricism demands the opposite: scientific integrity requires explicit discussion of metaphysical and philosophical ideas as an integral part of science.

(vi) At this point many scientists may feel that standard empiricism is very much to be preferred to aim-oriented empiricism just because the former view does emphatically *exclude* the irrational and stultifying miasma of metaphysics and philosophy from science. This ignores, however, that aim-oriented empiricism provides a new rational framework for the development and critical assessment of metaphysical and philosophical ideas relevant to science. Metaphysical ideas, and associated ideas about aims-and-methods, are to be assessed in terms of (*a*) their empirical fruitfulness,[33] and (*b*) their compatibility with the thesis that the universe is comprehensible in some way or other. Attempting to exclude metaphysical ideas from science, in accordance with the diktats of standard empiricism, cannot succeed; it merely suppresses rational— imaginative and critical—discussion of them within science. The result is that the metaphysical ideas that lurk implicitly in science at any given stage, influencing scientific thought, tend to be unhelpful to science, and tend to be upheld dogmatically as a result of being disavowed. (Those of our beliefs that we disavow are much more likely to be upheld dogmatically, precisely because disavowal makes critical examination of them impossible.) Thus Newton's theory of gravitation is initially found to be unintelligible, even untenable (in a sense even by Newton himself[34]), because of its incompatibility with the inappropriate metaphysics of the corpuscular hypothesis. Only a century later did Boscovich succeed in developing a point-particle atomistic metaphysics appropriate to Newton's theory. Likewise, understanding and acceptance of Maxwell's electromagnetic *field* theory were impeded by retention of inappropriate atomistic or mechanical metaphysical views, dogmatically upheld. And adequate understanding of the probabilistic quantum world is still today impeded by a dogmatic, but disavowed, allegiance to deterministic metaphysics more appropriate to nineteenth- rather than twentieth-century physics. Instead of the rational exploration of metaphysical ideas actually leading to the formation of good new scientific theories (which is what aim-oriented empiricism makes possible), the standard empiricist prohibition on the scientific discussion of metaphysics leads to the scientific retention of bad metaphysical ideas which *impede* the development, understanding, and acceptance of good new scientific theories. Science itself is damaged, and scientific progress is impeded.[35]

(vii) Aim-oriented empiricism provides science with a fallible, non-mechanical but *rational* method for the discovery of revolutionary new scientific theories. This involves modifying metaphysical ideas about physical comprehensibility or unity, in the way hinted at in (vi) above, until it proves possible to formulate one such idea with sufficient precision to become a new testable physical theory. It was this rational method of discovery that was employed by Einstein in creating special and general relativity (Maxwell 1993c: III). Nothing like this is at all possible granted standard empiricism. From this standpoint, the only scientifically rational way to assess metaphysical ideas would be to favour those ideas that are compatible with existing well-confirmed physical theories. But good new fundamental physical theories, and their associated metaphysical ideas, almost always *contradict* pre-existing theories. Standard empiricism leads us to favour precisely the wrong kind of metaphysical idea, from the standpoint of developing a good new scientific theory! No wonder such stalwart defenders of standard empiricism as Popper (1959: 31) and Reichenbach (1938: 381–3) both deny the possibility of a rational method of discovery for science. No wonder that most physicists and philosophers of physics find the whole process of the discovery of fundamental new physical theories a profound mystery! (See, for example, Wigner 1970, ch. 17.)

(viii) According to aim-oriented empiricism, science ought to exhibit *improving* aims and methods as scientific knowledge improves, within the framework of the fixed aim and fixed methods set by the basic assumption that the universe is comprehensible in some way or other. For aim-oriented empiricism, *evolving* aims and methods are the methodological *key* to the great success of science, and of the essence of the *rationality* of science. Evolving aims and methods are, of course, closely associated with all the features of aim-oriented empiricist science discussed above in points (i) to (vii). By contrast, standard empiricism, with its fixed aim and fixed methods for science, excludes the possibility of there being *evolving* aims and methods (at least at a fundamental level).

(ix) Aim-oriented empiricism does justice to a feature of physics, created by Einstein, that has come to dominate theoretical physics after Einstein. This feature involves giving a prominent role to fallible symmetry or invariance principles. These are *methodological* principles, which specify requirements that acceptable physical theories must satisfy. Thus the restricted principle of relativity, which played a vital role in the development of special relativity, demands that acceptable theories must be such that they work equally well in all inertial reference frames—in all of a set of hypothetical laboratories that are moving at constant velocity with respect to each other. This methodological principle is linked to the metaphysical principle that space is such that uniform motion with respect to it has no physical effects. The methodological principle is only acceptable if the metaphysical principle is true. If the metaphysical principle is false, and uniform motion through space does result in physical effects, all inertial reference frames will not be physically equivalent, and some correct part of physics will not conform to the methodological principle of relativity. Another such (closely related) methodological principle put forward by Einstein is Lorentz invariance, equivalent to special relativity. We have here a methodological principle which has played a profound role throughout the whole of modern theoretical physics; at the same time it is a piece of *physics*, equivalent to special relativity (equivalent to space-time being Minkowskian in character), and which might thus be wrong, or unacceptable. (Just this turned out to be the case with the development of general relativity: special relativity demands that space-time be flat or Euclidean, whereas general relativity postulates that space-time has *variable* curvature, depending on how much matter, or energy, is around.) Other fallible symmetry principles of great importance in modern physics are the principle of equivalence (associated with general relativity), the principles of parity, charge conjugation, and time reversal, and global and local gauge invariance.[36] Evolving, fallible methodological principles of this type, linked to metaphysical principles (which may well be false), are just what aim-oriented empiricism postulates to exist (see Figure 1). Standard empiricism, with its fixed aim and fixed methods for science, cannot begin to do justice to this important feature of modern theoretical physics.

   (x) In moving from standard to aim-oriented empiricism the demand that acceptable theories be simple, unified, or comprehensible is both emphasized and clarified. No longer can theories be accepted merely because they meet with empirical success. This has consequences for the status of theories that are at present accepted because of their great empirical success, but which are less than satisfactory from the standpoint of simplicity, unity, or comprehensibility. The classic example here is quantum theory. Granted standard empiricism, it is almost inconceivable that there could be grounds for rejecting quantum theory, given its astonishing empirical success. But from the perspective of aim-oriented empiricism, orthodox quantum theory is unacceptable, despite its immense empirical success, because of its grossly *ad hoc* character. Because it *evades* and does not *solve* the quantum wave/particle problem, orthodox quantum theory can only be a theory about the results of performing measurements on quantum systems such as electrons or atoms. This in turn means that the theory is made up of two conceptually incoherent parts, a quantum-mechanical part, and a classical part for the treatment of measurement. Quantum theory poses a serious challenge to aim-oriented empiricism, namely to indicate how an acceptable version of quantum theory may be developed, free of the defects of the orthodox version of the theory. In Chapter 7 I attempt to meet that challenge.

(xi) As long as science is pursued by scientists who believe in standard empiricism there will always be the danger that science loses sight of the noble goal to enhance our *understanding* of this mysterious universe in which we find ourselves. For, according to standard empiricism, the basic aim of theoretical physics is to develop theories of increasing empirical success—theories which predict more and more phenomena more and more accurately. But, even though predicting more and more phenomena more and more accurately may be *necessary* for increased scientific understanding, it is not *sufficient*. In order to increase our scientific understanding we need to increase our knowledge of the invariant *something*, U, present everywhere, which is, in some sense, responsible for all change and diversity. Only theories which can be interpreted as postulating some such U throughout the range of phenomena to which the theories apply are candidates for enhancing scientific understanding. An example of such a theory is general relativity: this postulates that the curvature of space-time varies in a fixed way (U) with variations in the presence of energy. All this is emphasized, in an absolutely essential way, by aim-oriented empiricism. Standard empiricism, by contrast, puts all the emphasis on the satisfaction of empirical requirements. Thus, as a result of taking this view for granted, scientists may come to accept a series of theories which successfully predict more and more phenomena more and more accurately, but which do *not* advance scientific understanding in that these theories all *fail* to postulate U's invariance throughout the domain of phenomena in question. And the classical example of this, again, is orthodox quantum theory. From the non-relativistic theory of Heisenberg and Schrödinger to the more recent relativistic field theories of Tomonaga, Schwinger, Feynman, Dyson, Salam, Weinberg, and others, orthodox quantum theory postulates two very different sets of laws, the quantum-mechanical and the classical (there thus being no invariant U running through all the phenomena to which the theories apply). Orthodox quantum theories predict an ever-increasing range of phenomena with ever-increasing accuracy but do not enable us properly to *understand* the quantum domain. What is the nature of quantum entities? Are the basic laws of the quantum domain deterministic or probabilistic? Elementary questions of understanding such as these are left unanswered by orthodox quantum theory. One physicist, indeed, has gone so far as to say, 'One understands quantum theory when one understands that there is nothing to understand.' Orthodox quantum theory and standard empiricism in this respect powerfully reinforce each other: they collude to create the nearly overwhelming impression that modern physics *predicts* phenomena but does not enable us to *understand*. The quest for scientific understanding, the supreme intellectual goal of science, going back over two and a half thousand years to the origins of science in the speculations of the Presocratic philosophers, is quietly betrayed and forgotten.[37]

11. CAN PHILOSOPHY OF SCIENCE HAVE IMPLICATIONS FOR SCIENCE?

The suggestion of the previous section that the *philosophy of science* has important implications for *science* may seem implausible. Examples of contributions to the philosophy of science that have fruitful implications for science itself, during the last 200 years or so, are hard to find. Scientists sometimes comment on the strange sterility of the philosophy of science as far as science itself is concerned.[38]

Two points need to be noted, however, about my claim that the move from standard to aim-oriented empiricism has important implications for science. First, as I have remarked above, aim-oriented empiricism is a philosophy of science, a view about the aims and methods of science that is already implicit in successful scientific practice, and more or less *explicit* in Einstein's extraordinarily successful scientific work in creating special and general relativity. Fruitful repercussions for science come from putting this view, which has already proved its scientific merit, into scientific practice in a much more explicit, thoroughgoing way. I am arguing for making much more explicit what is already implicit in the scientific endeavour. Secondly, if what I have argued so far is correct, then there is an immediate diagnosis for the scientific sterility of much philosophy of science. On the whole, philosophers of science work within the framework of, and seek to justify, versions of standard empiricism. In doing this they have sought to justify the unjustifiable, defend a conception of science which, if honestly put into scientific practice, would bring scientific progress to an instant stand-still.[39] No wonder philosophy of science tends to be scientifically sterile. I seek to free science from the harmful influence of a bad philosophy of science.

In attempting to get the argument of this book across to the scientific community, I do, however, face a problem. Standard empiricism bans serious discussion of the philosophy of science from science itself, in accordance with Popper's principle of demarcation. Thus the very thing that I am arguing against, standard empiricism, being already built into scientific practice, to some extent, will tend to ensure that my 'philosophical' criticisms, however valid, are excluded from serious scientific discussion. The ideas and arguments of this book will be deemed too 'philosophical', too lacking in empirical testability, to be worthy of receiving consideration in scientific journals. In this way, standard empiricism, once accepted by scientists, protects itself from criticism by excluding all such criticism from science.

12. THE LIMITATIONS OF PHYSICS

A few words now about *limitations* on what theoretical physics can be expected to achieve. Let us suppose that the universe *is* physically comprehensible, and that, one day, we will capture its comprehensible structure in the true theory of everything, T. In principle, T correctly predicts all phenomena. In practice, however, there will be severe limitations on the predictions that can be extracted from T.

First, it is all too likely that we will only be able to solve the equations of T exactly for a few, extremely simple systems; indeed, the situation may turn out to be even worse than this, in that the equations cannot be solved exactly at all, approximation methods being required even for the simplest of systems. As physics has advanced, successive theories have turned out to have equations that are more and more difficult to solve. Newtonian theory can be solved precisely for two-body systems, but cannot be solved precisely for all three-body systems. For systems with more than two bodies, approximation methods must, in general, be used. Maxwellian theory runs into difficulties in connection with the one-body system, because of the self-interaction of the particle via the field. And when it comes to quantum field theory, even the zero-body problem has become problematic, in that the vacuum has become so complex (being full of virtual particle creation and annihilation) that approximation methods are required. The predictive power of the true theory of everything, T, *in practice*, is likely to be severely limited.

Secondly, there will be limitations on the predictive power of T in practice due to the impossibility of obtaining precise knowledge of the initial physical state of any physical system. This will be the case even for the simplest systems; in the case of complex systems, such as those which include living things, obtaining even approximate knowledge of initial conditions for the purposes of predictions, using T, will be impossibly difficult. Even in the case of Newtonian theory, infinitesimal differences in the initial state of a system can rapidly turn into big differences in the way the system evolves. This is bound to be a feature of the true theory of everything, T. Discovering T will not, at all, bring physics, let alone science, to an end.

There is a third limitation on the predictive power of T that is a matter of principle rather than practice. Elsewhere I have argued that colours, sounds, smells as we experience them, and other experiential aspects of things (such as that aspect of processes going on inside our heads associated with consciousness) are in principle beyond the scope of physics. T may, in principle, predict all phenomena; but it only predicts the *physical* aspects of phenomena, not those aspects that have to do with human experience, human consciousness, and meaning. Furthermore, T is only capable of explaining phenomena in *one* kind of way. In order to understand a purposive being, whether an ant or an antelope, as a purposive being we need to appeal to a quite distinct mode of explanation and understanding not reducible to physical explanation and understanding. This is above all the case when it comes to understanding people. Understanding conscious, freely acting persons embedded in this physically comprehensible universe is compatible with, but irreducible to, physical understanding.[40]

13. PLAN OF THE BOOK

In developing the argument of this book in more detail, I proceed as follows. In Chapter 2 I argue that standard empiricism fails to account for the success of science, and deserves to be rejected. In Chapter 3 I fill in some further details about aim-oriented empiricism, and consider what metaphysical assumption needs to be made about the nature of the universe granted that current physics contains genuine theoretical knowledge (in an appropriate sense of 'knowledge'). In pursuing this question I am led to distinguish a number of metaphysical theses which assert that the universe is physically comprehensible (i.e. has a unified dynamic structure) in progressively stronger and stronger senses. In Chapters 4 to 6 I argue that aim-oriented empiricism is able to solve problems of simplicity, induction, progress, and discovery, mentioned in point 3 of Section 9 above, which standard empiricism fails to solve; this argument, if successful, provides decisive grounds for accepting aim-oriented empiricism as an intellectually rigorous conception of science which contains the methodological key to the explosive growth of scientific knowledge and understanding. I conclude Chapter 6 by considering a number of progressively stronger versions of aim-oriented empiricism, each of which asserts that the universe has a unified dynamic structure, but in progressively stronger senses of 'unified'. I consider whether the strong version of aim-oriented empiricism that I defend throughout most of the book is required to solve problems of simplicity, induction, progress, and discovery, or whether some weaker version of the view would suffice. In Chapter 7 I tackle the challenge posed by quantum theory. According to aim-oriented empiricism, the universe is comprehensible, and yet quantum theory seems to tell us the exact opposite. Does this count against aim-oriented empiricism? Might an aim-oriented empiricist perspective help to render the quantum world comprehensible? I argue that the key to making sense of the quantum domain is to see it as fundamentally probabilistic in character, and I put forward a version of quantum theory, designed to make sense of the quantum world which, in addition, yields predictions distinct from those of the orthodox version of the theory for experiments not yet performed (but in principle at least capable of being performed). I conclude with an appendix introducing some mathematical and physical ideas appealed to in the book, having to do with such things as Maxwell's field equations, group theory, and symmetry.

2

The Failings of Standard Empiricism

1. FAILURE OF STANDARD EMPIRICISM TO DO JUSTICE TO ACHIEVEMENTS OF MODERN SCIENCE

The achievements of modern science are extraordinary. What is so impressive is the combined scope and accuracy of modern scientific knowledge, the broad understanding combined with a wealth of detailed, precise knowledge. Three basic theories (general relativity, quantum electroweak dynamics, and quantum chromodynamics) apply, in principle, with astonishing accuracy, to all known phenomena, all known forces, particles, and fields.[1] Darwin's theory of evolution postulates two basic mechanisms (inherited variations and natural selection) behind the evolution of all life on earth, in all its amazing richness, complexity, diversity.[2] The Watson and Crick model for the structure of DNA, together with knowledge of the genetic code, provide us with the basis for an understanding of the mechanisms of inheritance for all life on earth.[3]

And before our very eyes, scientific knowledge continues to grow apace. During my lifetime, whole new domains of phenomena have come within the grasp of science, new sciences being created as a result, such as cosmology[4] (with the discovery of the big bang) and molecular biology (with the discovery of the structure of DNA). And science continues to lead to the creation of radically new technologies, in electronics, chemistry, agriculture, and medicine. Modern science is astonishing, both in the scope and detailed accuracy of its theoretical understanding, and in the wealth of its practical applications. There is grandeur in the modern scientific conception of the universe and our place in it.[5]

But if standard empiricism is accepted, all these achievements of modern science become incomprehensible. Not only can we make no rational sense of scientific progress; even worse, it becomes impossible to justify the claim that science does provide us with genuine knowledge about the world. Science becomes irrational. Some historians and sociologists of science (and a few philosophers) have actually arrived at this conclusion (such is the hold that standard empiricism has on contemporary thought about science and its history).[6]

2. BARE AND DRESSED STANDARD EMPIRICISM

Standard empiricism (SE), remember, is the doctrine that in science no substantial thesis about the world can be accepted as a permanent part of scientific knowledge *independent of the evidence*, and certainly not *in violation of the evidence*. In so far as factors other than evidence are appealed to in assessing the acceptability of theories—factors such as the simplicity or explanatory capacity of a theory—this must be done in such a way that no assumption about the nature of the world is permanently upheld, explicitly or implicitly, in science, as a part of knowledge, entirely independently of evidence.

We can, in fact, distinguish two versions of SE which differ on just this question of whether, in the end, empirical considerations ought *alone* to determine choice of theory in science, or whether simplicity considerations are important and legitimate *in addition* to empirical considerations. Let us call the first view *bare* SE and the second *dressed* SE.[7]

Almost everyone concedes that simplicity plays an important role in deciding what theories are accepted in science; few people, in other words, defend SE in its bare form. An exception is early Karl Popper. In his *The Logic of Scientific Discovery*, first published in 1934, Popper defends a version of bare SE: the central aim of the book is, in effect, to defend 'what may be called "the fundamental thesis of empiricism"'— the thesis that experience alone can decide upon the truth or falsity of scientific statements' (Popper 1959: 42).[8] It is true that Popper argues that, other things being equal, that theory is to be preferred which is the most empirically falsifiable; this, on the face of it, amounts to choosing theories on the basis of a consideration other than that of mere empirical success or failure. However, the *rationale* for this rule is that, by giving preference to theories that are the most falsifiable, we maximize the capacity of evidence to decide what theory should be chosen. The idea is, in other words, that giving preference to highly falsifiable theories, far from violating bare SE, is actually required if bare empiricism is to be implemented to maximum effect. Popper also concedes that, in science, preference is given to *simple* theories; however, according to the theory of simplicity developed in Chapter 7 of *The Logic of Scientific Discovery*, simplicity is to be equated with falsifiability: thus persistent preference for simple theories, in this sense, does not violate bare SE either.

Subsequently, Popper shifted his ground and went on to defend a version of dressed SE. In Chapter 10 of his *Conjectures and Refutations*, first published in 1963, Popper demands that an acceptable 'new theory should proceed from some *simple, new, and powerful, unifying idea* about some connection or relation (such as gravitational attraction) between hitherto unconnected things (such as planets and apples) or facts (such as inertial and gravitational mass) or new "theoretical entities" (such as field and particles)' (Popper 1963: 241). This new 'requirement of simplicity' (as Popper calls it) cannot be reduced to the earlier requirement of falsifiability: thus in demanding that theories must satisfy this new requirement in order to be acceptable, Popper shifts to defending dressed SE.

A second and more recent case of someone defending bare SE is provided by the philosopher Bas van Fraassen (1980). As it happens, even van Fraassen is prepared to admit that simplicity has a limited legitimate role to play in science: in deciding what research projects to work on, scientists may be influenced by the simplicity or complexity of rival hypotheses: see van Fraassen (1980: 87–8). However, van Fraassen is emphatic that *only* empirical considerations can legitimately decide what is accepted as scientific *knowledge*, simplicity having here no role to play whatsoever (1980: 87, and especially 12): it is this that makes him a proponent of bare SE.

3. HOW WIDELY HELD IS STANDARD EMPIRICISM?

How widely held, and how influential, is SE—whether bare or dressed? It is very widely upheld, I maintain, by scientists and non-scientists alike—far more so than may at first be appreciated. SE is the current official, orthodox, public conception of science, and is immensely influential for that reason.

But if this is correct, there is at once a problem. A basic thesis of this book is that it is aim-oriented empiricism (AOE), and not SE, which captures the inherent methodology and rationality of science, scientific progress being the result of AOE, and not SE, having been put into practice. If SE were put rigorously into scientific practice, science would come to an instant standstill. Does this not rather tell against the idea that SE is widely upheld by scientists? For if it were, how would scientific progress be possible?

The answer is that for much of scientific activity, putting AOE into practice does not differ too much from putting SE into practice, as long as SE is put into practice in a sufficiently *unrigorous* way. As long as SE is put into practice in such a way that simple, unifying, explanatory theories are accepted, and infinitely many complex, disunifying, non-explanatory rival theories are rejected even though they are all just as successful empirically, or even more so, scientific progress is possible. But putting SE into practice in this way involves permanently assuming, *implicitly*, that the universe is comprehensible (or at least approximately comprehensible in the bit of it that we inhabit). The basic tenet of SE is violated. Implementing SE in this unrigorous way nevertheless has the merit that it makes scientific progress possible and, for much of the time, does not differ too much from implementing AOE. The big difference is that, whereas AOE science conjectures that the universe is comprehensible *explicitly*, SE science assumes this *implicitly*. This difference only really matters in scientific practice if progress requires that the current best level 3 blueprint idea[9] concerning comprehensibility needs to be changed, that is, if a revolution in theoretical physics is required. In this case, AOE science, which can explicitly formulate and scrutinize rival blueprint ideas within the framework provided by the level 4 thesis of physical comprehensibility, is better off than SE science, which cannot do this because all non-empirical, metaphysical knowledge is explicitly denied. To put the point in Kuhn's terminology, much of science is 'normal' science, a kind of science that does not need (for the time being) to challenge the basic paradigm upon which it is based (Kuhn 1970, chs. ii–v); for this kind of science SE, if sufficiently unrigorously implemented, will be all but indistinguishable from AOE, as far as scientific practice is concerned. In other words, for much research, but by no means for all, appropriate versions of SE are almost as good as, and almost indistinguishable from, AOE. (These versions of SE, each corresponding to an epoch of 'normal' science, will differ from each other, in that each will appeal to a different notion of 'simplicity', corresponding to different 'paradigms' or level 3 blueprints.)

This, then, explains how it is possible for scientists to believe in such a scientifically stultifying doctrine as SE: as long as SE is put into practice in a sufficiently unrigorous way, for much of the time research can proceed in a way which is sufficiently close to AOE to make progress possible.

One might suppose that those scientists[10] who have expressed the conviction that the universe is ultimately physically comprehensible, in the sense that some yet-to-be-discovered unified pattern of law runs through all phenomena, reject SE; but no, this is not necessarily the case. Such a belief is entirely compatible with SE, as long as it is upheld as a personal conviction only, and not as an item of objectively established scientific knowledge. SE demands only that in the so-called *context of justification*,[11] the context in which decisions are reached as to what does, and does not, constitute scientific knowledge, no thesis about the world must be permanently upheld as a part of scientific knowledge independently of empirical considerations. SE allows that in the *context of discovery*, the context of inventing new theories, the context of personal conjecture and conviction, scientists may, quite legitimately, hold, and be influenced by, all sorts of beliefs, dogmas, and prejudices: none of this matters as long as such personal convictions do not influence what is accepted and rejected as knowledge, in the context of justification.

It might be thought that Thomas Kuhn (1970) and Imre Lakatos (1970) reject SE, in that both hold that, within a period of normal science, or within a research programme, certain basic assumptions about the world, constituting the 'paradigm' or 'hard core', are upheld in an almost dogmatic fashion, even when such assumptions run into empirical difficulties. SE can be regarded, however, as permitting retention, in the short term, of a paradigm or hard core, even when ostensibly refuted by evidence, as long as empirical considerations decide their fate in the long term. In the end, all that SE does *not* permit is the *permanent* retention of substantial theses about the world independently of, or against, empirical considerations. Both Kuhn and Lakatos hold that, in the end, empirical considerations must decide what paradigms or hard cores are maintained in science: both defend versions of SE.[12]

Again, one might suppose that those historians of science, such as Burtt (1932) and Koyré (1958, 1968), who have argued that modern science makes metaphysical presuppositions about the world, reject SE. But this is not the case. For what Burtt and other like-minded historians of science have meant by 'the metaphysical presuppositions of modern science' is something like the following. The thinkers who helped to create modern science tended to uphold diverse versions of a certain metaphysical view of Nature; this view played an influential role in the development of modern science, in the context of discovery; it is a view that we need to refer to in seeking to understand how and why modern science emerged; the metaphysical view sets a programme of research for science, and modern science may indeed be seen, in part, as the outcome of triumphantly fulfilling this research programme, metaphysics being transformed into empirically successful scientific theory. All this is entirely compatible with SE, as long as metaphysical pre-suppositions are not thought to play a role in the acceptance of theories as constituting scientific knowledge, in the light of their empirical success.

Many historians and sociologists of science, and students of science policy, emphasize that, in addition to evidence and simplicity, all sorts of other, less rational, human factors influence science:[13] the passionate curiosity of the scientist; his ambition, or his concern to help alleviate human suffering; availability of funds; public opinion; metaphysical, philosophical, religious, social, or even political ideas and objectives. And, indeed, is it not obvious that science is a part of the fabric of society, and is thus open to being influenced by all sorts of social factors? One might suppose that views such as these conflict with SE; but again, this is not necessarily the case. As long as the above 'external' social factors only influence choice of research aims and priorities, in the context of discovery, SE is not violated. There is a sense, of course, in which *all* science is personal and social in character, even for SE, in that all scientific activity is the activity of *persons*, acting on their own and in communication with one another. Even the actions of assessing theories in the light of evidence and simplicity are *personal* and *social* actions. The intellectual, methodological, and rational features of science are all irredeemably *social* in character—and in holding this to be the case one does not imply that the (potentially) rational character of science is thereby undermined.[14] Popper, an ardent upholder of SE, has gone further, and argued that the social character of science is not just compatible with its rationality, but is actually an essential prerequisite for rationality,[15] rationality itself being *essentially* social in character (Popper 1962: 224–7).

It is important to appreciate that SE is not put forward as a factual account of what actually goes on in scientific practice: it is put forward rather as a prescriptive doctrine—a specification of the requirements that science must satisfy if it is to be intellectually rigorous or rational. Thus SE is not repudiated by the observation that some scientific prac-tice does not conform to its methodological prescriptions. This may only establish that such scientific practice is less than rational.

By no means all those involved in the creation and development of modern science have believed in SE. As we saw in Chapter 1, two traditions of thought can be distinguished, *empiricism* and *rationalism*, the latter holding that *some* general assertions about the world can be established as knowledge by reason, independent of experience.[16] Two factors have served to make all versions of rationalism seem wholly implausible today.

First, there is the apparent impossibility of *proving*, by reason alone, independent of experience, any substantial thesis about the world. Any such proof must proceed from *postulates* or *axioms*, which cannot themselves be established by reason without introducing an infinite regress. There are, of course, so-called analytic propositions like 'All bachelors are unmarried', true merely in virtue of the meaning of constituent terms, and which can, as a result, be known to be true with certainty by inspection: but such propositions fail to tell us anything about the world. As Einstein once put it: 'Insofar as a proposition refers to reality, it is not certain; and insofar as it is certain, it does not refer to reality.'[17] From Plato onwards, rationalists have not been able to get round this difficulty—and this includes Kant, despite the heroic obscurity of his effort (as set out in his *Critique of Pure Reason*).

Secondly, the best candidates for items of scientific knowledge about physical reality established by reason alone have, it seems, been shown to be *false* by the advance of science itself. Once, the paradigmatic candidate for rationalist knowledge was Euclidean geometry, which seemed to be derivable by reason alone from a few postulates which could be seen to be obviously true, by inspection as it were, independently of any experience. *Substantial* knowledge about the physical world is involved here; and yet it seemed to be possible to establish its truth by reason alone. Subsequent scientific developments have demolished this idea. First, the idea that physical space is non-Euclidean becomes a *possibility* with the development of non-Euclidean geometry by Gauss and others; then the idea becomes a part of scientific *knowledge* with the acceptance of Einstein's general theory of relativity. The *paradigm* of rationalist knowledge has been overthrown by the advance of science itself: no substantial thesis about the nature of the universe which is claimed to be known by an appeal to reason alone can hope, it seems, to survive the revolutionary march of science.

In the end, SE has become the official, orthodox conception of science, unthinkingly upheld by most scientists, because of three factors: the collapse of rationalism; the apparent lack of a viable alternative to SE; and the apparent capacity of SE to do reasonable justice to much actual successful scientific practice. Even though they may not have given the matter much thought, the basic argument in support of SE has seemed, to most scientists, wholly convincing. It can be put like this.

All our knowledge about the world must, in the end, come via our *experience* of the world (however this is interpreted). For we cannot obtain any genuine scientific knowledge about the world entirely *independently* of all experience. (The collapse of rationalism enshrines this point.) Thus, in science, no assertion about the world can legitimately be upheld permanently, as constituting knowledge, on grounds that are independent of empirical success and failure.

Scientists rarely teach or discuss SE explicitly (to do so would violate the edicts of SE); rather, SE is implicit in what is taught and discussed in science.[18] Scientists leave it to philosophers to overcome objections to SE. This philosophers strive, but fail, to do; scientists interpret this failure as yet another indication of the general incompetence of philosophers. Indeed, the failure of philosophy to overcome objections to SE is almost regarded by scientists as yet another sign that SE is absolutely correct: for it seems to confirm that *philosophy*—the discussion of untestable ideas—is an inherently sterile activity, just what SE leads one to expect![19]

Philosophers of science persist in the hopeless endeavour of trying to justify the unjustifiable doctrine of SE, not suspecting, it seems, that what they are trying to establish as rational is hopelessly irrational. This heroic, quixotic effort is regarded by scientists as an incompetent attempt to defend the obvious. Some contemporary historians and sociologists of science have come, however, to the opposite conclusion: the failure of philosophy to justify SE—to solve the problem of induction within the framework of SE—means that science is non-rational. For these historians and sociologists, the history of science reveals changing *beliefs* but not evolving *knowledge*, and they look for explanations for changing scientific beliefs in economic, political, religious, and other social factors.[20]

Historians and sociologists of this persuasion would vehemently deny that they take seriously a doctrine as crudely 'rationalist' as SE; and yet they are, in an important way, massively influenced in their thinking by SE. For they accept, in effect, that SE provides the *only hope* of showing science to be rational. Without this assumption, they would not be able to conclude that the downfall of SE spells the downfall of scientific rationality. Thus the currently fashionable 'sociological' approach to understanding science rests upon the assumption that SE is the only possible way in which science can be shown to be rational. The whole *raison d'être* of this sociological approach to science disappears if the basic argument of this book is correct, namely that AOE solves the problem of induction and successfully exhibits science as rational. (See Maxwell forthcoming, *a*.)

The same point can be made in connection with the notorious anti-rationalist and methodological anarchist Paul Feyerabend (1978, 1982). Feyerabend vehemently rejects the idea that science is rational: for him, the best methodological policy in science is 'anything goes'. Given this, it might seem absurd to hold that Feyerabend is influenced in his thinking by the (would-be) rationalist doctrine of SE. But it is precisely because Feyerabend is committed to the idea that SE is the only possible ideal of rationality for science that he is led to hold that science is irrational on discovering that SE is untenable. As others do, Feyerabend overlooks the possibility of AOE.

The common thread running through all these diverse views and approaches, whether for science and reason or against, is the shared assumption that SE represents the only possible *ideal* of scientific rationality—in so far as there *is* any such ideal.

It may be held that SE is explicitly rejected by one well-known contemporary approach to understanding scientific method, namely Bayesianism. According to Bayesianism, scientists hold scientific hypotheses to be more or less probable prior to any consideration of empirical success or failure, different scientists quite properly giving different 'prior' probabilities to one and the same hypothesis. The process of empirical testing then leads to the different prior probabilities being modified, in accordance with the postulates of probability theory (and in accordance in particular with Bayes's theorem), this process ideally converting differing initial, prior probabilities into one common 'posterior' probability, *the* probability of the hypothesis in the light of the available evidence (Howson and Urbach 1993).

Bayesianism acknowledges that scientists hold beliefs about the world independently of, or prior to, evidence: to this extent, Bayesianism involves the rejection of SE. A basic task for Bayesianism, however, is to show that differing prior probabilities are converted into some common posterior probability by the process of empirical testing. (Without this, Bayesianism cannot hope to account for the manner in which science comes up with agreed, objective scientific knowledge.) For Bayesianism, we might say, the initial non-rational preferences of scientists are converted into sound, objective, rational preferences by empirical testing. To this extent, evidence provides, for Bayesianism, the only objective, rational means for assessing hypotheses in science and thus, to this extent, Bayesianism amounts to a version of SE. Bayesianism is an attempt to rescue as much as possible of SE, given that empirical considerations *alone* cannot possibly account for the way in which theories are accepted and rejected in science.

Having made out the case for holding that SE is widely held and influential, influencing even those who reject the whole idea that science is rational, I must immediately add that by no means *all* contemporary thinkers defend SE. A few courageous thinkers have argued for rationalism, in some form or other; for example, John Lucas (1985), Nicholas Rescher (1992, ch. 7), and Roger Trigg (1993). It is worth remembering that even Bertrand Russell, at times an extreme empiricist, came in the end to defend a 'postulational' version of rationalism (Russell 1948, pt. VI).

4. TEN PROBLEMS STANDARD EMPIRICISM CANNOT SOLVE

I now provide grounds for holding that all versions of SE, including Bayesian versions, are untenable. There are ten problems which cannot be solved within the framework of SE even though, as I shall argue in Chapters 4 to 6, all ten can be solved within the framework of AOE. If correct, this provides decisive grounds for rejecting SE, and accepting AOE in its stead. The ten problems are:

Three Problems of Induction

  (i) The practical problem of induction.
 (ii) The theoretical problem of induction.
(iii) The methodological problem of induction.

Two Problems of Simplicity

 (iv) The problem of what simplicity *is*.
  (v) The problem of the rationale of preferring simple to complex theories.

Two Problems of Evidence

 (vi) The problem of the theoretical character of evidence.
(vii) The problem of the rejection of evidence when it clashes with theory.

Three Problems of Scientific Progress

(viii) The problem of the meaning of scientific progress (i.e. the problem of verisimilitude).

(ix) The problem of progress in knowledge about the nature of fundamental physical entities.

(x) The problem of scientific discovery.

5. THE TEN PROBLEMS CONCERN NATURAL SCIENCE AS A WHOLE AND NOT JUST THEORETICAL PHYSICS

In arguing that SE fails, and AOE succeeds, in solving these ten problems, in the rest of this chapter and the four that follow, I will be concerned almost exclusively with theoretical physics, even though what is at issue is the rationality of natural science as a whole. How can this emphasis be justified? The answer has to do with the fundamental character of theoretical physics within natural science as a whole.[21] The problems that we are discussing arise in a particularly clear, explicit way in connection with theoretical physics just because this is the fundamental science, with no more fundamental empirical science available which can be presupposed. By contrast, the biological sciences presuppose parts of physics and chemistry; and sciences such as chemistry, geology, and astronomy all presuppose parts of physics. This means that laws and theories of these less fundamental sciences are quite clearly not accepted on the basis, exclusively, of evidence acquired within the science in question: compatibility with physics is also required. Darwin's theory of evolution, or Watson and Crick's model of DNA, would be rejected if they clashed with basic physics. In the case of theoretical physics, however, no more fundamental science exists to be appealed to in this way; as a result it is in this context that the problem of induction, and the other problems we are discussing, arise in a particularly sharp form. The problems we are discussing concern the whole of natural science but, for the sake of clarity, need to be formulated and discussed in connection with theoretical physics.

Without more ado, let us plunge into a discussion of the problems.

6. FUNDAMENTAL OBJECTION TO STANDARD EMPIRICISM

The fundamental objection to SE amounts to this. SE comes in two forms, bare and dressed. Bare SE is an honest doctrine that is hopelessly untenable: evidence *alone* cannot conceivably determine choice of theory in science. Dressed empiricism does much better justice to scientific practice, and is not quite so obviously untenable, but is dishonest: if simple theories are persistently preferred to complex theories, independently of and even in opposition to the evidence, then science in practice does make a persistent, substantial assumption about the world independently of the evidence—namely that the world behaves more or less as if simple—and the basic tenet of SE is violated. It is this baldly stated argument that I spell out in more detail in what follows, taking the above ten problems in turn.

7. THREE PROBLEMS OF INDUCTION

The basic objection to bare SE is that theoretical knowledge in science cannot possibly be established by an appeal to evidence alone. Any law or theory in physical science is a universal statement; it applies, potentially, to infinitely many occurrences. But we can only hope to verify such a law or theory for finitely many occurrences; we must always remain infinitely far away from verifying the law or theory itself. We can have no grounds, so it seems, for holding that theories that have been successful in the past will continue to be successful in the future, especially when applied to new sorts of phenomena.

Bare SE is untenable, in short, because it creates and fails to solve the problem of induction.

In order to appreciate the force of the argument against all versions of SE, dressed as well as bare, it is important to understand the various ways in which the problem of induction can be elaborated and intensified.

We need to appreciate, to begin with, that all the observational and experimental evidence that we can ever possess in support of any physical theory must always be highly restricted and atypical, verifying at most an almost vanishingly small, non-random sample of the predictive content of the theory. Theories such as Newtonian theory or quantum theory that apply at all times and places can only be verified by means of phenomena that have occurred on earth during the past 300 years or so. We cannot *now* verify these theories as far as the future is concerned, or as far as the present or increasingly distant past is concerned for increasingly spatially distant events. Ordinarily we suppose that our telescopes enable us to observe distant stars and galaxies undergoing motion and other changes that happened long ago. But this is only the case if our present optical theories that we use to interpret these observations are more or less *true* when applied to distant places in the past;

and it is of course just these applications of these theories that we cannot verify observationally *without assuming as true the very theories we seek to verify* (since we cannot dispense with these theories unless we return to the past). Granted that we do not rely on unverifiable predictions of this type, we are confined to our observations of events in our immediate environment. But if our current theoretical knowledge is even remotely correct, this restricts us to a minute, and highly atypical, portion of the history of the universe (see Figure 2). If we possessed a finite number of verifications of a theory scattered at random throughout the

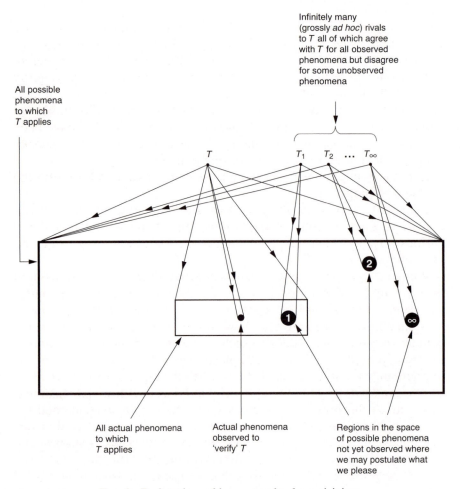

Fig. 2. Refutation of bare standard empiricism

history of the universe, the situation might not be so bad (even if we were infinitely far away from verifying *all* the predictions of the theory). This is not our situation at all. All our observations are restricted to a tiny and highly atypical pinprick of space-time. Furthermore, within this pinprick, any physical theory can only be verified to some limited degree of accuracy, infinitely far away from verifying *precisely* the predictions of the theory.

But the situation is even worse than this would suggest. For physical theories like Newtonian theory or quantum theory do not merely make predictions about what actually occurs; they contain an infinite wealth of counterfactual predictions—predictions about states of affairs that could, but do not, exist. Newtonian theory predicts the path a rocket would pursue were it to be fired at such-and-such a time and place with such-and-such a velocity, even though it is not fired at all. The capacity to make counterfactual predictions of this type is what distinguishes genuinely *lawlike* statements from so-called accidental generalizations.[22]

A genuine physical theory, in short, makes predictions about an infinity of *possible* physical states of affairs, almost all of which will never occur in reality. Furthermore, it is vital that accepted physical theories make correct predictions for *possible* (or counterfactual) phenomena as well as for *actual* phenomena. This is required if physical theories are to serve their function when used for practical, technological purposes. Whenever we employ physical theory in connection with technology we have created, we apply the theory to circumstances which would not have arisen but for our intervention. We need the theory to be correct for a range of *possible* phenomena we consider during the process of design and planning but which never occur *in actuality*.

It follows that even if a physical theory could be precisely verified for all actual phenomena throughout the entire history of the universe, we would still be infinitely far away from verifying the theory itself, for we would not have verified its predictions for an infinity of *possible* phenomena. Our universe is but one of an infinity of *possible* universes, infinitely many of which would differ from ours (if they existed) in only minor ways (such as that a pin on a table somewhere in the universe is half an inch from its actual position). It is vital that we take such possibilities, such possible universes, seriously in life, in considering alternative lines of action. In pondering alternative lines of action, we require our theories to be as correct in such (slightly different) possible universes as in the actual universe. But we can only conceivably verify any theory for just *one* of these infinitely many possible universes (and we cannot even remotely do that). The prospects of verifying a physical theory *empirically* seem utterly hopeless.

As David Hume (1959, sect. xii) well knew, it does not help to argue merely that theories can be verified if we accept a principle asserting that nature is uniform, for at once the question arises as to how we can justifiably accept this principle. We cannot argue that it is verified by experience, for this would require that we assume the very principle we seek to verify. Nor does it help, as Hume (1959, sect. xii) again understood, to argue that we should forgo *conclusive verification* and accept instead *probable verification*: the above considerations apply with equal force to any such probabilistic version of SE.

Bayesianism tries to get round Hume's arguments by interpreting probabilities of scientific hypotheses as being *subjective* in character, recording no more than the subjective confidence, or lack of it, of the individual scientist in this or that theory. But there are two major difficulties. First, we may doubt that Bayesianism really can show how diverse prior probabilities, which different scientists give initially to an untested scientific hypothesis, gradually converge on some common posterior probability, as a result of subsequent empirical testing. Secondly, and much more seriously, Bayesianism cannot hope to generate rational grounds for preferring one (unrefuted) scientific theory to another, just because it restricts itself to considering subjective probabilities only. According to Bayesianism, there is in science nothing more than the different *prejudices* of individual scientists, partly clashing and partly in accord with one another, prejudices which are modified somewhat by the results of empirical testing. Why should the mere prejudices of professional scientists be taken any more seriously than the prejudices of (consistent) madmen? Every time we cross a bridge, take medicine, or fly in an aeroplane we entrust our lives to the prejudices of scientists; and yet Bayesianism fails completely to explain why it is rational to do this, why the prejudices of scientists deserve to be taken any more seriously than those of lunatics. In so far as the judgements of experienced scientists *do* deserve to be taken seriously, there must, surely, be some objective reason for this; Bayesianism cannot begin to provide any such reason—a point admitted by Bayesians themselves when they concede that their doctrine does not solve the problem of induction.[23]

It does not help, either, to forgo verification altogether and accept, with Popper, that there is at most empirical falsification of theory in science (Popper 1959, 1963, ch. 1). For, given any theory, however massively empirically successful, the above considerations in effect show that there will always be infinitely many rival theories which agree precisely with the given theory for all available evidence but which disagree for some as yet unobserved phenomena. All we need to do in order to construct such 'aberrant' versions of an accepted empirically successful theory, T (such as Newtonian theory in the last century, let us say, or quantum theory or general relativity today), is to modify T *for as yet unobserved phenomena* in any way we please. In this way we can always construct endlessly many of the following five kinds of aberrant rival theories to T. These aberrant rivals to T would never be taken seriously for a moment in scientific practice; but bare SE, whether verificationist or falsificationist (i.e. Popperian), can provide no grounds for their wholesale exclusion from science. Indeed, the following aberrant theories become increasingly scientifically acceptable, as we move down the list, from the standpoint of bare SE—a devastating indictment of the position.

1. The new aberrant theory T_1 agrees with T for all observed phenomena, disagreeing only for phenomena within some as yet unobserved space-time region. Example: Suppose that T is Newtonian theory (NT), and consider Newton's law of gravitation $F = Gm_1m_2/d^2$. (Here F is the force of attraction due to gravity between two objects, masses m_1 and m_2, distance d apart, and G is the gravitational constant.) NT asserts that this law applies to all objects with mass everywhere, at all times and places. In order to formulate an aberrant version of NT, which we may call NT_1, we need only modify Newton's law of gravitation to read: '$F = Gm_1m_2/d^2$ for times before 12 p.m., 31 December 2050 and $F = Gm_1m_2/d^3$ for times at or after 12 p.m., 31 December 2050'. Until 12 p.m., 31 December 2050, the aberrant theory fits all the available evidence just as well as NT does, although after that date it yields drastically different predictions. Doubtless NT_1 will be decisively refuted when the year 2051 dawns, but there will always remain infinitely many further aberrant theories of this type to be refuted.

2. The aberrant theory T_2 agrees with T for all observed *kinds* of phenomena (wherever and whenever they may occur) but disagrees for some *kind* of phenomenon never observed. We saw, above, that almost all the possible states of affairs to which a theory such as NT refers will never occur, thus remaining unobserved even if all of space and time is observed. Thus we can easily specify endlessly many different *kinds* of physical states of affairs to which the theory applies that will never have been observed, and may never *be* observed, but *could* be observed. For example: 'Six spheres, within such-and-such size and accuracy, made of

solid gold, to such-and-such degree of purity, move without colliding under gravitation in a vacuum, of such-and-such degree, within such-and-such a spatial region'. If the spheres must have a mass greater than 1 million tons (and permitted departures from precision are minute), it is quite likely that no technologically advanced civilization anywhere, in the entire history of the cosmos, will create the six-gold-spheres system specified in the way indicated. One particular example, then, of this second type of aberrant theory is: 'For all systems that are not six-gold-spheres systems, $F = Gm_1m_2/d^2$ holds, but for all six-gold-spheres systems, $F = Gm_1m_2/d^3$ holds'. There is an infinity of such aberrant versions of NT which, though violently at odds with NT, will nevertheless never clash with NT for anything that actually occurs, anywhere in the history of the cosmos.

3. The aberrant theory T_3 agrees with T for all observed kinds of phenomena but disagrees for some particular kind of phenomenon observed many times *except for some irrelevant, bizarre detail*. Let us suppose that the phenomenon in question is Galileo's experiment: balls roll with (nearly) constant acceleration down inclined planes. This confirms NT. The unobserved phenomenon is the following variant of Galileo's experiment: 5 lb. of gold dust is sprinkled around the inclined plane on the laboratory floor. Instead of Newton's law of gravitation, NT_3 asserts: 'For phenomena except this particular kind of phenomenon, $F = Gm_1m_2/d^2$, but for this modified-Galileo kind of phenomenon, $F = Gm_1m_2/d^3$'. Any kind of experiment (or phenomenon), however often observed to confirm some theory T, can always be modified in this sort of bizarre, irrelevant way, in endlessly many different ways, so as to ensure that *precisely* this kind of (modified) phenomenon has never been observed, and no doubt never will be observed. This third kind of aberrant theory, in other words, is a special case of the second kind of aberrant theory—one that is especially easy to test experimentally.

4. Taking T_3 as our starting-point, we may add some independently testable and confirmed postulate, h, to T_3 to form $T_3 + h = T_4$, the fourth kind of aberrant variant of T. Thus to NT_3 we might add: 'Copper expands when heated (between such-and-such a temperature range, in such-and-such conditions)', in this way forming a new theory, NT_4. Here, NT_4 has greater empirical content than NT_3, the excess content being in part corroborated empirically.

5. So far it has been assumed that T yields nothing but correct predictions. This assumption is unrealistic. All actual physical theories, however empirically successful, have their limitations and problems.

For even the most empirically successful physical theory, a more realistic assessment of overall empirical support would be something like the following: the predictions of T are accurate for phenomena A, more or less accurate for phenomena B, not forthcoming for phenomena C (because here the equations cannot be solved), apparently incorrect for phenomena D (perhaps because the derivations from T are incorrect, or the experiments have not been done properly), and not forthcoming for phenomena E because beyond the scope of T (see Figure 3). There are now infinitely many aberrant variants of T which assert: everything occurs as T predicts in A; in B phenomena occur well within experimental error (and this is specified piecemeal); in C the observed phenomena occur (and this is specified piecemeal); and so too for D and E. All theories of this type are vastly more empirically successful than T, in

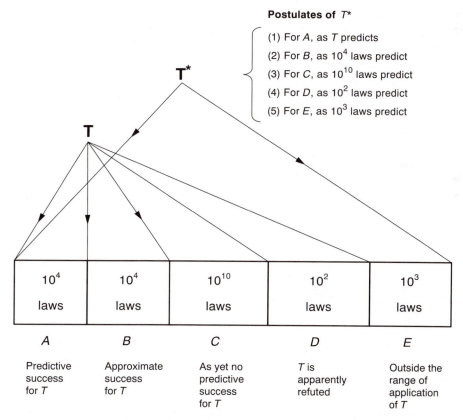

FIG. 3. The standard situation in physics

that they successfully predict everything that T does; they are not refuted where T is (in B and D); and they make accurate predictions where T yields no predictions (in C and E).[24]

It is important to appreciate that empirically successful aberrant theories, of types 1 to 5, arise all the time, even when firmly established physical laws and theories are applied in utterly standard circumstances to standard phenomena, in order to design or manufacture a transistor radio, let us say, a bridge or an aeroplane. No one bridge is exactly like any other, in all details, especially if we take the environment of the bridge into account. We ordinarily assume, of course, that the differences are irrelevant from the standpoint of the trustworthiness of physical laws that determine the strength of steel and so on. The above considerations show that it will always be possible, however, to formulate rival (aberrant) laws, just as well verified empirically as ordinary, accepted laws, if not more so, which postulate that, in the precise circumstances of such-and-such a bridge, unprecedented phenomena occur: steel will become soft as butter, and the whole edifice will collapse.

There are *infinitely* many aberrant rivals to T in each of 1 to 5 above, each aberrant rival to T being just as empirically successful as T, at the very least. Indeed, each one of the infinitely many aberrant rivals to T in 4, and in 5 is actually *empirically more successful* than T. We can of course set out to refute experimentally these aberrant theories, but as there are infinitely many of them, there will always remain infinitely many unrefuted. How, then, can it be justifiable to accept any physical law or theory as constituting knowledge, even conjectural knowledge, on the basis of empirical success and failure *alone*? This is the fully fledged problem of induction.

Three versions of the problem can be distinguished.

(i) T*he practical problem of induction*. What justification can there be for accepting any physical law or theory, however empirically successful, granted that our aim is to use the law or theory as a basis for action?

(ii) T*he theoretical problem of induction*. What justification can there be for accepting any physical law or theory, however empirically successful, granted that our aim is to improve our theoretical knowledge and understanding of the universe?

(iii) T*he methodological problem of induction*. What methods enable us to select physical laws and theories on the basis of empirical considerations in a way which does justice to what goes on in science?

These three versions of the problem are different because, in each case, the *aim* (for which theories are to be selected) is different.

As far as the practical problem is concerned, our aim is to have lawlike knowledge that is as trustworthy as possible and relevant to the actions we intend to perform (whether this is walking across a field, building a bridge, or prescribing medicine). But all lawlike knowledge is, it seems, entirely untrustworthy: however firmly verified a law or theory may be, there will always exist infinitely many (aberrant) rivals even more firmly established. Rational action becomes impossible.

As far as the theoretical problem is concerned, our aim is to improve our theoretical knowledge and understanding of the universe. Here, it may be much more important that a theory is fruitful than trustworthy. False, testable speculations (about the big bang, for example) may constitute important contributions to scientific knowledge. But eschewing trustworthiness does not help; the above arguments seem to show that this type of conjectural theoretical knowledge is impossible as well.

The third, methodological version of the problem is the most modest. The aim is simply to select theories on the basis of evidence in a way which reflects what goes on in science, irrespective of whether this delivers knowledge, in any sense. But even this highly modest aim seems to be unrealizable. If theories are selected on the basis of empirical success and failure, surely infinitely many empirically successful aberrant theories ought to be preferred to non-aberrant but empirically less successful theories? In scientific practice, it is rare indeed for an aberrant theory to receive any attention whatsoever, however empirically successful it might be.

In order to solve the practical and theoretical problems of induction we need to *justify* the methods of science (methods which determine choice of theory on the basis of evidence) from the standpoint of obtaining trustworthy, or theoretically fruitful, knowledge. In order to solve the methodological problem, something much more modest is required: we simply have to *specify* what the methods of science are, without bothering with their justification. It needs to be appreciated, in short, that the problem of induction is as much about *what* the methods of science are as it is about how such methods are to be *justified*.

Bare SE fails to solve all three versions of the problem of induction. One might think, perhaps, that the very absurdity of the above kinds of aberrant theory—their obvious scientific unacceptability—means somehow that the above *argument* against bare SE is somewhat absurd, not to be taken seriously. Actually, the matter is all the other way round. The argument is all the *stronger* for the absurdity of the theories that bare SE fails to exclude from science. If bare SE failed to exclude theories from science that are only unacceptable in some unobvious or uncertain way, the failure might not be too serious. The trouble is that aberrant theories are glaringly unacceptable, and yet bare SE fails to exclude them from science, or even recommends them for acceptance. Bare SE is hopelessly inadequate.

8. TWO PROBLEMS OF SIMPLICITY

Why, in practice, is science not overwhelmed by infinitely many well-verified, aberrant theories, of types 1 to 5 above? Because in scientific practice all such aberrant theories are not even formulated, let alone seriously considered or put to the test of experiment. Merely in order to qualify as a scientific theory at all, a system of testable statements must possess a certain degree of simplicity. As dressed SE asserts, *two* criteria govern choice of theory in science: *empirical success* and *simplicity*. Empirically successful but aberrant 'theories', of the five kinds considered above, do not get considered in science because of their gross lack of simplicity.

At once, two new problems arise.

(iv) *The problem of what simplicity is.* Granted that simple theories are preferred in science to complex (or aberrant) theories, what *is* simplicity?

(v) *The problem of justifying choice of simple theories in science.* How is persistent preference for simple, explanatory theories in science to be justified?

'Simplicity' is being used here as a blanket term, to cover a number of other terms used in this context, such as 'explanatoriness', 'non-*ad hocness*', 'non-aberrance', 'unity', 'symmetry', 'beauty', 'elegance', 'conceptual coherence', 'inner perfection'. Whether there is just one relevant notion here, or two or more notions, I leave open at the present stage of the argument. The common idea lurking behind the diverse terms is that there are non-empirical criteria for the selection of theories in science, which have to do with the form or nature of theories, rather than their empirical success or failure.

A solution to problem (iv) would suffice to solve problem (iii)—the methodological problem of induction. Appropriate solutions to problem (v) would suffice to solve the practical and theoretical problems of induction—problems (i) and (ii). Thus, in a sense, the problems of simplicity *are* the problems of induction. Solutions to the two problems of simplicity suffice to solve the three problems of induction.

Dressed SE is, however, incapable of solving these problems. The reason is straightforward. In persistently rejecting (or failing to consider) empirically successful but aberrant theories, of types 1 to 5 above, we are in effect making a persistent, substantial assumption about the world, namely that the world (or that bit of it that we are investigating) is not aberrant, or behaves, to a sufficient degree of approximation, as if not aberrant. (In a world that *is* aberrant, in some characteristic way, empirical progress would require us to favour the corresponding kind of aberrant theories.) In order to *justify* our persistent preference for simple (or non-aberrant) theories we need to justify our persistent assumption that the world behaves more or less as if simple (or non-aberrant). Indeed, in order merely to explain what simplicity *is*, in the relevant sense, we need to explain what the persistent assumption *is* that we are making about the world—this assumption that we hold onto so firmly in science that theories which clash with it are not even formulated, whatever their empirical success might be were they to be formulated. Solutions to the two problems of simplicity, (iv) and (v), in other words, require that we recognize entirely explicitly that science does, in practice, make a substantial, persistent *assumption* about the nature of the world, upheld independently of, or even in violation of, empirical considerations. But this violates the basic idea of SE: see Figure 4. Thus, no version of SE, whether bare or dressed, can solve the two problems of simplicity (or the three problems of induction).

Dressed SE is caught in a trap. The more a notion of simplicity is developed whose use in science is compatible with SE, the more useless such a notion becomes from the standpoint of ruling out empirically successful aberrant theories, of types 1 to 5, and so the more hopeless the notion becomes from the standpoint of helping to solve the problem of induction. On the other hand, the more a notion of simplicity is developed which does effectively rule out empirically successful aberrant theories, the more its use in science becomes incompatible with the basic idea of SE.

Let us now look at one or two attempts to solve the above two simplicity problems within the framework of SE.

One approach to these problems is that of conventionalism or instrumentalism. The persistent preference for simple theories in science is harmless because all that theories do in science is to systematize or organize empirical knowledge in as convenient a way as possible. Only at the observational level is there knowledge: at the theoretical

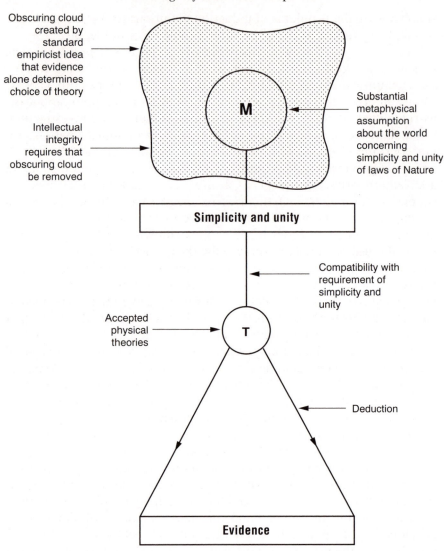

Obscuring cloud created by standard empiricist idea that evidence alone determines choice of theory

Intellectual integrity requires that obscuring cloud be removed

M

Substantial metaphysical assumption about the world concerning simplicity and unity of laws of Nature

Simplicity and unity

Compatibility with requirement of simplicity and unity

Accepted physical theories

T

Deduction

Evidence

FIG. 4. Refutation of dressed standard empiricism

level there are merely more or less convenient or 'simple' ways of organizing or systematizing this knowledge. Naturally that theory is chosen which systematizes empirical knowledge in the most convenient or simple way; persistent preference for the 'simplest' theory is entirely harmless, and does not at all involve making the metaphysical assumption that Nature herself is simple.[25]

This approach might be adequate if all that is at issue is choosing between a number of theories which systematize the *same* body of evidence in different, more or less simple ways. But this is not the problem that confronts us at all. Rather, the problem has to do with the grounds for choosing a simple theory, *T*, in preference to infinitely many rival, aberrant theories, which yield (some) empirical predictions which *clash* with those of *T*, and which seem to be just as firmly verified empirically as *T* or, as in the case of aberrant theories of types 4 and 5, even more firmly verified than *T*.

Another possible approach involves arguing that, in order to be acceptable, a physical law or theory must satisfy the simplicity requirement of being strictly universal, in the sense that it refers to no particular places, times or objects (Popper 1959: 62–70).

This fails on all counts. It rules out aberrant theories of type 1, but fails to exclude aberrant theories of types 2 to 5 (which are strictly universal). Furthermore, adopting such a simplicity requirement commits science to making the permanent metaphysical assumption that there are no special places, times, or objects, and this clearly violates SE. The universe might be such that there *are* special places, times, or objects, in which case, so it would seem, our theories should refer to them. The requirement is not strong enough to rule out aberrant theories of types 2 to 5; and yet it is too strong to be compatible with SE. The requirement is not even compatible with the historical record: Kepler's laws of planetary motion, major contributions to science, do refer to a special object (as it was then conceived to be), namely the sun.

Another possible approach is to argue that non-aberrant theories are inherently more verifiable than aberrant ones—or that it is only the non-aberrant part of an aberrant theory that is amenable to verification. This view is sometimes known as 'induction-to-the-best-explanation'. Given a number of rival theories it is always, other things being equal, the most explanatory theory that is the best verified. Aberrant theories, because of their grossly *ad hoc* character, are inherently non-explanatory and are thus, in comparison with their non-aberrant rivals, not amenable to empirical verification.[26]

But why should non-aberrant or explanatory theories be inherently the most verifiable? In a universe that *is* aberrant in some characteristic way, it would be theories that reflect this characteristic aberrance which would be empirically successful; non-aberrant, explanatory theories would all be false. If it were a case of choosing between an explanatory theory *T*, and a non-explanatory (aberrant) theory *T**, both having, on the face of it, equal empirical support, then there might be a case for favouring *T* to *T**. But this is not what is at issue. If *T** is a type 4 aberrant version of T, then T^* is *better verified* than T in the sense that T^* successfully predicts everything that T predicts but also successfully predicts phenomena about which T is silent. If T^* is a type 5 aberrant version of T, then the matter is even worse: T^* successfully predicts everything that T predicts; it successfully predicts phenomena about which T is silent; and it is not refuted whereas T *is* refuted. It is difficult to see what sense it can make to say that, in these circumstances, despite overwhelming appearances to the contrary, T is better verified than T^*. Persistently to choose explanatory (or non-aberrant) theories in this way, in preference to aberrant theories, *in the teeth of the evidence*, must be to make a persistent assumption about the world, to the effect that it behaves, at least approximately, as if non-aberrant; and this violates SE.

Yet another approach is Popper's idea, mentioned above, that simple theories deserve to be given preference in science, not because they are more verifiable, but because they are more *falsifiable*. If simplicity could indeed be equated with falsifiability, then this would constitute a magnificent vindication of Popper's version of bare SE. For we could argue that, in order to comply with SE, we need to maximize the capacity of the evidence to choose theories, and this in turn means giving preference to those theories most amenable to being chosen in this way, namely the most empirically falsifiable theories, which means in turn the simplest theories. Biasing our choice of theory in the direction of simplicity looks as if it violates impartial empiricism, but actually maximizes the capacity of evidence to choose theories impartially.

Unfortunately, the basic idea is untenable: simplicity cannot be equated with falsifiability. Aberrant theories of type 4 above are counter-examples: they are all more falsifiable than T, and at the same time much less *simple*. For Popper, T^* is more falsifiable than T if it predicts everything that T predicts, and more besides. Type 4 aberrant theories are more falsifiable than the given theory, T, in this sense, and yet much less simple, to an unacceptable extent.

Popper has also suggested that the relative falsifiability, and hence simplicity, of two theories can be assessed by comparing, roughly, for each theory, the maximum number of observation statements which, taken together, just fail to falsify the theory: the less this number is, the more falsifiable the theory is. Thus in order to refute the hypothesis that planets move in circles we need (in general) to determine four distinct positions of a planet, *three* being just insufficient, whereas in order to refute the hypothesis that planets move in ellipses we need in general six determinations of position, *five* being just insufficient. The hypothesis of circular orbits is thus more falsifiable, and so simpler, than the hypothesis of elliptical orbits, as our intuitions tell us (Popper 1959: 126–45).

It seems that, even for this simple case, the idea does not quite work: just *three* positions in a straight line suffice to refute both hypotheses. A much more serious difficulty is that this second method for comparing simplicity turns out to be untenable for exactly the same reason as the first method. Given two distinct theories, T_1 and T_2, with T_2, let us suppose, simpler than T_1 when compared by means of Popper's second method, then $T_1 + T_2$ will, by this same method, be simpler than T_1 (just because T_2 is). But this is absurd; $T_1 + T_2$ is, in general, a type 4 aberrant theory much less simple than T_1.

Subsequently, as we saw above, Popper shifted his ground and stipulated that an acceptable theory must comply with his informally stated *requirement of simplicity* (see Section 2 of this chapter). As an explication of what simplicity *is* this does not help much in that it uses the very terms, namely 'simple' and 'unifying', that we are trying to explicate. If, however, it can be interpreted in a sufficiently coherent and strong sense to exclude from science aberrant theories of types 1 to 5, then implementing the principle violates SE. For implementing the principle involves persistently rejecting infinitely many theories, of types 4 and 5 let us say, and persistently accepting *less empirically successful*, or even *empirically refuted*, theories in their stead, merely because these latter theories all *unify* (whereas the aberrant theories do not). To do this *is* to make a big, permanent metaphysical assumption about the world along the lines of: the phenomena behave, to a considerable degree of approximation at least, as if they all occur in accordance with some unified pattern of law. This violates SE. It is not just that Popper fails to provide a justification (or a 'rationale', to use more Popperian language) for his requirement of simplicity; its use is incompatible with SE, and therefore with falsificationism.

One way of trying to avoid the insuperable problem of justifying simplicity on SE grounds is to construe simplicity as something which is as formal, abstract, logical, or linguistic as possible, thus deflecting attention away from the existence of substantial metaphysical assumptions being built into the scientific use of the concept.

This strategy cannot work. In order to be adequate, the principle of simplicity must exclude aberrant theories of types 1 to 5. In choosing theories in accordance with such a principle we make a big metaphysical assumption (whether we acknowledge it or not), which clashes with SE. Hence no adequate conception of simplicity can be compatible with SE.

The fact that the strategy cannot work has not deterred people from trying it out. Examples are Jeffreys and Wrinch (1921), Goodman (1972), Popper (see above), Sober (1975), Friedman (1974), Kitcher (1981), and Watkins (1984: 203–13). What is interesting is that these attempts fail even to say, coherently, what simplicity *is*, quite in addition to the foregone failure to *justify* its use in science.

One might suppose, naively perhaps, that simplicity can be equated with the number of postulates in the deductive structure of the theory. But however many postulates a theory may have, it can always be reformulated as having just one postulate. Richard Feynman (Feynman *et al.* 1965: ii. 25. 10–11) gives this delightful recipe for converting any theory, with however many postulates, into an apparently beautifully unified theory, with just one postulate. Consider an appallingly aberrant universe governed by 10^{10} quite different, distinct laws. Even in such a universe, the true 'theory of everything' can be expressed in the dazzlingly simple, unified form: $A = 0$. Suppose the 10^{10} distinct laws of the universe are: $F = ma$, $F = Gm_1m_2/d^2$, and so on. Let $A_1 = (F - ma)^2$, $A_2 = (F - Gm_1m_2/d^2)^2$, and so on for all 10^{10} distinct laws. Let $A = \Sigma_{r=1}^{10^{10}} A_r$. The 'theory of everything' of this universe can now be formulated as: $A = 0$. (This is true if and only if each $A_r = 0$.)

We cannot say, either, that simplicity has something to do with *terminological* simplicity, with the simplicity or complexity of the *postulates* of the theory, for there stands Feynman's recipe as a demolition of the idea: what could be simpler than '$A = 0$'? Or, again, given any function, $y = f(x)$, however horribly complex, we can always reduce this to the wonderfully simple equation $y = z$. We simply implement a judicious change of variable: $x = f^{-1}(z)$. We then have $y = f(x) = f(f^{-1}(z)) = z$ (i.e. $y = z$).

Aberrance, too, can be got rid of by means of a modified version of what might be called Goodman's recipe, after his discussion of predicates 'grue' and 'bleen', aberrant variants of 'blue' and 'green' (in a type 1 way): see Goodman (1954).

Suppose we have a unified theory, T, and an aberrant variant, T^*, which is made up of two parts, T_A and T_B, which are restricted to applying to the mutually exclusive domains of phenomena, A and B, which together make up the domain of applicability of T. Suppose, further, that $T_A = T$ within A, but that $T_B \neq T$. All this we presume to be formulated in terms of language (or mathematical or conceptual scheme) L. We now put consequences of T_B into one-to-one correspondence with consequences of T within B, and introduce a new language, L^*, which is such that: (*a*) consequences of T_A and T have the same form within domain A in both L and L^*; and (*b*) any consequence of T_B formulated in L^* has the same form as the corresponding consequence of T in B. This means that the aberrant theory T^*, when formulated in the (aberrant) language L^*, has a form just like that of T, which is presumed to be unified throughout A and B. We can, in short, always *formulate* any theory, however grossly aberrant, in such a way that the *form* of the theory is wholly non-aberrant. (We can do this, at least, as long as we can establish a one-to-one mapping between the clashing consequences of the two theories, aberrant and non-aberrant, when both are formulated in the original language.)

The prospects for explicating simplicity in linguistic, terminological, or axiomatic terms do not look good.

There is, however, an important suggestion along these lines put forward by Jeffreys and Wrinch (1921). Their idea, essentially, is to count the number of constants, and equate simplicity with paucity of constants. Thus $y = ax^2$ is simpler than $y = ax^2 + bx$, where a and b are constants.

That there is something right in this idea is indicated by the fact that theoretical physics is indeed guided (in part) by this principle of simplicity. A case in point has to do with the so-called 'standard model' of contemporary theoretical physics. The standard model sums up our theoretical knowledge of the fundamental particles and forces apart from gravitation. It consists of the quantum field theories of the electromagnetic, weak, and strong forces plus a specification of those properties of particles, electrons, quarks, and so on not specified by theory, such as their mass. The standard model contains at least nineteen independent fundamental constants (Kaku 1993: 13–14) having to do with such things as the mass of particles, which are not determined theoretically. It is regarded as lacking in simplicity (or unity) for this very reason (at least in part).

However, interpreted as a theory of simplicity which applies to the terminological form of equations or theories, this 'number of constants' proposal is as hopeless as the other suggestions made along these lines. Given a non-aberrant theory, T, and an aberrant variant, T^*, then T^* will (in non-aberrant formulations, L) have more constants than T. These will be required in order to specify at what value of place, time, mass, relative velocity, or whatever, the form of the laws 'abruptly changes' (when viewed from a non-aberrant perspective). But when T and T^* are formulated in the appropriate aberrant language, the form of T^* becomes non-aberrant and it is T that becomes aberrant in form, and hence must have the additional constants. Number of constants varies with formulation. Indeed, given any set of equations with N independent constants, new terminology can always, quite trivially, be introduced which is able, artificially, to reduce N to 1 (or to turn 1 into N, to take the opposite case).

One might seek to explicate the distinction between non-aberrant and aberrant theories by means of the idea that in the first case the 'form' of the laws remains constant throughout all phenomena, whereas in the second case the 'form' changes. And one might stipulate, further, that functions specified by equations of non-aberrant theories must be *analytic*, in the mathematical sense of being representable as a power series. Granted that a function is analytic, then, given the form of the function for some restricted range of variables, the form of the function everywhere else is uniquely determined, by analytic continuation. (Given that $y = f(x)$ is analytic and has the form $y = 3x^2 + 4x$ for $2 \leq x \leq 5$, it follows that $f(x)$ must have the same form for all other values of x.) This provides, it seems, an unambiguous distinction between non-aberrant and aberrant theories.

All the usual difficulties arise in connection with this proposal. If it were substantive, it would be impossible to justify within SE. But difficulties arise in connection with the claim that it is substantive. We have already shown, above, that a change of language, from L to L^*, can change the form of the functions of a theory, from the non-analytic to the analytic, or vice versa. (All one requires is appropriate non-analytic functions specifying the change of variables as one goes from L to L^*.) And quite apart from analyticity being relative to choice of units, variables, concepts, or language, there is the difficulty that given any theory, however discontinuous and non-analytic it may be as one goes into, and out of, some sub-domain d of the domain of phenomena to which the theory applies, there will always be an *analytic* theory which approximates as close as one pleases to the given aberrant theory.[27]

The point would seem to be quite general. Given any theory, however complex, we can always transform it into an ostensibly simple theory by an appropriate choice of terminology, of language; and vice versa, any simple theory can, in the same way, always be made to appear as horribly complex or aberrant as we choose. The simplicity or complexity of theories is, it seems, language-dependent. We might try to overcome the problem by specifying a definite language, L, in which all theories are to be formulated, for example the Newtonian language of point-particles and forces that vary in a fixed way with distance. But to proceed in this way cannot be compatible with SE, since adopting a definite theoretical language in which to formulate theories amounts to adopting some kind of metaphysical thesis about the world. And if the historical record is anything to go by, adopting a fixed language for theoretical physics would be the *wrong* thing to do: sooner or later it would block progress. Just because we are ignorant of the ultimate nature of the universe, we don't know what is the appropriate language in which to formulate theories; any choice we make in our state of ignorance is almost bound to be the wrong choice, one in which physical phenomena cannot ultimately be described by a 'simple' theory.

Here, to conclude this discussion, are three more suggestions as to what simplicity might be.

The first is due to Michael Friedman (1974). Friedman's key example of unification is the case of Newtonian theory (NT) unifying (and hence explaining) Kepler's laws of planetary motion (KL), Galileo's laws of terrestrial motion (GL), Boyle's law (B), and Graham's law (G), all taken to be logical consequences of NT. We have $NT \rightarrow KL \& GL \& B \& G$. But we also have $KL \& GL \& B \& G \rightarrow KL \& GL \& B \& G$. Why does 'NT' unify and explain, whereas 'KL & GL & B & G' does not? Friedman's answer is that, whereas NT reduces the number of 'independently acceptable' sentences in that which we seek to unify, KL & GL & B & G does not (since it just reproduces the sentences we seek to unify).

There are a number of things wrong with this proposal. Friedman assumes that NT logically implies each of KL, GL, B, and G. But it does not. NT is logically incompatible with KL and GL, as we shall see below. This situation is, furthermore, typical of what happens in physics when one theory, T, unifies two other theories, T_1 and T_2: T is almost invariably incompatible with T_1 and T_2, but is nevertheless capable of yielding the forms of T_1 and T_2 when appropriate limits are taken (as we shall see in more detail in Chapters 4 and 6). But even if this objection is ignored, and we pretend that NT does imply the laws to be unified, there is still the problem of why NT can be held to have fewer independently acceptable sentences than KL & GL & B & G. We can easily divide the domain of phenomena to which NT applies into n sub-domains, and reformulate NT as n distinct theories about these n sub-domains; n, here, can be any number we please, even infinity. What justifies the claim that these n theories are not independently acceptable? One reply might be that the n fragments of NT all have the same form, whereas KL, GL, etc. do not; this ensures that the n fragments of NT are *not* independently acceptable. But first, what grounds can there be for holding that the same laws, in this sense, hold throughout a range of phenomena? And secondly, we can easily introduce new terminology to render the forms of the laws KL, GL, B, and G all somewhat similar, but the form of the *n* fragments of NT all dissimilar: we should then have to say that KL & GL & B & G is more unified than NT. Friedman's proposal fails.[28]

The second idea is due to Philip Kitcher (1981, 1989). For Kitcher, *T* unifies $T_1, T_2, \ldots, T_n$ if these theories can be derived from *T* and the derivations exhibit the same pattern of argumentation.

There are a number of objections to this proposal. First, doubts may be entertained as to whether the key notion of 'same pattern of argumentation' can be made sufficiently precise to be coherent. Secondly, it may be objected that the idea faces the same difficulty that faced Friedman's proposal: typically, in practice, unifying theories are incompatible with the laws or theories they unify (whereas Kitcher presupposes deducibility). Thirdly, it may be objected that, in practice, it seems to be the case that a genuinely unifying theory (such as NT, classical electromagnetism, or quantum theory) provides a rich store of *diverse* patterns of argumentation in predicting diverse phenomena, this if anything being a feature of unification rather than detrimental to unification. Even in the elementary case of 'deriving' KL and GL from NT, for example, different limits need to be taken: in the case of KL, one lets the masses of the planets tend to zero, whereas in the case of GL, one may keep the mass of the earth a constant and let its density tend to zero (its radius tending to infinity). To this extent, the arguments are different. In the case of quantum theory, a much richer range of diverse patterns of derivation are employed by physicists to obtain diverse phenomena predicted by the theory, and yet quantum theory does not seem the less unified as a result. Fourthly, even if this objection is ignored, Kitcher's proposal falls foul of the standard terminology-change objection. Given a *T* that unifies $T_1 \ldots T_n$ in Kitcher's sense, one could readily formulate *T* in some new (aberrant) terminology so that, when formulated in terms of this new terminology, quite different patterns of argumentation have to be employed in deriving each of $T_1 \ldots T_n$. The unity or disunity of a theory is hopelessly terminology-dependent. For these reasons, Kitcher's proposal fails.

The third idea is due to John Watkins (1984: 203–13). The idea, here, is that a putative theory, *T*, is sufficiently unified to constitute a genuine theory (as opposed to some arbitrary collection of postulates) if and only if when the axioms of *T* are split into any two parts, T_1 and T_2 (so that $T = T_1 + T_2$), then the testable content of T_1 plus the testable content of T_2 is less than the testable content of *T*. This proposal suffers from the defect that, as it stands, any genuinely unified scientific theory, such as Newtonian theory or general relativity, can always be axiomatized in such a way as to fail this requirement for unity. In order to overcome this defect, Watkins restricts attention to axiomatizations of (potential) theories that satisfy five requirements for being 'natural'. T is unified if and only if, when 'naturally axiomatized', the testable content of T_1 plus that of T_2 is less than that of T, where T_1 and T_2 consist of all the 'natural' axioms of T.

Watkins's five requirements for 'natural' axiomatization are the following:

1. Each axiom must be logically independent of the conjunction of the others.

2. No predicate or individual constant may occur inessentially in the axioms.

3. No axiom may contain a (proper) component that is a theorem of the theory, or becomes one when its variables are bound by the quantifiers that bind them in the axiom.

4. If axioms containing only theoretical predicates (and no observational predicates) can be separately stated, without violating other rules, they should be.

5. The axioms must be such that they cannot be made more numerous without violating one or other of the above rules.

The basic objection to this proposal is that it leaves entirely unaffected the *physical content* of the axioms or postulates. Given a theory, T, whose N postulates satisfy Watkins's requirements, we can easily formulate a grossly aberrant, disunified theory, T^*, whose N postulates are just like those of T except that a postulate which, in T, consists of a simple, non-*ad hoc*, *unifying* equation expressing the basic dynamics of the theory, becomes, in T^*, a horribly complex, *ad hoc*, *disunified*, aberrant equation expressing the dynamics of the theory. For example, T might be NT, one postulate of which asserts the basic law of Newtonian gravitation, namely: $F = Gm_1m_2/d^2$. In T^*, this may take as horribly complex a form as we choose, for example:

$$F = G\left[\left(m_1m_2/d^{5.7} + m_1^{3.5} + m_2^{3.5}\right)^{-\frac{3}{2}} + \left(m_1/m_2d + m_1^{3.5}m_2^{3.4}\right)^{2.5}\right].$$

(Watkins's five constraints do not require that the form of the equations are invariant with respect to changes of units: hence we need not bother to respect this invariance principle. The principle can always be complied with, however, if we so desire, by adding appropriate constants.)

There is no difficulty in ensuring that T^* satisfies Watkins's unity requirement just as well as T does and yet, clearly, T^* fails horribly as a 'simple' or 'unified' theory. Watkins's proposal fails to provide a sufficient condition for unity.[29]

To sum up the argument so far: bare SE cannot solve the three problems of induction and is thus untenable; dressed SE cannot solve the two problems of simplicity which means, in addition, that it cannot solve the two justificational problems of induction; it, too, is untenable. In persistently rejecting (or failing to consider) infinitely many empirically successful *aberrant* theories science does make a persistent substantial assumption about the world: in denying this SE, in all its versions, commits its fatal blunder.

Continuing our discussion of the ten problems SE fails to solve, we come now to:

9. TWO PROBLEMS ABOUT EVIDENCE

Any experimental result is, at the very least, a claim about a repeatable phenomenon. The same result will be obtained, so the implicit claim runs, whenever and wherever the experiment is performed, as long as it is performed properly. This means that even experimental results embody law-like, universal statements. Thus all the problems, considered above, that arise in connection with the acceptance of theories in science arise also in connection with the acceptance of experimental results.

The actual situation is much worse than this would suggest. For, as Duhem (1954, ch. IV) argued so cogently many years ago, actual experimental results are highly theoretical in character. What can be observed in the laboratory by a non-scientist with the unaided eye is of little scientific interest. It is not the observable results of an experiment that are of interest but the theoretical interpretation that is put upon these results. Theory is, in this way, built into evidence. We thus have:

(vi) *The problem of the theoretical character of evidence.* The evidence, in terms of which laws and theories are accepted and rejected, is itself highly theoretical in character. Thus, all the problems that arise in connection with the acceptance of *theories* on the basis of *evidence* also arise in connection with the acceptance of *evidence* on the basis of *things done in laboratories.*

This problem becomes all the more severe when one takes into account the frequency with which scientists reject evidence and hold onto theory when the two clash. SE would lead one to believe that evidence must be sacrosanct in science, it always being deplorable to reject experimental results because they clash with the theory one is testing. But scientists do this all the time! It may take months to get an experiment to work properly; during this period, results are rejected on the basis that the experiment is not working properly, just because the results do not meet with theoretical expectations. A famous example of this has been described by Gerald Holton (1978, ch. 2). Millikan, in determining the charge of the electron, repeatedly rejected observations which did not fit with his theoretical expectations. We thus have:

(vii) *The problem of evidence being rejected when it clashes with theory.* SE would lead one to expect that, whenever there is a clash between experimental results and theory, it is theory which gives way to experimental results. Frequently in science the reverse of this occurs; experimental results are rejected because they clash with theory. How can SE account for this as good scientific practice?

We come now to:

10. THREE PROBLEMS OF SCIENTIFIC PROGRESS

So far we have considered a number of problems about how it is possible to achieve scientific progress, and how we can ever *know* that scientific progress has been achieved. There is, however, an even graver problem about what it can *mean* to say that science makes progress.

One striking feature of scientific progress, already mentioned, is that new theories often correct, and therefore, strictly speaking, contradict their predecessors. As remarked above, NT corrects both Kepler's laws of planetary motion and Galileo's laws of terrestrial motion. If it is assumed that the sun is motionless, and the planets do not attract each other gravitationally, then NT predicts that the planets move in ellipses as prescribed by Kepler's laws. But both assumptions are false: according to NT, the planets attract the sun and each other gravitationally. This means that NT predicts deviations from Kepler's laws, as Newton himself demonstrated. In brief, NT contradicts Kepler's laws. Again, if it is assumed that bodies near the surface of the earth experience a constant gravitational force as they fall, then NT implies Galileo's law that bodies fall with constant acceleration. (This follows at once from

$F = ma$.) But Newton's law of gravitation tells us that, as bodies fall, the force of gravitation increases; thus NT contradicts Galileo's law. Again, Einstein's general theory of relativity yields very nearly the same predictions as NT for phenomena that involve sufficiently weak gravitational fields and velocities that are sufficiently slow with respect to the velocity of light. But even here, the predictions are not precisely the same; and for strong gravitational fields and/or velocities near to the velocity of light, general relativity can differ dramatically from NT. Once again, the new, better theory, general relativity, corrects, and thus contradicts, NT. This is a quite general pattern of development in theoretical physics.

In brief, theoretical physics advances from one false theory to another, each new theory revealing its predecessor to be false. At once the question arises:

(viii) *The problem of the meaning of scientific progress (i.e. the problem of verisimilitude)*. What can it mean to say that theoretical physics makes progress if it advances from one false theory to another?

The obvious intuitive answer is that to say physics makes progress is to say that its successive theories, though all false, do nevertheless progressively capture more and more of the truth. They get closer and closer to the truth. Popper (1963, ch. 10 and 391–7) attempted to make this intuitive idea a little more precise in the following way. First, we split the consequences of any false theory T into two mutually exclusive classes: those that are true, which in sum are the truth-content of T, and those that are false, which in sum are the falsity-content. We can represent factual propositions by points on the plane, a *theory* being a closed line which encloses those points that stand for the consequences of the theory. The plane can be divided up into two parts (see Figure 5), all factually true propositions on the right, all factually false propositions on the left. All false theories overlap the line dividing off the false from the true. It may be, however, for certain pairs of theories, that one theory, T_2, has more truth-content in it, and less falsity-content, than the other theory, T_1. We can take *this* to be what it means to say that T_2 is closer to the truth than T_1. In general, there are just three sorts of case to consider; these are depicted in the figure.

Unfortunately, this simple idea does not work.[30] If T_2 has greater truth-content than T_1 then, as a matter of logic, it also has some falsity-content *in addition* to the falsity content of T_1. And likewise, if T_1 has greater falsity-content than T_2 then it has some truth-content *in addition* to the truth-content of T_2 (see Figure 5). The conditions for two false

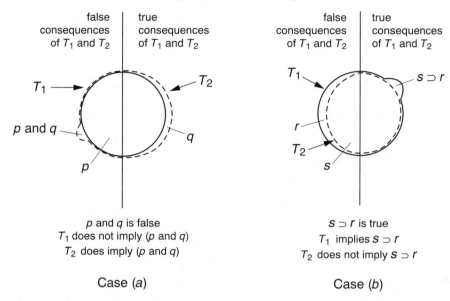

Case (*a*)

p and q is false
T_1 does not imply (p and q)
T_2 does imply (p and q)

Case (*b*)

$s \supset r$ is true
T_1 implies $s \supset r$
T_2 does not imply $s \supset r$

T_1 and T_2 are two false theories, with both true and false consequences. In the above figure, true and false consequences are represented as points inside circles (that lie on both sides of the line dividing true consequences from false).

If T_2 is to have greater verisimilitude than T_1, then *either*:

Case (*a*): the false consequences of both are the same but the true consequences of T_1 are a proper subset of those of T_2; *or*:

Case (*b*): the true consequences of both are the same but the false consequences of T_2 are a proper subset of those of T_1; *or*:

Case (*c*): T_2 has both greater truth-content and smaller falsity-content than T_1.

But if T_2 has excess truth-content over T_1, for example q, it must also have excess falsity-content, for example 'p and q'; and likewise, if T_1 has excess falsity-content over T_2, for example r, then it must also have excess truth-content, for example '$s \supset r$'. This means merely 'not both s true and r false'. Thus neither case (*a*) nor case (*b*) is possible; and hence nor case (*c*). The verisimilitude of the two false theories, T_1 and T_2, cannot be compared.

Fig. 5. Impossibility of comparing verisimilitude of two false theories

theories to be comparable with respect to closeness to the truth can thus never arise. Popper's proposed solution to the problem of what scientific progress can mean, granted that it proceeds from one false theory to another, does not work.

The 'problem of verisimilitude', as Popper christened it, remains unsolved.[31]

Even if the problem of verisimilitude can somehow be solved, there is still:

(ix) *The problem of progress in knowledge about the nature of fundamental physical entities.* A basic task of science, so it would seem, is to improve our knowledge of the basic constituents of the physical universe, the fundamental physical entities out of which everything is made. A glance at the historical record, however, appears to pose a serious problem for the view that science has progressively improved our knowledge of the nature of fundamental physical entities.

In the seventeenth century, fundamental physical entities were held to be corpuscles—tiny, impenetrable, particles interacting only on contact. By the early nineteenth century, fundamental physical entities had become point-particles, with mass, interacting at a distance by means of rigid, centrally directed, spherically symmetric forces. After the work of Faraday, Maxwell, Lorentz, and the young Einstein in developing electromagnetic theory and special relativity, the idea of the *field* was added to that of the point-particle. The field is spread in a continuous fashion throughout all of space-time; its continuously varying *strength* evolves in accordance with partial differential equations, of the type formulated by Maxwell in putting forward his electromagnetic theory. The field strength at any space-time point determines the *force* that a test particle would experience were it to be at that point. After Einstein's general theory of relativity, this field–particle view is transformed either into the view that there is just *one* entity, the self-interacting field spread out in space-time or, more radically, that there are *no* physical entities in addition to space-time, the whole of physical reality being the outcome of *variable space-time*—variable geometrically, and possibly topologically. This is in turn added to by quantum theory: embedded in variable space-time there are quantum objects, utterly mysterious, probabilistic wavelike *and* particle-like entities. These then change into quantum fields—particles corresponding (roughly) to different quantized excitation levels of the field. Then, with the development of superstring theory, the particle-like aspects of quantum fields become minute *strings* in ten or twenty-six dimensions of space-time. The possibility arises that the *one* fundamental physical entity is some kind of dynamic, probabilistic space-time geometry, of four or ten or twenty-six or some other dimensions (even, possibly, fundamentally dimensionless or of uncertain dimension). This, in turn, no doubt, will transmute into quite different and even stranger physical entities as theoretical physics continues to develop.

The question at once arises: What justifies us in holding that these changing ideas constitute *progress*? Is it even possible to describe such a succession of ideas as steadily moving towards some basic idea, which is progressively depicted more and more accurately? If not, then it seems we are entitled only to speak of *changing* ideas about the nature of fundamental physical entities; we have no grounds whatsoever for holding that there is *progress*, the step-by-step *improvement* in knowledge about the nature of fundamental physical entities. This, at least, seems to be the conclusion to draw if SE is adopted. There appears to be change but no progress in scientific knowledge of the nature of fundamental physical entities.[32]

Finally, there is a problem about scientific discovery.

Many, though by no means all, proponents of SE reject the idea that there is a rational (if fallible and non-mechanical) method of discovery in science. Thus Popper (1959: 31), in a well-known passage, declares: 'The initial stage, the act of conceiving or inventing a new theory, seems to me neither to call for logical analysis nor to be susceptible to it.' There are good reasons why the process of inventing new theories should appear to be non-rational, granted SE. The rational way to proceed, granted SE, would seem to be to try to extend or generalize existing empirically successful theories so that they cover a wider range of phenomena. In this way, new theories could perhaps be developed which would be based on, and be compatible with, predecessor theories. But almost always in physics, as we have seen, fundamentally new theories clash logically with their predecessors. Thus, almost always, attempting to develop new theories that are compatible with existing, empirically well-established theories would lead nowhere. At once arises:

(x) *The problem of scientific discovery.* How can it be possible for scientists, again and again, to discover or invent new theories that turn out to contain a wealth of amazingly accurate predictive and explanatory content, when the only guideline for the development of new theories—namely existing theories—turns out to point in the wrong direction?

Granted that there are infinitely many useless theories that scientists could develop, how do scientists manage, after finitely many failures, to pick on, or stumble across, the very few theories capable of meeting with empirical success? From the perspective of SE, scientific discovery must be a deep mystery.

One especially mysterious feature of scientific discovery is the way in which mathematical ideas, developed, it would seem, independently of theoretical physics, nevertheless subsequently turn out to be exactly what is needed in order to delineate some aspect of physical phenomena. Thus Menaechmus, in 350 BC, invents the idea of conic sections—curves that can be created by intersecting a solid cone with a plane. These curves include the circle, the hyperbola, the ellipse, and the parabola. Over 1,000 years later, Kepler discovers that the planets move in ellipses round the sun, while Galileo discovers that terrestrial projectiles move along parabolas. Again, Gauss and Riemann, in the nineteenth century, develop the idea of curved non-Euclidean or Riemannian geometry: decades later, Einstein discovers that space-time is Riemannian in character. Yet again, the mathematician David Hilbert develops the idea of 'Hilbert space', a 'space' of functions, a purely mathematical notion. Subsequently, it turns out that it is just this that is needed in order to formulate quantum theory. It almost seems that the minds of mathematicians and the nature of physical reality are mysteriously in harmony with one another. How is this possible? How can this be understood? Viewed from the standpoint of SE, discovery in theoretical physics is inexplicable. (For a classic formulation of the problem, see Wigner 1970, ch. 17.)

11. CONCLUSION

I conclude that, in view of the failure of SE to solve the above ten problems, SE is untenable and must be rejected.

3

Comprehensibility

1. INTRODUCTION

Having demolished standard empiricism (SE), I now set out to establish that aim-oriented empiricism (AOE) is a viable, rigorous conception of science that solves the problems that SE so strikingly fails to solve.

The most controversial feature of AOE is probably the assertion that it is a basic part of current theoretical scientific knowledge that the universe is comprehensible, even *physically* comprehensible. This chapter is largely devoted to explicating what it means to assert that the universe is comprehensible.

I begin by explaining in a little more detail[1] what I mean by the (level 5) thesis that the universe is comprehensible, and the (level 4) thesis that it is physically comprehensible. Then, after a few words on the Presocratics (who may be said to have invented the idea that the universe is physically comprehensible), I say something about ideas about physical comprehensibility from the history of physics at level 3, at the level of blueprints. I then consider what the thesis that the universe is physically comprehensible adds to the thesis that it is non-aberrant, in the sense discussed in Chapter 2: I distinguish eight facets of theoretical unity, which will play an important role in the next chapter. Finally I argue that if science accepts that the universe is non-aberrant, then it ought to accept that the universe is physically comprehensible. I must stress, however, that this is only a preliminary skirmish: the real argument for the comprehensibility of the universe begins in the next chapter.

2. WHAT DOES COMPREHENSIBILITY MEAN?

As understood here, the level 5 thesis that the universe is comprehensible consists of the following two assertions, (A) and (B).

(A) The universe is such that it has two aspects, U and V. U is present everywhere, at all times and places, throughout all phenomena, in an unchanging form; V varies from place to place, and changes from time to time. Furthermore, the diverse ways in which V can change are precisely determined by U, so that were V to change differently from the way it does, this would mean that U does not exist at all. Given U and the state of V everywhere at any instant, all subsequent states of V are precisely determined (or probabilistically determined, given probabilism). U and V are dovetailed together, in that V must change in the way in which it does everywhere, for U to exist anywhere.

If (A) is true, then there is a sense in which precise knowledge of the evolution of any small, isolated *bit* of the universe, whatever happens to be going on in that bit, contains some information about the entire universe. For this knowledge will include knowledge of U; and U is such that it is the same everywhere, at all times and places, throughout all phenomena. Furthermore, knowing the nature of U enables one to know, in principle, all possible ways in which states of affairs can differ, everywhere, and how all these different states of affairs change. To this extent, the truth of (A) guarantees that the universe is partially knowable.

(A) does not, however, guarantee that the universe is partially knowable to beings like us who do not possess *precise* knowledge of the evolution of any bit of the universe, however small. At most, we possess imprecise, approximate, fragmentary knowledge of the way states of affairs evolve in the bit of the universe we inhabit. If the universe is to be partially knowable *to us* we need to add to (A):

(B) U is, in principle, knowable *to us*.

For U to be knowable to us we require that our current knowledge contains the means for generating a sufficiently wide range of ideas to include the correct idea about the nature of U; and we require that our current knowledge contains the means to assess the relative merits of these ideas, from the standpoint of correctly characterizing the nature of U. We require, in other words, something like the following:

(B$_1$) Current knowledge contains, explicitly or implicitly, ideas and rules for the generalization of ideas, such that the correct idea, T, of the nature of U can be generated in a finite number of steps.

(B$_2$) Current knowledge contains, explicitly or implicitly, methods for the assessment of theories, especially experimental methods, that can be developed sufficiently to make it possible to choose T as the best idea for the nature of U from the many rival ideas that can be generated by means of the procedures referred to in B$_1$.

As understood here, in other words, the thesis that the universe is comprehensible implies that its nature, U, is in principle knowable.

There are a number of different ways in which the universe might be comprehensible, as I indicated in Chapter 1. If U = God, the God-like aspect of things, then everything is, ultimately, to be explained and understood in terms of the will of God. If U = disposition to realize the ultimate goal of the universe, then everything is to be explained and understood in a quasi-Aristotelian way, as being required to fulfil an ultimate cosmic goal. But if, as AOE asserts, U and V are *physical* in character,[2] then everything is to be explained and understood (in principle) in terms of some yet-to-be-discovered physical theory of everything, T.

In this last case of physical comprehensibility, the basic equations of T, essentialistically interpreted,[3] specify the nature of U; in determining how events unfold, these equations also reveal how U determines the way in which V changes. T, and thus U, determine *how* things change, but do not, of course determine *what* is changing at any instant. That is, T implies (in principle) conditional statements of the kind 'If the changeable state of the universe (or of an isolated system) is V_1 at one instant, it will be V_2 at such-and-such a later instant'.

As an elementary model of a universe that is physically comprehensible in this sense consider a (possible) universe in which there is only the classical electromagnetic field in the (classical) vacuum. The changeable V of this universe is made up of the different values of the electromagnetic field at different space-time points. The unchangeable U is that dispositional or necessitating property of the electromagnetic field, the same everywhere, which 'ensures' that the varying aspect of the field, V, changes as it does, in accordance with Maxwell's equations of the electromagnetic field in the vacuum. The nature of U, and the manner in which U determines the way V varies, is specified by Maxwell's equations.[4]

For the universe to be physically comprehensible, U must possess the mysterious feature of 'unity'; it must not, for example, be made up of two parts, $U_1 + U_2$, so that, for the determination of some phenomena U_1 suffices, and for the determination of some other phenomena U_2 suffices (even if for the determination of many other phenomena $U_1 + U_2$ is required). Both the (level 3) corpuscular and point-atom blueprints are inadequate in this respect, in that both permit empty space (determined by U_1) on the one hand, and regions or points of space occupied by particles (determined by U_2) on the other hand. These blueprints thus fail to satisfy the above requirement for unity.

Any field theory (interpreted as a theory of everything and not made up of two or more separate fields) that has non-zero values everywhere fares better. But, as we shall see, even such a theory may be said to lack unity in so far as space-time on the one hand, and the field on the other, constitute two distinct physical entities.

3. UNITY THROUGH DIVERSITY: THE PRESOCRATICS

Some may find physicalism inherently baffling because of its basic assertion that there exists something, U, which is *precisely the same*, at all times and places, throughout all change and diversity, and which *determines* the way that which changes does change. How can there be anything which is precisely the same everywhere, given the immense diversity of what there is? What can the centre of the sun have in common with empty space, or what exists inside our heads? Furthermore, how can the unchanging U remain the same everywhere, and yet produce this startling diversity of phenomena, of changes, throughout the world? The idea is all but a contradiction! To say this is of course to reinforce the basic tenet of AOE: that the basic *aim* of theoretical physics is inherently problematic. Theoretical physics, one might almost say, is the subject which ponders the paradoxes of *unity through diversity* or, more specifically, *unity through diversity determining change*.

The struggle to make sense of this idea goes back at least 2,000 years, to the Presocratics. The Presocratic philosophers sought precisely to specify that something, of which everything is made, which persists through all change and diversity, and which determines change and diversity.[5]

For Thales, the something was water: heated, it becomes steam, or air; cooled it becomes ice, rock, earth, or other solid substances. For Anaximander the unchanging something was the *apeiron*, the 'boundless' (roughly, space itself): compressed and rarefied, this becomes the diverse substances we observe. For Anaximenes, for whom, evidently, Anaximander's unobservable, abstract *apeiron* was unacceptable, the unchanging something was air, which, when compressed, becomes progressively water, then earth. For Pythagoras, everything was made of number, an extraordinary idea which is, in a way, at the heart of modern theoretical physics. For Empedocles, the ultimate unchanging stuff was fire + air + water + earth: mixed in different proportions, these become the diverse substances we observe. For Heraclitus, it was fire, or 'change' or 'process' itself (the *unchanging something* itself being *change*). For Parmenides, reacting against Heraclitus' thought with that reckless lucidity that was so characteristic of the ancient Greeks, the very idea of change involved a contradiction. Change means that something that does not exist comes to exist; but nothing can come of nothing; hence prior to existing, nothing must have been something after all, which means that that which does not exist does exist, which is a contradiction. Hence change is an illusion. The unchanging something is *everything*, the entire cosmos being a homogeneous, unchanging sphere with no outside. Democritus, in turn, found Parmenides' denial of change unacceptable. Change does exist; hence, granted the validity of Parmenides' argument, the nothing must exist after all. Surround Parmenides' universe with the nothing, the vacuum, shrink the universe down to a minute speck, and populate the nothing with other such Parmenidean universes in relative motion. The outcome is atomism (an idea which Feynman once called the single most important idea of modern science).[6] The coexistence of the changing and the non-changing has become possible because they are precisely segregated from each other. The absolute properties of the atoms—the ones they possess when alone in space—are unchanging (each atom being a minute Parmenidean universe). All *change* is confined to relative properties between atoms: relative position and motion.[7]

Extend Democritus' idea a little, and one can provide a possible illustration of how the unchanging can *determine* change. Let the unchanging properties of the atoms be mass, shape, rigidity. These properties determine the way relative positions and velocities change: mass determining uniform motion in the absence of collision; rigidity, shape, and mass determining changes in velocity as a result of collisions.

It is doubtful that the ancient Greeks conceived of such a *dynamic* version of atomism, due to their failure to solve mathematical problems associated with motion, having to do with such things as continuity, the realm of real numbers such as $\sqrt{2}$, the differential calculus. They failed to develop the mathematical means to come to grips with the idea of acceleration. Nevertheless, as a result of struggling with the fundamental problem of natural philosophy of specifying the nature of something *impersonal* conjectured to persist through all change and diversity, the Presocratics did come up with a number of brilliant possible solutions, some of which anticipated aspects of modern science.

4. BLUEPRINTS FOR A PHYSICALLY COMPREHENSIBLE UNIVERSE

I turn now to a consideration of some of the level 3 blueprint ideas as to how the universe is comprehensible that can be associated with modern science. I give here only a very brief, informal sketch of some of these ideas. One point to note is that as physics develops there is not mere discontinuity in ideas, as a reading of Kuhn (1970) would lead one to suspect: new blueprint ideas invariably emerge as modifications and generalizations of pre-existing ideas.

The first great blueprint of modern science was the corpuscular hypothesis of the seventeenth century, essentially dynamic atomism as characterized above, upheld in various versions by such figures as Galileo, Descartes, Huygens, Locke, Gassendi, and Boyle.[8] This vividly depicts how it might be possible to reduce the vast diversity of substances and processes in the world to just one kind of entity, and one process: atoms variously arranged, and in various kinds of relative motion.

The corpuscular hypothesis does, however, have its problems. First, it is difficult to understand how sensory qualities, consciousness, meaning, and value can be accommodated within the view—a problem that haunts theoretical physics down to the present day. Secondly, it is not easy to see how attractive and cohesive forces can be accounted for by the view: it clashes horribly with Newton's theory of gravity. Thirdly, the infinite rigidity of the corpuscles introduces discontinuity—instantaneous, infinitely repulsive forces when corpuscles collide. Fourthly, the blueprint may be regarded as making an illegitimate appeal to sensory experience—to our familiarity with the tactile properties of solid objects. If we strip this away, and consider corpuscles merely as exemplifying (more or less adequately) the basic idea of physicalism, then corpuscles should be specified as follows. Associated with each corpuscle there is a closed surface of some definite invariant shape and size, which is such that the instant two such surfaces touch, the two corpuscles experience an infinitely repulsive force.

Reformulated in this way, it is at once clear that the corpuscular blueprint is nothing more than an extremely arbitrary special case of a much more general blueprint, expounded by Boscovich in 1763 (see Boscovich 1966). Instead of conceiving of a corpuscle as a closed surface upon which there is an infinitely repulsive force that is zero everywhere else (extreme discontinuity), we conceive of it as a point-particle surrounded by a rigid, spherically symmetric, centrally directed field of force which varies *continuously* with distance, only being infinitely repulsive where the point-particle is. The corpuscle is an arbitrary, discontinuous special case of Boscovich's point-atom. The force, which for the corpuscle is infinite on a rigid closed surface, becomes, for Boscovich, finite everywhere, and continuously varying with distance, being infinitely repulsive at one point only, namely where the particle is.

This more general charged point-particle blueprint possesses three major advantages over the peculiar, corpuscular special case. First, the infinitely repulsive force, the point of discontinuity, has become harmless: it just means that no two corpuscles ever occupy the same spatial point. Secondly, attractive and cohesive forces can be accounted for by the blueprint in a simple, non-*ad hoc* fashion, without any departure from spherical symmetry, by attributing to point-atoms alternating regions of attractive and repulsive forces. Thirdly, Newton's theory of gravity partially exemplifies the blueprint (even if it is incompatible with the idea that the force between particles is repulsive at short distances).

Boscovich's blueprint can be modified by introducing the idea that there are forces (e.g. electric and magnetic) in addition to that of gravitation; the idea of positive and negative charge may be introduced, like charges repelling, unlike charges attracting. This facilitates the construction of cohering macro-objects with no net charge from charged point-atoms.

The point-particle blueprint assumes that the force field surrounding each point-particle is *rigid* (a feature inherited from the corpuscular blueprint), so that the point-particle always remains at the centre of its force field, however it may move. This means that changes in the force field, due to the motion of the point-particle, are transmitted instantaneously, throughout space.

We may argue that, other things being equal, our blueprint ideas ought to be as general as possible. Other things being equal, then, we ought to prefer a blueprint capable of incorporating the general case of changes in the force due to the motion of the associated point-particle being transmitted at finite or infinite velocity. Only in the infinite velocity case will the force field associated with each point-atom be rigid. This generalization introduces, however, a new complexity. We can no longer specify initial conditions solely in terms of the relative positions and velocities of point-atoms; we must, in addition specify the force field associated with each point-atom at each point in space (its spatial character depending on the past motions of the point-atom).

This new complexity can be simplified somewhat if we adopt one further modification. Instead of postulating a number of distinct force fields, one to each point-atom, we may instead postulate just one, single, unified field, created by point-atoms, and in turn acting on point-atoms. We have arrived at a new blueprint: the particle–field blueprint (a simplified version of the blueprint which may be associated with Maxwell's theory of the electromagnetic field, as we shall see in the next chapter).

But can we really make sense of the idea of a field that has no underlying material or mechanical substratum or ether? What the above line of argument has shown is that the idea of a field with no underlying ether is simpler, more intelligible, and more acceptable than the idea of a field with an underlying ether. Granted the account of necessitating physical properties to be expounded in Chapter 4, we can say, simply, that the etherless field is a physical entity whose variable properties are such that they determine, at each spatial point, the way a charged test particle would accelerate were it to be placed at that point. The unchanging property of the field is the same everywhere, at all times and places, and determines the way the variable properties change. All this beautifully exemplifies the basic idea of physicalism. Such a physical entity, spread out continuously in space and varying in intensity with time, may well seem unfamiliar and strange granted that we are primarily familiar with solid objects located in definite spatial regions; such considerations have nothing to do with comprehensibility as this arises within the context of theoretical physics.

If, now, we postulate that such a field possesses an underlying material ether, we will be obliged to develop a further theory specifying the manner in which the particles of the ether interact with one another; we will need to postulate a Boscovichian force, which we may in turn need to interpret in terms of a force field, a step which threatens to lead to an infinite regress. Even if the ether is continuous, we still need some infinitesimal analogue of force to account for the properties of the ether. A field without an ether is, in short, a far more comprehensible physical entity than a field with an ether.

Two problems do, however, arise in connection with this new particle–field blueprint.

First, a major problem arises in connection with the interaction between charged point-particle and field: the point-particle creates an infinitely intense field at the point where it is located in space, which means, in turn, that the field produces infinitely strong forces on the particle. No such problem arises within the Boscovichian blueprint, precisely because each point-particle is only acted on by the force fields of other point-particles. The problem arises when the distinct force fields of the distinct particles are unified to form *one* field, so that each particle both creates and is acted on by one and the same field. It is this step of unification, in the transition from Boscovichian to particle–field blueprint, that creates the problem.

Einstein hoped to overcome this problem by developing a self-interacting, non-linear unified field theory according to which 'particles' would simply be especially intense regions of the field. This Einsteinian 'unified field' blueprint has not (so far) met with success.

Secondly, a problem arises in connection with the *velocity* of transmission of influences through the field. In moving from the Boscovichian to the particle–field blueprint, we have not changed the key notion of force, given by the equation $F = ma$ (where m is mass, and a is acceleration). The strength of a force is an absolute quantity; hence acceleration too is an absolute quantity (and not merely a question of choice of reference frame). Velocity, however, can be regarded as something which depends merely on choice of reference frame. With respect to what, then, is the velocity of transmission of influences through the field to be measured? This question goes to the heart of the particle–field blueprint, since the idea that influences in the force field take time to travel, and therefore have some finite velocity, is the key distinction between the particle–field and Boscovichian blueprints. Let the velocity of transmission of the particle–field blueprint tend to infinity, and the blueprint reduces to some version of the Boscovichian blueprint. One possibility is to let the velocity of transmission be a constant relative to an underlying ether, but this, as we have seen, only introduces further complications, and destroys the field as a fundamental physical entity. Another possibility is to let the velocity of transmission be a constant relative to the *source particle*. This, however, violates the *unification* of the distinct force fields of the Boscovichian blueprint, the second crucial step in moving from the Boscovichian to the particle–field blueprint. The existence of different *velocities* of changes in the field, associated with the different velocities of source particles, would be close to associating a different *field* with each source particle. The *unified* particle–field blueprint postulates that, within the unified field, changes in intensity and/or direction of the field travel at some *finite* velocity, and thereby creates the profound dilemma as to *what it is* that this velocity is lawfully related to.

Einstein solved this second problem by means of the extraordinary proposal that changes in the field travel at the velocity of light, which has one and the same value when measured in *all* inertial reference frames. This is the nub of the special theory of relativity (SR).

One may see SR as arising out of an attempt to unify (to some extent at least) Newtonian theory (NT) and classical electromagnetism (MT). From NT Einstein extracted the (restricted) principle of relativity: the laws of nature have the same form relative to a set of reference frames all moving with constant velocity with respect to each other (so-called inertial reference frames). From MT he extracted the principle (implied by MT, and basic to the field concept, as we have seen) that it is a law of nature that the velocity of light in the vacuum is a constant, c. These postulates, taken together, imply the apparent absurdity that one flash of light will have the *same* velocity c with respect to two frames travelling at velocity c/2 with respect to each other, let us say.

But if relative velocity changes measured lengths of rods and rates of clocks, and hence measured velocities, it becomes just about conceivable that light does have the same velocity c with respect to *all* inertial frames.[9] Given a few very natural assumptions about how measurements of length and time, made in different frames, are related to one another (such as that the relationship is linear, symmetric, and isotropic), it turns out that there is just *one* way to arrange for light to have the same velocity c in all reference frames: this is contained in the so-called Lorentz transformations, the physical nub of SR. They specify how measured length and time intervals change, as we go from one frame to another, in uniform motion with respect to each other.

Soon after Einstein proposed SR in 1905, Minkowski showed that SR can be interpreted as partially 'unifying' space and time, to form what is now known as 'Minkowskian space-time'.

Given any two points, P_1 and P_2, in three-dimensional Euclidean space, the distance r between them is given by $r^2 = x^2 + y^2 + z^2$, where x, y, and z are distances as measured along the X, Y, and Z axes of some reference frame. Rotate the frame, and x, y, and z will change but r will remain the same.

Somewhat analogously, given any two events, E_1 and E_2, in four-dimensional Minkowskian space-time, then the space-time 'distance' s between them is given by $s^2 = x^2 + y^2 + z^2 - c^2 t^2$, where x, y, and z are, as before, spatial distances between the events as measured along the axes of some reference frame, and t is the temporal distance between the events as measured in that frame. Rotate the frame in four-dimensional Minkowskian space-time in such a way that this corresponds physically to giving the frame a uniform velocity in some direction, and the values of x, y, z, and t change, but s, the space-time interval between E_1 and E_2, remains the same. The value of s is frame-independent.

So far it looks as if SR unifies space and time completely, the very distinction between space and time disappearing. But this is not the case: a distinction remains. According to SR, there are three kinds of space-time intervals to consider, depending on whether s^2 is greater than, equal to, or less than zero. If $s^2 > 0$, the interval between E_1 and E_2 is 'spacelike' and no causal influence can connect up E_1 and E_2:[10] for one set of frames at rest with respect to one another, the two events occur simultaneously ($t = 0$), but for others, E_1 occurs before E_2, and for others, E_2 occurs before E_1. If $s^2 = 0$, then a ray of light can connect up E_1 and E_2. (SR has the extraordinary consequence that, when you view a distant star, the space-time distance between the emission of light from the star and its absorption by your eye is zero.) If $s^2 < 0$, the interval between E_1 and E_2 is 'timelike'; a material body can travel from one event to the other, one event occurring before the other in all frames.[11]

SR embodies a dramatically new blueprint idea, a new metaphysical idea, concerning the nature of space and time as a result of modifying and generalizing pre-existing Newtonian ideas. At the same time, SR embodies a new methodological principle: in order to be acceptable a fundamental physical theory must be Lorentz invariant (i.e. must conform to the Lorentz transformations). In linking together in this way, so explicitly, the metaphysical and the methodological, SR illustrates graphically a basic tenet of AOE (as I have mentioned in Chapter 1).[12]

The line of argument indicated so far in this section, taking one from the corpuscular to the point-particle–field blueprint, and from Newtonian to Minkowskian space-time, can be regarded as being more or less explicit in the work of Newton, Boscovich, Kant, Faraday, Maxwell, Lorentz, Einstein, and others; it is this that made it possible for the corpuscular hypothesis to evolve into Newtonian mechanics and Maxwellian electrodynamics, reinterpreted in terms of SR. And during the twentieth century new blueprint ideas have been developed, partly in response to empirical discoveries, partly as a consequence of the search for unity, but always as a result of modifying and generalizing pre-existing ideas, as indicated above.

Most notably, there is the profound generalization in our ideas about gravitation, space, and time brought about by Einstein's general theory of relativity (GR), capitalizing on earlier work of Gauss, Riemann, and others (to be discussed in the next chapter). In sharp contrast to GR, there is quantum theory (QT). Whereas GR emerged from a prior blueprint idea, QT was developed in the absence of such an idea, largely because of the failure to solve the problem of the nature of quantum entities, such as electrons and atoms, due to the fact that they seem to have both wave-like and particle-like properties. In Chapter 7 I sketch a possible blueprint for the quantum domain; this emerges, somewhat as blueprints considered above, as a result of generalizing from determinism to probabilism.

Despite the lack of a consistent, agreed blueprint associated with QT, nevertheless blueprint ideas have arisen as QT has developed, and as physicists have struggled with the problem of unifying QT and GR. There is the locally gauge invariant quantum field blueprint, suggested by contemporary quantum field theories (see Moriyasu 1983). There is John Wheeler's geometrodynamical blueprint, according to which everything is made up of empty curved space-time which is, in any minute region, a quantum superposition of topologically complicated space-times, particles and forces being nothing more than topological or geometrical features of space-time (see Wheeler 1968). There is the supergravity blueprint. There is what may be called Lagrangianism (to be discussed in a moment). And there is the superstring blueprint, according to which particles have the form of minute strings embedded in space-time of ten or twenty-six dimensions, those in excess of four being curled up into a minute size (Davies and Brown 1988).

If theoretical physics put AOE into practice, new (level 2) theories would tend to emerge from previously articulated (level 3) blueprints. Apart from the genesis of GR, this is not the way that new fundamental theories in physics have emerged; from NT to QT, appropriate blueprints have only been developed some time after the new theory (if at all). My claim is, of course, that this is due to the general acceptance of SE, which discourages sustained metaphysical speculation as an integral part of science. The result is that our best insights into the way the universe is physically comprehensible are provided, not by our best level 3 blueprints, but rather by the few great level 2 fundamental theories of physics: NT, MT, SR, and GR, non-relativistic QT, quantum electrodynamics (QED), quantum electroweak dynamics (QEWD), quantum chromodynamics (QCD), and, combining these last three, the so-called standard model (SM). As I shall argue in the next chapter, where I give an informal account of these theories, each constitutes an extraordinary feat of unification. According to AOE, each theory provides a partial, distorted glimpse of the underlying physical unity, U.

But if successful fundamental theories embody our best knowledge about the nature of U, it is often the case, nevertheless, that it is by no means obvious what a new theory should be interpreted to be telling us about U, about how the universe is physically comprehensible. As I have in effect indicated, even the creators of new theories may interpret their creations in ways which turn out to be thoroughly misconceived decades or even centuries later. The proper way (according to AOE) to specify what it is that a level 2 theory, T, is asserting about U is to specify a level 3 blueprint, B, got from T by retaining what is taken to be the central insight of T into the nature of U (e.g. the kind of entities or forces postulated by T, or the symmetries exhibited by T), and dropping all other features of T. There are, however, any number of different ways in which any T may be generalized in this manner, each way arriving at a different (level 3) blueprint that may be said to correspond to T. Consider, for example, the endlessly many blueprints that can be created from NT by generalizing progressively, and in different ways, from the specific equations and assumptions of NT. (Generalizing from such theories as QED and GR may be more difficult, but it can still be done.)

Given this point, the task of arriving at *one* best blueprint for the whole of physics may seem hopeless. But the many different blueprints that correspond to NT treat NT in isolation from the rest of physics, as if gravitation is the only force and NT is a theory of everything. The task of constructing a blueprint which (*a*) exemplifies physicalism, and (*b*) accords with all currently accepted fundamental physical theories and all known physical phenomena is so demanding that it is all but impossible to fulfil. Indeed, in our present state of only partial knowledge and understanding, the task can only be imperfectly fulfilled.

Before the advent of NT, the best that could be done was to speculate about the nature of U in the manner of the Presocratics (until, that is, some research programme, such as that developed by Galileo and his contemporaries, based on some specific idea about the nature of U, began to meet with unprecedented empirical success). After the advent of NT, the best blueprint would generalize NT just sufficiently to (*a*) exemplify physicalism as adequately as possible, (*b*) take into account all physical phenomena other than gravitation. Thus, in order to take electricity and magnetism into account, it would be necessary, initially at least, to recognize the existence of two additional forces besides gravitation, both capable of being repulsive as well as attractive. But as we have seen, and as Faraday was perhaps the first to realize, this would not suffice: granted that changes in electric and magnetic forces travel through space with a finite speed, and not with an infinite speed as with Newtonian gravitation (which as a consequence can be regarded as a rigid force), it becomes necessary to develop the theory of these forces as a *field* theory.

After the advent of MT, a new situation emerges: there are now two incompatible fundamental theories, NT and MT, which give rise to two incompatible blueprints. And this is the situation today: there are two fundamental incompatible theories, SM and GR, that give rise to two incompatible blueprints.

In these circumstances, what overall blueprint, for the whole of physics, ought to be accepted as a part of knowledge, according to AOE? Let the two clashing theories be T_1 and T_2, and the two corresponding clashing blueprints be B_1 and B_2. These two blueprints both exemplify physicalism, P_4, more or less adequately. As a result of progressively dropping clashing postulates of B_1 and B_2 we eventually arrive at the same metaphysical thesis, namely P_4. We will, however, arrive at a common blueprint idea, B, *before* we reach P_4. We may be able to formulate a number of such common blueprint ideas: the task then becomes to pick that common blueprint idea that holds the greatest hope of promoting progress.

What, it may be asked, is the best available blueprint as far as current physics is concerned? This is clearly both an immensely important and difficult question to answer. (Indeed, if we knew how to specify the *correct* blueprint, supposing that such a thing exists, at a reasonably substantial level below physicalism, the task of formulating the true theory of everything would be all but solved.) Does one put one's faith in the basic metaphysical idea of some contemporary research programme attempting to unify SM and GR, such as superstring theory? Or does one choose a blueprint that is, as far as possible, no more than common ground between accepted fundamental theories? It is the latter that we require; according to AOE, the best blueprint governs acceptance of current level 2 theories (along with empirical considerations), and is not just the best current guess as to how these theories are to be unified.[13] The best blueprint is a part of scientific knowledge; it belongs to the context of justification, and not just to the context of heuristics and discovery.

These considerations prompt me to suggest that the best blueprint currently available is a thesis that may be called *Lagrangianism*.

All fundamental, dynamical theories accepted so far in physics (NT, MT, GR, QT, QED, QEWD, QCD, and SM) can be formulated in terms of a Lagrangian and Hamilton's principle of least action. In the case of NT, this takes the following form. Given any system, we can specify its kinetic energy, KE (energy of motion), and its potential energy, PE (energy of position due to forces), at each instant. This enables us to define the Lagrangian, L, equal at each instant to KE − PE. Hamilton's principle states that, given two instants, t_1 and t_2, the system evolves in such a way that the sum of instantaneous values of KE − PE, for times between t_1 and t_2, is a minimum value (or, more accurately, a stationary value, so that it is unaffected to first order by infinitesimal variations in the way the system evolves). From the Lagrangian for NT (a function of the positions and momenta of particles) and Hamilton's principle of least action, we can derive NT in the form familiar from elementary textbooks.

It is this way of formulating NT, in terms of a Lagrangian, L, and Hamilton's principle, that can be generalized to apply to all accepted fundamental theories in physics. Lagrangianism, then, asserts that the universe is such that all phenomena evolve in accordance with Hamilton's principle of least action, formulated in terms of some unified Lagrangian (or Lagrangian density), L. We require, here, that L is not the sum of two or more distinct Lagrangians, with distinct physical interpretations and symmetries, for example one for the electroweak force, one for the strong force, and one for gravitation, as at present; L must have a single physical interpretation, and its symmetries must have an appropriate group structure. We require, in addition, that current quantum field theories and general relativity emerge when appropriate limits are taken.[14]

Even if the level 4 thesis of physicalism is true, it is more than likely that Lagrangianism is false. This is the case if space-time is discontinuous in the very small. In fact recent developments in quantum gravity, having to do with 'duality', suggest that Lagrangianism may well be false (see Isham 1997: 194–5).

5. ASPECTS OF PHYSICAL COMPREHENSIBILITY

The downfall of SE makes clear that physics does, and must, accept some substantial thesis about the nature of the universe as a part of knowledge independently of the evidence, even in violation of the evidence, implicit in the methods of science, if empirically successful aberrant theories are to be excluded. But must this thesis be physicalism? Does it not suffice to assume that the universe is *non-aberrant*? By a non-aberrant universe I mean a universe that is such that some physical theory of everything, T, is true, T not being aberrant in any of the five senses discussed in Section 7 of Chapter 2. Physicalism is a much stronger assertion than the thesis that the universe is non-aberrant.[15]

Let us, then, consider the following two questions. First, what does physicalism *add* to non-aberrance? Secondly, granted that we know somehow that the universe is non-aberrant (so that we have grounds for excluding empirically successful aberrant theories from science) what justifies holding that physicalism is a part of scientific knowledge?[16]

At first sight the thesis that the universe is non-aberrant may seem a quite different kind of proposition from the thesis that the universe is physically comprehensible, i.e. such that it has a unified dynamic structure. The leap from non-aberrance to physicalism, to unity, will seem all the more unjustified as a result. But in what follows I shall argue that non-aberrance is just a part of what we should mean by unity; aberrance is, in other words, just a particularly severe kind of disunity.

There are at least eight different distinctions to be drawn between (possible) universes that have unified and disunified dynamic structures, just two of these corresponding to the five distinctions between non-aberrance and aberrance considered in Chapter 2.

For some (but not all) cases, the unity/disunity distinction can be indicated as follows. Let the candidate theory of everything, T, whose degree of unity is being assessed, predict possible phenomena R. If T is disunified to degree N then there are N distinct subordinate regions, $R_1 \ldots R_N$, in the space of all possible phenomena R, different component theories, $T_1 \ldots T_N$, applying in each $R_1 \ldots R_N$. For unity we require that $N = 1$. Different kinds of disunity arise depending on how the subordinate regions $R_1 \ldots R_N$ are distinguished. Here are eight possibilities.

1. $R_1 \ldots R_N$ are different regions of space-time. This corresponds to type 1 aberrance of Section 7 of Chapter 2.

2. T postulates that, for distinct ranges of physical variables, such as mass or relative velocity, in distinct regions $R_1 \ldots R_N$ of the space of all possible phenomena, distinct dynamical laws obtain. This corresponds to type 2 to 5 aberrance of Section 7 of Chapter 2.

3. In addition to postulating non-unique physical entities, T postulates, in an arbitrary fashion, N distinct, unique, spatially localized objects, each with its own distinct, unique dynamic properties. In this case there will be $N + 1$ regions of R, $R_1 \ldots R_{N+1}$, one containing no

unique object, and each of the rest containing just one unique object, a different one for each region. In each of these regions, R_n, a special case of T applies, T_n, specialized to apply either to no unique object, or to the unique object to be found in that region. But in addition to this, there will be regions of R where more than one of the N objects are to be found. In this case, in other words, $R_1 \ldots R_N$ do not exhaust R.

4. T postulates physical entities interacting by means of N distinct forces, different forces affecting different entities, and being specified by different force laws. In this case one would require one force to be universal so that the universe does not fall into distinct parts that do not interact with one another.[17] Somewhat as in 3, there will (in general) be M regions in R, $R_1 \ldots R_M$, with $M \leq N$, such that in each region, the universal force alone, or the universal force plus one other, is operative. In each of these regions, R_n, a special case of T applies, T_n, specialized to the particular forces to be found in that region. But in addition to this, there will be regions of R where more than two forces operate (assuming that there are more than two forces). In this case, in other words, $R_1 \ldots R_M$ do not exhaust R.

5. T postulates N different kinds of physical entity,[18] differing with respect to some dynamic property, such as value of mass or charge, but otherwise interacting by means of the same force. Somewhat as in 2, there will be N regions of R, $R_1 \ldots R_N$, which contain just one type of particle only. In each of these regions, R_n, a special case of T applies, T_n, specialized to the particular value of mass, charge, or whatever, to be found in that region. But in addition to this, there will be regions of R where more than one kind of entity is to be found. In this case, in other words, $R_1 \ldots R_N$ do not exhaust R.

6. Consider a theory, T, that postulates N distinct entities (e.g. particles or fields), but these N entities can be regarded as arising because T exhibits some symmetry.[19] If the symmetry group, G, is not a direct product of subgroups, we can declare that T is fully unified; if G is a direct product of subgroups, T lacks full unity; and if the N entities are such that they cannot be regarded as arising as a result of some symmetry of T, with some group structure G, then T is disunified.

The way in which relativistic classical electromagnetism unifies the electric and magnetic fields is an example of this kind of unity. Given the electric field, then the magnetic field must be adjoined to it if the theory is to exhibit the symmetry of Lorentz invariance. Again, the way in which chromodynamics brings unity to the eight gluons, and to quarks that differ with respect to colour charge, postulated by the theory, provides another example of this kind of unity. The diverse gluons and colour-charged quarks of the theory are required to exist if the theory is to have its distinctive locally gauge invariant character, in this case the symmetry group being $SU(3)$. The electroweak theory of Weinberg and Salam is an example of partial unity of this type, in that, in this case, the symmetry group, corresponding to the locally gauge invariant character of the theory, is $SU(2) \times U(1)$—a group that is a direct product of subgroups. The theory only partially unifies the diverse quanta of the associated fields, the photon of electromagnetism, and the vector bosons of the weak force.[20]

Note that disunity of this type may conceivably obtain even though there are *no* non-overlapping regions, $R_1 \ldots R_N$, the whole theory, T, applying throughout R (in this case T demanding that all N entities be simultaneously present). In this respect, this case differs from (1) to (5).

7. If (apparent) disunity has emerged as a result of a series of cosmic spontaneous symmetry-breaking events, there being manifest unity before these occurred, then the relevant theory, T, is unified. If current (apparent) disunity has not emerged from unity in this way, as a result of spontaneous symmetry-breaking, then the relevant theory, T, is disunified.[21]

8. According to GR, Newton's force of gravitation is merely an aspect of the curvature of space-time. As a result of a change in our ideas about the nature of space-time, so that its geometric properties become dynamic, a physical force disappears, or becomes unified with space-time. This suggests the following requirement for unity: space-time on the one hand, and physical particles and forces on the other, must be unified into a single self-interacting entity, U. If T postulates space-time and physical 'particles and forces' as two fundamentally distinct kinds of entities, then T is not unified in this respect.

As we go from 1 to 5, the kind of disunity involved becomes less and less severe. It is reasonable to interpret 1 to 5 in such a way that disunity of type R, where $1 < R \le 5$, presupposes unity $N = 1$ for $1 \ldots R - 1$. For these cases, unity requirements are accumulative, in other words. As far as 6 and 7 are concerned, if there are N distinct entities which are not unified by a symmetry, whether unbroken or broken, then the degree of disunity is the same as that for 4 or 5, depending on whether there are N distinct forces, or one force but N distinct kinds of entity. The kind of disunity involved in 8 is the least severe. Or, put the other way round, type 8 unity is the most demanding to fulfil.

1 to 8 throw further light on what it means to assert that the universe is physically comprehensible, but are not to be regarded as *defining* what

dynamic unity or physical comprehensibility means. This has a bearing on 8. If the above sought to define dynamic unity, it would be inadequate because 8 requires that space-time and particles-and-forces be 'unified', thus including the very term to be defined. But as 1 to 8 are not to be regarded as defining what dynamic unity means, we can leave open the possibility that space-time and particles-and-forces may be unified in some way that differs, at least to some extent, from ways 4 to 7.

Let us, however, in an attempt to keep the argument to manageable proportions, assume that 1 to 8 constitute all the different kinds of unity/disunity distinctions that we need to consider.[22] (I assume that other analogous distinctions are possible which would be intuitively acceptable;[23] and I assume that the same arguments, to be indicated in a moment, would apply.)

The question before us is: Granted that current physics includes, as an item of theoretical knowledge, that the universe is unified in senses 1 and 2, which we may call 'weak' unity, what justification is there for the claim that it includes the much stronger item of knowledge that the universe is unified in senses 1 to 8, which we may call 'strong' unity?[24]

One point can be made straight away. It hardly makes sense to assume that the world is non-aberrant in senses 1 and 2, and yet allow that it may be aberrant in sense 3. This is because any disallowed theory, aberrant in sense 1 or 2, can always be mimicked by an appropriate theory aberrant in sense 3—one which postulates appropriate, dynamically unique objects. We may as well assume, then, that 'weak' unity consists of non-aberrance in senses 1, 2, *and* 3.

6. FROM NON-ABERRANCE TO UNITY

I have ten points to make, (A) to (J), in favour of adopting strong unity, given that science at least accepts weak unity.

(A) 1, 2, and 3 are arbitrary special cases of the more general idea of strong unity, exemplified in 1 to 8. Thus type 1 disunity is a special case of type 6 disunity, in that space-time aberrance violates space-time symmetries, in particular, invariance with respect to location in space and time. Before the advent of SR, it is understandable that violation of invariance with respect to location in space and time should receive particular attention from philosophers struggling with Hume's problem of induction; but after SR, it is no longer clear that these two symmetries deserve to be put into a different category from other space-time symmetries, such as invariance with respect to orientation or uniform motion, or from more general physical symmetries, such as those of GR or SM. Again, it is clear that type 3 disunity is a special case of type 4 or 5 disunity. One can go further and regard type 1 or 2 disunity as a special case of type 4 or 5 disunity, in that types 1 and 2 disunity can always be redescribed as new entities, with new dynamical properties, coming into existence as one enters a new space-time region (case 1), or a new range of phenomena (case 2). 1 and 2 are simply the most serious kinds of disunity, which have been given undue prominence through the accidents of intellectual history. Philosophers, in discussing the problem of induction, have followed Hume in giving prominence to the problem of why theories that are type 1 disunified should be dismissed as false; this may then be extended to take in the case of theories that are type 2 or 3 disunified. But as far as physics is concerned, all eight kinds of disunity function as an indication of inadequacy or falsehood, and it is artificial to put the first two into a special category.

(B) This is borne out by the historical record. Almost all laws and theories proposed in physics since Newton are unified in senses 1, 2, and 3: these requirements for unity apply so universally within physics that their ubiquitous influence may escape notice. But the influence of the other requirements for unity, 4 to 8, is hardly less ubiquitous: here are some famous examples of new theories exemplifying one or other kind of unity, this influencing the acceptance of these new theories (along with empirical success).

Newton's unification of Kepler and Galileo is, explicitly, a type 1, 2, 3, and 4 unification. (Galileo's laws of terrestrial motion and Kepler's laws of planetary motion refer to different spatial regions, and different unique objects, and are made up of different laws; Newton replaces this with one set of laws that applies universally to all objects that have mass at all times and places.) MT after Einstein's SR unifies the electric and magnetic forces in a type 6 way. (In order to conform to the symmetry of Lorentz invariance the electromagnetic field must be treated as one entity, and not two distinct entities, the electric and magnetic fields which, separately, fail to exhibit Lorentz invariance.) Quantum theory unifies disparate laws of physics and chemistry in a type 5 way. (At the macroscopic level of chemistry and solid state physics there are millions of different substances obeying millions of different laws; atomic theory and QT reduce all this to just four entities, the electron, proton, neutron, and photon, obeying one set of laws, those of QT or, a little more accurately perhaps, those of QED.) GR is a step towards type 8 unification. QEWD unifies the electromagnetic and weak forces in type 6 and 7 ways. (This theory is locally gauge invariant, the symmetry group being $U(1) \times SU(2)$; and the theory also exploits the idea of spontaneous symmetry-breaking.) QCD brings some type 5 unity to hadrons (in that the number of distinct kinds of particle with distinct dynamic properties is reduced); it also brings some type 6 unity to quarks and gluons, in that the theory exhibits local gauge invariance, the symmetry group being $SU(3)$.

The historical record reveals, in short, that the demand for unity, in senses 1, 2, and 3, is an important special case of the stronger demand for unity in senses 1 to 8.

(C) In order to make progress, science needs to modify metaphysical assumptions and methods (at levels 3 to 8) in the direction of those assumptions and associated methods which seem best to promote progress in knowledge. This idea of improving knowledge-about-how-to-improve-knowledge in the light of improving knowledge is of the essence of scientific rationality, according to AOE. It is on just these grounds that science is justified in accepting, as a part of conjectural knowledge, that the universe is unified in senses 1 to 8, granted that it already accepts that the universe is unified in senses 1 to 3. The concept of unity in senses 1 to 8 is a natural generalization of the arbitrarily restricted conception of unity in senses 1 to 3, as we saw in (A) above. Furthermore, the stronger thesis of unity, in senses 1 to 8, has proved to be even more fruitful, heuristically and methodologically, than the weaker thesis of unity, in senses 1 to 3, as we saw in (B) above. These are just the circumstances in which the weaker thesis should be replaced by the stronger. Not to do so is to violate the basic idea of learning from success and failure what metaphysical assumptions and associated methods to adopt.

(D) In doing theoretical physics we need to be both optimistic and pessimistic, wildly speculative and fiercely sceptical. In the present context, the way to fulfil these all but contradictory impulses is to adopt relatively specific assumptions, with relatively specific associated heuristic and methodological rules, at levels 3 and 4, and at the same time adopt as unspecific assumptions as possible, at levels 9 and 10, that are compatible with the idea that some knowledge exists and can be acquired. But this idea of ten distinct levels can be regarded as only a crude first approximation of how we should represent scientific knowledge. In finer detail, we may think of knowledge as consisting of a nearly continuous path stretching from our current accepted fundamental physical theories (GR + SM), via Lagrangianism, physicalism, and so on, to level 10, so that there are as many theses as we please between levels on what is conjectured to be the best path. (Any thesis located at a point on this path ideally implies all theses located on points higher up on the path.) Granted that the thesis that the universe is unified in senses 1 to 3 lies on the path corresponding to scientific knowledge, it makes good sense that we should put the more substantial, specific thesis that the universe is unified in senses 1 to 8 at a point lower down on the path representing knowledge. This makes good sense granted (A) above; it becomes even better sense granted (B) and (C).

(E) A fundamental, all-pervasive heuristic and methodological rule in science is: try to develop testable conjectures that are explanatory; other things being equal, favour that theory that is explanatory. The search for explanation and understanding is, in other words, fundamental to science, and science would be lost without it. But this demand that acceptable physical theories be *explanatory*, pushed to the limit, becomes the demand that the universe be assumed to be unified in senses 1 to 8.

(F) In response to (E), it might be argued that accepting that the universe is unified in senses 1 to 8 because of the persistent preference for *explanatory* theories in science is to accept a conjecture about the nature of the universe that is far in excess of what is required. All that is required is a much vaguer, less substantial thesis that asserts something like: the universe is such that the search for explanatory theories can meet with some empirical success. Caution is indeed a part of scientific rationality; but so is audacity. The great advantage in adopting (conjecturally) much more substantial and specific theses about the universe than 'the universe is such that the search for explanatory theories can meet with some success' is that this may well facilitate scientific progress. As a result of making explicit a hierarchy of much more substantial, specific theses, we make it possible to subject such theses to critical scrutiny, in the light of the empirical success or failure of testable theories developed in conformity with such theses. This is the basic idea of the principle of intellectual integrity, discussed in Chapter 1; it is also the fundamental idea of AOE.

(G) Assume that we do not yet have complete, precise theoretical knowledge about the nature of the universe, and that we still have much, at this level, to discover. Other things being equal, the more nearly the universe is such that the true, yet-to-be-discovered theory of everything, T, is unified in senses 1 to 8, so the more discoverable T will be; and the more T departs from unity (other things being equal), the more difficult it becomes to discover it. (Other things being equal, *one* theory is easier to pin down than *one hundred* theories, let us say; the assumption that the true theory of everything, T, is unified in senses 1 to 8 provides us with much more powerful heuristics and methodology than the assumption merely that T is unified in senses 1 to 3 only.) On these grounds alone we should adopt, as a working hypothesis, that T is unified in senses 1 to 8—just as the drunk who drops his key after dark should assume, to begin with at least, that it fell into the illumination of the street lamp.

(H) The argument given at the end of Section 5 for accepting sense 3 given acceptance of senses 1 and 2 may be extended to provide grounds for accepting 4 and 5, given 1 to 3. Any aberrant theory, rejected because it clashes with senses 1 to 3, could presumably be mimicked by a theory compatible with 1 to 3 but incompatible with 4 or 5.

(I) For unity in senses 1 to 8 to be the scientifically correct assumption to make, it is not necessary that physicalism be true; it is enough that the universe is 'nearly physically comprehensible', the physicalistic version of the level 6 thesis of AOE.

(J) In order to solve disunity problems of current theoretical physics it is necessary to bring unity to SM, and to unify SM and GR. Experiments most relevant to this task involve observing phenomena at energies close to that associated with the big bang, when quantum effects become directly relevant to those of GR. Such experiments are impossible. The task of unifying SM and GR, in other words, is confronted by a situation new in physics: the experiments that most need to be done cannot be done. Given this state of affairs, our only hope of discovering that theory which covers phenomena predicted by both SM and GR is that the theory satisfies the harsh requirement of being unified in senses 1 to 8. Relax this requirement, and all hope of making further theoretical progress all but disappears. (It may be, of course, that once a candidate unification of GR and SM has been formulated, the theory itself may indicate low-energy experimental tests that can be performed; the chances are, however, that we will only be able to imagine such experiments once the theory has been formulated.)

From considerations (A) to (J), I conclude that if 'the universe has a unified dynamic structure in senses 1 to 3' is a part of (conjectural) scientific knowledge, then so is 'the universe has a unified dynamic structure in senses 1 to 8'. But the former *is* a part of scientific knowledge; hence so is the latter. We have some (preliminary) grounds for holding that the thesis 'the universe is physically comprehensible' is a part of current (conjectural) scientific knowledge.

Many theoretical physicists will not be entirely surprised by this conclusion. Most theoretical physicists assume that neither GR nor SM as
they stand can be true, despite the wealth of empirical success achieved
especially by SM. They assume this because GR + SM is disunified. SM
is disunified in that it postulates too many different kinds of particle,
and too many forces (three rather than one); and GR + SM is disunified
because the two theories are incompatible, and only become compatible
if arbitrarily restricted in scope (so that they are not applied to the
interior of black holes, for example, or to the big bang state). Theoretical physicists assume, in short, that the universe is unified in senses 1 to
8, and any fundamental theory, or group of such theories, which fails to
be compatible with this assumption of unity cannot be true *whatever its
empirical success may be*! In effect, the thesis that the universe is unified
in senses 1 to 8 is regarded as being more firmly established than either
GR or SM.

The incompatibility of GR + SM with the thesis of strong unity (unity
in senses 1 to 8) may be thought by some, however, to be grounds for
contesting the argument of the present section (contained in points (A)
to (J) above). GR + SM is, it seems, compatible with weak unity (unity
in senses 1 to 3). In order to find an accepted physical theory that is
incompatible with weak unity we need to go back to a time before
Newton, to Kepler and Galileo. How, then, can we argue from the
acceptance of weak unity, long compatible with theoretical knowledge
in physics, to the acceptance of strong unity, which has always been
incompatible with such knowledge? (GR + SM violates all of 4 to 8 of
strong unity.)

I have four points to make in reply.

(W) If the argument from weak to strong unity involved the claim
that weak unity *entails* strong unity, then it would, of course, be a
disaster that weak unity is compatible with, and strong unity incompatible with, current physical theory. But the argument, contained in (A) to
(J), makes no such claim. It cannot; strong unity has more content than
weak unity.

(X) It is not entirely clear that GR + SM is compatible with weak
unity. As I have remarked above, there is a sense in which the *scope* of
GR and SM needs to be restricted in an *ad hoc* fashion in order to
avoid logical inconsistency. Quantum field theory, an essential part of
SM, implies (roughly) that vacuum fluctuations, fluctuations in energy,
become larger and larger as smaller and smaller space-time regions
are considered. Eventually such fluctuations become so large that GR

comes into play, and virtual black holes are formed (with dire consequences for the smoothness, the differentiability, of space-time). Such extreme implications of quantum field theory must be ignored if the theory is to be viable. On the other hand, GR predicts that singularities in space-time form inside black holes; but such singularities fall within the scope of quantum theory. For singularities, the implications of GR conflict with those of QT or SM. The same point arises in connection with the big bang state of the universe. Such collisions between GR and SM are only avoided by arbitrarily restricting the scope of GR and SM, which is to run foul of type 2 unity.

(Y) So far it has been assumed that weak unity, unity of types 1, 2, and 3, is made up of sacrosanct principles which physics could not conceivably overthrow. But recent physics has shown that particular symmetry principles, even when apparently trivially obvious, may well be overthrown by the advance of knowledge—even though the search for strong unity is not thereby undermined. The overthrow of parity and time-reversal are cases in point. It is conceivable, then, that unity of types 1, 2, and 3 might be overthrown—at least if too narrowly interpreted—even though strong unity is retained. Unity of type 1 may be interpreted as implying that space itself is causally inefficacious, so that a mere change of location cannot affect the way phenomena evolve. But, according to GR, space (or space-time more generally) is not, in a sense, causally inefficacious: space (or space-time) has a variable curvature, which affects motion differently in different places (space-time regions). Type 1 unity can be reformulated so that it does not contradict GR; but a reformulation is required for this to be the case! Again, according to the electroweak theory, theories of cosmic inflation, and other theoretical speculations that involve spontaneous symmetry-breaking and phase changes that affect the nature of space, different spatial regions have inherently different physical features associated with them. (Some theorists even believe that boundaries form between different spatial regions.) Once again, type 1 unity only survives such theoretical developments if reformulated. In effect, type 1 unity becomes subsumed into type 2 unity, as space-time acquires variable dynamic properties. If types 7 and 8 unity are correct, then it is to be expected that space-time has variable dynamic properties, which means that any version of type 1 unity which presupposes dynamically invariant space-time cannot be correct. In other words, unity of types 7 and 8 may be incompatible with type 1 unity as this has been interpreted above (although type 1 unity can be reinterpreted to become subsumed into type 2 unity in such a way that it is no longer incompatible with unity of types 7 or 8). It is conceivable that the advance of theoretical physics might even lead to the overthrow of type 3 unity, in that the true theory of everything might refer, quite essentially, to *one unique object*, namely the big bang state—all subsequent diverse phenomena being a consequence of subsequent spontaneous symmetry-breaking.

(Z) It needs to be appreciated that being incompatible with current theoretical knowledge, far from being a vice in any acceptable level 4 thesis, is actually a virtue. It is to be expected that the true theory of everything, T, which turns the true level 4 thesis into a precise, testable dynamical theory, will contradict currently accepted physical theory (even if, in a certain sense, it yields current theories when certain limits are taken). NT contradicts Galileo's laws of terrestrial motion and Kepler's laws of planetary motion; GR contradicts NT; SR contradicts pre-relativistic physics based on Galilean invariance; QT contradicts classical physics; QED contradicts classical electrodynamics. (In each case, however, as we saw in the last chapter, the new theory yields a theory empirically equivalent to the old theory if certain limits are taken and the resulting theory is reinterpreted physically. Thus NT yields Kepler's laws in the limit when the masses of the planets tend to zero, and the resulting laws are reinterpreted to apply to planets of non-zero mass.) It is reasonable to hold that this mode of advance will continue, and the true theory of everything, unifying GR and SM, supposing such a thing is possible, will contradict GR and SM.

Thus, the fact that strong unity (physicalism) contradicts current theory speaks in its favour. But there is a stronger point to be made. If strong unity is *true*, it is all but inevitable that theoretical physics should advance in the way just indicated. For if strong unity is true, no dynamical theory can be precisely true of any restricted range of phenomena without being generalizable in a trivial way to be precisely true of all physically possible phenomena. This is built into the idea that that which determines how events unfold does not change throughout the space of all possible physical phenomena. Thus, any theory that applies (within the limits of experimental accuracy) to some restricted range of phenomena only cannot be precisely correct if strong unity (physicalism) is true. Granted that theoretical physics advances by developing theories of greater and greater scope, it will advance by developing theories that *correct* their predecessors—if physicalism is true. That theoretical physics since Galileo and Kepler has just this overall feature, required by physicalism if it is true, provides grounds for favouring physicalism to rival doctrines that fail to account for this pervasive feature of progress in theoretical physics. Weak unity (unity in senses 1 to 3) does *not* imply that theoretical physics must advance in this way!

So far we have been comparing weak and strong unity considered as rival metaphysical doctrines; but we really need to consider the relative merits of weak and strong AOE (incorporating weak and strong unity respectively at level 4) when considered within the framework of what may be called 'generalized AOE' (the view that scientific knowledge includes *some* hierarchy of increasingly contentless cosmological assumptions, without being those specifically of AOE). According to this framework, four considerations ought to govern choice of thesis at level N, where $2 < N < 8$.

(C1) The thesis must be the best available exemplification of the best thesis at level $N + 1$, and ought, ideally, to entail this thesis.

(C2) The thesis ought to be potentially more fruitful, heuristically and methodologically, than any rival.

(C3) The thesis ought to be actually more fruitful than any rival.

(C4) The thesis ought to have the least possible content.[25]

Let us now consider what adjustments need to be made to strong AOE to form the best version of weak AOE, with the thesis of weak rather than strong unity at level 4.

One possibility is to have, at level 5, the thesis that the universe is comprehensible in some way other than physically comprehensible, e.g. because God exists, but in such a way that weak physical unity also holds. But this is hardly an acceptable position, in that such a level 5 thesis, in so far as it differs from physicalism, shows no sign of being associated with an empirically progressive research programme within physics. (The hypothesis that God exists would become heuristically and methodologically fruitful if, for example, empirical data began to show that prayer is efficacious. Not only has this not happened as yet; if it did, it would involve, so it would seem, the occurrence of miracles, which would violate weak unity.)

Granted weak unity at level 4, and granted generalized AOE, the best conjecture to accept at level 5 is, it seems, a thesis that might be called *weak comprehensibility*. This generalizes weak unity to kinds of explanation other than physical explanation, and asserts that there are M unchanging entities (gods or whatever) in terms of which phenomena can, in principle, be explained and understood. Weak comprehensibility does not, however, imply near comprehensibility since this, in turn, implies that the best level 5 and 4 theses to accept are comprehensibility and physicalism, which collapses the position into strong AOE. At levels 6 and 7 we have theses that are implied by weak comprehensibility; and at level 8 we have the strong AOE thesis of meta-knowability.

It is here that objections to weak AOE arise. If weak AOE accepts the level 8 thesis of meta-knowability, it accepts (as a working hypothesis) that the universe is such that there is some discoverable assumption that can be made about the nature of the universe which aids the growth of knowledge. It accepts that the universe is such that, as knowledge improves, knowledge-about-how-to-improve-knowledge can improve as well; there can be positive feedback between improving knowledge and improving aim-and-methods, improving metaphysical conjectures linked to improving methods. Granted this, and granted the thesis of weak unity and the considerations spelled out above, the case for adopting strong unity (to replace weak unity) seems quite good. Not to adopt strong unity is tantamount to rejecting meta-knowability at level 8. It is of course possible to defend weak AOE in this way; but this entails rejecting the basic idea of generalized AOE. The success of science is, I suggest, based quite fundamentally on the highly optimistic conjecture that the universe is such that we can discover improved methods for the improvement of knowledge.

4

Simplicity

1. INTRODUCTION

In this and the next two chapters I set out to show that aim-oriented empiricism (AOE) solves the ten problems, discussed in Chapter 2, which standard empiricism (SE) fails to solve. In the present chapter I argue that the problem of what the simplicity of a theory *is* can be solved within the framework of AOE. (This also disposes of the methodological problem of induction.) In Chapter 5 I argue that AOE solves the justificational problems of induction (and thus, also, the problem of justifying preference for simple theories); and in Chapter 6 I argue that AOE solves the remaining five problems on the list.

2. PRAGMATIC AND EPISTEMOLOGICAL NOTIONS OF SIMPLICITY

'Simplicity'[1] in the present context apparently means the simplicity of the *form* of a law or theory—the extent to which the *functions*, the *equations*, of the theory are simple. But it also means the extent to which a theory is non-*ad hoc*, or *explanatory*, or *elegant*, or *unified*, or *conceptually coherent*, or possessing what Einstein called *inner perfection* or, in other contexts, *beauty*, *comprehensibility*, or *intelligibility*.

In judging some theories to be 'simple' and others to be 'complex', physicists may mean only that some theories are such that it is an easy matter to solve their equations and extract their empirical predictions, whereas other theories have equations that are fiendishly difficult, if not impossible, to solve. This highly pragmatic meaning of simplicity is, of course, of immense importance in physics—especially in less fundamental, more phenomenological parts of physics, where the aim is primarily the instrumentalist one of predicting phenomena as easily and accurately as possible. There is, however, no particular reason why simplicity, in this pragmatic sense, should be an indication of truth. In this chapter our concern is only with simplicity in so far as this *is* (or is taken to be) an indication of truth.

Those who uphold bare SE are in the comfortable position of being able to deny that there is any such epistemologically significant sense of simplicity; but bare SE is untenable. Most supporters of SE acknowledge that simplicity considerations, in addition to empirical considerations, play an essential role in science in deciding what theories are to be accepted as the best attempt at knowledge of truth, and what are to be rejected as false. They defend, that is, versions of dressed SE. And as a result, they face the two problems of simplicity, where simplicity is interpreted to be epistemologically significant, relevant to a determination of what is, and what is not, knowledge of truth. Dressed SE is confronted by, and is unable to solve, the two problems from Chapter 2, Section 8:

(iv) What *is* simplicity?
(v) What is the rationale for preferring simple to complex theories?

3. DIVERSE ASPECTS OF THE PROBLEM OF WHAT SIMPLICITY IS

Problem (iv) breaks up into the following subordinate problems.

(iv*a*) *The terminological problem.* Whether a theory is simple or complex appears to depend on how the theory is formulated, the terminology, or concepts, used to formulate it. But how can such a terminology-dependent notion of simplicity have any significant methodological or epistemological role in science? What determines the 'correct' terminology, in terms of which theories are to be formulated so that their simplicity may be appraised? How can there possibly be any such thing as the 'correct' terminology? If there is not, does not the whole notion of simplicity of theories collapse? On the one hand, the simplicity or complexity of a theory must, it seems, depend on the terminology used to formulate it, but on the other hand, this cannot, it seems, be the case if simplicity is to be significant as an indication of truth.

(iv*b*) *The problem of degrees of simplicity.* How can theories be (partially) ordered with respect to their degree of simplicity, in a way that is unaffected by the way they are formulated?

(iv*c*) *The problem of changing notions of simplicity.* As science develops, what simplicity means changes. What it meant to Newton is different from what it would have meant to a nineteenth-century physicist, which is different again from what it would mean to a late twentieth-century physicist. How can justice be done to the changing nature of simplicity (and to variability from one discipline to another)?

(ivd) *The problem of the multifaceted nature of simplicity.* 'Simple' is the generic term that philosophers of science tend to use for a whole family of notions that scientists appeal to in assessing the non-empirical merits of theories, as I have indicated above. An acceptable theory of simplicity ought to pick out just one concept as fundamental, but at the same time do justice to the role that the other concepts appear to have in assessing theories in physics.

(ive) *The problem of ambiguity.* An indication of the complexity of the notion of simplicity in physics is given by the fact that one theory may be, in an obvious sense, much more complex than another, and yet, at the same time be, in a much more important sense, much simpler. The classic case of this ambiguity of simplicity is provided by a comparison of Newton's and Einstein's theories of gravity. In one obvious sense, Newton's theory is much simpler than Einstein's; in another sense, Einstein's theory is the simpler. An adequate theory of simplicity must resolve this puzzling state of affairs.

(ivf) *The problem of doing justice to the intuition of physicists.* Physicists are by no means unanimous in their judgements concerning the simplicity of theories, but there is a considerable level of agreement. An acceptable theory of simplicity must do justice to such agreed intuitions.

(ivg) *The problem of improving on the intuitions of physicists.* An acceptable theory of simplicity ought to be able to improve on the intuitions of physicists, if it provides a genuine clarification of the nature of simplicity.

The first of these problems, the terminological problem, (iva), is by far the most serious. It has the form of a paradox. The simplicity of a theory both must, and cannot possibly, depend on terminology.

In Chapter 2 we saw that SE fails to solve problem (iv) in the main because of a failure to solve the terminological problem;[2] but SE also fails to solve other aspects of the problem, (ivb) to (ivg).

It is worth noting in passing that Einstein, who came close to accepting AOE (Maxwell 1993c: III), fully recognized the importance of the problem of what simplicity is, and yet did not know how to solve it. This is apparent from a passage of Einstein's 'Autobiographical Notes' during which he discusses ways in which physical theories, quite generally, can be critically assessed (Einstein 1949: 20–5).

Einstein emphasizes that theories need to be critically assessed from *two* distinct points of view: from the standpoint of their empirical success, and from the standpoint of their 'inner perfection', the 'naturalness' or 'logical simplicity' of the postulates. Einstein stresses that the theories that need to be considered are those 'whose object is the *totality* of all physical appearances', that is, 'theories of everything', in modern parlance. And Einstein acknowledges that 'an exact formulation' of the second point of view (having to do with the 'inner perfection' of theories) 'meets with great difficulties' even though it 'has played an important role in the selection of theories since time immemorial'. Einstein continues:

The problem here is not simply one of a kind of enumeration of the logically independent premises (if anything like this were at all unequivocally possible), but that of a kind of reciprocal weighing of incommensurable qualities. . . . The following I reckon as also belonging to the 'inner perfection' of a theory: We prize a theory more highly if, from the logical standpoint, it is not the result of an arbitrary choice among theories which, among themselves, are of equal value and analogously constructed. (Einstein 1949: 23)

And Einstein comments:

I shall not attempt to excuse the meagre precision of these assertions . . . by lack of sufficient printing space at my disposal, but confess herewith that I am not, without more ado, and perhaps not at all, capable of replacing these hints with more precise definitions. I believe, however, that a sharper formulation would be possible. (Einstein 1949: 23)

In two important respects, Einstein formulates the problem of what it means to say of a theory that it has 'inner perfection', 'explanatoriness', or 'unity' in AOE terms. First, Einstein makes it quite clear that 'inner perfection' is a feature that a theory must possess, if it is to be acceptable, that is entirely *in addition* to empirical success. Secondly, he makes it clear that the problem of what 'inner perfection' *is* needs to be considered in connection with theories that purport to be 'theories of everything'. Nevertheless, Einstein did not know how to solve the problem.

4. HOW AIM-ORIENTED EMPIRICISM SOLVES THE PROBLEM OF WHAT SIMPLICITY IS

According to AOE, *the* non-empirical requirement that the totality of fundamental theories, T_n, in physics must satisfy in order to be ultimately acceptable is that T_n is a precise version of the vague, level 4 thesis of physicalism, or strong unity. The key notion is thus *unity*—unity of the *content* of the totality of fundamental dynamical theory. Given two rival total theories, T_n and T_{n+1}, T_{n+1} is simpler than T_n if and only if T_{n+1} exemplifies physicalism better than T_n does. In other words, if T_n is more disunified than T_{n+1} in one or other of the eight different ways discussed in Section 5 of Chapter 3, then T_n is less simple. Furthermore, the kind of disunity becomes increasingly serious as we move from sense 8 to sense 1, with 7 and 6 being, in this respect, equal. If T_n is disunified in a more serious kind of way than T_{n+1}, in this sense, then T_n is more disunified, less simple.

This account of simplicity can be extended to individual theories in two different ways. An individual theory, T^*, is 'simpler' than a rival, T^{**}, if $T_m + T^*$ exemplifies physicalism better than $T_m + T^{**}$ does, where T_m is the conjunction of all other current, accepted, fundamental theories. We can also, however, treat an individual theory as if it is a 'theory of everything', ignoring all phenomena which lie outside the domain of the theory. Given two rival individual theories, T_1 and T_2, we can regard them as rival 'theories of everything' and consider their relative simplicity, i.e. unity, i.e. their success, when so regarded, at being precise versions of physicalism.

Furthermore, this account can be straightforwardly extended to do justice to the point that notions of simplicity evolve with evolving knowledge. Theoretical physics does not just, in practice, presuppose physicalism; as we have seen, at any given time it presupposes a blueprint, B, a more precise version of physicalism, which will almost certainly be false, and will need to be changed as physics makes progress.

In accepting the blueprint B, we accept that the fundamental physical entities and force(s) are as specified by B; we accept a set of invariance or symmetry principles, specific to B, related to the geometry of space-time, and the general dynamical/geometrical character of the fundamental physical entity (or entities), postulated by B.

Thus, the Boscovich blueprint may be so understood that it asserts that fundamental physical entities (point-particles with mass) are all of one type (symmetric with respect to particle exchange), their surrounding field of force being rigid throughout all motions, and rotationally symmetric. The time *evolution* of any physical system is invariant with respect to translations in space and time, changes of orientation, and changes in fixed velocity with respect to some inertial reference frame. By contrast, the field–particle blueprint, associated with classical electrodynamics, postulates the existence of two distinct kinds of fundamental entity, point-particles and fields of force; it asserts that force fields are non-rigid (changes in the field travelling at some definite, finite velocity). This means that spherical symmetry will be restricted to the case when a charged particle is motionless in a spatial region within which the field is otherwise zero. Again, whereas the Boscovich blueprint may be taken to imply Galilean invariance, the field–particle blueprint may be taken to imply Lorentz invariance.

A level 2 theory, T, may clash with physicalism and yet exemplify physicalism to some degree, in that it is disunified to some degree in one or other of the eight ways of being disunified specified in Chapter 3. Analogously, T may clash with a blueprint, B, and yet exemplify B to some degree, in that it postulates B-type entities, forces, and symmetries, but at the same time violates, to some degree, and in one or other way, the specific kind of unity postulated by B. The ways in which T may violate B may differ in some respects from the eight ways in which T may violate physicalism. If B is the Boscovichian blueprint, only the first five of the eight unity/disunity distinctions specified in Chapter 3 are relevant. In this case, B does not postulate anything like a force exhibiting local gauge invariance (6); it does not postulate spontaneously broken symmetries (7); and it does not unify space-time and matter (8). Consequently, even though T fails to be unified in ways 6, 7, and 8, this does not mean that T lacks B-type unity. If, on the other hand, the point-particles postulated by T have force fields that lack rigidity and spherical symmetry, this would constitute a violation of B-type unity or simplicity, even though this does not, as such, violate physicalism.

Given two distinct blueprints, B_n and B_{n+1}, which postulate entities, forces, and symmetries of somewhat different kinds (even though there is some overlap), we have two distinct notions of simplicity, B_n-simplicity and B_{n+1}-simplicity. A theory, T, may have a high degree of B_n-simplicity, and a low degree of B_{n+1}-simplicity.

Blueprints can themselves be assessed with respect to simplicity, with respect, that is, to how well they accord with physicalism.

The simplicity of level 2 theories can, in short, be assessed in two distinct ways, in terms of what may be called P-simplicity and B-simplicity (degree of exemplifying physicalism and some blueprint, B, respectively).[3] The P-simplicity of a theory, T, assesses how successfully T realizes physicalism, and remains fixed as long as physicalism does not change its meaning. The B-simplicity of T assesses how well T realizes the best available overall blueprint for physics; B-simplicity evolves with evolving blueprints. Furthermore, that blueprints evolve with evolving knowledge is, according to AOE, essential to the rationality of science, a vital, necessary component of scientific progress (granted that we are ignorant of what version of physicalism is true). There is thus, according to AOE, no mystery about evolving notions of simplicity; that the notion of simplicity should evolve is essential to rationality, a vital component of progress. Simplicity criteria, associated with level 3 blueprints, do not merely *change*; they can *improve*. We learn more about the precise way in which Nature is simple or unified as science progresses.

This, in barest outline, is the AOE solution to the problem of what simplicity *is*.

5. CONTENT AND FORM

Why does this proposed AOE solution to the problem of what simplicity is succeed where all SE attempts at solving the problem fail? The decisive point to appreciate is that, according to AOE, in assessing the relative simplicity of two theories, T_1 and T_2, what matters is the *content* of the two theories, not their *form*. It is what theories *assert* about the world that must accord, as far as possible, with physicalism, with the thesis that a unified *something* runs through all phenomena. Thus questions of formulation, axiomatic structure, etc. are essentially irrelevant when it comes to assessing the simplicity of theories in a methodologically significant sense. The fact that a theory may seem simple when formulated in one way, highly complicated or *ad hoc* when formulated in another way—a fact that defeated SE attempts at solving the problem—has, according to AOE, no bearing whatsoever on the simplicity or unity of the theory in an epistemologically and methodologically significant sense, which has to do exclusively with *what the theory asserts about the world* (which remains constant throughout mere terminological reformulations). What matters, in short, is the simplicity or unity, not of the *theory itself*, but of what the theory *asserts to be the case*. A perfectly simple or comprehensible possible universe may be depicted by a theory that is formulated in a horribly complex fashion; and vice versa, a horribly complicated or incomprehensible universe may be depicted by a theory formulated in a beautifully simple way.

The point is a quite general one. We have no reason to suppose that the simplicity, symmetry, or unity of *objects* (e.g. possible universes) is reflected in the simplicity, symmetry, or unity of *true descriptions of these objects* (e.g. theories). Suppose we are given a number of wooden objects, $O_1 \ldots O_N$, to be graded with respect to their simplicity, symmetry, or unity: a sphere, a cube, and examples of the other four regular polygons (the tetrahedron, the octahedron, the dodecahedron, and the icosahedron), a spheroid, an egg-shaped object, and various awkward and arbitrary-looking objects, some made up of loosely connected bits and pieces. We confidently grade the objects as required. We are now given a series of descriptions of these objects, $D_1 \ldots D_N$, and we are asked to order *these* with respect to their simplicity, symmetry, or unity. There need be no correspondence at all between the ordering of the *objects* and the ordering of the *descriptions*. The simplest object might have been given a horribly complicated description, and vice versa. It is only if we ignore the nature of the *descriptions themselves*, and concentrate exclusively on the *content* of the descriptions, the nature of what the descriptions describe, that the two orderings will be the same.[4]

Traditional SE approaches to the problem of simplicity, such as those of Goodman, Friedman, Kitcher, and Watkins (see Chapter 2), have been barking up the wrong tree. They have been concentrating on theories themselves, their structure, their axiomatic form, or whatever, and thus missing the point: what matters, for science, is the content of theories, what theories assert, and not primarily their structure or form.[5] The simplicity or complexity of a theory, a theoretical description, may quite generally, as we have seen, have nothing to do whatsoever with the simplicity or complexity of what is described. It cannot therefore be scientifically significant. In order to get at a scientifically significant conception of simplicity, we must attend to the content of the theory. But this means recognizing, quite explicitly, that in persistently choosing simple, unified, or comprehensible theories in science we are persistently choosing theories that accord with a metaphysical thesis about the world, namely that the world itself is simple, unified, or comprehensible.[6] And this violates SE. It is thus the attempt to find a solution to the problem of simplicity within the confines of SE which renders the problem insoluble. The problem can only be solved by violating SE, by accepting that science presupposes that the universe is simple, unified, or comprehensible in some meaningful and substantial sense, which in turn requires that one adopts some version of AOE.[7]

6. TERMINOLOGICAL SIMPLICITY

It may be objected that the point just made establishes too much. Simplicity of formulation *does* matter in physics! What is so puzzling about simplicity in science is that even though simplicity of formulation clearly cannot matter, it nevertheless does matter. In deciding what theories to accept and reject, scientists are constantly, and quite properly, guided by the simplicity or complexity of the *formulation* of theories.

But this too can easily be accounted for by the present AOE theory of simplicity. The acceptability or unacceptability of theories $T_1 \ldots T_n$, from the standpoint of simplicity or unity, depends upon how well or ill the physical content of these theories satisfies the symmetries of the best available blueprint for physics, which in turn depends on the physical content of the blueprint (and not on its formulation). So far formulation or language is entirely irrelevant. However, the decision to employ a set of basic concepts, C, to formulate physical theories in effect amounts to adopting a blueprint B_C. The better the physical content of a theory, T, satisfies the symmetries of B_C, the simpler the formulation of T will tend to be, when formulated in the corresponding concepts C. Thus the simplicity or complexity of the formulation of a theory, T, is relevant to the acceptability of T if the concepts, C, used to formulate T correspond to the best available blueprint for physics; otherwise the simplicity or complexity of the formulation of T is irrelevant to the acceptability of T. Here, in a nutshell, is the solution to the problem—utterly baffling when viewed from the perspective of SE—of how the simplicity or complexity of *formulation* of a theory can be both *highly relevant* to the acceptability of the theory, and *utterly irrelevant*.

What does it mean to say that a set of concepts, C, or a language, L, corresponds to a blueprint B? The answer is straightforward. L corresponds to B when the physical terms of L (the physical concepts of C) have meanings which presuppose the truth of B—as when Newtonian concepts of space, time, mass, and force presuppose the truth of the corresponding facets of the Newtonian blueprint. Furthermore, L corresponds to B when the symmetries of B are reflected in L.[8] Granted that the most acceptable blueprint for physics postulates that space-time is Minkowskian in character, then the fact that a theory T takes on a simple form when formulated in a Lorentz invariant language, which incorporates the symmetries of Minkowskian space-time, is highly significant from the standpoint of the acceptability of T.[9] The fact that T has a highly complex form when formulated in some other language, not related to Minkowskian space-time, whereas another theory T^* has a highly simple form in this other language, is neither here nor there from the standpoint of acceptability (granted that space-time *is* Minkowskian, or at least is asserted to be so by the most acceptable blueprint).

One way in which simplicity of form registers itself in a methodologically significant way in physics is through *relative* simplicity. Given an empirically highly successful theory, T, about some range of phenomena, it is methodologically significant that a new theory, T^*, about some different range of phenomena, has a *simple* form relative to T—i.e. has a simple form when formulated in the language L within which T has a simple form. The fact that both T and T^* have simple forms in L indicates that they satisfy well the symmetries of the best blueprint B, corresponding to L (or implicit in the choice of L as the basic language of theoretical physics). In line with this, theoretical physicists strive to formulate new theories in a way which is as close as possible to the form of pre-existing, empirically successful theories, modifications being introduced only to the extent that these are necessary to accommodate the different circumstances with which the new theory deals. An example is the way in which classical electrodynamics can be regarded as arising as a result of a series of modifications to Newtonian theory (see Section 4 of Chapter 3, and below). Other examples, to be discussed below, are of the way in which quantum electroweak theory and quantum chromodynamics arose as a result of keeping as close as possible to the form of the pre-existing, empirically highly successful theory of quantum electrodynamics, only those modifications being introduced which were necessary in order to accommodate those features of the weak and strong forces that differ from the electromagnetic force.

Furthermore (in line with this same point) theoretical physicists were highly encouraged, a decade or so ago, when they realized that the three fundamental theories of physics have one symmetry feature in common with one another—local gauge invariance. (Even general relativity has a local gauge invariant aspect.) This common symmetry feature was taken to be an indication of the underlying unity of Nature, and a sign that theoretical physics was on the right road. All this makes perfect sense according to the AOE theory of simplicity or unity developed here.

It might seem, at first sight, that a theory of simplicity which concentrates on unity at the level of fundamental theory can have little to say about simplicity at the humble level of empirical laws, remote from fundamental theory. But the considerations just mentioned show that this is not the case. An empirical law, however complex, can always be turned into a law that is as simple as we please by an appropriate change of concepts. (The demand for simplicity appears to be vacuous.) What prevents us from doing this in scientific practice is the demand for unity: we require that, as far as possible, diverse laws are formulated in terms of the *same* basic concepts. The introduction of new concepts at the empirical level needs to be kept to a minimum, and such concepts need to be related to, or explicated in terms of, concepts associated with the best available blueprint (as when the notion of temperature of a gas is related to average kinetic energy of the constituent molecules). It is the demand for theoretical unity, in other words, which makes the demand that empirical laws should have a simple form a non-vacuous demand (and one which often cannot be fulfilled).[10]

7. FURTHER QUESTIONS

So far I have indicated how AOE solves the first three problems concerning what simplicity is: the terminological problem, the problem of specifying degrees of simplicity, and the problem of changing, or evolving, conceptions of simplicity. What about the remaining four problems indicated above? I take these in turn.

(ivd) *The multifaceted problem.* AOE is quite clear: the key notion behind the generic term 'simplicity' is unity or explanatoriness. These two notions are connected as follows. The more *unified* a dynamical theory is, other things being equal, so the more *explanatory* it is. To explain, in this sense, is, ideally, to show that apparently diverse phenomena are really just different versions of the *one* kind of phenomenon, differing only with respect to initial conditions but otherwise evolving in accordance with the same force. Thus Newtonian theory explains the diverse phenomena it predicts by revealing that these phenomena all evolve in accordance with Newtonian gravitation. As long as the totality of physical theory is disunified, explanation is inadequate; the explanatory task of physics is only at an end when all physical phenomena have been shown to be just *one* kind of phenomenon, all differences being differences of initial conditions of the *one* kind of entity or stuff.[11]

Other terms bandied about—simplicity, symmetry, elegance, beauty, comprehensibility, etc.—all devolve, more or less straightforwardly, from the central notion of unity throughout diversity, or explanatoriness. In Chapter 3, Sections 5 and 6 we saw, briefly, how the demand for symmetry is related to the demand for unity: see Sections 11–13 below and the Appendix for a more detailed discussion of the role of symmetry in physics, and its connection with unity. Above, we have seen how terminological simplicity[12] of individual laws or theories can always be concocted by an appropriate choice of concepts, but that the simplicity of a number of laws when formulated in terms of the same concepts cannot, this being an indication of unity.

It may be asked: Does simplicity (in the non-generic sense) play a role in distinguishing between physically comprehensible and incomprehensible universes? If it does, it takes second place to considerations of unity. This point is best discussed in connection with the fifth problem.

(ive) *The problem of ambiguity.* General relativity (GR) is, in a quite straightforward sense, a much more complicated theory than Newton's theory of gravitation (NT). NT determines the gravitation field by means of *one* equation, whereas GR requires a system of *six* equations.[13] Furthermore, NT is a linear theory, in the sense that, as one adds more massive bodies to a system of bodies, the gravitational forces due to the new bodies merely add on to the forces already present. GR, on the other hand, is non-linear: the gravitational field interacts with itself. Finally, the equations of GR are vastly more difficult to solve than those of NT; GR is much more complex than NT in terms of the pragmatic notion of simplicity considered above.

GR has, however, much greater unity than NT. According to NT, gravitation is a force that exists as something entirely distinct from, and in addition to, space and time; according to GR, gravitation is nothing more than the variable curvature of space-time. The field equations of GR specify how the presence of mass, or energy more generally, causes space-time to curve. According to GR, bodies 'interacting gravitationally' do not, in a sense, interact at all; all bodies move along the nearest thing to straight lines in curved space-time, namely curved paths called geodesics (the four-dimensional analogue of great circles on the earth's surface). A geodesic is a curve such that, between any two points, its length is unchanged to first order by small changes in the curve. Ordinarily one would think of the earth's motion round the sun as constituting a spiral in four-dimensional space-time; according to GR, the mass of the sun causes space-time near the sun to be curved in such a way that the path executed by the earth is a geodesic.

GR unifies by annihilation (see below); space-time has a variable curvature, as a result of the presence of matter or energy, and this variable curvature affects what paths constitute geodesics, and thus what paths bodies pursue; gravitation, as a force distinct from space-time, vanishes. As a result, GR does not need an analogue of Newton's second law, $F = ma$; all that is required is a generalization of Newton's first law: every body continues in its state of rest or uniform motion in a straight line, except in so far as a force is imposed upon it. ('Uniform motion in a straight line (in Euclidean space)' needs to be generalized to become 'geodesic in Riemannian space-time'.)

Despite its greater complexity, GR exemplifies physicalism better than NT because of its greater unity. And there is a further, crucial point. Given the basic unifying idea of GR, namely that gravitation is nothing more than a consequence of the variable curvature of space-time, the equations of GR are just about the simplest that are possible. The complexities of GR are not fortuitous; they are inevitable, granted the fundamental unifying idea of GR.

From this discussion of NT and GR we can draw the following general conclusion. Given two theories, T_1 and T_2, if T_2 has greater unity than T_1 then, other things being equal, T_2 is the better theory from the standpoint of non-empirical considerations, even if T_2 is much more complex than T_1. This will be the case, especially, if the greater complexity of T_2 is an inevitable consequence of its greater unity. Simplicity considerations may have a role to play, on the other hand, if there are two theories, T_1 and T_2, that are unified equally, in the same way, so that, at a certain level, T_1 and T_2 have a common blueprint, but T_1 is much simpler than T_2. In this case, T_1 is a better theory than T_2 on non-empirical grounds. A universe that exemplifies unity in a way that is highly complex in comparison with other possible universes (other possible dynamic structures) unified in the same sort of way is, we may argue, not fully comprehensible. To this extent, comprehensibility requires simplicity. (We have here a ninth way of drawing the distinction between unity and disunity, to be added to the eight indicated in Section 5 of Chapter 3.)

The extent to which simplicity considerations, of this limited type, ultimately play a role in what it means to say that the universe is comprehensible depends, to some extent, on the character of the true theory of everything, T. Given T, there are, we may assume, any number of rival theories, $T_1 \ldots T_n$, that exemplify physicalism just as well as T does, as far as the eight requirements for unity indicated in Chapter 3 are concerned. It is conceivable that a level 3 blueprint, B, can be specified which is such that T, together with a proper subset of $T_1 \ldots T_n$, are all equally well B-unified, as far as the eight requirements for unity are concerned, but *one* of these B-unified theories is much simpler than the others. In this case we could declare that, for unity, we require that the simplest of these theories is true.

What does simplicity (in the non-generic sense) mean in this context? I return to this question in Section 16 below.

I consider now the two remaining problems, (iv*f*) and (iv*g*).

One beautiful accomplishment of the theory of simplicity being put forward here is that it accounts effortlessly for the fact that it is above all those physicists who have the best understanding of the *whole* of fundamental theoretical physics who will be in the best position to make good judgements concerning the relative simplicity of theories. In order to make such good judgements it is necessary to have a good understanding of the *content* of physics at levels 2 and 3—which is just what the specified kind of physicist will possess. Granted SE, the ability to make good judgements concerning simplicity can only be the outcome of some mysterious intuitive capacity; granted AOE, on the other hand, grounds for simplicity judgements can be spelled out explicitly, and assessed objectively and rationally, in terms of rival blueprint proposals. We see, here, in essence, how the AOE theory of simplicity can both account for existing intuitions of physicists, and indicate how such intuitions can be improved.

Here are a few slightly more detailed comments concerning these two issues.

(iv*f*) *The problem of doing justice to the intuition of physicists.* I consider just five points (five items of data, as it were, that any theory of simplicity ought to be able to account for). First, physicists are generally at a loss to say what simplicity is, or how it is to be justified. Secondly, despite this, much of the time most theoretical physicists are in broad agreement in their judgements concerning the non-empirical simplicity requirements that theories must satisfy to be accepted, at least to the extent of agreeing about how to distinguish non-aberrant from aberrant theories (although of course they do not use this terminology). If this were not the case, there would be no generally accepted theories in physics. But thirdly, in addition to this, non-empirical simplicity criteria intuitively accepted by physicists tend to change over time. Fourthly, during theoretical revolutions there are often spectacular, irreconcilable disagreements (Kuhn 1970, chs. VII–XII). Rationality tends to break down during revolutions, as graphically described by Kuhn. But fifthly, despite all this, intuitive ideas concerning simplicity, at least since Newton, have enabled physics to meet with incredible (apparent) success.

According to the account of simplicity being advocated here, the more nearly the totality of fundamental dynamical theory exemplifies physicalism, so the greater is its degree of simplicity. In practice physics accepts physicalism, even though this may be denied by physicists (because it clashes with the official doctrine of SE). This view accounts for the above five points as follows.

The failure of physicists to say what simplicity is, or how it should be justified, is due to the fact that most physicists accept some version of dressed SE; within this framework no adequate account of the role of simplicity in physics can be given, as we have seen. The general, more or less implicit acceptance of physicalism in practice means that there is, in practice, at any given time, broad agreement concerning judgements of simplicity. (Physicists may merely require that any acceptable theory must be such that it can be given some more or less specific kind of formulation: but, as we have seen, this in practice is equivalent to demanding that any theory accord with some blueprint corresponding to the concepts, the language, of the formulation.)

According to AOE, even if at level 4 there is no change of ideas, at level 3 it is entirely to be expected that there will be changes over time. (It would be astonishing if, at level 3, the correct guess was made at the outset.) The historical record reveals just such an evolution of blueprint ideas, from the corpuscular hypothesis, via the Boscovichian blueprint, the classical field blueprint, the empty space-time blueprint (with variable geometry and topology), the quantum field blueprint, Lagrangianism, to the superstring blueprint. Thus, over time, judgements concerning simplicity both do, and ought to, evolve with evolving level 3 blueprint ideas. During theoretical revolutions, it is above all level 3 blueprint ideas that change. During such revolutions, some physicists will hold on to the old, familiar blueprint, while others will embrace the new one. This means that physicists will assess the competing theories in terms of somewhat different conceptions of simplicity, related to the different, competing blueprints. General agreement about simplicity considerations will, in these circumstances, break down. Arguments for and against the competing theories will be circular, and rationality will tend to break down in just the way described so graphically by Kuhn. Finally, the success of physics is due, in large part (1) to the acceptance in practice of physicalism (or some fruitful special case such as the corpuscular hypothesis or Boscovichianism), and (2) to the fact that physicalism is either true or, if false, 'nearly true' in the sense that local phenomena occur as if physicalism is true to a high degree of approximation.

(iv*g*) It deserves to be noted that AOE does not merely account for basic facts about physicists' intuitions; as I have indicated, it clarifies and improves on those intuitions. Once AOE is generally accepted by the physics community, the breakdown of rationality during theoretical revolutions, noted by Kuhn, will no longer occur. If the revolution is a change from theory T_1 and blueprint B_1 to theory and blueprint T_2 and B_2, an agreed framework will exist for the non-empirical assessment not only of T_1 and T_2, but of B_1 and B_2 as well. Kuhn argues that the breakdown of rationality during revolutions is due to the fact that, ultimately, only empirical considerations are rational in science. During a revolution, empirical considerations are inconclusive; the new theory, T_2, will not have had time to prove its empirical mettle (etc.). Thus rational assessment of rival theories must be highly inconclusive. In so far as physicists appeal to rival paradigms, B_1 and B_2, as Kuhn calls them, the arguments are circular, and thus irrational (persuading only those who already believe). Accept AOE, and this situation changes. Rational considerations do exist for the (tentative) assessment of the relative merits of B_1 and B_2; we are justified in assessing how adequately they exemplify physicalism. This means, in turn, that we can judge rationally whether we are justified in assessing T_2 (or T_1) in terms of B_2. Such judgements, though rational, will be fallible, even if physicalism is true: acceptance of AOE thus makes clear that dogmatism, at the level of paradigms, or level 3 blueprints, is wholly inappropriate. This in itself promotes rationality in physics.

Acceptance of AOE would also mean that theoretical physics need not be dominated by mere fashion. Granted SE, a new blueprint, a new approach to developing a theory of quantum gravity for example, can only be rationally assessed when the research programme is sufficiently completed to yield empirical predictions. Before empirical predictions have emerged, there are no objective criteria for assessing new blueprints and, as a result, one particular blueprint may come to dominate, almost for no better reason than it is the fashion: a recent example is the massive upsurge of work on superstring theory in the 1980s. Granted AOE, rival blueprints or research programmes can be objectively and rationally (if fallibly) assessed in the absence of empirical predictions: critical discussion and not mere fashion can decide priorities for research.

8. IS PHYSICALISM MEANINGFUL?

The correct theory of simplicity ought itself to be simple. Some may feel, however, that the above is altogether too simple, in that it is circular. The unity of *theories* is explicated in terms of the unity of *physicalism*. What has been achieved?

If the task was to give some sort of philosophical analysis of the concept of unity, this objection might be well-founded, but this is not what is required in order to solve the problem of simplicity. The task, rather, is to solve the problems—(iv*a*) to (iv*g*)—that arise in connection with attributing degrees of simplicity to theories. In order to solve these problems, it is essential to associate simplicity with content and not form. But this means that we require, at some level, a substantial thesis about the nature of the universe, the content of which is taken to be paradigmatic of simplicity (or unity). We cannot take some level 2 theory as paradigmatic of unity because, in our present state of ignorance, any theory we pick out is almost bound to be false (the associated notion of unity being inapplicable to the actual universe). Nor, for the same reason, can we take a level 3 blueprint to exemplify unity. The conjecture is that, as long as the level 4 thesis of physicalism is sufficiently *imprecise*, it will turn out to be true; it thus constitutes the best paradigm of unity that we are in a position to formulate in our present state of partial knowledge and ignorance. (The next chapter justifies adopting this conjecture.[14]) As long as the metaphysical thesis of physicalism is a *meaningful* assertion, explicating the unity of theories in terms of how well or ill they exemplify physicalism does not introduce an illegitimate circularity into the proposed solution to the problems of attributing unity to theories.

But is physicalism meaningful? In the last chapter I suggested, in effect, that physicalism should be interpreted as asserting that the universe is such that the true dynamic theory of everything is unified in the eight ways indicated in Section 5. But it is important, for reasons just indicated, not to tie down the meaning of physicalism to these specific eight points. We need to leave open the possibility that further facets of unity will be discovered in the future (and that some of the eight facets indicated in Chapter 3 will be discovered to be irrelevant). A number of doubts may be raised about the meaningfulness of physicalism when this thesis is interpreted in the open-ended way indicated in Section 2 of Chapter 3.

1. Does it really make sense to assert, as physicalism does, that there exists something which is *the same* everywhere?

2. Granted that extraordinarily diverse blueprints or paradigms for theoretical physics have been put forward at various times, does it really make sense to say that they all exemplify one common idea, namely physicalism? Is not this all the more the case if one takes into account that successive theories, paradigms, or blueprints in physics are

incommensurable? (See Kuhn 1970, chs. x, xii, and postscript, sect. 5; Feyerabend 1978.)

3. Is physicalism meaningful given its extreme vagueness? Granted that the universe is such that it is in principle possible to formulate a true, unified theory of everything, T, it is quite likely that major mathematical and conceptual developments will need to take place before T can be formulated. We might be as far from being able to formulate T today as Descartes was, in his day, from being able to formulate general relativity, quantum field theory, or string theory. Physicalism must be sufficiently vague and open-ended in its meaning to accommodate all such future conceptual developments, so that T, despite being dramatically different from anything we can conceive of today, is nevertheless a precise version of physicalism, as it has been formulated here. Can a thesis that is as vague as this be genuinely meaningful?

4. Physicalism asserts that there exists something, U, which *determines* (perhaps probabilistically) the way events unfold. Does this assertion make sense, given Hume's arguments designed to show that it does not? How are Hume's arguments concerning the impossibility of there being necessary connections between successive events to be countered?

5. How does the above account of simplicity meet Goodman-type arguments concerning 'grue' and 'bleen' (Goodman 1954), which seem to show that there is a strong element of arbitrariness in the distinction between 'remains the same' and 'does not remain the same'?

6. How does one go about deciding the extent to which a new theory, formulated perhaps in terms of radically new mathematical and physical concepts, is or is not a precise version of physicalism?

In the rest of this chapter I answer these, and related questions; and I indicate how the great unifying achievements of theoretical physics, from Newton to Weinberg and Salam, exemplify beautifully the theory of simplicity sketched above.

9. UNITY THROUGHOUT DIVERSITY

Can physicalism be meaningful granted that it asserts that there exists a unified something which is the *same* everywhere, throughout all change and diversity? I have already shown, in effect, that the answer to this question is: Yes. In Sections 3 and 4 of Chapter 3 I indicated a number of meaningful versions of physicalism, from the Presocratics to the ideas of modern physics, which more or less adequately embody the idea that an aspect of physical reality persists unchanged throughout all change and diversity. This key notion of physicalism of there being an unified something persisting throughout all change and diversity will be further clarified by the discussion, below, of the unifying achievements of theoretical physics.

Can physicalism be meaningful granted the extraordinary diversity of blueprints claimed to be more or less adequate exemplars of physicalism—especially when one takes Kuhn's and Feyerabend's arguments concerning incommensurability into account? Yes. That exemplars of physicalism are extraordinarily diverse in character indicates merely that physicalism is an idea of great generality, not that it is meaningless. Exemplars of the notion of 'object' or 'entity' are also extraordinarily diverse in character: this indicates that these are rather general notions, but not that they are meaningless.

As for arguments concerning incommensurability, all new ideas in physics and mathematics are never utterly new (or they would be meaningless). They invariably arise as modifications of pre-existing ideas (in the kind of way indicated in Sections 3 and 4 of Chapter 3); or they arise as a result of making explicit what has been implicit in what has gone before. It may be, however, that the illusion of incommensurability is created by restricting attention to the two levels of SE, and refusing to consider the multiple levels of AOE: the higher one ascends the hierarchy of levels postulated by AOE, the more one finds continuity through even the most violent and radical of revolutions in thought.

10. THE PROBLEMATIC VAGUENESS OF PHYSICALISM

It may be objected that physicalism is much too *vague* to be meaningful. In order to render it meaningful, it would be necessary to provide some precise *definition* of physicalism; but this would tie the notion down to some definite conceptual framework which would make it impossible to apply the notion to all the very different conceptual frameworks found in the ideas of such diverse thinkers as Thales, Anaximander, Democritus, Boscovich, Faraday, Einstein, Wheeler, Penrose, and Schwartz and Green[15] (let alone to conceptual frameworks, or blueprints yet to come).

The request for a *precise* definition of physicalism, of 'unity-throughout-diversity-determining-change' is, of course, a trap. As I have remarked above, the scientific acceptability of the level 4 thesis of physicalism depends on this thesis being *open-ended* in what it asserts, so that it is *not* tied down to making precise, specific assertions about the world (such as the assertions found at level 3 or level 2). Philosophers, physicists, mathematicians, and philosophers of science are inclined to believe that only those assertions whose meanings are absolutely precise are meaningful at all. This rests on a false theory of meaning. Meaningful assertions can be more or less precise, more or less vague. Furthermore, it is vital, in order to make sense of science (and for other reasons as well) to acknowledge the legitimacy of imprecise meaning. If one does not, it becomes impossible to grade assertions about the comprehensibility of the universe in terms of their precision in the sort of way required by AOE. The meaning of 'unity-throughout-diversity-determining-change' has been explicated at the required level of generality and vagueness; and diverse, more precise exemplars of the general, vague idea have been provided: what more could be required in order to establish the meaningfulness of the general notion?

I have three further points to make in connection with the meaningfulness of physicalism.

First, it is important to appreciate that physicalism is a special case of an even more general thesis, namely the level 5 thesis that the universe is comprehensible in some way or other. I have already indicated how this more general thesis is to be understood. More could be said; further examples of more and less comprehensible (possible) universes could be given; the world's religions and mythologies could be ransacked to provide colourful comprehensibility ideas. One would need to be in the grip of a very narrow conception of meaningfulness to declare this wealth of ideas all meaningless. False, yes; but meaningless, no. Granted, then, that the general level 5 thesis is meaningful, it is difficult to see how the more specific level 4 thesis of physical comprehensibility can fail to be meaningful.

Secondly, not only is physicalism assured of meaning from above (in terms of the hierarchy of levels of AOE); it is also assured of meaning from below. As I have already stressed, a number of distinct, more precise, more or less adequate level 3 versions of physicalism can be exhibited, such as atomism or Boscovich's point-atomism, which are undeniably meaningful. Indeed, level 2 physical theories can be exhibited which are still more precise (more or less adequate) versions of the general idea of physicalism, and which are undeniably meaningful. Granted the meaningfulness of these diverse, precise versions of physicalism, it is difficult to see how physicalism as such could be meaningless.

Thirdly, one reason why physicalism might be judged to be meaningless is that it is so vague that nothing is excluded: however physically incomprehensible or chaotic the universe might be, it could still be construed to exemplify physicalism. But this is not the case: in Section 3 of the next chapter, I indicate twenty rivals to physicalism, twenty kinds of possible universe in which physicalism would be false (infinitely many possible universes corresponding to each kind).

A final point concerns the meaning of 'unity' of dynamic structure. The key notion here is not just 'unity', but rather 'unity throughout diversity'. The greater the amount of *diversity* through which there is unity, the more richly comprehensible the universe is. The Parmenidean universe is, in a sense, not a comprehensible universe at all in that it excludes all possibility of diversity.

11. TWO EXAMPLES OF THEORETICAL UNIFICATION FROM THE HISTORY OF PHYSICS

In order further to clarify what it means to assert that the universe has an underlying unified dynamic structure (a unified U running through all phenomena), and in order to show that the account of simplicity being proposed here can do justice to judgements of unity as these are made in physics, let us look, briefly, at some of the great acts of unification achieved so far in the history of theoretical physics, beginning with those associated with Newton and Maxwell.

The first great act of theoretical unification achieved by modern physics was Newton's unification of Kepler's laws of astronomical motion and Galileo's laws of terrestrial motion. Kepler's laws assert that: (1) the line from the sun to any planet sweeps out equal areas in equal times; (2) planets move in elliptical orbits around the sun with the sun at one of the two foci of each ellipse; and (3) the ratio a^3/T^2 is the same for all planets, where a is the average distance of the planet from the sun and T is the period of revolution of the planet round the sun. Galileo's laws of terrestrial motion assert that a freely falling body falls with constant acceleration, the same for all bodies, and that bodies with some initial horizontal motion, but otherwise freely moving, move along parabolas. It was Newton's great achievement to show that these ostensibly different laws, astronomical and terrestrial, all follow from, or exemplify, *one common set of laws*, namely (1) $F_{total} = ma$, (2) $F_{12} = Gm_1m_2/d^2$, and (3) $F_{total} = \Sigma F_i$. (Here, F is force, m is mass, a is acceleration, G is a constant, and d is the distance between two objects whose masses are m_1 and m_2. Equation (1) asserts that the total force on an object is equal to the object's mass times its acceleration; equation (2), Newton's famous law of gravitation, specifies how the force of gravitation between two objects varies with the masses of the objects and the distance between them; and equation (3) tells us that the total force on a particle is the vector sum of all the constituent forces.)

Newtonian theory (NT), of course, goes far beyond this somewhat local act of unification. It also unifies the motion of double stars, moving around their common centre of mass, the motion of the millions of stars of our galaxy, and the motions of endlessly many other variously evolving systems interacting in accordance with Newton's laws.

From a mathematical point of view, NT is able to unify these disparately evolving systems because the theory has the form, mathematically, of a *differential equation*. In general, a differential equation specifies a whole family of curves, or of functions, with infinitely many members. It specifies, in *one* equation, what all the curves, or functions, have in common. It is in this way that the three equations of NT are able to imply, to *unify*, the widely diverse motions associated with terrestrial projectiles, the solar system, double stars, and galaxies.[16]

Consider, for example, the derivation of Galileo's law of freely falling bodies. We consider a body, mass m, moving freely up and down near the surface of the earth. In this case we have $ma = F = GmM/d^2$, that is, $a = GM/d^2$. Here, M is the mass of the earth and d is the distance to the centre of the earth. If we assume that the distance moved by the body is tiny with respect to d, we may regard the latter as a constant, and we have: $a = g$, where g is a constant equal to GM/d^2. We have derived Galileo's law of free fall, in the form of the differential equation $d^2s/dt^2 = g$. This is equation (*b*) of Section 1 of the Appendix; and as I indicate there, its solutions are the doubly infinite family of functions $s = \frac{1}{2}gt^2 + v_0t + s_0$ (where s is vertical distance at any time t, v_0 is initial velocity, and s_0 is initial height). Somewhat similar procedures, usually considerably more complicated mathematically, yield different evolutions for different initial states of affairs (such as the rotation of a planet round the sun, or the rotation of two stars round their common centre of mass).[17]

It is worth noting that NT, in unifying Kepler's and Galileo's laws, also reveals that these laws are only approximately true (as we have already seen). Galileo's law of free fall is not quite true, given NT, partly because the value of g varies from place to place, but also because g varies as the moving object changes its distance from the centre of the earth. Likewise, Kepler's laws are only approximately true, given NT; as in the case of Galileo's law, they arise as limiting cases, as some quantity tends to zero (1/radius of the earth, and the density of the earth in the case of Galileo's law; the mass of the planets, in the case of Kepler's laws). This rather widespread feature of theoretical unification in physics will be discussed further in Chapter 6 in connection with the problem of verisimilitude.

There is a sense in which the theoretical unification brought about by NT is paradigmatic for all subsequent theoretical physics down to the present day. Fundamental physical theories all have the form of differential equations which unify by specifying what is common in the way things change throughout the vast range of apparently diverse phenomena to which the theories apply.[18]

A second great example of theoretical unification from the history of physics is that brought about by James Clerk Maxwell's theory of the electromagnetic field (MT) in the form it acquired after Einstein's special theory of relativity (SR), put forward in 1905.[19] This achieved *two* great feats of unification. It unified *electricity* and *magnetism* to form *one* entity, the *electromagnetic* field; and it unified electromagnetism and light by revealing that light is nothing more than an aspect of the electromagnetic field.

In a sense, these Maxwellian unifications are much more impressive than that achieved by NT. In the case of NT, the same *kind* of phenomena, namely objects moving through space, are all shown to obey the same few simple laws. In the case of MT, apparently quite different phenomena were shown to be the same phenomenon, or different aspects of the same phenomenon. Ordinary phenomena associated with *light* give us no reason to suppose that this has anything to do with *electricity* and *magnetism*: and the latter two phenomena seemed, initially, quite distinct.

The two cases of Maxwellian unification differ in the following crucial respect. The unification of light and electromagnetism is, in a sense, unification by annihilation: from the standpoint of fundamental theoretical physics, light is revealed to be nothing more than wavelike changes in the intensity of the electromagnetic field, of a certain restricted range of wavelengths, which travel through a vacuum with a definite velocity c. All this applies as well to radio waves, infrared waves, ultraviolet waves, X-rays, and γ-rays: these are, according to Maxwellian theory, exactly the same phenomenon as light, differing from light only with respect to wavelength. (It deserves to be noted that any one of these phenomena can be transformed into any other by a mere change of reference frame, which has the effect of changing the measured wavelength of electromagnetic waves.)

The unification of electricity and magnetism is rather different: what it reveals is not that one is reducible to the other, but rather that *both* are aspects of *one, unified* entity, the electromagnetic field. We may call the first *unification by annihilation* (or unification by reduction), and the second *unification by synthesis*.[20]

It is the second kind of unification that is problematic. It is problematic because it is by no means obvious what, in general, must be done to show that *two* entities, or *two* forces, are really nothing but two aspects of *one* entity, or *one* force. Let us, then, take a closer look at the way in which MT succeeds in unifying electric and magnetic forces.

We need to consider two theories. First, we have electromagnetic theory after Coulomb's contribution but before the work of Oersted, Ampère, and Faraday; let us call this CT. Secondly, we have electromagnetic theory after the work of Maxwell, Fitzgerald, Heaviside, Lorentz, and Einstein, which we will call, as before, MT.

CT is concerned with forces between static electrically charged bodies, and between magnetized bodies. It asserts that there are *two* forces, the electric force and the magnetic force. These two forces are similar, according to CT, to the extent that each obeys an inverse-square law, namely $F = k_1 q_1 q_2 / d^2$ for the case of two electric charges, q_1 and q_2, distance d apart, and $F = k_2 m_1 m_2 / d^2$ for the case of two magnetic poles of strength m_1 and m_2, distance d apart. k_1 and k_2 are appropriate constants. In both cases the forces are attractive or repulsive, depending on whether the charges or poles are unlike or like.

The case for holding that CT postulates two distinct forces (and not two aspects of one force) rests on the following considerations. Different sorts of substance become electrically and magnetically charged, this being the result of different processes, electric and magnetic charges being conserved in different circumstances. Positive and negative electric charges exist independently of one another in a way which does not obtain for magnetism (in that positive and negative charges, or poles, are always linked together in a magnet). CT says nothing about the interdependence of the two forces, the capacity of one kind of force to create the other, and before Oersted nothing was known about this. In these circumstances, there is hardly a greater case for declaring the electric and magnetic forces to be two aspects of one unified force than there is for declaring the electric and gravitational forces to be two such aspects of one unified force.

Let us now consider how MT succeeds in unifying by synthesis the two forces of CT. The fundamental difference between the Newtonian or Boscovichian notion of force and the post-Maxwellian, post-Einsteinian notion of force is that, whereas the former is *rigidly* attached to the charged object that creates it, the latter is *not* rigid. As far as MT is concerned, any change in the electric or magnetic force, due to change in the motion of the charged object that creates the force, travels at a finite velocity (the velocity of light) rather than at an infinite velocity (required for rigidity). This means that in order to specify the instant-aneous state of a physical system, the strength and direction of the electric and magnetic forces must be specified at each spatial point in addition to a specification of the positions and velocities of charged objects. The electric and magnetic forces become *fields of force*,[21] which vary continuously through space and time; MT specifies how these fields vary in space and time, and how they are created by, and act upon, charged objects. In order to specify how the fields vary continuously in space and time, MT needs to be formulated in terms of so-called *partial differential equations*.[22]

MT can be summed up in the following five postulates:

(1) $\nabla \cdot E = 4\pi\varrho$ (2) $\nabla \cdot B = 0$

(3) $\nabla \times E = -\dfrac{1}{c}\dfrac{\partial B}{\partial t}$ (4) $\nabla \times B = \dfrac{1}{c}\dfrac{\partial E}{\partial t} + \dfrac{4\pi}{c}\mathbf{j}$

(5) $F = q\left(E + (v/c) \times B\right).$

Here, c is the velocity of light, q is electric charge, ϱ is electric charge density, and j is electric current density. Postulate (5), the Lorentz force law, gives the force F on a charge q with velocity v as a result of an electric field strength E and magnetic field strength B.

All this presupposes SR. This means that Newton's force law $F = ma$, or $F = d(p)/dt$ where $p = mv$ (Newtonian momentum) has to be replaced with:

(6) $F = d(p)/dt$ with p interpreted relativistically, so that: $p = mv/\sqrt{(1 - v^2/c^2)}$, where m is rest mass.

In order to see how MT unifies the two distinct forces of CT, let us first consider the form that MT takes in the vacuum, when there is no charge and no current, so that $\varrho = j = 0$. In this case the above equations reduce to:

(1*a*) $\nabla \cdot \boldsymbol{E} = 0$ (2*a*) $\nabla \cdot \boldsymbol{B} = 0$

(3*a*) $\nabla \times \boldsymbol{E} = -\dfrac{1}{\text{c}} \dfrac{\partial \boldsymbol{B}}{\partial t}$ (4*a*) $\nabla \times \boldsymbol{B} = \dfrac{1}{\text{c}} \dfrac{\partial \boldsymbol{E}}{\partial t}$.

There are three points to note. First, (3*a*) and (4*a*) specify how a magnetic field changing with respect to time creates a circulating electric field, and an electric field changing with respect to time creates a circulating magnetic field. The two fields, *E* and *B*, are no longer distinct; a change in the one creates the other. Interestingly enough, it is this interdependence of the electric and magnetic fields that is responsible for the other great feat of unification achieved by MT, namely the unification of light and electromagnetism. What these two equations imply is that once periodic changes in the electric or magnetic field have been set up they travel through space with the velocity of light, changing *E* producing a changing *B*, in turn producing a changing *E*, and so on. This, according to MT, is what light is.

The second point to note is the symmetry that exists between the way *E* affects *B*, and *B* affects *E*. And the third point is that, given any specific space-time chunk of electromagnetic field evolving in accordance with the above four postulates, the way in which the field divides up into *E* and *B* depends on the choice of reference frame. But, according to SR, nothing of absolute (or theoretically fundamental) significance can depend on the choice of reference frame. Any specific way of dividing up the electromagnetic field into *E* and *B* has as much absolute significance as a choice of velocity for some object. We cannot, in short, think of the electromagnetic field as being made up of two distinct fields, *E* and *B*, since any specific choice of *E* and *B* is arbitrary in that it amounts to an arbitrary choice of reference frame. There is thus the *one* entity, the electromagnetic field, made up of two symmetrically interdependent aspects, *E* and *B*.

(In a somewhat similar way, as I indicated above, the apparently distinct phenomena of radio waves, infrared rays, visible light, ultraviolet rays, X-rays, and γ-rays are, in a sense, unified by synthesis. It is not just that MT unifies these apparently distinct phenomena by annihilation, by showing that they are all nothing more than electromagnetic waves differing only with respect to the inessential attribute of wavelength; in addition, MT shows that *one and the same* pulse of electromagnetic waves is a pulse of radio waves, light, X-rays, or γ-rays *depending on choice of reference frame*. The differences are entirely reference-frame-dependent.)

As I mentioned in Section 2 of the last chapter, the fragment of MT that we are considering, made up of postulates (1*a*) to (4*a*), provides us with a (somewhat depleted) picture of a (possible) comprehensible universe, consisting exclusively of the electromagnetic field in the vacuum. That which varies, V, is the varying values of the electromagnetic field; that which does not vary, U, is the dispositional (or necessitating) property of the field to change in accordance with (1*a*) to (4*a*). The *unity* of this U (the physical comprehensibility of the possible universe of which it forms a part) has nothing to do with the structure or form of the corresponding theory as such; it has to do with the nature of the (possible) physical reality that the theory postulates (the key point of Section 5 above).

Let us now return to the full version of MT, postulates (1) to (5) above. This is a very much richer theory, in that it specifies the way in which charged objects, whether at rest or moving, create the electromagnetic field, via postulates (1) and (4), and the way in which the electric and magnetic fields exert force on charged objects, via postulate (5).

In one way, the *unity* of the electric and magnetic forces is further confirmed by the fact that the magnetic force is created entirely by a changing electric field and/or by electrically charged objects in motion, as specified by (4). Magnetic poles disappear. Electrically charged and magnetically charged objects differ in that the latter are merely the former *plus motion*. (There is here a whiff of unification by annihilation.)

In other ways, the introduction of *electric charge* somewhat disrupts the unity of the fragment of MT concerned only with the electromagnetic field in the vacuum. The symmetry between the two fields, apparent in (1*a*) and (2*a*), and (3*a*) and (4*a*), somewhat disappears. MT postulates *two* very different sorts of physical entity, the *electromagnetic field* on the one hand, and *charged objects with mass* on the other hand. Very much worse, there is a problem of consistency, due to the problem of self-interaction. A charged object both creates the field, and is acted upon by the field that it creates (something that does not happen as far as rigid, Newtonian or Boscovichian forces are concerned); if the charged object is a point-particle, the absurd outcome is an infinite self-interaction.

What we may hope to learn from Maxwellian unification about unification in general is, then, the following. The apparent diversity of entities and forces in the world is to be reduced to *one* kind of entity and force by means of unification by annihilation, or by synthesis. In the case of unification by synthesis, the new unifying theory must do one or other, or both, of the following two things.

(*a*) It must show how the distinct entities or forces, $E_1 \ldots E_N$, interact with one another in a symmetric way, so that the existence of any *one* of E_1 to E_N implies the coexistence of all the others.

(*b*) It must show that the manner in which the *unified* entity or force, E, splits up into the distinct entities or forces, $E_1 \ldots E_N$, depends on nothing more than the adoption of an arbitrary convention from a range of equivalent possibilities—such as, in the case of the electromagnetic field, the adoption of one reference frame from infinitely many other, equally good reference frames in uniform relative motion with respect to each other.[23]

Unification of $E_1 \ldots E_N$ exploiting (*a*) is immensely strengthened if (*b*) is satisfied as well. As we saw above, the Maxwellian unification of the electric and magnetic fields by the fragment of MT specified by (1*a*) to (4*a*), brought about by exploiting (*a*), is immensely strengthened as a result of satisfying (*b*) as well. On the other hand, (*b*) on its own may, in certain circumstances, be quite sufficient to bring about all the unification one could require. This point was illustrated by the case of the unification of the apparently distinct entities: radio waves, infrared rays, visible light, ultraviolet rays, X-rays, γ-rays. *One and the same pulse of electromagnetic waves* is all of these entities, simultaneously as it were, but with respect to different reference frames. Here (*b*) alone brings about a striking kind of unification by synthesis.

Maxwellian unification can be regarded as carrying yet another lesson for theoretical *unity* in physics in general, namely: an acceptable conception of a unified U (or T) must be such as to solve the Maxwellian field/particle problem. The *field* and the *particle* must be unified, either by annihilation or by synthesis.[24]

Given the above two great theoretical unifications of classical physics, there is at once a new problem: how to unify NT and MT. This gives rise to a preliminary problem: how to unify *blueprints* associated with NT and MT. Elsewhere I have argued that this was, fundamentally, Einstein's problem, his attempts at solving the problem giving rise to his major contributions to theoretical physics, such as special and general relativity, his theory of Brownian motion, and his 'light quanta' explanation of the photoelectric effect: see Maxwell (1993*c*: III). We see here the rational (if fallible and non-mechanical) method of discovery of AOE being put into explicit and successful scientific practice for the first time: see Maxwell (1993*c*: I, II).

12. GLOBAL AND LOCAL GAUGE INVARIANCE OF MAXWELL'S EQUATIONS

There is a further feature of MT, not yet mentioned, which has turned out to be a vital ingredient of subsequent theoretical developments: so-called global and local gauge invariance. Maxwell's equations can be rewritten in terms of a scalar potential, $\phi(x,t)$, which assigns a number to each space-time point, and a vector potential, $\mathbf{A}(x,t)$, a vector field. These are defined in terms of the electric and magnetic fields, E and B, as follows:

$$\mathbf{B} = \nabla \times \mathbf{A}; \quad \mathbf{E} = -\nabla \phi - \frac{1}{c}\frac{\partial \mathbf{A}}{\partial t}.$$

The value of ϕ may be changed by an amount k that is the same at all space-time points, and this will not affect the electric or magnetic fields, since $\nabla(\phi + k) = \nabla\phi$. This feature of MT—the fact that it is unaffected by a constant change of ϕ—is known as global gauge invariance, 'global' because the change is the same everywhere.

It is also possible to change ϕ in a way which varies, smoothly but otherwise arbitrarily, from space-time point to space-time point. But in this case, if E and B are to remain the same, the vector field, $\mathbf{A}$, must also be changed in a related way, varying from space-time point to point, to compensate for the changes in ϕ. The precise way in which these interrelated, compensating, but otherwise arbitrary changes in ϕ and $\mathbf{A}$ need to be made can be represented as follows. Let $f(x,t)$ be any function of space and time, differentiable, but otherwise arbitrary. Then ϕ can be changed to ϕ^*, where:

$$\phi^* = \phi + \frac{1}{c}\frac{\partial f(x,\ t)}{\partial t},$$

as long as $\mathbf{A}$ is simultaneously changed to $\mathbf{A}^*$, where $\mathbf{A}^* = \mathbf{A} - \nabla f(x,t)$. That E and B are unchanged by such interlinked, compensating, but otherwise arbitrary changes of ϕ and $\mathbf{A}$ means that MT exhibits what is known as a local gauge invariance—'local' because changes in ϕ can differ from place to place and time to time, as long as compensating locally varying changes are simultaneously made to $\mathbf{A}$. Because of the way ϕ and $\mathbf{A}$ are linked to E and B, the locally gauge invariant character of MT can be regarded as strengthening further the unification by synthesis of E and B.

Local gauge invariance, variously interpreted, is a feature of all the fundamental theories of physics, and thus would seem to be a powerful unifying idea for the whole of theoretical physics. It has proved especially important in the development of quantum field theories of the weak and strong forces, as we shall see.

13. FURTHER UNIFYING ACHIEVEMENTS OF MODERN PHYSICS

Before continuing with the main task of this chapter (to solve remaining problems concerning the meaningfulness of physicalism), I feel I ought at least to indicate, if only very briefly and informally, some main triumphs of unification achieved by physical science since Newton and Maxwell, and something of the problems of unification that remain to be solved.[25]

The gradual discovery, during the eighteenth and nineteenth centuries, that all substances are made up of ninety or so elements is a major contribution to unification.[26] So too is Mendeleev's discovery of a pattern in the chemical properties of the elements, which led to the periodic table of the elements.[27] The discovery of conservation principles—conservation of momentum, energy, and mass—which cut across diverse branches of physics and chemistry, brought further unity to physics. Atomic theory, in chemistry, the kinetic theory of gases, and statistical mechanics, began to hold out great promise as a unifying theory[28] during the second half of the nineteenth century.[29]

Einstein's special theory of relativity (SR) helped to unify the electric and magnetic forces, as I have explained above; but it brought unity to physics in other ways as well. SR implies that mass is a form of energy, enshrined in the most famous equation of modern physics: $E = mc^2$. This means that conservation of mass ceases to be a separate principle, and becomes a part of the principle of conservation of energy. SR can be interpreted as partially unifying, by synthesis, time and space in that, according to the theory, the way in which space and time are distinguished is, to some extent, a frame-dependent matter.[30] The distinction between time and space nevertheless remains: according to SR two events can either be connected by an irreversible causal process, or they cannot; in the former case the separation is timelike, in the latter case spacelike, and this distinction is a frame-independent matter. SR is also, it must be noted, one of the great unifying ideas of physics in that it is a feature of all the fundamental theories of physics. (In the case of general relativity, SR emerges in the limit as the gravitational field goes to zero.)

Einstein's general theory of relativity (GR) is of profound significance in the search for unity in physics, in that it strongly suggests that the underlying unity of the physical universe is much more radical and surprising than anyone (apart from Parmenides) would have supposed before the advent of the theory.[31] According to GR, gravitation is nothing more than a consequence of the curvature of space-time. GR unifies by annihilation: gravitation, as a force distinct from space-time, disappears, and we are left with bodies moving along the nearest thing to straight lines in curved space-time. GR indicates the possibility of a new blueprint for unity in physics: not just the force of gravitation, but all other forces, and all other aspects of physics, are but geometrical, or topological, features of space-time, there being, ultimately, nothing more than empty space-time.[32] At the very least, GR strongly suggests that the fundamental problem of unification in physics is the problem of unifying space-time on the one hand, and matter on the other.[33]

Perhaps the most far reaching act of unification in physics ever made is that achieved by the theory of atomic structure and quantum theory (QT), developed by Rutherford, Bohr, Heisenberg, Schrödinger, and others during the first three decades of the twentieth century. According to this theory, almost all the chemical and physical phenomena we ordinarily come across, the chemical and physical properties of the billions of different substances that exist in Nature and in the laboratory, are the outcome of interactions between just *four* particles: the electron, the proton, the neutron, and the photon. This is unification by annihilation with a vengeance: instead of billions of different sorts of substance, there are just *four*.[34]

All of the billions of different sorts of substance are made up of around 100 elements, each element being made up of its characteristic kind of atom. The atom consists of a central nucleus, made up of protons (positively charged) and neutrons (no charge) closely bound together, surrounded by a cloud of negatively charged electrons. Atoms of different elements are distinguished by having different numbers of protons in their nuclei, and hence different numbers of electrons in the cloud of electrons surrounding the nuclei (when the atom is in its electrically neutral state). In addition to the electromagnetic force between protons and electrons and the strong force between protons and neutrons (which binds them into nuclei), two features of QT, especially, account for the amazing diversity of properties of different atoms.

First, there is the wave aspect of electrons. This ensures that electrons in atoms only exist in certain discrete, stable orbits around the central nucleus. In order to persist in an orbit around the central nucleus of an atom, a whole number of electron waves must exist around the nucleus to form a standing wave (in a way that is analogous to standing waves of sound formed in organ pipes). Electrons jump up from the smallest orbit to a larger orbit as a result of absorbing an appropriate amount of energy, perhaps in the form of light; after a short time, electrons in excited orbits jump down to a smaller orbit, emitting light of a characteristic frequency as they do so.

Secondly, there is Pauli's exclusion principle, which forbids two electrons to be in the same quantum state. The wave aspect of electrons, and Pauli's exclusion principle, working together, ensure that the electrons of atoms exist, in a stable way, only in certain discrete orbits; the number of electrons in the outer orbit largely determines the chemical properties of the atom. It is this that is responsible for the fact that atoms, of definite types, stick together in diverse, precise ways to form the myriad of different kinds of molecule that go to make up the material world around us, and go to make up our own bodies. Thus, two atoms of hydrogen, each consisting of one proton and one electron, and one atom of oxygen, consisting of eight protons and eight neutrons in the nucleus surrounded by a cloud of eight electrons readily combine together to form one molecule of water, H_2O. All the macroscopic physical and chemical properties of all the billions of different sorts of substance that there are in the world are a consequence of just *three* kinds of particle, the electron, proton, and neutron, interacting with one another by means of the electromagnetic and strong force, and in accordance with quantum theory. To this one should add a fourth particle, the photon, the particle of electromagnetism and light.[35]

Non-relativistic QT (which is what we have been considering so far) treats forces in a classical fashion, as influencing the way in which the quantum state of particles evolve. The next great unifying theory, quantum electrodynamics (QED), brings together MT, SR, and QT: it is, in effect, a quantum theory of the electromagnetic field and the charged particles, such as the electron, that create, and are acted upon by, the field. The first step towards the creation of QED was taken by Paul Dirac in 1927; after over twenty years of painful development, during which physicists struggled to overcome the infinities predicted by the theory, QED was brought to a reasonably satisfactory form by Tomonaga, Schwinger, Feynman, and Dyson. One of the new predictions of QED is that, corresponding to each particle, there is an oppositely charged antiparticle—particle and antiparticle being created and annihilated in pairs. The antiparticle of the electron is called the positron. According to QED, two sufficiently energetic photons in the same spatial region can transform into an electron–positron pair; and vice versa, a colliding electron–positron pair can transform into two photons.[36]

Whereas non-relativistic QT is unable to describe processes of particle creation and annihilation, QED is, above all, a theory of creation and annihilation processes. Even the vacuum is, in a sense, according to QED, full of such processes. One of the implications of QT is that, as one considers more and more minute intervals of space and time, momentum and energy become increasingly uncertain (in accordance with Heisenberg's uncertainty relations). Within sufficiently minute regions of space-time, momentum and energy are sufficiently uncertain for so-called virtual electron–positron pairs to be created and annihilated. One can, indeed, regard QED as a theory that is primarily about the vacuum; add momentum and energy to the vacuum, and the result is semi-permanent excited states of the vacuum, which we experience as matter (Aitchison 1985). QED would seem to be another step towards unifying space-time and matter.

Another feature of QED that has an important bearing on its unity is its locally gauge invariant character (analogous to the locally gauge invariant character of MT, discussed above). QED is, in a sense, made up of two parts. On the one hand, there is the part that deals with matter, with the electron: this is based on Dirac's relativistic quantum equation for the electron. On the other hand, there is the part that deals with the electromagnetic field, and the particle of the field, namely the photon. Dirac's equation is invariant with respect to a global change of phase: it is globally gauge invariant. (Two wave systems, travelling in the same direction with the same velocity and having the same wavelength, differ with respect to phase if the crests and troughs of one wave system fail to coincide with those of the other system: if the crests and troughs coincide, the two wave systems have the same phase.) The quantum state of the electron can be conceived of as having a wavelike character that is extended in space. If this wavelike state is shifted by some fraction of a wavelength everywhere by the same amount, this leaves everything physical unaffected. Only a change of phase of one part of the wavefunction *relative* to another part has physical consequences: a change of phase of the whole wavefunction has no physical consequences.

We may, however, consider changing the phase of the wavefunction by different amounts at different space-time points, so that the change of phase is some arbitrary, but smooth, function of space and time. Such a change will, in general, have observable consequences. We can, however, consider inventing a field designed specifically to compensate for the change of phase that varies, arbitrarily, from place to place and time to time. If such a field is added to Dirac's wave equation, it has the effect of rendering the equation *locally* gauge invariant. The equation is invariant, not just with respect to *global* changes of phase (the same everywhere) but to *local* changes of phase (that vary from place to place and time to time). But in order to transform the theory in this way, from a *globally* to a *locally* gauge invariant theory, the added, compensating field must have very special properties. These turn out to be precisely those of the other half of QED—the electromagnetic field. We can, in other words, regard the electromagnetic field, the force between charged particles, as arising as a result of the demand that the globally gauge invariant Dirac equation of the electron be *locally* gauge invariant. The electromagnetic field (or the photon) is, in a sense, not something that is added on, arbitrarily, to the electron: it is, in a certain sense, implicit in the nature of the electron, conceived of as an entity divorced of its charge or field (but being, locally, and not just globally, gauge invariant in character). Just as the scalar and vector potential fields of MT are interrelated in such a way as to render the theory locally gauge invariant, so too the matter field and the electromagnetic field of QED are interrelated in such a way as to render QED locally gauge invariant.[37]

The locally gauge invariant character of QED turned out to be a vital clue for the subsequent development of quantum field theories of the other fundamental forces of particle physics.

Around 1930 there seemed to be relatively few fundamental particles: the electron, proton, neutron, and their antiparticles, and the photon (which is its own antiparticle).[38] Then in the 1940s, 1950s, and 1960s more and more particles began to manifest themselves, in cosmic rays, and in high-energy collisions in particle accelerators. One compensation was that there appeared to be just four forces in Nature: gravitation (which, according to GR, is not really a force), electromagnetism, the weak force, and the strong force. The weak force manifests itself when the free neutron decays into a proton, electron, and neutrino (an electron-like particle of zero charge and possibly zero mass). The strong force arises in connection with particles like the proton and neutron, called hadrons, and is responsible for binding protons and neutrons together in the nuclei of atoms against the repulsive electromagnetic force between the protons.

In 1954 Yang and Mills put forward a suggestion as to how QED might be generalized, based on the idea of local gauge invariance. In the case of QED, local gauge transformations involve changes of phase, compensated for by changes in the electromagnetic field. In the case of the more general locally gauge invariant theories, the transformations involve a change in the nature of particles, these changes being compensated for by changes in the force fields. Quantum field theories, of the type proposed by Yang and Mills, required there to be new particles, associated with the forces, having charge but zero mass. Neither the weak nor the strong force appeared to have particles of the required type associated with them. Despite this, quantum field theories of the weak and strong forces were subsequently developed, both of the general locally gauge invariant type suggested by Yang and Mills. The two theories overcame the objection that particles of the right kind had not been observed in very different ways.

Steven Weinberg and Abdus Salam, independently, put forward a Yang–Mills type quantum field theory that unifies (by synthesis) the electromagnetic and weak forces. According to this theory, quantum electroweak dynamics (QEWD), at very high energies, such as those that existed soon after the big bang, the electroweak force has the form of two forces, one with three associated massless particles, two charged, W^- and W^+, and one neutral, W^0, and the other with one neutral massless particle, V^0. According to QEWD, the two neutral particles, W^0 and V^0, are intermingled in two different ways, to form two new, neutral particles, the photon, γ, and another neutral massless particle, Z^0. As energy decreases, the W^+, W^-, and Z^0 particles acquire mass, due to a mechanism known as spontaneous symmetry-breaking (involving another, hypothetical particle, not yet detected, called the Higgs particle), while the photon, γ, retains its zero mass.[39] There appear to be two new, very different forces, the weak and electromagnetic. The particles associated with the weak force had not been detected because of their large mass, relative to that of the proton; subsequently, all three particles have been detected experimentally.[40]

The reason for the non-detection of the particles associated with the strong force is quite different. According to the Yang–Mills theory of the strong force, quantum chromodynamics (QCD), protons and neutrons are not fundamental particles but consist of three more fundamental particles, with fractional charge, called quarks. Quarks can never exist in isolation, but only in quark-antiquark pairs or threesomes. The strong force is only secondarily a force between proton and neutron; primarily it is a force between quarks. According to QCD, there are eight new particles associated with this force, called gluons. Gluons are not observed because they, like quarks, are confined to hadrons. The dozens of different hadrons that had been observed during the 1950s and 1960s are, according to the quark theory and QCD, different states of relatively few quarks.[41]

QEWD unifies the electromagnetic and weak forces by synthesis. It is highly significant, in this context, that the theory is a Yang–Mills-type theory, locally gauge invariant in a way that is a generalization of the locally gauge invariant character of MT and QED. Nevertheless, the unification achieved by QEWD is not altogether satisfactory: the theory is obliged to postulate two forces, with distinct strengths (or coupling constants) and distinct associated particles, W^-, W^+ and W_0, on the one hand, and V^0 on the other. This lack of unity is reflected in the group structure of the locally gauge invariant character of the theory.[42] These two forces then become intermingled to produce the two forces that are observed, the weak and the electromagnetic.

In considering the unifying power of QCD, unification both by annihilation and by synthesis need to be considered. Unification by annihilation is involved in that, instead of the dozens of different kinds of hadronic particle that had to be regarded as 'fundamental' before the advent of the theory, only six different sorts of quark, each with three possible 'colour' charges, and eight different sorts of gluon needed to be recognized as fundamental after the advent of the theory. All the hadronic particles could be built up from these twenty-six kinds of particle. Unification by synthesis is also involved in that QCD is a Yang–Mills-type theory, a locally gauge invariant theory: the eight gluons of the theory and the three kinds of 'colour' state of the quarks are not arbitrary: their number and properties are dictated by the gauge invariant character of the theory. The eight gluons become eight aspects of the one entity, the strong force, unified by synthesis, along with the three 'colour' states of the quarks; the final count of entities might be said to be six quarks plus the chromodynamic force.[43]

In one important respect, the weak and strong forces differ from the electromagnetic force. Whereas the photon, the particle associated with electromagnetism, does not itself carry charge, and does not change the character of the matter particles that it interacts with (such as the electron), particles associated with the weak and strong forces do carry charge and do change the character of the matter particles with which they interact.

In connection with this point, it is worth noting that unity considerations, as these arise in connection with a Boscovichian (or Newtonian) kind of theory that postulates particles that are neither created nor destroyed, differ in one important respect from unity considerations as these arise in connection with locally gauge invariant quantum field theories. In the former case, the *fewer* the number of different sorts of fundamental particle, the simpler or more unified the corresponding theory is. In the latter case, if a number of different sorts of particle are all interrelated by means of *one* locally gauge invariant force, which transforms the different sorts of particle into each other, then the different sorts of particle can be held to be unified by synthesis, in a manner which is distantly related to the way MT unifies the electric and magnetic fields. It is only when different sorts of particle are not unified by synthesis in this way that the increasing number of particles goes against unity.[44]

The two unifying Yang–Mills-type quantum field theories of matter, QEWD and QCD, are together called 'the standard model' (SM). For a summary of the diverse particles that are postulated by SM, see Table 1.

SM appears to be able, in principle, to account for all phenomena not associated with gravity. Its unifying power is extraordinary. The two constituent theories, though different, are nevertheless of the same type; both emerge as generalizations of QED. Despite these desirable features, SM is clearly unsatisfactory, both from the standpoint of AOE, and in the judgement of physicists. There are two forces (or even three), and not one; there are too many particles; and various properties of the particles, such as mass, are not determined by the theory itself.[45]

The fundamental problem of unification confronting theoretical physics is, however, the problem of unifying SM and GR. If we regard SM as the quantum theory of matter and its forces, and GR as the theory of space-time, then the problem is to unify matter and space-time. One approach to this problem is that of superstring theory, according to which fundamental particles are tiny strings rather than point-particles, moving in ten or twenty-six dimensions of space-time, the dimensions that we do not observe being curled up, everywhere, into a minute six- or twenty-two-dimensional sphere, too small to be observed. So far this approach, and others, have not met with empirical success.[46]

After this thumbnail sketch of the achievements and problems of unification in theoretical physics, illustrating the account of unification expounded above and in Chapter 3, I return to a discussion of the philosophical problems about what unification, in general, *means*.

TABLE 1. *Fundamental particles of the standard model*

Particles of matter

Three generations of fermions (spin = $\frac{1}{2}$)

		First generation		Second generation		Third generation	
		Name	Electric charge	Name	Electric charge	Name	Electric charge
Leptons		electron	e− −1	muon	μ −1	tau	τ −1
		electron-neutrino	ν_e 0	muon-neutrino	ν_μ 0	tau-neutrino	ν_τ 0
Quarks		down	d $-\frac{1}{3}$	strange	s $-\frac{1}{3}$	bottom	b $-\frac{1}{3}$
		up	u $+\frac{2}{3}$	charm	c $+\frac{2}{3}$	top	t $+\frac{2}{3}$

Note: These 'matter' particles all have mass (except possibly for neutrinos which may have zero mass). Each of these 16 particles has its anti-particles. Quarks exist only in groups of three (as in the proton and neutron) or as a quark-anti-quark pair (known as mesons). The proton consists of two up quarks and one down quark (u, u, d), and the neutron is made up of two down and one up (u, d, d). All ordinary matter is made up of just three particles, the electron, and the down and up quarks (plus particles associated with forces).

Particles associated with forces

Bosons (spin = 1)

	Forces	
The photon γ	Electromagnetic force	
Three vector bosons W^+, W^-, Z^0	Weak force	} Electroweak force
Eight gluons $G_{R \to G}$, $G_{G \to R}$, $G_{R \to B}$, $G_{B \to R}$, $G_{G \to B}$, $G_{B \to G}$, G_1, G_2.	Strong force (chromodynamics)	

Note: Quarks and six of the eight gluons carry the charge of the strong force, so-called 'colour' (red, green, and blue). A 'red' quark, emitting gluon $G_{R \to G}$, is thereby changed from being 'red' to 'green'. G_1 and G_2 do not change the colour of quarks with which they interact.

14. HOW CAN WHAT EXISTS AT ONE INSTANT NECESSARILY DETERMINE WHAT EXISTS SUBSEQUENTLY?

Physicalism asserts that the universe is such that what exists at any instant determines necessarily (but perhaps only probabilistically) what exists at subsequent instants. There is, however, a famous argument due to Hume which claims to show that this is impossible. In order to establish that physicalism is meaningful, I must show that Hume's argument is not valid.

Hume's argument has been immensely influential. Not only philosophers, but physicists too, accept the main implication of Hume's argument, namely that theoretical physics can at most specify *laws*, *regularities*, or *rules*, to which physical phenomena conform, and cannot specify anything that exists which determines, necessarily, that these laws or regularities are observed.

According to the orthodox, Humean view, a theory such as Newton's specifies laws or regularities such as: $F = ma$ and $F = Gm_1m_2/d^2$, which postulate regularities in the motions of bodies when interacting by means of gravitation. We might call this orthodox view *lawism*; any quasi-Popperian version of this view, which holds that all scientific knowledge is, ultimately, conjectural in character, might be called *conjectural lawism*.

The obvious objection to *lawism* is that, unless we can make sense of the idea that there is something *that actually exists* which, in some sense, determines or is responsible for lawfulness, it is difficult to see how the lawfulness that physics has revealed in the world around us can possibly be intelligible. It would become one gigantic, wildly implausible cosmic accident. The more physics explains, by showing how restricted regularities are consequences of more widely obtaining regularities, the more *inexplicable* the existence of these regularities becomes.

Many philosophers of science, who take lawism for granted, ignore this problem. Instead they worry about the following, related, more technical puzzle: how does one distinguish between *genuine physical laws*, such as $F = Gm_1m_2/d^2$, on the one hand, and so-called 'accidental generalizations', such as 'all solid lumps of gold are less than 10,000 tons' on the other hand? If a universal statement is true and a law, it cannot be falsified however hard we try; if it is true but only an accidental generalization then nothing in the constitution of things, as it were, would prevent us from falsifying the statement, if we so wished. In this respect 'all lumps of gold are less than 10,000 tons' differs dramatically from 'all lumps of gold are less than ten times the mass of the sun', since in the latter case attempts to refute the law would create, not a large lump of gold, but a black hole. *Lawism* faces the problem of distinguishing between *genuine physical laws* (which seem to have physical necessity associated with them) and *mere accidental generalizations* (which do not).

Both problems are solved by the view I now expound and defend, which I call *conjectural essentialism*. According to conjectural essentialism, it is legitimate to interpret (appropriate) physical theories as attributing *necessitating properties* to postulated physical entities—properties in virtue of which the entities must, of necessity, obey the laws of the theory. Theories interpreted in this essentialistic way postulate the existence of that which determines, of necessity, that the laws of the theory are obeyed; such theories *explain why* the laws of the theory are obeyed. The true, unified theory of everything, T, interpreted essentialistically, would specify an unchanging aspect of things, U, which would, of necessity, determine the way things change.

Philosophers have, unfortunately, made a great mystery out of something that is actually quite simple, and ought readily to be understood by everyone, namely: the idea of a *property* determining *change*. Almost all—perhaps *all*—physical properties have this character. That is, they are *dispositional* or *necessitating* properties which determine how things change. This is true of such common-sense properties as rigid, elastic, solid, sticky, heavy, rough, opaque, transparent, inflammable. It is also true of such theoretical properties as electric charge, electromagnetic intensity and direction (of the electromagnetic field), inertial rest mass, spin, gravitational charge. In all such cases, if an object has the property (rigidity, charge, or whatever) then, in such-and-such circumstances, of necessity, the object participates in change (or resistance to change) in such-and-such a way. To say of an object that it is inflammable is to say that it is such that if it is exposed to a naked flame then, of necessity, it burns. There is nothing mysterious about the notion of necessity that is involved here. It is straightforward *analytic* necessity. In other words, it is built into the *meaning* of 'inflammability' that inflammable objects burn when exposed to naked flames. Just as 'If X is a bachelor then X is unmarried' is true analytically (and therefore necessarily) in virtue of the meaning of 'bachelor', so too 'If X is inflammable and exposed to a naked flame then X burns' is true analytically (and therefore necessarily) in virtue of the meaning of 'inflammable'.

We cannot know for certain that any object, O, is inflammable in this sense, even if we have established that O does always as a matter of fact burn when exposed to naked flames. But this does not make this notion of 'inflammable' meaningless. (Only those who believe in the verification principle of logical positivism could believe this.)

Two notions of 'inflammable' can be distinguished, namely: inflammable$_1$ which means 'in fact burns whenever exposed to a naked flame'; and inflammable$_2$ which means 'of necessity burns whenever exposed to a naked flame'. An object O may be inflammable$_1$ and yet not inflammable$_2$. It might just so happen that O burns on all those occasions when it is exposed to a naked flame but would not have so burnt on a number of other possible occasions; it might be simply that O is never exposed to a naked flame, the condition 'burning whenever exposed to a naked flame' being satisfied vacuously. In either case, O is inflammable$_1$ but not inflammable$_2$. 'O would burn if it were exposed to a naked flame' may be interpreted in such a way that it is true if and only if O is inflammable$_2$ (O being inflammable$_1$ being insufficient). In what follows, 'inflammable' is to be understood to mean 'inflammable$_2$'.

The thesis that O is inflammable provides only a very inadequate *explanation* of the fact that O burns when exposed to a naked flame. But this does not mean, as some have thought, that necessitating properties such as inflammability have no proper place in science. The explanation is inadequate because it is extremely restricted in scope. A more adequate explanation would refer to necessitating properties much more widely possessed by physical entities. Such an explanation would link combustion to other phenomena; it would explain why some materials are inflammable, others not, and why objects become and cease to be inflammable in the circumstances in which they do. All this is achieved, at least in principle, by QT applied to chemistry: as a result of attributing a few precise, theoretical necessitating properties, such as charge and spin, to electrons and nuclei, it is possible, in principle, to predict and explain a wide range of physical and chemical properties of substances. Inflammability turns out to be the possession of a molecular structure which is such that, at a sufficiently high temperature, in the presence of sufficient oxygen, oxidization proceeds rapidly and in a self-sustaining way, with the emission of gas, heat, and light. A highly theoretical quantum-mechanical description of combustion provides a very much better explanation because, as a result of attributing very few necessitating properties to a very few different kinds of entity (just *four*!), a vast range of apparently diverse phenomena can in principle be predicted, including phenomena associated with inflammability. In order to get good explanations, in other words, we do not need to get rid of references to necessitating properties; we need rather to discover necessitating properties that determine a wide range of phenomena, of kinds of change.

We may regard the quantum-mechanical explanation as providing the underlying mechanism involved in combustion—as telling us what inflammability really is, in our world. It is important to appreciate, however, that in attributing the necessitating property of inflammability to something, we do not thereby require there to be some such underlying mechanism, some such theoretical explanation. It is logically possible that the world is such that all the diverse observational necessitating properties that there appear to be in the world around us do really exist, and yet there exists no mechanism underlying these properties—nothing in terms of which a theoretical explanation of the properties can be couched. In calling something inflammable, we leave open, but do not require, that inflammability can be explained, or explained away, in terms of more widely possessed properties. Necessitating properties exist in possible worlds that are *incomprehensible*, in other words, as well as in physically comprehensible possible worlds.

This point is important because if we make possessing a necessitating property dependent on there being a theoretical explanation to be discovered (or, ultimately, dependent on physicalism being true), then we cannot interpret fundamental physical theories (or versions of physicalism) essentialistically, as attributing essentialistic properties to postulated entities. From the standpoint of theoretical physics, the entire *raison d'être* for having the notion of necessitating properties disappears.

Any fundamental physical theory amenable to being interpreted realistically can also be interpreted essentialistically, as attributing necessitating properties to postulated entities—properties which require, as a matter of logic, that the entities obey the laws of the theory. NT interpreted realistically as a theory about point-particles with inertial mass subject to Newton's laws asserts, when interpreted essentialistically: (1) Everything is made up of point-particles with invariant inertial mass m and gravitational charge g, with $m = g$. Here (2) $F = ma$ is true analytically, in virtue of the meaning of 'inertial mass' and 'force'; and likewise (3) $F = Gg_1g_2/d^2$ is true analytically, in virtue of the meaning of 'gravitational charge'. This does not make NT itself analytic, for (1) is a massively contingent assertion (which is in fact false given GR or QT). We have in fact any number of different interpretations of NT, from the maximally essentialistic, just indicated, at one extreme, to the more and more anti-essentialistic, the meaning of 'force', 'inertial mass', and 'gravitational charge' becoming progressively more and more vague, presupposing the truth of laws that are more and more vague, as we move from the essentialistic to the anti-essentialistic. Thus if the meaning of 'gravitational charge$_1$' is such that '$F = Gg_1g_2/d^2$' is true analytically, the meaning of 'gravitational charge$_5$' might be such that no more than 'objects with gravitational charge$_5$ tend to move towards each other in some way that is some function of mass and distance' is true analytically. Any such more or less essentialistic theory is only true if the entities of the theory really exist with all the necessitating properties which the theory attributes to them.

Alternatively, consider the fragment of Maxwellian theory, discussed above, which is restricted to the electromagnetic field in the vacuum without charge. This theory, interpreted essentialistically, postulates the existence of the electromagnetic field, a physical entity spread out continuously throughout space and time. The four postulates of the theory, $(1a)$ to $(4a)$, are analytic statements: taken together, they specify a physically necessitating property which might be termed: being the electromagnetic field. If such an entity with such a property exists, then of necessity that which changes, intensities and directions of the electric and magnetic fields, does so in accordance with $(1a)$ to $(4a)$. The necessitating property, corresponding to the postulates $(1a)$ to $(4a)$, remains the same everywhere at all times, and determines necessarily the way that which changes, E and B, does change.

The basic idea of physicalism—a unified U, invariant throughout all change and diversity, itself determining change—is exemplified much more adequately by this fragment of MT, than by NT. In the case of NT, in moving around in space and time we encounter *two* quite different kinds of state: the point-particle, or empty space imbued with forces created by particles: given the fragment of MT, we encounter only *one* thing, the electromagnetic field.

In a deterministic universe governed by a deterministic physical theory, T, which is true even when interpreted in a maximally essentialistic manner, what exists at one instant determines necessarily what exists at subsequent instants. Let S_0 and S_1 be complete, precise specifications of the state of the universe at times t_0 and t_1 with $t_0 < t_1$. Then as long as the universe is such that T is only true when interpreted non-essentialistically, S_0 does not imply S_1. It is rather S_0 *plus* T that implies S_1. S_0, a highly theoretical description, couched in the language of T, will carry implications about how entities behave at time t_0; it will not however, on its own, imply subsequent states of affairs. Suppose now that the universe is such that T is true even when interpreted in a maximally essentialistic way, so that all the laws of T are true analytically (the entire contingent import of T being confined to the assertion that everything is made up of the entities of T with the necessitating properties attributed to them by T). In this case S_0, in order to give a complete specification of what exists at time t_0, must attribute necessitating properties to entities at t_0 which presuppose that the entities obey the laws of T. In other words, S_0 must include the laws of T implicitly in specifying what exists at t_0. Thus in this case S_0 on its own implies S_1. There are logically necessary connections between successive states of the universe S_0 and S_1, in the sense that what exists at t_0 is such that any set of propositions which correctly and completely describes it (and no more) logically implies propositions which describe subsequent states of the universe. If we try to weaken S_0 so that it becomes S_0* let us say, with $S_0 \to S_0$* but S_0* $\nrightarrow S_0$, and S_0* $\nrightarrow S_1$, then an aspect of what exists at t_0 described by S_0 is not described by S_0*. It is thus *what exists* at t_0 that necessarily determines the subsequent state of affairs at time t_1 (even though the logically necessary connection is between the propositions S_0 and S_1).

This deterministic notion of necessitating property can be generalized to form a probabilistic notion of necessitating property.[47]

Most philosophers, even today, reject the whole idea that necessitating properties of the above type might really exist. They do this because they take it for granted that Hume, long ago, in 1738, showed decisively that the whole idea of a necessitating property, discussed above, does not make sense (Hume 1959). It has not been noticed just how crudely defective Hume's arguments are. The entire argument is based on a phenomenalistic criterion of meaning: all meaningful ideas must be analysable into sense-data terms—or, as Hume put it '*all our ideas are copied from our impressions*' (Hume 1959: 76). Being unable to trace the notion of necessitating property or necessary connection, as conceived of here, to sense impressions, Hume concludes that there is no such notion, the whole idea of there being necessary connections between successive events in Nature being meaningless. But phenomenalism quite generally, including Hume's version, is wholly untenable—as everyone today agrees. This demolishes Hume's argument.

Few philosophers even today seem to appreciate just how defective Hume's arguments are, even though I sought to point this out over a quarter of a century ago (Maxwell 1968a). A few philosophers have subsequently argued for the anti-Humean idea that laws of nature are necessary; for example, Dretske (1977); Tooley (1977); and Armstrong (1978, 1983). However, as van Fraassen (1989, pt. i) has pointed out, these philosophers fail to explain how laws can be both *necessary* and *empirical* (or factually contingent). They overlooked the solution to this problem, provided in my 1968 paper, and reproduced above: if T is interpreted essentialistically, all the *laws* of T are analytic, and thus entirely non-factual; the whole factual content of T resides in the assertion that entities, of the specified type, with the specified necessitating properties, do actually *exist*.

It may be asked: If *all* the laws of T are analytic, can T be meaningful? To say that a law is analytic is to say that it is an implicit definition of a notion used by the law—just as the analyticity of 'All bachelors are unmarried' may be regarded as an implicit definition of 'bachelor'. But if *all* the laws of T are analytic, this would seem to imply that all the concepts of T are implicitly defined in terms of each other; and this would seem to imply that they are all meaningless. Being defined in terms of each other, there is no room for meaning to enter in from outside the circle of definitions.

The reply to this objection is straightforward. As I have already remarked, given a theory such as NT, we can distinguish any number of different versions of NT, from the highly non-essentialistic at one extreme to the fully essentialistic at the other. As we move from the less to the more essentialistic, so more and more becomes analytic, more and more theory is, in effect, built into the meaning of the constituent concepts. Thus the meaning of 'gravitational charge$_5$' might be such that no more than 'objects with gravitational charge$_5$ tend to move towards each other in some way that is proportional to their mass' is true analytically; the meaning of 'gravitational charge$_2$' might be such that '$F = Gg_1g_2/d^n$' is true analytically, where n is some positive integer; and, finally, the meaning of 'gravitational charge$_1$' is such that '$F = Gg_1g_2/d^2$' is true analytically. As we move from the non-essentialistic towards the wholly essentialistic, the meaning of the Newtonian concepts, such as 'mass', 'gravitational charge', and 'force', are more and more tightly interrelated with one another; but we have no reason whatsoever to hold that meaning gradually drains away as we approach the wholly essentialistic, and no reason to hold that meaning abruptly disappears at the last step, when we arrive at the fully essentialistic interpretation of NT. It is entirely wrong to think of Newtonian concepts, such as 'mass' etc., in the essentialistic case, acquiring their meaning entirely via their analytic relationships with each other; if there is any doubt about the meaning of the Newtonian concepts in the fully essentialistic case, we can go through the process of approaching the essentialistic case, step by step, from some non-essentialistic starting-point agreed to be meaningful. This process can be regarded as giving meaning to the concepts in the fully essentialistic case, and specifying precisely what these meanings are, and how they are related to meanings associated with non-essentialistic versions of NT. The process progressively *constrains* and *makes more precise* the already meaningful; it in effect builds more and more theoretical content into the meaning of 'gravitational charge' etc.; but it does not annihilate meaning. The analyticity of *all* the laws of NT would only imply that these laws are meaningless if the only way the associated Newtonian concepts acquire meaning was via their analytic relationships with each other; but, as we have seen, this is not the case. The objection to the meaningfulness of the fully essentialistic version of NT collapses. The fully essentialistic version of NT, I might add, asserts *more* than all non-essentialistic versions (via its existence postulate), and thus logically implies all non-essentialistic versions of NT (which would be a difficult feat were essentialistic NT meaningless!).

Once phenomenalism is rejected, and once the above objection is rejected, all that remains of Hume's argument is something like the following: just as whatever object happens to exist at one *place* cannot determine necessarily what exists at another place, so too whatever object (instantaneous event or state of affairs) exists at one *time* cannot determine necessarily what exists at another time.

There are two ways in which one may seek to demolish this argument. The first challenges the *validity* of the argument: time, it may be argued, need not be sufficiently like space for the argument from space to time to be valid. The second leaves the validity of the argument unquestioned and challenges the *premiss*. Necessary connections between different parts of *space* are possible. And hence, too, it is possible to have necessary connections between different *times*.

In my 1968 paper I developed the first argument. Here I sketch the second argument. It is a rather more powerful argument in that it transforms an argument *against* the possible existence of necessary connections between successive events into an argument *for* the possible existence of such connections.

The argument for the possible existence of necessary connections between distinct *places* (spatial as opposed to temporal necessary connections) proceeds as follows. If we have two distinct objects each confined to one of two distinct spatial regions, r_1 and r_2, then it may well be true that what exists at r_1 cannot necessarily determine what exists at r_2. But suppose we have *one* object occupying both r_1 and r_2. And suppose that this object is such that (*a*) it cannot overlap spatially with any other object, and (*b*) the nature of the whole object is determined necessarily by any spatial part of the object, however small. In this case what exists in r_1 *would* necessarily determine what exists in r_2.

There are, here, two kinds of object to consider: spatially *contingent* objects and spatially *necessary* objects. A spatially contingent object is an object which can be specified precisely and completely by a specification of what exists at each spatial point the object occupies, the omission of a specification of what exists at any one occupied point being sufficient to render the specification of the whole object incomplete. Spatially necessary objects are objects for which this is not true. One kind of spatially necessary object is an *any-point-self-determining* object. This object is such that what exists at any occupied point is such that it necessarily determines what exists at all other occupied points. The object, O, is such that at each occupied point, x, there is a particular value, $P(x)$, of a necessitating property, P, which determines necessarily that O and P exist throughout all occupied points, and determines necessarily what $P(x)$ will be at each x.

The Newtonian gravitationally charged point-particle, conceived of in a maximally essentialistic way, is a spatially necessary object (ignoring that it fails to exclude other objects). This object, via its gravitational charge, occupies all of space (since the gravitational force created by the charge has a value greater than zero throughout all of space). This entire object is, however, determined necessarily by what exists at the point occupied by the point-particle—the value of the Newtonian gravitational charge, or inertial mass, at that point. Any specification of this essentialistic Newtonian point-particle which satisfies the requirements for spatial contingency must be incomplete because it cannot specify the spatially necessitating property of gravitational charge which the point-particle possesses at the point it occupies.

A variety of different kinds of spatially necessary object is conceivable. There is the object that is determined necessarily by what exists in some particular proper part of the space it occupies. There is the object that is determined necessarily by what exists within any volume, dV, of occupied space, however small. There is the object that is determined necessarily by what exists at one unique point. And there is the object that is determined necessarily by what exists at any N points—with $N = 1$ as a special case. The important point here, however, is that the mere possibility or conceivability of any of these spatially necessary objects suffices to establish that it *is* possible that what exists at one place does necessarily determine what exists at another place. Not only does the above remnant of Hume's argument fail to establish that it is impossible for temporally necessary connections to exist; it actually establishes that it *is* possible for temporally necessary connections to exist (granted the validity of arguing from space to time).

One great advantage that this argument has over my earlier argument (Maxwell 1968*a*) is that it renders the existence of necessary connections entirely compatible with SR. The earlier argument, in requiring there to be a special sort of distinction between space and time, makes the existence of necessary connections problematic granted SR or GR. No such difficulty arises with the argument presented here.

The two arguments can, however, be brought together to form one coherent argument, which may be outlined as follows. It is possible that physical space is such that it renders spatial necessary connections impossible. But even if space is like this, it is also possible that time is sufficiently different from space so that temporal necessary connections *are* possible. There are grounds, however, for holding that spatial necessary connections are only impossible in *some* possible physical spaces but not in *all*. In order to exclude spatial necessary connections— or spatially necessary objects—space needs itself to possess a necessitating property: one which necessarily excludes spatially necessary objects. Strikingly enough, such a necessitating property, in order to exclude spatially necessary objects *in* space, must be such that it turns *space itself* into a spatially necessary object. In other words, in order to deny the possibility of spatially necessary objects we need to assert that physical space itself is a spatially necessary object. It is quite possible that space is *not* this kind of spatially necessary object (which excludes the existence of all other spatially necessary objects). If this is the case, then spatially necessary objects (and connections) become entirely possible (as indicated above). In this case we do not at all need to draw a distinction between space and time in order to make possible *temporal* necessary connections.

Essentialistic physics is able to explain *why* regularities exist in Nature. Lawful regularities are the outcome, the necessary consequences, of physical entities possessing appropriate necessitating properties. But anti-essentialistic physics, by contrast, can provide no such explanation. That there should be precise, universal regularities in Nature must remain a mystery, a persistent miracle. It cannot help at all to 'explain' regularities that are restricted in scope by demonstrating that they are consequences of much more universal regularities. Such 'explanations' only deepen the mystery—in that the more universal a mere regularity is so the more inexplicable it becomes. It is, in short, absurd to suppose that there could be precise, universal regularities in Nature, and yet nothing in existence which is responsible for such regularities. Yet it is just this absurdity to which anti-essentialistic physics commits itself (assuming that no other agent, such as God, is called upon to be responsible for maintaining the lawfulness of Nature).

The outcome is clear: physics must be interpreted essentialistically. Of course, if Hume were right, and no meaning could be given to the notion of necessitating property, this whole line of reasoning would collapse. We have seen, however, that Hume is wrong. Given the *possibility* of necessitating properties, it becomes absurd not to commit physics to the essentialistic task of discovering the nature of that ultimate necessitating property, invariantly present everywhere, which is responsible for determining how things change.

Once the possibility of necessitating properties is acknowledged, it becomes clear how genuine *laws* are to be distinguished from mere accidental generalizations. 'All lumps of gold are less than 10,000 tons', interpreted as a statement of a law of nature, in effect amounts to attributing a necessitating property to gold which renders it impossible for a lump of gold to have a mass equal to, or greater than, 10,000 tons. If no such necessitating property exists, then 'All lumps of gold are less than 10,000 tons' is *false*, interpreted as a physical law, even though it may be *true*, interpreted as an accidental generalization (which does not require the existence of any necessitating property in order to be true).

Physicists, as well as philosophers, have rejected conjectural essentialism for bad reasons (leaving Hume's arguments on one side). There are at least four. They stem from (1) anti-Aristotelianism, (2) belief in God, (3) respect for Newton, and (4) acceptance of SE. I take these in turn.

1. In creating modern science, Galileo and others appreciated that it was necessary to reject Aristotelianism and put in its stead a mechanistic, mathematical or atomistic view of Nature—i.e. some version of physicalism. This meant in particular rejecting the 'occult' properties of Aristotelianism and the pseudo-explanations that they provide. But occult and necessitating properties seem superficially to be very similar. In vehemently opposing the former, scientists created a psychological barrier to the idea that science might need to refer to the latter—essentialism being in this way excluded from consideration.

2. Most of those who created modern science believed in the existence of God. Belief in God even played an important role in the creation of science: it inspired belief in the order and knowability of the universe (see, for example, Hookyas 1973). But belief in God

renders belief in necessitating properties redundant: one can believe that lawfulness exists because God wills it. As a result, natural philosophers were able to develop physics as a science of natural *laws* or *regularities* without there being any scientific explanation as to why lawfulness exists—the explanation lying (so it was believed) beyond science in religion. Later, when science became dissociated from its Christian, theological context, the anti-essentialistic mode of thought, which no longer made sense, had, within science, hardened into a dogma.

3. Newton, notoriously, vehemently rejected any essentialistic interpretation of his law of gravitation. For Newton, this law described the actual motions of objects, but did not *explain* these motions, and did not assert the existence of a real physical force of gravitation acting at a distance. Not surprisingly, given the immense prestige of Newton, this anti-essentialistic attitude became enshrined in subsequent physics.

4. Most physicists after Newton have taken some form of SE for granted. SE requires that science be sharply dissociated from philosophy and metaphysics. But in order merely to *distinguish* essentialism and anti-essentialism, and in order to develop and assess arguments in support of the former and against the latter, it is necessary to do philosophy and metaphysics. SE thus excludes from physics just that which needs to be brought into physics if anti-essentialism is to be reconsidered.

Conjectural essentialism has a number of advantages over conjectural lawism.

First, essentialism clarifies the nature of the relationship between physical entities and their properties on the one hand, and acceptable dynamical equations on the other hand. Granted lawism, it is not at all clear what this relationship is. A physical theory, T, construed as a set of dynamical equations or laws, may be realistically interpreted as being about physical entities of such-and-such a type: but it remains obscure as to what the physical *properties* of these entities are, and how these properties relate to the dynamical laws governing the way the entities evolve and interact. Granted essentialism, the nature of the relationship between dynamical laws and entities and their properties is crystal clear: the necessitating properties of the entities determine how the entities interact: the dynamical laws simply specify precisely what these properties are. If we confine our attention to *good* fundamental physical theories, then there is a straightforward correspondence between *theories* on the one hand (specifying dynamical laws) and *entities and their properties* on the other hand. (This is not true of all theories. Orthodox QT cannot be interpreted as specifying entities with precise properties because it fails to solve the great quantum wave/particle mystery. But precisely for this reason, orthodox QT is seriously defective, as we shall see in Chapter 7.)

One bad consequence of the failure of the scientific community to grasp the simple relationship between theories on the one hand, and entities and their properties on the other (as a result of adopting lawism), is that, repeatedly in the history of science, persistent and entirely wrong-headed attempts have been made to understand *new* theories in terms of *old* entities and properties, appropriate to an earlier theory. Adequate understanding of NT and MT was delayed by decades because of the failure to grasp the simple point that new theories demand to be understood in terms of new metaphysics—a point that is entirely obvious granted essentialism. Adequate understanding of QT is still lacking, over seventy years after the birth of the theory, for this reason (as I shall argue in Chapter 7).

Misguided attempts to understand a new dynamical theory in terms of old physical entities and properties inevitably fail; such failures, all too often, are then interpreted as demonstrating the inherent *unintelligibility* of the physical entity corresponding to the new theory. Thus the failure of attempts to interpret Newton's law of gravitation in terms of the corpuscular hypothesis was taken to demonstrate the inherent unintelligibility of the gravitational force; the failure of attempts to interpret MT in terms of the quasi-materialistic ether was taken to demonstrate the inherent unintelligibility of the classical electromagnetic field; and the failure of attempts to interpret QT in terms of the classical point-particle and/or field is still taken to demonstrate the inherent unintelligibility of quantum objects. In this way, lawism creates spurious mysteries; it spawns the idea that the physical universe is inherently unintelligible. Essentialism clears all this up at a stroke. There is nothing inherently unintelligible about the Newtonian gravitationally charged point-particle, or the Maxwellian electromagnetic field: in so far as these entities exist, they are just what the corresponding essentialistically interpreted dynamical theories say they are; they have precisely the necessitating properties that the theories attribute to them. And this may even be true of apparently inherently baffling quantum objects, once QT has been properly formulated (see Chapter 7 and Maxwell 1988*a*, especially 41–4).

There is another, more general way in which essentialism makes theoretical physics more understandable than lawism does. According

to essentialism, the aim of theoretical physics is to depict entities and
properties that persist through change: the dynamical equations of
physics simply give precision to the nature of postulated physical
entities and their properties. From the standpoint of lawism, by contrast, theoretical physics seeks to discover dynamical equations which
specify laws governing natural phenomena. But for most of us, dynamical equations are much more difficult to understand than entities with
properties that persist through change. Our ordinary understanding of
the natural world is built up out of the idea of material objects persisting
through change. Understanding essentialistic physics involves imagina-
tively transforming our ordinary ideas of objects and their properties
until they become the entities of theoretical physics—corpuscles, point-
particles, fields, probabilistic quantum objects. Thus essentialistic
physics embodies knowledge and understanding of the universe in a
form which lends itself to intuitive comprehension—even intuitive,
imaginative visualization. Anti-essentialistic physics, by contrast, does
none of this: it represents knowledge as *equations*, and as a result leaves
most of us profoundly baffled. Instead of theoretical physics being a
clear glass designed to help us clearly see the universe, it becomes an
opaque barrier set up between us and the world. The universe is difficult
enough to understand as it is; we do not need a gratuitously incomprehensible *physics* imposing itself between us and the universe, so that
effort that should go into understanding the universe must go instead
into trying to decode an unnecessarily baffling *physics*. And it is not only
non-physicists who are baffled by anti-essentialistic physics; physicists
too have lost their way among their equations. In order to *improve*
theoretical knowledge and understanding of the universe, we need to
represent our knowledge in a form which is as intuitively understandable as possible. In doing this, essentialism aids the discovery of
new physical theories; it is heuristically fruitful, in other words.

Third, essentialism helps solve the mind/body problem or, more
fundamentally, the human world/physical universe problem. For essentialism tells us precisely what *kind* of aspect of things theoretical physics
is concerned with: it is that aspect which (*a*) everything has in common
with everything else and which (*b*) determines how things change.
There is no reason to believe that a complete, precise specification of
this specific aspect of things would be a complete specification of all that
there is. It is entirely possible that there are other aspects, to do with
how things look, sound, feel, or smell for example, or to do with how it
is to have certain sorts of thing occur in one's own brain, which require
no mention granted that one is concerned exclusively to specify that
which satisfies (*a*) and (*b*).[48]

The fourth advantage that essentialism has over lawism is of course that it makes sense of the thesis that the universe is physically comprehensible. If we accept lawism, we cannot make sense of the crucial idea that what *exists* determines how things change; accept essentialism, and this crucial idea becomes fully meaningful.[49]

In order for the universe to be physically comprehensible, then, we require there to be a necessitating property which remains invariant as we move around in the space of all possible physical phenomena, and which determines, necessarily, the diverse ways in which events unfold. One problem remains concerning the meaningfulness of this idea.

15. GOODMAN-TYPE OBJECTIONS

The main point of the above proposed solution to the problem of simplicity is that by assessing the simplicity of a theory, T, in terms of the extent to which T is a precise version of physicalism, the terminological simplicity or complexity of T becomes irrelevant to the question of its simplicity in a physically or methodologically significant sense, only the content of T being relevant. But does this shift from terminology to content really help? We have seen, in Chapter 2, that the same theory, T, can be terminologically simple or complex, depending merely on what terminology is chosen for the formulation of T. Does not exactly the same point arise in connection with the content of T? Suppose T asserts that there is a fundamental necessitating property, P, which persists in an unchanging way throughout all phenomena, and which determines the way phenomena unfold. T accords beautifully with physicalism. Consider, now, aliens who, for reasons of their own, decide that properties only remain invariant throughout all possible phenomena if, in our terms, they change as one enters or leaves (in thought) some region r in the space of all possible phenomena predicted by T.[50] For the aliens, T is a grossly *ad hoc* theory; they would hold that it is a different theory, T^*, which accords with physicalism which, for us, would be grossly *ad hoc*, in that the determining property, P^*, postulated by T^*, would change its character as one enters and leaves the region r (according to our ideas about invariance). Granted this arbitrariness in what it means to assert that a property changes, or remains the same, and hence in what it means to assert that a theory, T, postulates the existence of something *invariant* throughout all change, does not this mean that the above proposed solution to the problem of simplicity collapses?

The answer is No. In putting forward physicalism I am appealing to our current, human, non-alien conceptions of 'invariance' and 'change', 'same' and 'different'. Alien notions are excluded.[51] Indeed, as we shall see in the next chapter, the argument for accepting physicalism as a part of current scientific knowledge only goes through if physicalism is interpreted in such a way as to presuppose our current, human notions of 'invariance' and 'change', 'the same' and 'different'. What science presupposes is that the universe is physically comprehensible *to us* and not *to aliens* with weird Goodmanesque notions of invariance.

Concepts of invariance and change must not themselves change as physics develops (at least not to the extent of becoming Goodmanesque). In saying this I am not, of course, saying that our ideas about *what* changes, and what does not change, remain the same. Changing our ideas about *what* does, or does not, change is quite different from changing our *concept* of change (into an alien, Goodmanesque conception).

Before Newton, weight was perhaps considered to be an intrinsic, unchanging property of objects; after Newton, it is obvious that weight is variable but that mass is invariant (granted the correctness of NT). After Einstein's SR it becomes clear that mass varies with velocity, and even rest mass can be converted into energy, in accordance with $E = mc^2$. Before Einstein's GR, it was generally taken for granted that space itself does not change from place to place; GR asserts that the curvature of space-time varies from one space-time region to another. GR does, however, postulate the existence of a necessitating property that is *unchanging*: this is the disposition of energy-density to change the curvature of space-time in the *fixed* way specified by the basic dynamic equation of the theory, discovered by Einstein. The variability of curvature is linked in a fixed way to variability in energy-density: it is this, rather than curvature itself, which does not change from space-time point to point. The outcome is *unification*: gravitation becomes space-time curvature.

In all these cases, *what* is deemed to be unchanging changes, but the concept of change does not itself change. In deciding that weight, far from being invariant, is variable as an object is moved from place to place, we employ the same notion of change, of varying and remaining the same. And the same point arises in connection with mass and space-time curvature. Furthermore, whenever it is discovered that some property, hitherto thought to be invariant, is actually variable, some other property is postulated to be *invariant*.

Merely in order to state that some property, hitherto deemed to be invariant, is actually variable, we need to appeal to the same notions of invariance and variability.

16. SIMPLICITY

We saw above, during the discussion of NT, GR, and the problem of the ambiguity of simplicity, (iv*e*), in Section 7, that it is reasonable to suppose that simplicity, in the non-generic sense, is an ingredient of unity, in addition to the eight facets of unity introduced in Chapter 3. At once we have the question: What *is* simplicity, in this non-generic sense?

Let us suppose that we have before us a set of more or less physically comprehensible universes (each with its own distinct, more or less unified dynamic structure), and we want to know how to order them partially with respect to simplicity (in the non-generic sense). Let us suppose each universe is such that it can be represented as:

1. a differentiable manifold (representing a possible space-time);
2. each with a distinctive topological character;
3. each with a distinctive geometric character;
4. each with a distinctive tensor field of such-and-such uniform type;
5. each with a set of differential equations which specify an invariant way in which 2, 3, and 4 vary;
6. a set of symmetries, S, with symmetry-group G.

Here are some ways in which we can grade such structures with respect to simplicity (in the non-generic sense).

The dynamic structure is simpler as, other things being equal:

(*a*) the number of dimensions of the manifold decreases;
(*b*) the topological unconnectedness, global and/or local, of the manifolds decreases;
(*c*) the rank of the tensors in point 5 decreases;
(*d*) the order of point 5 decreases;
(*e*) the simpler the equation of point 5 becomes;
(*f*) the smaller the order of G, the more nearly it is simple (i.e. not a product of subgroups), and the more nearly it is simply connected.[52]

Points (*a*) to (*f*) are not to be understood as *defining* (non-generic) simplicity. On the contrary, 'simplicity' is to be understood in its ordinary, non-technical, open-ended sense. What 'simplicity' is being applied to, here—possible dynamic structures—is highly technical and specialized; but this does not mean that 'simplicity' must itself have a highly technical, specialized meaning. On the contrary, it is vital that 'simplicity' has its ordinary, open-ended meaning, so that the term can be meaningfully applied to possible dynamic structures different from anything that we have conceived of so far. It is all too likely that the universe is not comprehensible along the lines presupposed by points 1 to 6. Granted, however, that it has *some* kind of dynamic structure, we ought to be able to grade dynamic structures of more or less similar types with respect to their relative simplicity or complexity. Points (*a*) to (*f*) are put forward merely as illustrative of the way that this can be done.

It deserves to be noted that, in entertaining the possibility that considerations of (non-generic) simplicity *are* important, in addition to considerations having to do with other facets of unity or comprehensibility, I am not reintroducing, by the back door, all the problems of simplicity that I have claimed, already, to have solved. Arguments developed above, in connection with 'unity', apply also in connection with 'simplicity'. Let me quickly indicate what these arguments are, as they arise in connection with (non-generic) simplicity.

First, in assessing the relative simplicity or complexity of two theories, T_1 and T_2, we are concerned, not with the form of the theories, but only with their content, the possible, physical, dynamic structures that they depict, the possible universes they specify. Questions of terminological or axiomatic simplicity or complexity are irrelevant. Points (*a*) to (*f*) use technical terms, such as 'tensor', in their ordinary sense, but physically interpreted to refer to possible physical realities. Secondly, as I have just emphasized, 'simplicity' and 'complexity' are to be interpreted in their ordinary, open-ended, vague sense, to allow for the possibility that physics may need to consider new kinds of dynamic structure, whose relative simplicity and complexity cannot be assessed in precisely the same way in which we might make such assessments today, in connection with dynamic structures specified by means of physics and mathematics available to us today. It is important to appreciate that a word, such as 'simple', can be entirely meaningful even though its meaning is vague and open-ended in this sort of way; meaning does not need to be precise and technical. Thirdly, it is, no doubt, quite possible for Goodmanesque aliens to give meanings to 'simple' and 'complex' (or their nearest linguistic correlates) which match our ordinary meanings near enough in some contexts, but then mean exactly the opposite for some other contexts (so that in these contexts 'simple' means complex, and 'complex' means simple). In asserting that the universe has a 'simple, unified dynamic structure', I am employing the word 'simple' (and all other words) in their ordinary, human, non-alien sense. Finally, what the terms 'simple' and 'complex' refer to may change as mathematics and physics develops, but this does not mean that the *meanings* of 'simple' and 'complex' change—certainly not, at least, to the extent of any such change being equivalent to adopting some alien meanings of these terms.

17. HOW IS THE PHYSICAL COMPREHENSIBILITY OF A NEW THEORY TO BE ASSESSED?

We are, let us suppose, confronted by a new physical theory, T, a potential theory of everything that may be formulated in terms of new physical and mathematical concepts. How do we decide whether T depicts a comprehensible universe?

The first step is to establish that T is meaningful, and what, precisely, it asserts. If there were a conceptual gulf between our pre-existing ideas and the new notions of T, it might be difficult to see how the meaningfulness of T could be assessed. But, as I have already argued, new ideas in mathematics and physics are never wholly new, never the outcome of a leap across a conceptual gulf; they always arise as a result of pre-existing ideas being modified.

Sometimes this comes about as a result of ideas that are implicit in what has gone before being made explicit. Thus, Babylonian mathematicians studied various patterns of arithmetical relationships which we, employing algebra, would now write down as, for example: $a^2 - b^2 = (a + b)(a - b)$. The Babylonians, however, did not use letters to represent any numbers; they studied algebra implicitly, but never made it explicit. Algebra arose, in part, in order to specify arithmetical patterns, of the kind just indicated. Similar remarks can be made concerning the idea of function, first used implicitly, then made explicit and generalized; and the same point can be made concerning the calculus. Another example is the idea of a group. Group-theoretic notions did not appear from nowhere, like magic; they made explicit what until then had been implicit.

Another way in which new ideas can emerge from old is as a result of pre-existing ideas being modified, usually in the most conservative way possible, to cope with some new circumstance or set of problems.

An example is the way in which the system of integers is modified to become the system of real numbers so that number may be extended, from being applicable to discrete entities like stones, to being applicable to length, area, volume, and other such continuous magnitudes. Granted that lengths can have numbers associated with them one is immediately forced to acknowledge that the diagonal of a square with unit length sides must have a length; its length is $\sqrt{2}$, which cannot be represented as a whole number fraction. The profound mathematical problem of how to come to grips with a number like $\sqrt{2}$ is created by the act of extending number from counting objects to counting lengths and areas. The real number system, one might say, is the most conservative modification that can be made to the system of integers so that number may apply in the new context of continuity.

Examples of new physical ideas emerging as a result of earlier ideas being modified or generalized have been given in Section 4 of Chapter 3, where I indicated how the corpuscular blueprint gave rise to Boscovich's point-atom blueprint, which in turn gave rise to the field blueprint. Mathematical developments required to specify field theories, such as MT (involving the transition from ordinary to partial differential equations), came about via attempts to describe such things as the flow of liquid and heat.[53]

Another striking example is the emergence of Einstein's idea that space-time has a variable curvature. The basic mathematical ideas were developed by Gauss and Riemann some decades before Einstein began to tussle with the problem of gravitation in the years 1907–15. Gauss was set the task of surveying a hilly area of land. He found a way of characterizing the geometry of the land in terms of measurements performed on the land. In other words, given any continuous surface curved in some way in three-dimensional space, Gauss discovered how the curvature of the surface can be specified in terms of measurements performed on the surface. This, in effect, generalizes the whole idea of two-dimensional Euclidean geometry. Before Gauss, curved surfaces in three-dimensional Euclidean space are merely a fragment of three-dimensional Euclidean geometry; after Gauss, one can think of the study of curved surfaces as a generalization of the study of flat, Euclidean surfaces.

Riemann's contribution was then to generalize Gauss's achievement to N dimensions, thus generalizing the whole idea of Euclidean geometry (Lanczos 1970, chs. 3, 6). N-dimensional Riemannian geometry can always be conceived of as a fragment of $N + 1$ dimensional Euclidean geometry, and this possibility indicates that the new Riemannian notion of geometry is a modification of the old Euclidean notion of geometry;

the crucial point, however, is that this interpretation is not necessary, and it is this which ensures that Gauss's and Riemann's contributions amount to a profound generalization of geometry. What the advent of Riemannian geometry illustrates so beautifully is the manner in which a radically new idea is nevertheless tightly related to the old idea it generalizes. Gauss and Riemann entertained the possibility that physical space might be Riemannian; it was only some decades later, and after SR, which has the effect of blurring, to some extent, the distinction between space and time, that Einstein was able to capture the idea that space-time is Riemannian in his theory of gravitation. Later, the French mathematician Cartan formulated a non-relativistic version of GR, one which preserves the Newtonian distinction between space and time, and postulates that space is curved in a way closer to what Gauss and Riemann had envisaged as a possibility.

If the new theory, T, is to be meaningful, it needs to be related to pre-existing mathematical and physical ideas in the kind of way in which Riemannian geometry is related to Euclidean geometry, and the ideas of GR are related to those of NT. In addition we require at least a proof of relative consistency,[54] and relevant existence and uniqueness proofs (which establish that T does indeed specify a possible dynamic structure of the intended type).

Granted that T passes these preliminary tests, we next require that it is a precise exemplification of physicalism: it must unify space-time on the one hand, and matter on the other; it must unify particle and field aspects of reality; it must unify GR and SM (QCD and QEWD). What T specifies must be characterizable in terms of a system of differential equations, or some appropriate generalization of such a system of equations. What T specifies must exhibit symmetry, along the lines discussed above. Ideally, T ought to be such that the symmetry group of T, together with one evolution, determine all other possible evolutions predicted by T. If T is one among many, perhaps infinitely many, other theories that satisfy the symmetry group of T, then T must be the simplest of these possible theories, in the sense discussed in Section 16. If, at a fundamental level, T postulates the existence of two variable, interacting entities, X and Y (the prototypes, perhaps, of space and matter, or forces and particles), then X and Y must interact in a symmetric fashion in appropriate circumstances.

Having established that T is meaningful, and depicts a dynamic structure that is unified and comprehensible, the next step is to assess the empirical adequacy of T. We require of T that it is a theory of everything; that is, it must be such that it applies to all phenomena. Even though T will contradict pre-existing empirically successful theories, nevertheless T ought to be able to explain the empirical success of such theories—GR and SM. If, in addition, new predictions of T, that clash with predictions of earlier theories, are confirmed experimentally, no predictions of T are falsified, and there is no rival theory of everything in sight, then T will be accepted as scientific knowledge. The hope, of course, would be that T is the *true* theory of everything, T thus, in principle, predicting accurately all physically possible phenomena.

There is an important additional requirement that T ought to satisfy, partly structural, partly empirical. We do not just require that T explains the empirical success of pre-existing theories; we require, in addition, that these theories, appropriately interpreted, can be extracted from T by an appropriate process of taking limits.

As we have seen above, and as we shall see in more detail in Chapter 6, even though NT and Kepler's laws are, strictly speaking, incompatible, nevertheless the form of Kepler's laws can be derived from NT when appropriate limits are taken. Equally, even though GR and NT are incompatible, the form of NT can be extracted from GR when appropriate limits are taken. A version of NT emerges from GR if GR is restricted in its application to infinitely weak gravitational fields (so that the curvature of space-time disappears), and to objects that are moving infinitely slowly compared to the velocity of light (so that relativistic effects disappear). In these limiting conditions, the evolutions of bodies predicted by GR become evolutions predicted by NT. The symmetries of GR become the symmetries of NT. What cannot be derived from GR by this process is the Newtonian *force of gravity*, since GR dispenses with the notion of force. It is nevertheless correct to say that the structure of NT emerges from the structure of GR when appropriate limits are taken. This structural relationship between GR and NT must hold if GR is going to be able to *explain* NT.

This is the kind of structural relationship that must hold between T and current fundamental physical theories, GR and SM. As a result of taking appropriate limits it must be possible to derive versions of GR and SM; as these limits are taken, so the symmetry group of T becomes the symmetry group of GR, or of SM.

In short, if the universe is to be comprehensible, its unified dynamic structure must be such that it contains the dynamic structure of our current theoretical knowledge in physics, GR and SM, as limiting cases, much as the structure of Kepler's and Galileo's laws are contained, as limiting cases, within NT.

If the universe is such that this requirement is satisfied, then we know much more about the ultimate nature of the universe than that some version of physicalism is true; we know that physicalism contains within it GR and SM as limiting cases. Our existing theoretical knowledge tells us something important, if distorted, about the ultimate nature of physical reality.

18. CONCLUSION

SE cannot solve the problem of what simplicity is, but AOE suffices to solve the problem. This must count as a powerful argument against SE, and for AOE.

5

Induction

1. INTRODUCTION

In this chapter I argue that AOE solves the problem of induction—the two justificational problems of induction that is, problems (i) and (ii) of Sections 4 and 7 of Chapter 2. (The methodological problem of induction, problem (iii), was solved in the last chapter.) The solution to these two problems also solves problem (v), the problem of justifying persistent preference for simple (i.e. unifying) theories in physics.[1]

What needs to be done, in order to establish that AOE solves these problems, is to justify accepting, as a part of theoretical scientific knowledge, the cosmological conjectures, at levels 3 to 10, specified in Section 4 of Chapter 1 and subsequently clarified. We cannot justify the claim that these conjectures are *true*; but we can justify, I shall argue, accepting these conjectures as a part of scientific knowledge, granted that the aim of science is to acquire knowledge about the world, knowledge of factual truth.

In tackling the justificational problems of induction we cannot, of course, assume that we possess level 2 theoretical knowledge; it is this that we seek to establish. At most we are permitted to assume that we possess knowledge of particular matters of fact, knowledge of empirical data. The problem of induction is the problem of justifying claims to possess theoretical knowledge given knowledge of evidence.

It could be argued that in seeking to show that AOE solves the problem of induction I am tackling the wrong issue. In Chapter 1, Section 3, I argued that the basic justificational problem is what I called 'the fundamental epistemological dilemma of science'; it is only if SE is accepted that this becomes the malformed 'problem of induction'. My hope is, of course, that this will gradually become the generally accepted view. But in the meantime, the problem of induction is well known, while the fundamental epistemological dilemma is not. It is the former problem that needs to be tackled.

2. OUTLINE OF THE SOLUTION AND THREE OBJECTIONS ANSWERED

Cosmological speculation about the ultimate nature of the universe plays such a vital role in the rational acquisition, possession, and use of knowledge that it must be regarded as a part of knowledge itself, however epistemologically unsound it may be in other respects. The best such speculation available is that the universe is comprehensible in some way or other and, more specifically, in the light of the immense apparent success of modern natural science, that it is physically comprehensible. But both these speculations may be false; in order to take this possibility into account, we need to adopt a hierarchy of increasingly contentless cosmological conjectures concerning the comprehensibility and knowability of the universe until we arrive at conjectures so contentless that it would not be rational to reject them in any circumstances. In this way we maximize our chances of adopting cosmological conjectures that promote the growth of knowledge, and minimize our chances of taking some cosmological assumption for granted that is false and impedes the growth of knowledge. The hope is that as we increase our knowledge about the world we improve (lower-level) cosmological assumptions implicit in our methods, and thus in turn improve our methods. As a result of improving our knowledge we improve our knowledge about how to improve knowledge. Science adapts its own nature to what it learns about the nature of the universe, thus increasing its capacity to make progress in knowledge about the world. That, in seven sentences, is how AOE solves the problem of induction.[2]

In tackling the problem of induction it is important that we do not try to do the impossible. When I first learned of Hume's sceptical arguments concerning induction (from Sinclair 1945) when I was about 11 years old, I was convinced. *Of course* we cannot *know for certain* that the sun will rise tomorrow. It occurred to me that, until then, I had almost thought that we must possess secure knowledge because the universe would never dare disobey the august authority of the scientific community. What could be more absurd? Of course all our knowledge about the nature of the universe must ultimately be guesswork, simply because, for all that we can ever know, Nature may, at any moment, surprise us utterly. In attempting to establish that we do have secure (or probable) knowledge about the cosmos we do not defend the rationality of science; we undermine it, because we obscure the need to revise ideas all too likely to be more or less false. In order to give ourselves the best chances of improving our knowledge it is important that we recognize just how speculative are the cosmological assumptions that we make that exercise such an influence over methods for acquiring knowledge: only in this case can these influential assumptions, all too likely to be wrong, be improved.

The solution I advocate might be characterized as a modified version of Popper's well-known failed attempt to solve the problem.

The traditional approach to solving the problem of induction, and the problem of scepticism more generally, from Descartes and Locke to Russell and Ayer, is to give priority to that putative knowledge that seems the most *secure*, and use this as a basis for building up less secure putative knowledge, concerning theory, or concerning the past or other minds. Popper in effect turned this on its head and argued that, granted that our aim is the *growth* of knowledge, we should give priority to that putative knowledge which is the most *insecure*, namely that which is empirically falsifiable, just because here we can hope to discover that we are wrong, thus giving ourselves the hope of improving our knowledge. Whereas, according to the traditional approach, scepticism is the enemy to be defeated in order to salvage knowledge and reason, for Popper scepticism (the critical attitude) is at the very heart of reason, and is what makes the growth of knowledge possible. Popper is, however, insufficiently sceptical of scepticism itself. Scepticism is only rational in so far as it helps promote the growth of knowledge. If doubt can be shown not to help the growth of knowledge in any circumstances what-soever, then it becomes irrational. This is the nub of the revision I make to Popper's failed attempt at solving the problem of induction (and the problem of scepticism more generally). The revision is crucial; it turns failure into success.

My proposed solution belongs to another well-known approach to the problem of induction, the approach, namely, of appealing to a principle of the uniformity of Nature.[3] Theses at levels 3 to 9 (see Chapter 1, Section 4, and Figure 1) are all uniformity principles. Even the thesis of partial knowability, at level 10, may be regarded as a highly restricted, qualified uniformity principle. There are, however, on the face of it, three decisive objections to the idea that any such approach can solve the justificational problems of induction.

1. Any attempt to solve the problem in this way must rest on a hopelessly circular argument. The success of science is justified by an appeal to some principle of the uniformity of Nature; this principle is then in turn justified by an appeal to the success of science. As Bas van Fraassen has put it, 'From Gravesande's axiom of the uniformity of

nature in 1717 to Russell's postulates of knowledge in 1948, this has been a mug's game' (van Fraassen 1985: 259–60).

2. Even if, by some miracle, we knew that Nature is uniform in the sense that the basic laws are invariant in space and time, this still would not suffice to solve the problem of induction. Given any empirically successful theory, T, invariant in space and time, there will always be infinitely many rival theories which will fit all the available data just as well as T does, and which are also invariant in space and time.

3. We cannot even argue that the principle of uniformity, indicated in objection 2, must be accepted because only if the principle is true is it possible for us to acquire knowledge at all. One can imagine all sorts of possible universes in which knowledge can be acquired even though the uniformity principle, as indicated above, is false.

These objections may well be decisive against some traditional attempts to solve the problem of induction by appealing to a principle of the uniformity of Nature, but they are harmless when directed against aim-oriented empiricism (AOE).

What differentiates earlier 'uniformity' views from AOE is that whereas the earlier views appeal to just *one* (possibly composite[4]) principle of uniformity, AOE appeals to *eight* distinct uniformity principles upheld at *eight* distinct levels, these principles becoming progressively more and more contentless as we ascend from level 3 to level 10. This difference is decisive as far as the above three objections are concerned.

Reply to 1. It is obviously fallacious to justify the uniformity of Nature by an appeal to the success of science, and then justify the success of science by an appeal to the uniformity of Nature. Any view which appeals to just *one* (possibly composite) uniformity principle becomes fallacious in this way the moment it appeals to the success of science. The only hope of a valid solution to the problem along these lines is to justify accepting the specified uniformity principle on the grounds that there is no alternative: if the principle is *false*, all hope of acquiring knowledge disappears, and thus we risk nothing in assuming the principle to be true. Just this kind of justification is given by AOE for principles accepted at levels 10 and 9—a kind of justification which makes no appeal to the success of science, and thus entirely avoids the above fallacy. In addition, however, according to AOE, we need to choose between rival, much more specific, contentful uniformity principles in such a way that we choose those that seem to be the most fruitful from the standpoint of promoting the growth of empirical knowledge. Choice of principles, at levels 3 to 7 at least, *is* influenced by the (apparent) success of science, or the (apparent) success of research programmes within science. But this does *not* mean that AOE commits the above fallacy of circularity: principles at levels 9 and 10 are justified without any appeal to the success of science at all. Just because AOE appeals to eight principles, graded with respect to content, it becomes possible to give different justifications for these principles at different levels, something that is not possible if an appeal is made to only *one* uniformity principle.

Reply to 2. As a result of specifying eight uniformity principles, graded with respect to content, AOE is able to uphold, at level 3 or 4, uniformity principles much stronger than the principle that laws should be uniform in space and time, sufficiently strong indeed to pick out, at any given stage in the development of physics, that small group of fundamental dynamical theories that do the best justice (*a*) to the evidence and (*b*) to the best available level 3 or level 4 principle.

Reply to 3. Traditional 'uniformity' views that appeal to just *one* uniformity principle have the impossible task of formulating a principle which is simultaneously (*a*) sufficiently *strong* to exclude empirically successful aberrant theories and (*b*) sufficiently *weak* to be open to being justified along the lines that it is impossible to acquire knowledge if the principle is false. AOE, as a result of specifying eight principles, graded with respect to content, is not required to perform this impossible task. At levels 9 and 10 uniformity principles are accepted that *are* sufficiently weak to be justified along the lines that it is impossible to acquire knowledge if they are false; at levels 3 and 4 principles are adopted that are sufficiently strong to exclude empirically successful aberrant theories. These latter principles are not such that they must be true if any advance of knowledge is to be possible; circumstances are conceivable in which these strong principles ought to be revised in the interests of further acquisition of knowledge. Indeed, at level 3, such revisions have occurred a number of times during the development of modern physics.

3. RIVALS TO COMPREHENSIBILITY

In order to dramatize the point that science might well be possible even though the level 5 comprehensibility thesis is false, I now list twenty metaphysical theses about the nature of the universe, all different from, and most incompatible with, physicalism, P_4, and comprehensibility, P_5, even though all accord with scientific evidence just as well as P_4 and P_5 do. It would seem that these twenty theses deserve serious consideration alongside P_4 and P_5.

Compatible with P_4—and thus with P_5 as well (but failing to entail P_4 and P_5)

(*a*) *Lawfulness.* The universe is such that everything occurs in accordance with laws {L} that are invariant with respect to space and time.

(*b*) *Weak physicalism.* In addition to (*a*), the laws are invariant throughout the phenomena to which they apply.

(*c*) *Conditional physicalism. If* laws exist, they exhibit sufficient unity, sufficient comprehensibility, to make further progress in theoretical physics possible.

(*d*) *Heuristic physicalism.* Physicalism is upheld as a conjecture in the context of discovery, as a heuristic aid for the discovery of new theories, but *not* as a part of knowledge; in the context of justification *conditional physicalism* is maintained.

Incompatible with P_4—but not P_5

(*e*) *Deistic physicalism.* The physicalistic character of the universe, to the extent that it exists, is the outcome of the will of God.

(*f*) *Partially physicalistic comprehensibility.* The universe is ultimately comprehensible in some non-physicalistic way; this reduces, for many phenomena in the world we observe, to partial physicalistic comprehensibility, to a sufficient approximation at least to make the success of modern physical science possible. (*e*) is a special case of (*f*).

Incompatible with P_5—and thus with P_4 as well

(*g*) *Patchwork physicalism.* The universe is such that different theories apply in different space-time regions.

(*h*) *Local physicalism.* The universe behaves as if physicalism is true in the particular space-time region we have lived in and interacted with so far; elsewhere, the universe behaves differently.

(*i*) *Incomprehensible physicalism.* Physicalism is true, but incomprehensible to the human mind.

(*j*) *Accidental physicalism.* Events occur purely at random: the apparent partial physical comprehensibility of our world is a purely random occurrence in an ultimately chaotic universe.

(*k*) *Global accidental physicalism.* The universe behaves everywhere as if physicalism is true, but nothing exists which determines what exists next, so that behaving in accordance with physicalism is the outcome of pure chance.

(*l*) *Physicalism with partial unity.* All natural phenomena occur in accordance with a few different sorts of unified dynamic structure (such as those depicted by current fundamental physical theories, general relativity (GR) and the so-called standard model (SM)) but no true unification exists.

(*m*) *Inaccurate physicalism.* The universe is such that there is a unified final theory, *T*, which does better justice to the phenomena than any other, but nevertheless phenomena persistently deviate very slightly, in different ways, from the predictions of *T*.

(*n*) *Inaccurate physicalism without unity and progress.* The universe is such that GR + SM does better justice to the phenomena than any other group of theories, but nevertheless phenomena persistently deviate very slightly from the predictions of these theories.

(*o*) *Physicalism with intermittent miracles.* Phenomena occur in accordance with a unified final theory, apart from intermittent moments in restricted spatial regions, where arbitrary new physical states of affairs come inexplicably into existence.

(*p*) *Approximate physicalism.* The universe is such that, though physicalism is false, theoretical physics can still make some progress; new non-*ad hoc* theories can be formulated which would be empirically more successful than existing theories.

(*q*) *Asymptotic physicalism.* The universe is such that infinitely many theoretical revolutions are required before its ultimate structure can be correctly and completely captured by means of a true, unified 'theory of everything', *T*.

(*r*) *Complex physicalism.* The universe is such that further progress in theoretical physics requires successive revolutions (perhaps infinitely many), and after each revolution fundamental physical theory is more complex, more disunified, than before.

(*s*) *Threefold asymptotic physicalism.* The universe is such that there are three distinct forces in existence, each force being such that its nature can be specified increasingly accurately as a result of theoretical revolutions, infinitely many such revolutions being required, however, before any force can be specified precisely.

(*t*) *Asymptotic physical incomprehensibility.* The universe is such that theoretical physics can specify how phenomena occur with increasing accuracy as a result of undergoing endlessly many further theoretical revolutions, but after each revolution the number of distinct forces goes up by one.

(*a*) to (*t*) accord just as well as P_4 or P_5 do with the empirical success of science: on what grounds, then, are P_4 and P_5 to be preferred to all of (*a*) to (*t*)? Of course if P_5 is accepted, (*g*) to (*t*) at least can be rejected on the grounds of being incompatible with P_5; but what justifies acceptance of P_5? Each of (*g*) to (*t*) can be readily reformulated as level 5 rivals to P_5, by replacing the word 'physicalism' with 'comprehensibility thesis' (and making other relevant minor changes in the wording), to form (*g**) to (*t**), let us say. Thus (*g**) reads:

(*g**) *Patchwork comprehensibility.* The universe is such that different theories (exemplifying different notions of comprehensibility) apply in different space-time regions.

A part of what needs to be done, in order to solve the justificational problems of induction, is to justify accepting P_4 and P_5 in preference to any of (*a*) to (*t*), and any of (*g**) to (*t**).

One point that emerges from the above is that the relationship between the non-empirical *methods* of science and the corresponding *metaphysics* is one–many, and not one–one. Given that science adopts the basic non-empirical method *M*, 'choose that theory which accords best with physicalism', it may be argued that science thereby accepts one or other of a range of distinct metaphysical theses (not just P_4 and P_5, but (*a*) to (*t*) as well). A part of the reason for this situation is that there is a certain ambiguity in what 'such-and-such metaphysics is implicit in such-and-such methods' *means*. Granted, as before, that science adopts methods *M*, we may mean one or other of the following. (1) The world is such that it corresponds perfectly to the methods *M* in that adopting *M* enables science to discover the ultimate nature of the world. (2) The world is such that adopting *M* promotes progress in knowledge better than any rival method, of comparable generality. (3) The world is such that adopting *M* promotes progress as well as any rival method, of comparable generality *for a time*, or *to a certain extent*. (4) The world is such that the (apparent) empirical success achieved by science so far as a result, in part, of putting M into practice is possible and has occurred. Given sense (1), adopting M commits one to P_4 uniquely. Given sense (2), adopting M opens up the possibility that the universe is only partially comprehensible, but in such a way that physicalism, even if false, is nevertheless fruitful from the standpoint of the growth of knowledge. Given senses (3) or (4), adopting M leaves open (a) to (t) and (g^*) to (t^*) as possibilities.

It should be noted that if (s) is true, we could have rational grounds for preferring (s) to physicalism (P_4), and accepting (s) might well promote scientific progress better than accepting P_4. The same applies to (t); and there are other analogous possibilities. This establishes that accepting that the universe is physically comprehensible, or even comprehensible more generally, is not, in all possible circumstances, necessary, or even the best option, for scientific progress.

4. THE INDUCTION THEOREM

The solution to the justificational problem of induction offered here makes no attempt to establish that the cosmological theses, at the various levels, are *true*, or that we *know for certain*, beyond all doubt, that these theses are true. Rather, it sets out to establish that we are justified in accepting the various cosmological conjectures as a part of our (conjectural) knowledge because acceptance gives sufficiently good promise of aiding the growth of knowledge.

The chief consideration, then, that needs to be taken into account in deciding whether or not we are justified in accepting some cosmological thesis at some level is this: From the standpoint of the growth of empirical knowledge, how fruitful[5] is it to accept the thesis if it happens to be true, and how damaging if it happens to be false? As far as possible, we want to maximize the chance of fruitfulness and minimize the risk of damage. Ideally, of course, we would like to accept theses that are fruitful if true, but not damaging if false. (Even better would be a thesis that is fruitful whether true or false.[6])

Cosmological theses that are scarcely damaging at all to accept if false (since if false, acquisition of knowledge becomes impossible whatever we accept) do not require revision, and are put at the top of the hierarchy, at levels 10 and 9. Cosmological theses that promise to be immensely fruitful if true but severely damaging if (radically) false are put at the bottom of the hierarchy, at level 3, 4, or 5; these cosmological theses are revisable, in the light of their degree of fruitfulness (for the growth of empirical knowledge) in practice. By revising such low-level theses, in the light of the apparent[7] empirical success or failure of associated research programmes, we hope to be led to accept theses that are increasingly fruitful; we minimize the risk of being stuck with some thesis which, once accepted, blocks further progress in knowledge. In this way we maximize the chances of learning about how to learn as we proceed—the key idea of AOE.

The ten levels of AOE are labelled as before: P_1 = evidence, P_2 = fundamental physical theories, P_3 = level 3 blueprints, and so on up to P_{10} = partial knowability (see Figure 1). We then have:

The Induction Theorem

(1) The problem of induction presumes that we are justified in accepting evidence, P_1.

(2) We are justified in accepting P_r, given P_1 and P_{r+1}, for $r =$ 2, 3, . . . 8, as at least 'the best available bet, from the standpoint of the growth of knowledge, given the other options at this level, and our (apparent) successes and failures so far, even though (for some r) it may be a highly risky bet which could conceivably turn out to be disastrously wrong, to the extent, even, of leading us disastrously astray'.

(3) We are justified in accepting P_{10} since in making this assumption we have nothing to lose and may have much to gain, from the standpoint of the growth of knowledge.

(4) Given P_{10}, we are justified in accepting P_9, since in making this assumption we have almost nothing to lose and may have much to gain.

(5) Hence we are justified in accepting P_r, for $r =$ 1, . . . 10.

The all-important point, from the standpoint of the traditional problem of induction, is that the conclusion (5), includes the case $r = 2$, which corresponds to 'currently accepted physical theories': it is this, above all, which requires justification for the problem to be solved.

5. PROOF OF THE INDUCTION THEOREM

I repeat: in proving the induction theorem we are *not* proving, for each relevant r, that P_r is true, known to be true, or even merely known with some degree of probability to be true. We are only proving that, from the standpoint of the growth of knowledge of truth (at levels 1 and 2), we are justified in accepting P_r in preference to any rival, Q_r, at that level, relative to available evidence.[8]

At each level, the chosen assumption is to be justified on the grounds that it satisfies the following criteria better than any rival assumption at this level:[9]

   (i) It holds out greater hope of promoting the growth of knowledge than any rival (at that level) whether true or false.

  (ii) It holds out greater hope of promoting the growth of knowledge than any rival (at that level) if true.

 (iii) It does better justice to apparent scientific progress than any rival (at that level).

 (iv) It is inherently more plausible, more likely to be true, than any rival (if only because it has less content).

  (v) Accepting it does less damage to the growth of knowledge, if it is false, than any rival at that level.

 (vi) It is the best available exemplification of the best thesis at the next level up and, ideally, implies that thesis.

(It is to be expected that (ii) and (iv) will clash. The more an assumption promises to help the growth of knowledge, if true, the more the assumption is likely to assert, and vice versa. The more an assumption satisfies both (ii) and (iv), the better it is. It could be argued that it is on these grounds that the level 5 thesis of comprehensibility gains much of its *a priori* appeal.)

The logical relationships between the propositions at the various levels was discussed in Section 4 of Chapter 1. The important point is that, as long as we have not discovered an empirically successful unified theory of everything, level 2 will be incompatible with levels 3 and 4, and level 3 may not be fully compatible with level 4 (even if level r implies level $r + 1$ for $4 \leq r \leq 9$). The totality of level 2 theories will exemplify the best level 3 blueprint more or less adequately, and will exemplify physicalism more or less adequately; in other words, it will have some degree of P_3-simplicity (or unity), and P_4-simplicity. This can be extended to higher levels; level 2 theory has some degree of P_5-simplicity, P_6-simplicity, and so on. Equally, P_3 will have some degree of P_4-simplicity, and P_r-simplicity more generally, where $r \geq 4$.

In what follows essential use will be made of these notions of degrees of P_3-simplicity, P_4-simplicity, and P_r-simplicity more generally.[10]

Let us now consider the stages of the argument in turn.

$r = 2$. To prove: We are justified in accepting current *fundamental physical theories*, the standard model (SM) and general relativity (GR), P_2, given the *evidence*, P_1, and the best available level 3 *blueprint*, P_3.

As I have already mentioned, SM and GR are very different sorts of theory. SM is a conjunction of two quantum field theories, QEWD (the theory of the electromagnetic and weak force) and QCD (the theory of the strong force that acts between quarks). GR is a non-quantum-mechanical theory of gravitation according to which gravitation is nothing more than the curvature of space-time. SM is probabilistic while GR is deterministic. GR can be interpreted classically, as being about curved space-time, even in the absence of measurement; SM, in so far as it is formulated in terms of orthodox quantum theory (OQT), cannot be interpreted in this classical way, but must instead be interpreted as being about measurement. Time features very differently in the two theories, as Isham (1993) has emphasized. How can a level 3 blueprint be constructed which does justice to these very different sorts of theory?

As I have already remarked, one feature that SM and GR have in common is that they can both be formulated in terms of Hamilton's principle of least action, formulated in terms of distinct Lagrangians. Thus, we may adopt, as the best available blueprint for current physics, the Lagrangian blueprint indicated in Section 4 of Chapter 3.

Given P_1 (the evidence) and P_3 (this Lagrangian blueprint), we are justified in accepting SM and GR in that these theories are our best efforts so far at (*a*) successfully predicting P_1 by means of (*b*) theory that is a special case of P_3. A theory, *T*, some yet-to-be-discovered string theory perhaps, which satisfies these two criteria better than SM + GR, would thereby be hailed as a great contribution to theoretical physics.[11]

It is all too likely, however, that the Lagrangian blueprint is false, even though P_4 (physicalism) is true.

A general reason for holding this to be the case is simply that, as we have already seen, repeatedly in the past blueprints have been found to be false (or at least incompatible with well-corroborated, accepted theories). It seems reasonable to hold that the Lagrangian blueprint will, in turn, come to be rejected as a result of future developments in theoretical physics.

In Chapter 3 I hinted at a more specific reason for holding that the Lagrangian blueprint is false. QT suggests that as one considers ever more minute space-time regions so energy fluctuations (or energy uncertainties) increase without limit; given GR, this suggests that the continuity of space-time breaks down in minute regions. But, if correct, this would in turn mean that the Lagrangian blueprint, which presupposes continuity and differentiability of space-time, is false.[12]

Even worse, the Lagrangian blueprint, as characterized above, may be impossible: there may be no Lagrangian blueprint, whether true or false, which satisfies the above requirements for unity and which reduces to SM and GR in the required way.

The possible falsity, even impossibility, of the Lagrangian blueprint, plus the obscurity as to what to put in its place, poses a profound problem for theoretical physics. It is not, however, a problem for our proof of the induction theorem, as I shall show in a moment.

We come now to cases for which:

$r \geq 3$.

For these cases, a question immediately arises about what role evidence can play, since cosmological ideas at level 3 and above, unlike level 2 theories, are not in general open to empirical refutation. Of course, even in the case of level 2 theories, difficulties arise in connection with extracting empirical predictions, as we have seen; these difficulties can, however, be overcome, and level 2 theories can be refuted empirically. By contrast, level 3 blueprints, and cosmological ideas at levels above 3, are not in general open to straightforward empirical refutation. Exceptionally, a few blueprints may be falsified empirically; an example is the falsification of the corpuscular blueprint (which only permits repulsive forces by contact) by the observation of attractive forces at a distance. But cases of this kind are the exception rather than the rule.

In seeking to falsify empirically a level 3 blueprint, B, we could of course seek to falsify all precise, testable, level 2 versions of B, that is, all B-type theories. But even for level 3 blueprints, this may not be possible. For cosmological ideas at levels above 3 it is clearly, in general, impossible. And even when level 3 blueprints can be assessed empirically in this way, it is not relevant to physics since, as we have seen, in general accepted level 2 theories are *incompatible* with the best available level 3 blueprint. How, then, are cosmological ideas at levels 3 and above to be assessed empirically?

This can be done by assessing how empirically progressive or unprogressive rival research programmes are that are based on rival cosmological ideas. Given two rival cosmological ideas, C_1 and C_2, that give rise to two rival methodologies, M_1 and M_2, and thus to two rival research programmes, R_1 and R_2, we can assess the relative empirical success or failure of testable theories developed within these research programmes. If R_1 is more empirically progressive than R_2, then C_1 is better empirically than C_2.[13]

There is, however, a snag. R_2 may seek to keep abreast empirically with R_1 by accepting empirically successful theories generated within R_1, however awkwardly such theories accord with C_2 (i.e. with M_2). But even if R_1 and R_2 do accept the same theories in this way, and thus, in a sense, have the same empirical success, we can still assess C_1 and C_2 empirically; we can do this by assessing how well or ill the theories exemplify C_1 and C_2 (i.e. accord with M_1 and M_2). If the succession of theories exemplify C_1 better than C_2, then C_1 is better empirically than C_2.

It is, roughly, this version of the idea that I now develop in a little more detail in connection with level 3 blueprints. It is important to appreciate that the idea of assessing level 3 blueprints, and higher-level cosmological theses, along the lines just indicated (to be made more precise below) in terms of empirical progressiveness or fruitfulness, depends crucially on the solution to the problem of simplicity expounded in Chapter 4. Given a level r thesis, P_r, and a number of rival theories, $\{T\}$, we require that some of these theories exemplify P_r better than others, the theories of $\{T\}$ being partially ordered with respect to this notion of P_r-simplicity. Given this, the nub of the theory of simplicity developed in Chapter 4, it becomes possible to assess rival level r theses in terms of empirical progressiveness or fruitfulness.

Let us now consider the specific case:

$r = 3$. To prove: We are justified in accepting the Lagrangian *blueprint*, given the *evidence*, and *physicalism*, P_4.

Any acceptable blueprint must accord with, must be a special case of, physicalism. Given two blueprints which clash with physicalism, that one is to be preferred (other things being equal) which has the greater P_4-simplicity.

Blueprints can also be assessed with respect to what may be called their degrees of empirical 'adequacy'.[14] This measures the extent to which the blueprint in question renders a body of accepted level 2 theory that predicts level 1 evidence as unified or disunified. The more the accepted theory is unified with respect to a blueprint, the more empirically adequate the blueprint is; and the more disunified the theory, the less empirically adequate.

Degrees of empirical adequacy can be defined more precisely as follows. We are given, let us suppose, a body of evidence, E, and a set of theories, $\{T\}$, made up of the totality of fundamental physical theories,

T, which predict E to some considerable degree of success, together with all *ad hoc* variants of T (of types discussed in Chapter 2) of equal or greater empirical success, and any other rivals to T of at least equal empirical success. We are also given two distinct blueprints, B_1 and B_2. We then have:

> *Degree of empirical adequacy*: B_1 has a greater degree of empirical adequacy with respect to E and $\{T\}$ than B_2 does if and only if T_1 is more B_1-unified than T_2 is B_2-unified, where T_1 is the most B_1-unified theory in $\{T\}$ and T_2 is the most B_2-unified theory in $\{T\}$.

Corresponding to infinitely many empirically successful but grossly *ad hoc* theories in $\{T\}$ there will be infinitely many grossly *ad hoc* blueprints that will have high degrees of empirical adequacy. These blueprints can, however, be excluded on the grounds that they clash with the level 4 thesis of physicalism, P_4, or, more generally, that they have a low degree of P_4-unity. The dual demands of exemplifying P_4 and being empirically adequate severely limit choice of viable blueprint at any stage in the development of physics.

As an illustration of the idea of empirical adequacy, consider the Newton–Boscovich blueprint of point-particles, and the Faraday–Einstein blueprint of a classical point-particle–field. Let us suppose that we are given a body of evidence, E, predicted by classical electrodynamics, MT. The Newton–Boscovich blueprint demands rigid, spherically symmetrical, centrally directed forces and Galilean invariance, all of which are violated by MT. MT is highly disunified with respect to the Newton–Boscovich blueprint, highly unified with respect to the Faraday–Einstein blueprint. In other words, the Faraday–Einstein blueprint has a higher degree of empirical adequacy relative to E and MT than the Newton–Boscovich blueprint does.

The above definition of empirical adequacy assumes that it is possible to compare degrees of B_1-unity and B_2-unity. If this is not possible, the notion of empirical adequacy ceases to be applicable. We can, however, even in these circumstances, assess rival blueprints empirically in another way, in terms of what may be called their empirical 'fruitfulness'.

We are given, let us suppose, a period of development in the history of theoretical physics, from times t_1 to t_n, composed of successive predictive theories, $T_1, T_2, \ldots T_n$, and corresponding bodies of evidence, $E_1, E_2, \ldots E_n$. We then have:

Degree of empirical fruitfulness: B_1 has a higher degree of empirical fruitfulness than B_2 with respect to $T_1 \ldots T_n$ and $E_1 \ldots E_n$ if and only if the theories become increasingly B_1-unified as one moves from T_1 to T_n, but become increasingly B_2-disunified.

'Fruitfulness' is a legitimate word to use in this context since the more empirically 'fruitful' a blueprint is, in the above sense, so the better the blueprint would be from the standpoint of promoting the growth of knowledge. Suppose there are two rival blueprints, B_1 and B_2, B_1 having a higher degree of empirical fruitfulness, in the above sense, relative to $T_1 \ldots T_n$ and $E_1 \ldots E_n$. If this is the case then, at time t_1, when the evidence is E_1 and the current theory is T_1, B_1 would be a 'better', a more 'helpful' blueprint to adopt than B_2 because it would offer greater help with the task of developing T_n, granted that theoretical unity is persistently being sought. In these circumstances, B_1 leads one towards discovering theories of increasing empirical success while B_2 leads one away from discovering such theories.

Above I listed six requirements that a cosmological assumption needs to satisfy to be acceptable, the third being: (iii) It does better justice to apparent scientific progress than any rival. This idea of doing 'justice' to a period of scientific progress can be explicated in terms of empirical fruitfulness (for level 3 blueprints at least). Given a chunk of physics history, from time t_1 to t_n, B_1 does better 'justice' to it than B_2 if and only if B_1 is more empirically fruitful with respect to it than B_2 is. We have here, in short, a way of assessing the extent to which a period of development in theoretical physics supports, or undermines, a given blueprint. Or, equivalently, it can be regarded as a way of assessing rival philosophies of physics, in so far as a philosophy of physics is an aim linked to a set of methods, the aim being to turn a blueprint, B, into a precise, testable, and, it is hoped, true theory, the methods being those linked to B. Philosophy of physics, interpreted in this way, becomes an integral part of physics itself.

I conclude from this discussion that the Lagrangian blueprint is, at present, the best available in that it simultaneously exemplifies P_4 and is empirically adequate or fruitful to a greater extent than any rival blueprint so far proposed. A blueprint which satisfies these criteria better will, as a result, be more acceptable.

The argument so far, for the cases $r = 2$ and $r = 3$, can be much simplified if it omits all reference to level 3 blueprints, and collapses the two stages of the argument into one stage, designed to prove: given the evidence, P_1, and physicalism, P_4, GR + SM (i.e. P_2) is the best theory to accept. Put very briefly, the argument is just this: Given the evidence and physicalism, GR + SM is the best available theory because it (*a*) is the least disunified realization of physicalism that (*b*) has met with the greatest empirical success.

Despite the brevity of this version of the argument, I have sketched the longer, more complicated version in order to introduce the notions of empirical adequacy and fruitfulness, in order to indicate how physicalism provides a powerful methodology for the development and assessment of theories and blueprints within physics, and so that, in subsequent sections, I can show how the inductive argument is a generalization of the kind of reasoning that goes on within physics itself.

$r = 4$. To prove: Given the *evidence* and the *comprehensibility thesis*, P_5, *physicalism*, P_4, is the best level 4 conjecture to adopt.

P_4 is to be preferred to any other level 4 conjecture primarily because it does far better justice to the immense apparent empirical success of physics than any rival level 4 conjecture that is a version of P_5. P_4 is, in other words, vastly more empirically fruitful than any comparable, rival P_5-type conjecture.

Confronted by the many theoretical and metaphysical revolutions associated with the advance of physics, some people have concluded that there is no theoretical knowledge that can be regarded as persisting throughout these upheavals. They have concluded that physics cannot be regarded as progressively making more detailed, precise, and secure, some definite, fixed picture of the universe (see Kuhn 1970; Laudan 1980).

This conclusion is perhaps inescapable as long as one restricts one's attention to precise, level 2 theories; it may even be justified if one considers, in addition, much more imprecise blueprint ideas at level 3.[15] It ceases to be tenable, however, the moment one is prepared to consider the very much more imprecise level 4 idea of physicalism. (This point illustrates a basic theme of the induction theorem: as cosmological conjectures become increasingly imprecise and contentless, as one ascends the hierarchy of levels, so the chances of formulating a cosmological conjecture that is true, and thus not in need of revision, increase.) From the Presocratic philosophers some two and a half thousand years ago, via Galileo and Newton to theoretical physics today, a persisting aim has been to discover underlying unity running throughout the apparently disparate phenomena of Nature. Revolutions in theoretical physics, associated with Galileo, Newton,

Faraday and Maxwell, Einstein, Bohr, Schrödinger, Dirac, Tomonaga, Schwinger and Feynman, Weinberg and Salam, have all been unifying revolutions—revolutions that have brought greater unity to theoretical physics. *Far from obliterating the idea that there is a persisting theoretical idea in physics, revolutions do just the opposite in that they all themselves actually exemplify the persisting idea of underlying unity!* It is a basic task of theory in physics to unify disparate phenomena. Unity is sought as an essential part of the search for explanation, an all-pervasive feature of science. As long as some disunity remains, there remains something to explain which can only be eliminated with the development of a better explanatory theory which depicts underlying unity. Physicalism merely postulates that the universe is such that the kind of explanation sought by theoretical physics, even when pushed to the limit, exists to be discovered.

But physicalism is not just implicit in the aim of theoretical physics; as I have repeatedly emphasized, it is implicit in physics' methodology. As long as the only theories that are considered in physics are ones that bring about increasing theoretical unity, infinitely many empirically successful disunified theories being permanently ignored, physics implicitly accepts physicalism. From Galileo onwards, the task has been to develop a body of level 2 theory, T, which (a) is more and more comprehensively and precisely predictive of phenomena, and (b) is more and more unified. This means that as physics advances, T becomes more and more a precise realization of P_4; and this in turn means that P_4 is uniquely empirically progressive; P_4 does unique justice to the empirical success of physics. (Objections to this claim will be considered below.)

If P_5 was not, at this stage, being presupposed, the empirical fruitfulness of P_4 could be mimicked by various rivals to P_4, such as the 'aberrant' versions of physicalism indicated above in Section 3. But if we are given P_5, then most, but not all, of these rivals are eliminated.

What about rivals to P_4 which mimic P_4 as far as physics is concerned, but differ from P_4 elsewhere, though not so as to clash with P_5? Two possibilities, here, are that the universe is comprehensible because God exists, or is comprehensible in some other non-physicalistic way but in such a way that natural phenomena occur in accordance with some version of physicalism. These rivals to P_4 can do justice both to the idea that the universe is comprehensible, and to the immense apparent empirical success of science; they are, it seems, as empirically fruitful as P_4: on what grounds, then, are they to be rejected?

The conjecture that the comprehensibility of the universe devolves from God deserves special treatment: I discuss it below. Here I consider the more general conjecture, Q_4, that the universe is ultimately comprehensible in some non-physical way, even though all physical phenomena occur as if comprehensible physically (so that P_4 appears to be true as far as physics is concerned).

Q_4 and P_4 postulate identical cosmology-dependent methods for the material world, but Q_4 postulates the existence of a non-material spiritual world (encountered perhaps after death) in which quite different cosmology-dependent methods for acquiring knowledge need to be adopted. If Q_4-type cosmological assumptions are regarded as being just as acceptable as P_4 on the grounds that they are just as empirically fruitful and just as compatible with P_5, all hope of improving theoretical knowledge collapses. For we can then postulate infinitely many 'aberrant' rivals to P_4, concocted in such a way that, as physics advances, cosmology-dependent methods must arbitrarily change. As long as these aberrant versions of P_4 agree with P_4 as far as current theoretical physics is concerned, and do not violate P_5, they will all be just as acceptable as P_4. There would be no reason whatsoever to suppose that methods that have been successful in the past will have any sort of relevance to methods that will be required in future for success. We would have no grounds for supposing that the unchanging something, U, postulated by P_5 to be responsible for all change and diversity, is knowable. But, as P_5 was formulated in Chapter 3, U is in principle knowable to us. This means P_4 should be favoured over its aberrant variants, other things being equal.

Another, related argument can be given for favouring P_4 over Q_4-type rivals. Once we accept Q_4-type rivals to P_4 that agree precisely with P_4 as far as all physical phenomena are concerned, we cease to have a reason for rejecting Q_4-type conjectures which agree with P_4 for all observed phenomena but disagree for observable phenomena so far unobserved. Abrupt future change in physical phenomena that contradict P_4 need not contradict Q_4-type rivals, since that which is ultimately responsible for phenomena, God or whatever, may persist unchanged through the abrupt future changes (whereas that which is postulated by P_4 cannot so persist[16]). This means that we cannot possibly acquire theoretical knowledge of invariant features of the universe, and this in turn contradicts P_5.

Accepting Q_4-type aberrant variants of P_4 does not just contradict P_5; it contradicts the level 8 conjecture of meta-knowability. In the last but one paragraph I argued that if Q_4-type assumptions are acceptable, there would be no reason whatsoever to suppose that methods that have been successful in the past will have any sort of relevance to methods that will be required in future for success. But just this is required for meta-knowability. Meta-knowability implies that present success of methods is a guide to future success. Indeed, this is required for knowledge-acquisition quite generally. Without it, we could have no reason to suppose that past and present success is a guide to future success, and knowledge-acquisition would collapse. P_5 implies meta-knowability; accepting Q_4-type assumptions contradicts meta-knowability, and thus, again, contradicts P_5.

In effect we have here a seventh criterion for assessing cosmological assumptions to be added to the six already listed:

> (vii) At any level r, a cosmological conjecture that leads to 'cosmology-dependent' methods that remain the same through-out the development of knowledge is to be preferred, other things being equal, to a cosmological conjecture which leads to cosmology-dependent methods which change at different stages in the development of knowledge.

A basic idea of AOE, and a basic lesson to be learned from history, is that, as science advances so cosmology-dependent methods change. But it is also a basic idea of AOE that, if methods change at level r, then we need to step up a level in the hope of formulating, at level $r + 1$ (or above), cosmology-dependent methods which do not change, and which regulate changes in cosmological assumptions and associated methods at lower levels. The partial knowability of the universe depends on there being some level at which cosmology-dependent methods can be regarded as being at least implicit in the history of knowledge-acquisition up to now and invariant throughout all future developments. The lower the level at which this is true, the more knowable the universe becomes. It is this that provides the justification for accepting (vii) given P_5, or given the level 8 consequence of P_5, meta-knowability.

If some Q_4-type variant of P_4 is true, the nature of that which deter-mines how events unfold must remain utterly inscrutable to us, at least as far as doing physics is concerned. All that we can hope to discover, through doing physics, is the nature of that which P_4 postulates that determines all change but does not itself change. P_5 is violated.

$r = 5$. To prove: Given the *evidence* and the level 6 thesis that the universe is *nearly comprehensible*, the best level 5 conjecture is *perfect comprehensibility*, P_5.

This step is almost a tautology. Given that the universe is nearly comprehensible it follows, by definition, that the universe is such that the growth of knowledge is better promoted by acceptance of P_5 rather than any rival partial comprehensibility thesis. But quite generally, if choosing a hypothesis, H, in preference to any rival, $H_1 \ldots H_n$, better aids the growth of knowledge (through being, potentially, more fruitful empirically), then H is to be preferred. On these grounds, P_5 is to be preferred. The more H appears to be spectacularly successful in promoting the growth of knowledge, the more justified we are in accepting this conjecture. P_5, in the specific form of P_4, has indeed appeared to be spectacularly successful in promoting the growth of knowledge; we are, on these grounds, justified again in accepting P_5.

$r = 6$. To prove: Given the *evidence* and the level 7 thesis that the universe is *roughly comprehensible*, the best level 6 conjecture is *near comprehensibility*.

In Section 4 of Chapter 1 and in Section 3 of the present chapter, we saw that, in certain circumstances, we could have rational grounds for favouring some conjecture of partial comprehensibility rather than perfect comprehensibility (which we are justified in accepting, given near comprehensibility). The degree of P_4-disunity of the totality of theory might remain constant at some number, 3 or 15 let us say, across many theoretical revolutions that increase the predictive power and success of the theories; or, alternatively, the degree of P_4-disunity might increase by one after each theoretical revolution; and there are, of course, other possibilities. I claim that it is *only* in such circumstances that we should reject near comprehensibility at level 6 (and so perfect comprehensibility at level 5 and physicalism at level 4), given rough comprehensibility at level 7. Given a cosmological conjecture which leads to unchanging methods in line with criterion (vii) formulated above, and which, at the same time, is more fruitful empirically than physicalism, P_4, comprehensibility, P_5, and near comprehensibility, P_6, then it should be preferred to these latter conjectures. On the other hand, this is the *only* circumstance in which some roughly comprehensible version of P_4 should be preferred to the perfectly comprehensible version of P_4.

$r = 7$. To prove: Given the *evidence* and the level 8 thesis that the universe is *meta-knowable*, the best level 7 thesis is that the universe is *roughly comprehensible*.

In asserting that the universe is meta-knowable we are asserting that it is such that there is some discoverable assumption that can be made about the nature of the universe which aids, and does not hinder, the growth of knowledge. Meta-knowability guarantees that generalized AOE[17] is an appropriate methodology to adopt: the universe is such that, as we acquire new knowledge, we can improve the cosmological conjectures presupposed by our methods, this in turn enabling us to improve our methods. Just as in the case of comprehensibility, it only makes sense to say that the universe is (or is not) meta-knowable with respect to some specific body of knowledge together with its methods for improving knowledge (and possibly implicit meta-methods for improving existing methods). The body of knowledge in question is here taken to be the kind of pre-scientific knowledge possessed, for example, by hunting and gathering people. Given such a body of knowledge, the universe might be meta-knowable in a number of different ways, and to a greater or lesser extent.

The universe may be meta-knowable because it is comprehensible, or nearly or roughly comprehensible. But there are, it would seem, ways in which the universe might be meta-knowable even though not even roughly comprehensible. It might be meta-knowable because it is such that it is possible for us, by fasting, prayer, or meditation, to develop the capacity to see, with the mind's eye, events that are ordinarily inaccessible to us because they are concealed, minute, or far away, or because they occur in the past or future. The universe might be meta-knowable because instruments can be constructed which provide us with a clear view of what we do not, otherwise, know. Alternatively, the universe might be meta-knowable because there are gods who know everything (perhaps because they *are* the universe), and who will divulge their knowledge to us if properly consulted, by means of natural signs such as thunder, rainbows, drought; or by means of prophets, oracles, sacrificial ceremonies, dreams, drug-induced visions, or in other ways. But even if the universe is meta-knowable in one or other of these ways, it might nevertheless not be even roughly comprehensible. Even if fasting, prayer, some specially constructed instrument or whatever provides us with extensive knowledge of events occurring at other times and places, there might nevertheless be no explanation for the success of these methods for acquiring knowledge, and no explanation for the way the events themselves occur.[18]

If methods for acquiring knowledge, other than those based on the search for explanations, had met with the kind of extraordinary (apparent) success that science has met with, we might put our trust in such methods, and forgo the attempt to explain and understand. But no such methods have met with anything remotely like the apparent success of the scientific search for explanation. It is, in short, the far greater empirical fruitfulness of partial comprehensibility over any rival meta-knowable conjecture that justifies us in preferring this conjecture.

I now interrupt the orderly ascent from level 2 upwards, and jump to $r = 10$; I then consider $r = 9$, and conclude with the remaining case $r = 8$.

$r = 10$. To prove: Given the *evidence*, we are justified in accepting that the universe is *partially knowable*.

I have two arguments in support of the contention that, given the evidence, we are justified in holding that we have some genuine knowledge of particular things and processes in our immediate environment, and some capacity to improve this knowledge.

1. Having knowledge of particular things in our environment follows immediately from having knowledge of evidence. Once upon a time it was fashionable to construe evidence as reports of experienced sense-data. Nowadays, for good reasons, it is generally recognized that even our most experientially primitive, least theoretical empirical knowledge consists of, amongst other things, knowledge of macroscopic objects such as tables, pens, trees, bits of apparatus, and their typical macroscopic properties. Scientific evidence may be knowledge that lacks universality in that it pertains to particular things and events at particular times and places: nevertheless it presupposes knowledge of objects with various sorts of physical property—bits of apparatus, for example, made of glass, copper, rubber, or whatever with the usual macroscopic properties of these substances.[19] In so far as the problem of induction presupposes knowledge of evidence, it presupposes that we possess knowledge of this type.

2. We are justified in assuming that we have some knowledge of particular things in our immediate environment, and some capacity to improve this knowledge since, in making this assumption, we have nothing to lose. Doubt is rational only in so far as it can contribute to the improvement of knowledge. Doubting some specific item of factual knowledge, about some particular object or event, may well contribute to the improvement of knowledge, and thus may well be rational: in this case we can use our knowledge of other objects and events as a background against which we can test rival hypotheses about the object or event whose nature is in doubt. In this case, doubt can contribute to the growth of knowledge. But if we doubt *all* our knowledge of our environment we deprive ourselves of the possibility of acquiring knowledge: such doubt cannot conceivably contribute to the growth of knowledge, and is thus irrational. We are justified in ignoring it.

Granted that we have some factual knowledge of things and events of our immediate environment, it follows immediately that we have some meagre knowledge of the entire cosmos. We know that the universe is such that it makes our particular knowledge possible. We know that the entire cosmos is such that nowhere is there an explosion of chaos which will travel at near infinite speed to engulf our world.

It may seem paradoxical, even absurd, to claim that we undeniably possess knowledge about the entire universe, about the ultimate nature of reality (even before the advent of modern science). The claim may seem less shocking, however, when it is appreciated just how *meagre*, how relatively *contentless*, this postulated cosmological knowledge is. Once this point is grasped, the idea that we now possess cosmological knowledge about the ultimate nature of the universe may come to seem quite prosaic, even banal.

Consider the following statement about the cosmos: 'The universe is not a chicken'. It is of course just about conceivable that this is false, and that the galaxies that we see when we peer through telescopes into outer space are really the giant molecules of a cell of the body of the cosmic chicken. But this does not seem to be a very serious possibility. We can be sufficiently confident that the universe is *not* a chicken, surely, to declare that this is a part of knowledge (taking into account that, ultimately, all our knowledge is more or less conjectural in character). What makes it possible for us to possess this item of cosmological knowledge is that it is extremely *meagre* knowledge. In knowing that the universe is not a chicken, we know very little about the nature of the universe. There are an awful lot of ways in which the universe can *not* be a chicken. Nevertheless, in knowing this we do genuinely know *something* about the entire universe, about ultimate reality, even though it is knowledge without a great deal of content.[20]

As we descend from level 10, via levels 9, 8, . . . to level 2, so our claims to cosmological knowledge become increasingly contentful and, to that extent, increasingly likely to be false.

$r = 9$. To prove: Given the *evidence* and the level 10 thesis that the universe is *partially knowable*, the best level 9 thesis is that *the universe is non-malicious*.

This is, in a sense, the nub of the problem of induction, as traditionally conceived: what justification can we possibly have for holding that any regularity or order which holds locally, in the particular portion of space and time that we have examined (and which makes local knowledge possible), holds everywhere? At this stage in the argument the appeal to evidence is irrelevant; what is at issue is the justification for holding that evidence gathered in one portion of space and time has any relevance to what goes on at other times and places. Without the level 9 thesis of non-maliciousness, the empirical method breaks down.

I have three arguments in support of the contention that, given the level 10 conjecture of partial knowability, we are justified in accepting the level 9 conjecture that the universe is non-malicious.

1. If we assume that, at level 10, we have knowledge only of particular objects and processes that have existed in the particular region of space and time of our experience, adopting the level 9 conjecture of non-maliciousness—a conjecture about the entire universe—seems to amount to no more than a wild, unjustifiable leap into the dark. Why should our minute local patch in the history of the cosmos be typical of the whole? What conceivable justification could there be for making such a blind leap of faith?

In one respect, at least, this seriously misrepresents our epistemological situation. As I emphasized above, in assuming that we possess some knowledge of local objects and processes, and some capacity to improve this knowledge, we thereby make a cosmological assumption about the entire universe. We assume that the cosmos is such as to make such local knowledge possible. The transition from level 10 to level 9 is thus not the transition from an exclusively local to a global conjecture: it is the transition from a rather vague cosmological conjecture to a rather more contentful cosmological conjecture. A leap is involved, but it is not the blind leap represented above.

2. Granted that we take up the task of trying to improve our knowledge of the nature of the universe, we are justified in assuming that it is possible to do this. It would be irrational to attempt to acquire such knowledge knowing that this is impossible. But without the assumption of non-maliciousness, the project is impossible. However massively some cosmological theory, T, may be verified by evidence, we can have no grounds for preferring this theory to infinitely many aberrant rivals, which agree with T for all observed phenomena but disagree, in arbitrary ways, for some unobserved phenomena. There would be no way of ruling out cosmological hypotheses that assert that physicalism holds locally and *only* locally.[21] The empirical method disintegrates.

3. Put another way, we are justified in assuming that the universe is non-malicious since in making this assumption we have nothing to lose. If the universe is epistemologically malicious so that, despite the immense apparent empirical success[22] of science, in ten minutes' time

we will abruptly find ourselves living in an entirely different kind of world with no possibility of having any advanced warning of the change, it could not conceivably help to take such an eventuality seriously, prior to the event. Even if, by some miracle, we guessed correctly, prior to the event, when the change will occur, and what the new world will be like, nevertheless this could not form a rational basis for action as there would be an infinity of equally plausible (or implausible) conjectures which would postulate different changes at different times.

Arguments 2 and 3 depend on non-maliciousness being so contentless that it is the absolute minimum that has to be postulated for it to be possible to extend knowledge of the here and now to the rest of the cosmos. Non-maliciousness is a very weak uniformity principle. It does not imply that random aberrant phenomena never occur; it implies, rather, that if they occur elsewhere in the universe, they also occur in our immediate environment, in the here and now, so that, having experience of them, we have a basis for postulating their occurrence elsewhere. Non-maliciousness implies that there is *some* general feature of our immediate environment which makes it possible for us to acquire knowledge in our immediate environment, that exists everywhere, throughout the universe. What this general feature *is* is left entirely open by the thesis. It might be known local regularities; it might be an unknown unified pattern of physical law (physicalism); it might be God, or a tribe of gods; it might be the amenability of things to be known by means of clairvoyance, visions, or special instruments which reveal what occurs anywhere once the controls are suitably adjusted.

Under what circumstances ought epistemological non-maliciousness to be abandoned? It is conceivable that, even after millennia of intelligent and massive effort, no progress whatsoever has been made in extending knowledge from some more or less local region to the rest of the universe. Eventually it might be decided that the task is impossible; the universe is epistemologically malicious in such a way as to make it impossible for us to extend our knowledge beyond our more or less local region. And this might be correct. From the standpoint of the growth of knowledge, it would be advantageous, in these circumstances, to reject non-maliciousness, since this would lead us to concentrate on acquiring knowledge of our local, knowable part of the universe. (All this becomes a serious possibility if one takes the non-local to be regions such as: at, or before, the big bang; or after the big crunch, if there is one.)

But, even if millennia of effort to extend knowledge beyond the 'local' fails, it is still possible, for all that we can know, that some additional effort will meet with success. Without trying, we will not succeed; and nothing can tell us, indubitably, that we cannot succeed. Furthermore, it is always possible that we live in a comprehensible universe, even one that is comprehensible physically. In this case, knowing the general nature of what exists non-locally (beyond the earth, in ten centuries' time, before the big bang or after the big crunch) may be essential to knowing the general nature of what exists locally. In order to know the general nature of what existed at the big bang, we need to unify GR and QT; almost certainly, we need the true, unified theory of everything, T. It may be that T only yields predictions that differ radically from current fundamental theories for very extreme, highly non-local conditions, such as at the big bang (or inside black holes). Nevertheless, it is only by knowing T that we can know the precise nature of what exists locally. Whatever success (as we descend from level 10 to level 1) or failure we meet with, in short, in trying to extend knowledge beyond the 'local' (however specified), there will always be grounds for devoting some effort to the attempt to extend knowledge in this way, which means accepting the thesis of epistemological non-maliciousness as a working hypothesis at least, to be accepted as knowledge if the attempt to extend knowledge appears to meet with success.

We see here the first sign of the valid (and not circular) appeal to *apparent* empirical success. No attempt is made to justify the truth of non-maliciousness by an appeal to *real* empirical success[23] (which in turn requires the truth of non-maliciousness). Acceptance of non-maliciousness is justified on the grounds that there is no alternative: non-maliciousness plays such an irreplaceable role in the acquisition of knowledge that we are obliged to accept the thesis as a part of knowledge. But if the effort to extend knowledge beyond our locality persistently and obviously fails, we may come to doubt the thesis of non-maliciousness. Even then, we should retain the thesis as a working hypothesis, to be elevated to an item of (conjectural) knowledge the moment attempts to extend knowledge *appear* to succeed. There is, I repeat, nothing circular about this argument. No appeal is made to *real* empirical success (which would be circular); acceptance of non-maliciousness is justified on the grounds that the thesis plays an irreplaceable role in the acquisition of knowledge; *apparent* empirical success is only appealed to in order to reverse the decision to abandon all attempts to acquire knowledge of the cosmos because of earlier complete lack of even apparent empirical success.

$r = 8$. To prove: Given the *evidence*, the level 9 thesis that the universe is *epistemologically non-malicious*, and the level 10 thesis that the universe is partially knowable, the best level 8 thesis is that the universe is *meta-knowable*.

The thesis of meta-knowability asserts that the universe is such that we can discover how to improve our methods for the improvement of knowledge. Cosmological assumptions implicit in current methods can be modified, in a discoverable way, so as to lead to methods more conducive to the growth of empirical knowledge. The universe is such, in other words, that generalized AOE will meet with success.

The level 9 thesis of epistemological non-maliciousness allows for, but does not assert, this level 8 thesis. It is compatible with non-maliciousness that the universe is such that no improvement in methods is possible beyond those employed by early man of the Stone Age. It is even compatible with non-maliciousness that the universe is such that there are many ways in which existing methods can apparently be improved, such methods inevitably failing drastically after initial apparent success. Meta-knowability asserts that *some* new methods are discoverable for which this is not the case.

I have three arguments in support of the claim that we are justified in accepting meta-knowability, granted partial knowability and non-maliciousness.

1. Granted that there is *some* kind of general feature of the universe which makes it possible to extend knowledge from the local to the non-local (as guaranteed by non-maliciousness), it is reasonable to suppose that we do not know all that there is to be known about what the *nature* of this general feature is. It is reasonable to suppose, in other words, that we can improve our knowledge about the nature of this general feature, thus improving methods for the improvement of knowledge. Not to suppose this is to assume, arrogantly, that we already know all that there is to be known about how to acquire new knowledge. Granted that learning is possible (as guaranteed by partial knowability and non-maliciousness), it is reasonable to suppose that, as we learn more about the world, we will learn more about how to learn. Granted partial knowability and non-maliciousness, in other words, meta-knowability is a reasonable conjecture.

2. Meta-knowability is too good a possibility, from the standpoint of the growth of knowledge, not to be accepted initially, the idea only being reluctantly abandoned if all attempts at improving methods for the improvement of knowledge fail.

3. We are justified in becoming more confident in meta-knowability as our efforts at improving our factual knowledge *appear* to substantiate the thesis. Suppose that an empirical research programme has been developed, *apparently* increasingly successful empirically, the programme having some fixed cosmological thesis at level 4, 5, 6, or 7, compatible with non-maliciousness, and having a succession of cosmological theses at a lower level (at level 3, 4, 5, or 6), these different cosmological theses leading to somewhat different (non-empirical) methods for assessing theories. At the lower level, there is a succession of research programmes, each apparently more successful than its predecessor; at the higher level, there is one (meta-) research programme apparently becoming ever more successful empirically. Suppose, further, that the lower-level cosmological theses constitute better and better exemplifications of the higher-level, fixed cosmological thesis. Thus, as the lower-level cosmological theses exemplify the fixed, higher-level thesis better and better, so they *also* lead to methods that *appear* to be more and more successful empirically. These are just the kind of circumstances in which we should say that, as we *appear* to acquire new knowledge, so we also *appear* to acquire new knowledge about how to acquire knowledge (i.e. we develop new and better methods for the acquisition of new knowledge).[24] What has just been described is realized by the history of modern physical science, as pursued from the time of Galileo down to today;[25] but it could be realized by a research programme quite different from science (in a different universe perhaps). In these circumstances, it will certainly *appear* to be the case that meta-knowability is true. But without non-maliciousness, we have no grounds whatsoever for arguing from the *apparent* increasing empirical success of the research programme, from the *apparent* substantiation of meta-knowability, to *real* increasing empirical success, *real* substantiation of meta-knowability. Without non-maliciousness, we have no grounds for rejecting all those malicious cosmological theses which arrange for a series of research programmes (constituting one meta-programme) to meet with ever-increasing apparent empirical success for a time until, abruptly, everything discovered turns out to be utterly false empirically. But if non-maliciousness *can* be taken for granted, disasters of this kind are excluded. Non-maliciousness does not absolutely guarantee that *apparent* meta-knowability is *real* meta-knowability: but it does guarantee that *apparent* meta-knowability, involving an empirical research programme that becomes ever more successful empirically, in the way described, cannot suddenly and inexplicably collapse. Given non-maliciousness and a research programme

of the kind indicated, we are justified, I conclude, in adopting the thesis of meta-knowability at level 8.

But modern physical science has achieved immense *apparent* empirical success. This is undeniable. Hence we have every ground for accepting meta-knowability.

This last argument may seem to be invalidly circular; but it is not. The argument appeals only to the *apparent* empirical success of physical science, not to *real* success.[26] Apparent empirical success means that, alongside modern science, there are infinitely many (possible) *aberrant* research programmes, with aberrant theories, and aberrant higher-level cosmological assumptions, that are just as apparently empirically successful as orthodox science is. But these latter are all excluded by the level 9 thesis of non-maliciousness. It is the combination of non-maliciousness plus *apparent* empirical success of science that provides the valid (non-circular) justification for acceptance of the level 8 thesis of meta-knowability.

This concludes my proof of the induction theorem; I now indicate a few additional arguments, and rebut objections.

6. KNOWLEDGE MUST BE EXPLANATORY

At level 8 and above we consider the possibility that the universe is partially knowable but not even partially comprehensible. It can be argued, however, that factual knowledge of our environment, if it is to be a viable basis for action, for life, must be explanatory in character, to a certain extent at least.

By 'explanatory knowledge' I mean, at root, knowledge which carries implications, not just for what actually exists or occurs, but also for what would exist or occur if a range of other things had happened. I have explanatory knowledge of a piece of wood, at least to some extent, if I know how it would behave in a variety of counterfactual circumstances: if it were put on a fire, thrown into the sea, attacked with a sharp knife, or used to support a weight. This kind of explanatory knowledge involves knowing that things possess dispositional properties which persist throughout a range of circumstances and which determine how the things in question behave or interact in a variety of circumstances. In so far as I know that an object is heavy, light, brittle, solid, soft, inflammable, opaque, transparent, sticky, hard, hot, ductile, etc., I know how the object would behave or interact in a range of circumstances.[27] Such explanatory knowledge is not confined to inanimate things; it applies to living things, and to people. In knowing that an animal can fly, can run fast, can swim, is hungry, is flesh-eating, is frightened or defensive (perhaps because defending young), I know something about how the animal is likely to behave in a variety of circumstances: and all this becomes much more elaborate in connection with the knowledge that human beings, with a common language, can have of each other.

Knowledge of this type is *explanatory* because it enables us to 'explain' or 'understand' why things happen as they do (to some extent at least) as being the outcome of dispositional properties being 'realized' by particular states of affairs (as when the inflammable wood burns when it is thrown on the fire, or the hungry animal attacks when it sees its prey). What actually occurs is a part of a pattern of possible occurrences, and it is knowledge of this pattern of possibilities which makes this type of knowledge explanatory.

Such explanatory knowledge is, when compared to the explanatory character of scientific knowledge, primitive indeed. It is vague, restricted in scope, and highly piecemeal or *ad hoc*. With respect to this kind of explanatory knowledge, things come into existence, change, and cease to exist in all sorts of largely inexplicable ways. Nevertheless, even though primitive, it is vital for survival, for life. This is true, in a sense, for any living thing that must *act* appropriately in order to survive.

In order to survive we must be able to pursue certain basic goals more or less successfully in the environment in which we live: we must be able to eat, escape from those who seek to eat us, find a mate, rear young, etc. Successful goal-pursuing in a rather complex world requires that we have the capacity to do a variety of things, and the capacity to select out just that sequence of actions from our repertoire of possible actions that needs to be performed in order to give ourselves good chances of achieving our goals in the particular circumstances in which we find ourselves. This holds for anything that pursues goals through action in the real world, whether it is a person, an animal, an insect, or a robot. But this vital capacity to choose particular actions in response to particular circumstances from a repertoire of possible actions itself requires some, perhaps implicit, *explanatory* knowledge of aspects of the environment. In so far as the control system of the goal-pursuing thing considers a range of possible actions and selects out some particular line of action to perform as that which is most conducive to successful realization of the basic goal in the given circumstances, the thing must be able to determine how the environment would behave if any of the possible actions were to be performed: the ability to do this requires, in effect, explanatory knowledge of the type indicated above.

And the greater the range of possible actions that can be performed and need to be considered, so the more explanatory the knowledge needs to be.

Granted the fundamental role that primitive explanatory knowledge plays in being able to act in the world, in being able to survive, it is inevitable that, in attempting to improve knowledge, we will attempt to improve *explanatory* knowledge.

It does not, of course, follow that, just because we need explanatory knowledge, it exists, potentially, to be found. We might live in a world in which some primitive explanatory knowledge (of the kind we have been considering) is possible, there being, however, no more general explanation for this primitive explanatoriness. Objects might have their familiar dispositional properties, but when we try to explain why these objects and properties come into existence, persist, and cease as they do, in terms of more enduring and more universally possessed dispositional properties, we might meet with persistent failure.

What *does* follow, however, from our fundamental need, as purposive beings, for explanatory knowledge is that, inevitably, in seeking to improve knowledge, it is *explanatory knowledge* that we will be seeking to improve. And from this it follows that *explanatoriness*, of some kind or other, will in effect be taken as at least one basic clue to the kind of new knowledge to be sought.

And just as the usefulness, for action, of common-sense knowledge is related to its explanatory character, so too with scientific knowledge: in using scientific knowledge for technological purposes it is essential that we can envisage and explore all sorts of states of affairs that have never existed before, and may never come into existence: only explanatory knowledge, that can make reliable predictions about a wide range of counterfactual conditions, can enable us to do this. As I have already argued, in Chapter 2 and elsewhere, laws and theories of physics are profoundly explanatory in just this sense, in that they carry implications for an infinity of counterfactual states of affairs.[28]

What is involved in improving the explanatory aspect of explanatory knowledge? It involves drawing closer to the ideal of having a body of knowledge which, in principle, explains *everything*, nothing being left to be explained. We reach this ideal of perfect and complete understanding if we are able to show that, underlying the immense diversity of things, substances, properties, occurrences that there appear to be in the world, there is just *one* underlying entity with just one kind of unchanging property which determines the way in which the change-able aspect of the entity changes. As long as our knowledge postulates the existence of a number of different sorts of entity, with different sorts of property that determine the way in which the entities evolve or interact, we can ask: Why are there just these particular kinds of entity with these particular properties? Given the existence of one of these kinds of entity, what is there that determines that the other kinds of entity exist, with the properties that they have? Such questions only cease when we have traced explanations back to just *one* kind of entity, *one* necessitating property.

It might be thought that, even in a perfectly comprehensible universe, one problem of explanation would remain, namely why the one ultimate *something* exists, rather than something else, or nothing at all. But here we are asking for the impossible. In explaining *A*, *B*, and *C* we must appeal to the existence of *something*, *D* let us say, in terms of which *A*, *B*, and *C* are to be explained. When all phenomena have been explained in terms of just *one* underlying entity, the possibility for further explanation is at an end.

From these considerations we may draw the following conclusion. Given the fundamental role that explanatory knowledge has in our existence as purposive beings, and given (a closely related point) that much of the usefulness of scientific knowledge devolves from its (apparently successful) explanatory character, it is thoroughly understandable, even rational, that the search for knowledge in general, and science in particular, should adopt as a basic methodological idea that explanations exist to be found, the universe being at least partially comprehensible. Pushed to the limit this becomes: the universe is comprehensible.

7. NECESSARY CONNECTIONS

The strongest intuitive reasons for believing that the universe is comprehensible are, perhaps, along the following lines. Even prior to or independently of science, we can see all around us in the world amazing signs of order, design, pattern, regularity, intelligibility. (This is apparent in the seasons, the motions of heavenly bodies, the forms of living things, the constant properties of substances such as water, the forms of crystals, and even in the amazingly diverse, intricate patterns exhibited by snowflakes.) There is a great range of diverse phenomena which exhibit partial, fragmentary explanatoriness. All this becomes vastly more pronounced when one views the world through the spectacles of modern theoretical scientific knowledge. It is scarcely credible that all this more or less fragmentary order or explanatoriness should exist merely by accident. If the fragmentary explanations we give of things are genuine, and not entirely phoney, then there must exist deeper reasons for this; there must be better, more comprehensive explanations for the order and fragmentary explanatoriness that we now detect or see. It is wildly implausible to suppose that the world is such that partially comprehensible phenomena exist merely by accident, being embedded in more fundamental chaos and incomprehensibility. Limited, partial explanations, which explain by appealing to that which cannot itself be explained, in the end explain nothing: they are no better than pseudo-explanations. In short, pre-scientific, fragmentary explanatory knowledge is only plausible and authentic if the universe is such that, in principle, it can be given an ultimate explanation, the universe being ultimately comprehensible. And this argument for the comprehensibility of the universe becomes all the more powerful when we take the immense empirical success of scientific explanatory knowledge into account.

Is this argument valid? Does it justify rejecting various aberrant variants of P_5 which assert that the universe exhibits some partial, fragmentary comprehensibility but, overall, is not comprehensible?

In general the argument is not, I think, valid. Consider weak unity, which may be interpreted as asserting that the universe is such that everything that occurs is explicable in terms of the existence of some number $N > 1$ of distinct kinds of fundamental entity (forces or fields perhaps), each with its own distinct dispositional (or necessitating) properties. If this is how our world is, and N is not too large, there would still be genuine (partial) explanations for the fragmentary order and intelligibility we see around us. It is not clear how or why the above argument renders this possibility too implausible to be considered seriously. Why should weak unity only be plausible if $N = 1$, otherwise being increasingly implausible as N increases? If weak unity is true, and N is not too large, then there are genuine (partial) explanations for the fragmentary order or intelligibility we see in the world around us.[29]

There is, however, one version of the above argument that is, I think, valid. This version provides grounds for rejecting *accidental physicalism*, according to which the partial, fragmentary intelligibility that we appear to have discovered in the world is purely accidental, there being nothing in existence that determines what exists at the next instant. To suppose that the regularity that we observe in the world is the outcome of pure chance (anything being equally likely to occur at any instant as anything else, since there exists nothing that *determines* what must happen next) is, we may argue, to suppose the existence of a persistent, infinitely improbable miracle. Given any small region of space, the probability that, in the next instant, ordinary regularities will continue to hold is zero, in that there are infinitely many alternative states of affairs that could exist that are all equally probable. That this infinitely improbable occurrence of regularity should obtain, not just for an instant in a tiny region of space, but everywhere, all the time, is far too absurdly improbable to be considered for a moment. In such a world, there is no genuine explanation for observed regularity because this regularity is utterly incomprehensible, the outcome of an infinitely improbable statistical fluke.

There is a reply to the argument formulated in this way. We may assume that the universe endures for ever. In this case, eventually, we may argue, everything will occur, including wild statistical fluctuations that involve the persistent and utterly accidental observance of certain kinds of regularity. Our world is merely such a rare island of purely accidental order in a surrounding ocean of chaos.

However, if this is how the world is then nothing exists at one instant which can provide any kind of rationale for making an informed guess as to what will exist at the next instant. Past regularities can be no kind of reasonable guide to future regularities. At any moment absolutely anything may happen, and all imaginable occurrences are equally likely.

In such a world, as long as the infinitely improbable miracle of ordinary regularities persists, a kind of pseudo-explanatory knowledge is possible. But real explanatory knowledge is not possible because nothing exists which determines the manner in which events unfold: ultimately, they occur at random. In assuming that the universe is partially knowable, we are justified in rejecting this possibility of accidental order. For in assuming that we can improve our knowledge, to some extent at least, we assume that knowledge we have acquired at one time is relevant to what exists at later times. We are rationally entitled to make this assumption. This involves rejecting the nightmare possibility of accidental physicalism.

This argument requires that it is at least *possible* that what exists at one instant determines what exists at the next instant; it requires that it is at least *meaningful* to assert that this is the case. Hume may, however, be interpreted as denying that this is possible or meaningful. For, according to Hume (1959: 163–4), 'necessity is something that exists in the mind, not in objects . . . Either we have no idea of necessity, or necessity is nothing but that determination of the thought to pass from causes to effects, and from effects to causes, according to their experienced union.' If Hume is right, and the very idea of objective necessary connections existing between successive states of affairs is incoherent, it becomes incoherent to demand that connections actually exist. Indeed, comprehensibility and physicalism, as so far understood, become incoherent notions.

But Hume is wrong, as we saw in the last chapter. We can make perfect sense of the idea that what exists at one instant determines *necessarily* what exists at the next instant. Given that this is meaningful, and therefore possible, we should, given the above argument, accept as a basic tenet of human knowledge that the signs of explanatoriness that we see in the world around us indicate that the universe is such that what exists at one instant necessarily determines (perhaps probabilistically) what exists subsequently, our partial explanations for natural phenomena thus being genuine explanations.

This argument may establish that we are justified in rejecting accidental physicalism, but it does not justify rejecting weak unity in preference to strong unity. For that, we require the arguments given in Section 5 above.

We should conclude, then, from the argument of this section and the last one, that the project of acquiring knowledge about the world is justifiably committed, at a fundamental level, to seeking explanatory knowledge, some cosmological assumption of at least partial comprehensibility being quite properly built into the methods of science.

8. ALL THREE PROBLEMS OF INDUCTION SOLVED

Do the above considerations solve all three problems of induction—the theoretical, practical, and methodological, discussed in Chapter 2? My answer is: Yes.

The methodological problem (the problem of specifying what the methods of science are) was solved in the last chapter, at least as far as theoretical physics is concerned.[30]

The theoretical and practical problems are both problems of justification. In the first case, the problem is to justify accepting empirically successful theories, granted that the purpose is to acquire theoretical knowledge and understanding for their own sake. In the second case, the problem is to justify accepting such theories granted that the purpose is to use the theories for action, for practical applications.

The theoretical problem is solved by the discussion of Section 5 above. Granted that we seek theoretical knowledge and understanding we are justified in assuming that the universe is such that some such knowledge is possible (unless we have grounds for believing the opposite). On this basis, we are justified in holding that the universe is partially knowable, non-malicious, meta-knowable, and roughly comprehensible; granted the immense apparent empirical success of science we are then justified in accepting that the universe is comprehensible and, more specifically, physically comprehensible, for reasons given above. This solves the problem.

The practical problem is solved similarly. Throughout the assumption has been that, whatever else 'knowledge' may mean, it means at least 'a sufficiently good guess at the facts to provide a rational basis for action'. The argument of Section 5 above establishes (or justifiably assumes) that it is knowledge in this sense (knowledge as a rational basis for action) that we possess at both level 1 and level 10; we may conclude that the argument establishes that it is knowledge in this sense that we possess at the intervening levels, including $r = 2$.

Two objections may be made to this claim. First, it may be objected that in order that the predictions of accepted physical theories be a rational basis for action it is only necessary, at most, that we know, somehow, that our local bit of the universe behaves as if physically comprehensible to a sufficient degree of accuracy. The thesis that the whole universe is perfectly comprehensible physically is in excess of what is required. Secondly, and more seriously, it may be objected that the entire argument of Section 5 is based on the idea that if a cosmological thesis, at a certain level, appears to be *sufficiently fruitful for the growth of knowledge*, we are justified in accepting it as knowledge. This may be sufficient grounds for acceptance granted that we seek knowledge for its own sake, but it is not clear that it is sufficient grounds for acceptance granted that we seek knowledge as a basis for action.

As far as the first objection is concerned, it is important to appreciate, to begin with (as I have stressed above) that whenever we claim to know, or to be able to act, in however humble, limited, and local a way, there is always a cosmological dimension to any such claim. I only know that I can walk across the room if I know that the entire cosmos is such that it permits me to do this. Rational action contains the implicit cosmological presupposition that the cosmos is such that rational action is possible within it. But granted this, why should trusting predictions of accepted physical theories require that the cosmological presupposition that is accepted is physicalism? Why is it not sufficient to assume merely that our local bit of the cosmos behaves as if physicalism is true to a sufficient approximation? Section 7 above provides some grounds for holding that we cannot just make a cosmological assumption about our locality only; rational action requires the assumption that states of affairs that exist at one instant determine (necessarily) what exists subsequently (and, presumably, previously): in making this assumption we are in effect assuming that some aspects of local order exist globally. Secondly, the discussion of the inadequacies of weak unity in Section 6 of Chapter 3 provides grounds for holding that such weakened versions of physicalism do not suffice to exclude empirically successful aberrant theories from physics, and hence do not suffice to solve the practical problem of induction.

As far as the second of the above two objections is concerned, my reply is that if a cosmological thesis appears to be fruitful for the growth of knowledge, then this *does* provide grounds for holding that the thesis constitutes knowledge in the sense of being 'a sufficiently good guess at the facts to provide a rational basis for action'. Assume that we possess some factual knowledge, and some (perhaps implicit) methods, M, for the generation and assessment of potential new knowledge ('knowledge' throughout being understood to mean 'a sufficiently good guess at the facts to provide a rational basis for action'). If, now, some cosmological conjecture and associated methods lead to the generation of much new potential factual knowledge which satisfies the existing methods of appraisal, M, then this does provide grounds for regarding the cosmological conjecture as a part of knowledge (in the relevant sense of 'knowledge'). The argument of Section 5 above, appealing as it does to 'fruitfulness for the growth of knowledge' is just as relevant to the practical problem of induction as it is to the theoretical problem. The above 'proof' of the induction theorem solves both problems.

9. REPLY TO OBJECTIONS

I now consider additional objections to the claim that the above solves the problem of induction.

Objection 1. It may be, if we attend exclusively to physics, that physicalism is more acceptable than any of its rivals. But interpreted as a doctrine about everything that there is, physicalism is untenable. It cannot do justice to biology, and it is incompatible with the existence of consciousness, free will, reason, knowledge, meaning, and value in the world (and thus with physics itself considered as a meaningful discipline embodying knowledge).

Reply. This objection is, in my view, valid.[31] It demands that we reinterpret physicalism so that it becomes a doctrine that is about an *aspect* of everything, namely that aspect which everything has in common with everything else, and which determines (necessarily, but perhaps probabilistically) the way in which all events unfold. Elsewhere I have argued for such a version of physicalism, which I call *experiential physicalism*, according to which the world has many (compatible) aspects, above all (1) the physical, (2) the purposive, and (3) the experiential.[32] Experiential physicalism is the proper version of the comprehensibility thesis to adopt granted the success of natural science, and the nature, the quality, of human life.

Objection 2. In order to solve the problem of induction it is necessary to show that inductive reasoning is valid in all sorts of contexts, and not just in the context of physics. The solution proposed above, being restricted to physics, fails to solve the problem.

Reply. My reply to this objection is that in all contexts, whenever a law or theory is justifiably accepted on the basis of evidence, there are always more general theoretical, metaphysical, or cosmological assumptions lurking in the background justifying the rejection of infinitely many rival, empirically successful, aberrant laws or theories. If the context is practical and non-scientific, the lurking assumptions may be some relevant part of scientific knowledge. If the context is scientific but non-physical (e.g. social, biological, or chemical), the lurking assumptions may be some part of physics. If the context is phenomenological physics, the lurking assumptions will be more fundamental theoretical physics. In all these cases it may be possible to avoid appealing explicitly to the cosmological assumptions at levels 3 to 10 by appealing to some part of established scientific knowledge. It is only when we come to fundamental theoretical physics that this is no longer possible, and we are forced to confront the problem of induction in its naked form. Nevertheless, in *all* contexts, the cosmological assumptions at levels 3 to 10 lurk in the background, whether explicitly appealed to or not. The above solution to the problem of induction is completely general; the discussion has concentrated on theoretical physics because it is here that the problem arises without irrelevant distractions.

Objection 3. None of the above arguments tell against asymptotic physicalism.[33]

Reply. Asymptotic physicalism is a possibility, but it does not help much to take it seriously. And in any case, we are not entirely bereft of indications as to how far, or near, we are to discovering the true theory of everything. There are two questions to consider. First, how comprehensively and accurately do our current theories apply to all known phenomena? Secondly, how unified is our current theoretical knowledge? The better our level 2 theories satisfy these two requirements, the better the indications are that we are close to discovering the true unified theory of everything. In terms of these indications, current theoretical knowledge shows every sign of being very much closer to the true theory of everything than theoretical knowledge around 1900, or around 1930 (which would not be possible if infinitely many theoretical revolutions are required before the true theory of everything can be reached). A few physicists may, incautiously, have expressed the view around 1900 that fundamental developments in theoretical physics were at an end; if so, they should have known better. Theoretical physics at that time had no explanation whatsoever for the properties of matter, for chemistry, or even for such a vital process as the energy being produced by the sun. All this required quantum theory. In 1930 the strong force, responsible for holding the nuclei of atoms together, was a complete mystery. Today, however, three fundamental theories—GR, QEWD, and QCD—apply, in principle, to all ordinary phenomena going on around us; they fail only for such recondite phenomena as the first few instants after the big bang, processes going on inside black holes, and dark matter, responsible (it is believed) for the anomalous rotation of galaxies. We have objective grounds for conjecturing that a theory which successfully *unifies* GR, QEWD, and QCD, and which successfully resolves outstanding cosmological problems, will indeed be the true theory of everything.

Objection 4. Arguments 2 and 3 of step $r = 9$ of the proof of the induction theorem, intended to justify acceptance of non-maliciousness, appeal to the idea that only if phenomena exhibit a certain uniformity or invariance throughout space and time is it possible to acquire knowledge of the nature of the universe. But is this correct? Consider a possible universe that is meta-knowable because all phenomena occur in accordance with a unified (and therefore non-aberrant) theory T; and consider a possible universe which is malicious because phenomena occur in accordance with T^*, some aberrant variant of T. T^* agrees with T within the region of space-time open to our inspection so far, but disagrees with T at some other times and places. Could not a society of aliens hold no doubt somewhat perverse ideas about the nature of the universe, about 'meta-knowability' and 'methodology', such that, in doing science, a succession of characteristically *aberrant* theories, that eventually lead to the development of T^*, are persistently accepted, and non-aberrant variants, that lead to T, remain unformulated as too absurd to consider? In order to discover that the universe is 'meta-knowable', in their perversely aberrant sense of 'meta-knowable', the aliens must reject in an a priori fashion the possibility that the universe is 'epistemologically malicious', in their perverse, aberrant sense (which corresponds to our notion of non-maliciousness and meta-knowability). Is there not complete symmetry here, between *our* arguments for rejecting epistemological maliciousness and the alien's arguments for rejecting epistemological non-maliciousness?

Reply. No. Granted that we and the aliens adopt the same concepts of 'invariance' and 'sameness', we agree that only in the non-malicious universe, in our sense, do laws and necessitating properties remain invariant and the same throughout all of space and time. We agree that the content of the aliens' preferred theory, T^*, changes its form as we move from the region of space and time we have so far experienced to other regions. Whereas our version of non-maliciousness requires that any underlying *something* that determines how events unfold here and now is the same everywhere, being invariant in space and time, the aliens' version of non-maliciousness requires that that which determines how events unfold is *different*, from place to place and time to time. Granted the aliens' notion of non-maliciousness, there are infinitely many different ways in which our knowledge of the here and now may be extended to other times, other places, all equally legitimate and acceptable. Granted our notion of non-maliciousness, in extending our knowledge of the here and now to other times and places we are constrained by the requirement that that which determines how events unfold does *not* vary from time to time, and from place to place.

Objection 5. The above reply to objection 4 presupposes that we and the aliens uphold the same conception of 'the same' or 'the invariant'. But suppose this is not the case. Suppose the aliens' conception is such that T^* is invariant throughout space and time whereas T is not, having a form that changes; whereas for us, of course, exactly the reverse is true. In this case, given any argument that we can construct for favouring T to T^*, there will be an analogous, equally valid argument that the aliens will be able to construct for favouring T^* to T. Hence we can have no rational grounds for favouring invariant to aberrant theories of equal empirical success; we can have no rational grounds for favouring non-maliciousness to maliciousness.[34]

Reply. The level 10 thesis, argued for above, is that the universe is partially knowable *to us*, with respect to *our* system of knowledge containing, implicitly, *our* conception of 'the same' or 'invariant'. Again, in asserting that the universe is meta-knowable we are asserting that it is meta-knowable with respect to *our* pre-existing system of partial knowledge, containing, implicitly, *our* conceptions of 'the same' and 'invariant'. In so far as we have any rationale for extending and improving our pre-existing partial knowledge, this rationale must appeal to notions of 'the same' or 'invariant' that are implicit in *our* pre-existing partial knowledge. In seeking to extend and improve our partial knowledge it is *our* notion of 'meta-knowability' that we must attend to, and not some alien notion. Alien notions suffer from the disadvantage that there are infinitely many of them, all equally viable from a rational standpoint. Taking such notions seriously is equivalent to taking maliciousness seriously: it is equivalent to taking seriously the possibility that anything may occur at any moment.[35]

Objection 6. Strong unity or physicalism, P_4, is not necessary for the above solution to the problem of induction; the argument is even better if strong unity is replaced by weak unity. Granted that this is the case, the argument that strong unity is an item of current scientific knowledge collapses.

Reply. Cosmological theses, at levels 3 to 7, are to be selected on the basis of their potential and actual empirical fruitfulness; on both grounds, strong unity is superior to weak unity. Currently accepted fundamental physical theory, GR + SM, *both* exemplifies physicalism to an extent that is immensely superior to any earlier body of accepted fundamental physical theory *and* is vastly superior in its apparent empirical success. (Before the advent of quantum theory, it must be remembered, the whole of chemistry, the properties of matter, and solid state physics was a complete mystery, there being no hint of a theoretical explanation for this vast range of phenomena.) Physicalism (or strong unity) has thus been quite extraordinarily fruitful empirically (in terms of the notion of 'empirical fruitfulness' defined in step $r = 3$ of the induction theorem).

Weak unity, by comparison, has not been nearly so fruitful empirically. Whereas strong unity asserts that the true theory of everything, T, is fully unified, weak unity asserts merely that T is made up of N distinct, non-aberrant theories (aberrant in senses 1 to 3 of Section 5 of Chapter 3, N being any integer), each theory possibly being extremely complex in character (so that no individual theory belonging to T need be the simplest of its type), the only additional proviso being that the N theories are logically compatible with one another. It is not obvious that the current body of accepted fundamental physical theory,

GR + SM, exemplifies weak unity better than the corresponding body of theory accepted at any earlier time since Newton. Contemporary physical theory has far greater empirical content and success than the body of fundamental physical theory accepted at any earlier time, but to say this is not to say that it exemplifies weak unity better. It needs to be remembered, in addition, that GR + SM does not exemplify weak unity perfectly, even though weak unity is very much less demanding than strong unity. As we have seen, GR and SM are not consistent; in order to be made consistent, their domains of application must be restricted, which means, in effect, that GR and SM become *aberrant* theories, and thus violate weak unity!

Both Galileo's laws of terrestrial motion and Kepler's laws of planetary motion violate weak unity in that the laws refer to special objects (the earth or the sun). By contrast, Newton's laws do not violate weak unity. As far as the step from Galileo and Kepler to Newton is concerned, weak unity is empirically fruitful. It is not clear that it has been so fruitful subsequently, especially when one takes into account that GR + SM actually violates weak unity.

I conclude that strong unity is to be accepted at level 4 and weak unity is to be rejected.

Objection 7. In step $r = 4$ it was argued that, given P_5, the best available level 4 conjecture is P_4. Does this argument really suffice to reject the possibility that the universe is comprehensible because God exists, the material world conforming to physicalism because of the will of God?

Reply. This conjecture deserves to be taken seriously for a number of reasons. It appears to satisfy (i) to (vi) just as well as P_4 does.[36] It had an immense influence on the birth of modern physics in that all those who participated in bringing this birth about believed in some version of the thesis, and this belief influenced their thought, and even their work, in natural philosophy. This is true, for example, of Galileo, Kepler, Descartes, Huygens, and Newton. The 'God' conjecture even solves a problem that P_4 may seem inherently incapable of solving: if God exists, we can understand why the physical universe is comprehensible to us, but if God does not exist, the comprehensibility of the universe may seem to become all but incomprehensible. And finally, billions of people alive today still believe in God, or at least profess to do so, and in many ways the 'God' conjecture remains the official creed of humanity. (It may seem strange for religion to play a role in discussing the rationality of science. Given SE, it is clear why this seems strange. But given AOE, 'God' inevitably becomes a thesis that requires discussion.)

The conjecture that there is a God who is all-knowing, all-powerful, and all-loving is straightforwardly untenable, on *moral* grounds, given elementary facts of human life. If such a God exists, he is in charge of natural phenomena. Hence, whenever a child suffers and dies from natural causes (disease or accident), it is God who tortures and murders the child. Nothing can morally excuse the torturing and murdering of a child. Of course, in the case of God, one could argue that he provides life after death, and hence that murder is not really murder at all. When a child dies in agony of cancer, God is, as it were, performing surgery on the child; the outcome will be arrival in Heaven. But if a human surgeon were to perform such a protracted and painful operation, neglecting to use anaesthetics, we would regard the deed as a criminal one. So should we if the surgeon happens to be God. All traditional theological attempts to find excuses for God's crimes are intellectually and morally disreputable. As long as God is all-powerful and all-knowing, God's actions are unforgivable, and the fundamental religious problem, we might say, is not 'How can God forgive us?', but rather 'How can we forgive God?' The conjecture that an all-powerful, all-knowing, all-loving God exists is refuted by basic facts of human existence.

Despite all this, as I have mentioned, billions of people firmly believe in the existence of a God who is *both* all-powerful and all-loving. This belief is the outcome of our understandable need for that which has supreme power in the universe to be, also, supremely loving. This need arises not just for selfish reasons, such as fear of death, but also for more unselfish ones: God is needed to put right all the unspeakable injustices of this world. Ultimately, however, belief in the existence of an all-powerful, all-loving God is little better than the wishful hope that there should be a big, loving Parent in the sky, to take care of the horrifying aspects of human existence. What needs to be recognized is that, in our world, it is not possible to fuse together cosmic power and love, cosmic power and value; these two aspects of 'God' must be dissociated from one another. God must be split into two parts: the God of power, and the God of love or value.

Put another way, there are just two legitimate excuses for God's crimes: (1) God is all-powerful but incapable of loving because of his utterly *impersonal* nature, which precludes the possibility of knowing, let alone loving; or (2) God is all-loving but powerless; he knows what is going on but is powerless to prevent it. The first solution to the problem leads to the idea that the God of power is Einstein's God, that which determines, utterly impersonally, the way events unfold; it leads, that is, to physicalism. The second solution leads to the idea that the God of love is that which is of most value—most loving—potentially, in us; we see what goes on in the world (to some extent at least), but because of our limited knowledge and power to act, and our limited capacity for loving, we fail to avert human suffering.

Once God has been split into two in this way, into the impersonal, physicalistic God of power, and the human God of value (that which is best, potentially, in us), the problem then becomes how the two transformed parts are to be put together again. How is it possible to have persons, lovable and loving (to some extent at least), in a physicalistic universe? How can the God of value exist within the physicalistic God of power? I attempt to answer this question in Maxwell (1984*a*, ch. 10; forthcoming *b*).

Finally, it may be asked: Is the thesis that the universe is comprehensible an a priori conjecture, or not? According to AOE, the level 10 thesis of partial knowability is upheld as a permanent item of conjectural scientific knowledge on a priori grounds ('a priori', here, meaning merely 'non-empirical'); and the same holds for the level 9 thesis of non-maliciousness (unless there is persistent catastrophic failure to extend knowledge beyond our local world). These cosmological conjectures are required to get the empirical method off the ground. Granted this, the level 5 conjecture of comprehensibility, and the level 4 conjecture of physical comprehensibility, are accepted as being more empirically fruitful than any rival. These latter conjectures are thus accepted on a mixture of a priori and quasi-empirical grounds.

6

Evidence, Progress, and Discovery

1. INTRODUCTION

In this chapter I seek to show that aim-oriented empiricism (AOE) solves the remaining five problems concerning scientific progress which standard empiricism (SE) fails to solve, as we saw in Chapter 2. We begin with:

2. TWO PROBLEMS ABOUT EVIDENCE

As far as physics is concerned, an experimental result, a piece of evidence, has the form of a repeatable, lawlike phenomenon, often of a highly theoretical character. Thus the problem of induction arises at the level of the acceptance of *evidence*, let alone law or theory. SE fails to provide a rationale for accepting such 'evidence', to the extent that it is a more secure part of scientific knowledge than theory. SE fails to solve:

(vi) The problem of the theoretical character of evidence.

This problem vanishes given AOE. For, according to AOE, physicalism is a central, secure tenet of modern scientific knowledge, upheld on quasi-a priori grounds. Physicalism is implicit in all phenomena, and therefore implicit in all experimental phenomena. This justifies characterizing all experimental results as lawlike in character; and this in turn (given conjectural essentialism) justifies characterizing observable phenomena as the outcome of observable objects interacting in accordance with diverse (more or less observable) necessitating properties. Associated with physicalism there are physicalistic *methods*; these apply, not just to laws and theories, but to evidence as well (see Figure 1). Physicalism is a well-established part of scientific knowledge, and so too are carefully verified experimental regularities: what is still obscure is what lies in between: physicalism specified as a precise, true theory of everything, T, plus a detailed account of how this accords with all well-established experimental regularities. Given that discovering this is the basic task of theoretical physics, it is irrelevant to consider unrepeatable occurrences: such things are presumed, on rational grounds, not to occur.

Consider some particular occurrence, O, that happens to be an experiment. O can be described at different levels of universality and precision. At one extreme, there is the description provided by T, the (as yet unknown) true, unified theory of everything: this is completely universal, in that O is depicted as just another example of the universal phenomenon (namely, evolving in accordance with U, as predicted by T). Then there are increasingly *restricted* descriptions, which specify O as a special case of increasingly restricted ranges of phenomena predicted by T. And there are the increasingly inaccurate descriptions, which specify that O occurs in accordance with such-and-such regularities to such-and-such a degree of accuracy (i.e. within such-and-such experimental error). In this way we arrive at experimental (or observational) laws or regularities (or objects with observable, macroscopic necessitating properties). We can be much more confident of the truth of observational laws than we can of those asserted by any physical *theory* because of the vastly increased content of the latter. Knowledge of regularities, at some level of restrictedness and inaccuracy, is necessary for life to be possible at all: even amoebae need such implicit knowledge of aspects of their environment to survive. The art of experimental physics lies in extending the scope, the precision, and the reliability of our grossly restricted, inaccurate, and often unreliable common-sense knowledge of observable regularities, in tandem with advancing theoretical knowledge, so as to restrict, on experimental grounds, the range of theoretical possibilities.

The second problem about evidence is:

(vii) The problem of the rejection of evidence when it clashes with theory.

In scientific practice experimental results are constantly rejected because they clash with current theory (as we saw in Chapter 2). This poses a severe problem for SE since, according to that doctrine, the only grounds for accepting a theory, in the end, is compatibility with evidence.

From the standpoint of AOE, there is no problem. Two kinds of criteria legitimately govern choice of theory: compatibility with (*a*) physicalism and (*b*) experimental results. If a theory and an experimental result clash, this may be because (1) the theory is false, (2) the experiment has not been performed properly, (3) the derivation of the experimental prediction from the theory has not been carried out properly, (4) some other factual or theoretical assumption, used in the derivation, is false. A clash between a theory and experimental result indicates that there is a problem, but does not exclusively dictate that the problem is to be solved by the rejection of the theory. Precisely because there are grounds other than empirical success for accepting theories, clashes between theories and evidence do not automatically require that it is the theories which must give way. As the discussion of problem (vi) made clear, evidence is itself more or less theoretical in character; if it clashes with a good theory it may well be wrong.

3. TWO PROBLEMS ABOUT SCIENTIFIC PROGRESS

The first of the two problems about scientific progress is:

(viii) The problem of the meaning of scientific progress (i.e. the problem of verisimilitude).

This problem arises, it will be remembered, because physics proceeds from one false theory to another, thus rendering obscure what it can mean to say that science makes progress. Popper tried to solve the problem by suggesting that scientific progress, at the level of theory, takes place when successive theories, though all false, are nevertheless gradually approaching the truth in that they have more and more truth-content and/or less and less falsity-content. The problem became severe for (standard empiricist) philosophy of science with the discovery, by Miller and Tichý, that Popper's plausible attempt at a solution does not work.[1]

One point needs to be recognized at the outset: the fact that physics does proceed from one false theory to another, far from undermining physicalism, and hence AOE as well, is actually to be expected, granted physicalism (as I indicated in Chapter 3). For, if a theory, T_0, is precisely true throughout some restricted domain of phenomena D then, granted physicalism, T_0 must specify precisely that which does not change, U, throughout all phenomena in D, and the way U determines how things change in D. But, according to physicalism, U exists unchanged throughout all phenomena; furthermore, its nature or structure is given by the basic *form* of the theory which specifies how U determines change (assuming that appropriate conceptual conventions have been adopted, as indicated in Section 6 of Chapter 4). This means that if T_0 is correct in D, it will be easily possible to extend the interpretation and application of T_0 to *all* phenomena, keeping the *form* of T_0 unchanged, in this way arriving at the ultimately true theory of everything, T. Conversely, if T_0 cannot be extended in this way to apply correctly to all phenomena, then T_0 cannot be precisely true within D: T_0 must be *false*. In brief, physicalism implies that a physical theory can only be precisely true of *anything* if it is (capable of being) precisely true of *everything*.

Granted, then, that physics proceeds, not by attaining T in one bound, but rather by developing a succession of theories that apply, with ever-increasing accuracy, to ever wider ranges of phenomena until eventually a theory of everything is attained, it is inevitable, granted physicalism, that physics will progress by the development of theories that are all *false* throughout their domains of application until the ultimate, unified true theory of everything is attained (which will be precisely true about everything). Since physicalism predicts that physics will progress in this way, the fact that physics has so far thus progressed can only count in favour of physicalism: it cannot count against physicalism and AOE, as some have supposed. (See e.g. Laudan 1980; Newton-Smith 1981.)

There is just one conceivable exception to this argument. It is possible that the form of T (or the nature of U) might be such that T reduces to an especially simple form for an appropriately simple or symmetric kind of system. Thus two spherical bodies of equal mass rotating about the point midway between them exemplify a law much simpler in form than Newtonian theory.[2] In having only what remains of T when it has been reduced to just such an especially simple form for some simple or symmetric system, one would have a *true* theory, but a theory *not* easily extendable to recover T. However, even if such a simplified version of T were to be formulated, it is most unlikely, before the discovery of T, that it would be correctly interpreted to apply only to appropriately symmetric kinds of system. One would need to have T in order to know how to specify correctly systems to which the simplified version of T applies precisely. Interpreted to apply to a broader range of systems, the simplified version of T will not be precisely true.[3]

Given physicalism (and AOE), it is to be expected that physics advances by developing a succession of theories, $T_0, T_1, T_2, \ldots T_n$, which, though all false, and though all mutually incompatible, nevertheless deserve to be regarded as getting progressively closer and closer to the truth, T. But what does it *mean* to speak, here, of $T_0 \ldots T_n$ getting 'progressively closer and closer to the truth'?

AOE solves the problem as follows. $T_0 \ldots T_n$ get 'progressively closer and closer to the truth', T, if and only if: T_n can be 'approximately derived' from T (but not vice versa), T_{n-1} can be 'approximately derived' from T_n (but not vice versa), and so on down to T_0 being 'approximately derivable' from T_1 (but not vice versa).

In order to explicate the key notion, here, of 'approximate derivation' let us consider a special case. Let us take T_0 to be Galileo's version of the heliocentric theory (G), T_1 to be Kepler's laws of planetary motion (KL), T_2 to be Newtonian theory (NT), and T to be Einstein's theory of general relativity (GR). What does it mean to say that NT can be 'approximately derived' from GR, KL can be 'approximately derived' from NT, and G can be 'approximately derived' from KL? Let us take the case (considered briefly in previous chapters) of approximately deriving KL from NT.

This can be done in three steps. *First*, NT is restricted to N body systems interacting by gravitation alone within some definite volume, no two bodies being closer than some given distance r. *Secondly*, keeping the mass of one object constant, we consider the paths followed by the other bodies as their masses tend to zero. According to NT, in the limit, these paths are precisely those specified by KL for planets. In this way we recover the *form* of KL from NT. *Thirdly*, we reinterpret this 'derived' version of KL so that it is now taken to apply to systems like that of our solar system. (It is of course this *third* step of reinterpretation that introduces error: mutual gravitational attraction between planets, and between planets and the sun, ensure that the paths of planets, with masses greater than zero, must diverge, however slightly, from precise Keplerian orbits.)

The approximate derivation of G from KL is even simpler: only two steps are required. *First*, KL is restricted to systems for which the elliptical paths of planets take the form of circles; and *secondly*, this restricted version of KL is then reinterpreted to apply to all systems to which KL applies.

The approximate derivation of NT from GR is, by contrast, somewhat more complicated. *First*, GR is restricted to systems of bodies with mass travelling along geodesics. *Secondly*, we consider the paths of the bodies as relative velocities tend to zero, and the curvature of space-time tends to the limiting case of flat space and time. *Thirdly*, the resulting laws are reinterpreted to apply to bodies of any mass travelling at any relative velocities. In this way, we arrive at an instrumentalistic mimic of NT which asserts (in effect): bodies move *as if* there is a force of gravitation such that $F = ma$ and $F = Gm_1m_2/d^2$. According to GR, there is no force of gravitation; there is, rather, space-time that is curved by the presence of mass, or energy-density. Massive bodies travel along geodesics in this curved space-time, a geodesic being the equivalent of a straight line in curved space. The force of gravitation has disappeared. Since GR makes no reference to force, it is not possible to derive from GR a version of NT that asserts that the force of gravitation exists. It is possible, however, to derive a version of NT that makes precisely the same predictions as NT, which is all that we require. (For details, see Schutz 1989: 205–8 or Rohrlich 1989.)

Quite generally, we can say that T_{r-1} is 'approximately derivable' from T_r if and only if a theory empirically equivalent to T_{r-1} can be extracted from T_r by taking finitely many steps of the above type, involving (*a*) restricting the range of application of a theory, (*b*) allowing some combination of variables of a theory to tend to zero, and (*c*) reinterpreting a theory so that it applies to a wider range of phenomena.

This solution to the problem of what progress in theoretical physics *means* requires AOE to be presupposed; it does not work if SE is presupposed. This is because the solution requires one to assume (*a*) that the universe is such that a yet-to-be-discovered true theory of everything, T, exists, and (*b*) current theoretical knowledge can be approximately derived from T. Both assumptions, (*a*) and (*b*), are justified granted AOE; neither assumption is justifiable granted SE.

In one important respect, the above solution to the problem is unsatisfactory. If a series of theories, $T_0 \ldots T_n$, progressively approaches the truth, T, then, as we move from T_0 to T_n, more and more of the *form* of T will be captured by the successive theories. This justifies regarding $T_0 \ldots T_n$ as constituting improving theoretical knowledge of the nature of the basic dynamic structure of the universe. Nevertheless, $T_0 \ldots T_n$ are all false. We do not have progress in knowledge in the sense of a progressive capturing of more and more empirical truth.

We can, however, define a notion of 'empirical progress' granted the above notion of 'theoretical progress'. If $T_0 \ldots T_n$ constitutes theoretical progress towards T in the above sense then, corresponding to each T_r, there will be an approximate version of the theory, T^*_r, which will be *true*. Furthermore, $T \to T^*_n \to \ldots \to T^*_0$. The existence of the approximate, *true* theories $T^*_0 \ldots T^*_n$, associated with the precise, *false* theories $T_0 \ldots T_n$, enables us to interpret the latter series of theories as embodying progressively improving knowledge of the truth, T.

Consider the following example. For the sake of illustration, let us take NT as the truth, T, and let us consider KL*, the approximate version of KL, derivable from NT and, for the purposes of illustration, to be regarded as 'true'. KL* can be arrived at as follows.

As before, we consider only Newtonian systems that consist of N bodies interacting by gravitation alone within some definite volume, no two bodies being closer than some given distance r. Given the initial state of the system at time t_0, then at any time $t > t_0$, the state of the system as predicted by NT will diverge somewhat from the state predicted by KL. Let this divergence $d(t)$ at any instant t be the maximum distance between what NT predicts for any object of the system, and what KL predicts for that object. (We can put the origin of our reference frame at the centre of mass of the whole system.) There are now two possibilities to consider, the time-independent case, and the time-dependent case.

The time-independent case. We suppose that, for appropriately restricted systems, NT tends to KL in a time-independent way, as the masses of the planet-like objects tend to zero. That is, given $\delta > 0$, there exists $\delta m > 0$ such that, for all systems of the specified type with masses of each planet $< \delta m$, the predictions of NT diverge from those of KL by an amount $d(t) \leq \delta$ for all subsequent times.

Given this, we can formulate KL* to assert: 'For systems appropriately restricted, and further restricted by the requirement that the mass of each planet-like object $< \delta m$, the paths of the planets diverge from Keplerian orbits by no more than δ'. This is logically entailed by NT. If NT is true, so is KL*.

We may have set things up so that δm is very much smaller than the masses of actual planets. By demanding that r, the minimum distance between objects, is sufficiently increased, we can always arrange for δm to be increased by as much as we please. In order to ensure that the planet-like objects do not diverge from KL orbits by more than the given amount δ, we must ensure that these objects do not exert gravitational forces on each other, and on the sunlike object, by more than a certain amount. Given $F = Gm_1m_2/d^2$, we can arrange for this, either by having a sufficiently small δm or, where δm is large, by having a correspondingly large mass for the sunlike object, and ensuring that the minimum distance between the objects is sufficiently large.

The time-dependent case. It may be that NT tends to KL in only the following time-dependent sense: Given $\delta > 0$, and given $t_1 > t_0$, there exists $\delta m > 0$ such that, for all systems of the specified type with masses of each planet $< \delta m$, the predictions of NT diverge from those of KL by an amount $d(t) \leq \delta$ for all times t for which $t_0 \leq t < t_1$. In this case KL* must be formulated in a *time-restricted* manner, if KL* is to be logically entailed by NT.

The points just made concerning NT, KL, and KL* can be made, I suggest, quite generally. Whenever, within the physicalist programme of physics, an explanatory, empirically successful theory T_0 is superseded by a theory T_1 (so that T_1 has greater explanatory power, empirical content, and success than T_0, and is able to explain the partial empirical success of T_0), then T_0 can be 'approximately derived' from T_1 by means of steps analogous to the three steps involved in 'approximately deriving' KL from NT. Furthermore, this enables us to define T^*_0, an approximate version of T_0, which is logically entailed by T_1, even though T_0 is incompatible with T_1.

We have good reasons, I believe, to hold that these general points are true. Whenever a new theory, T_1, is proposed in physics, it is standard procedure to show how relevant pre-existing more limited laws and theories, T_0, can be 'derived' as approximations from the new theory. Strictly speaking, all such 'approximate derivations' are invalid, in so far as T_0 is incompatible with T_1. What entitles us to regard such 'derivations' as valid is that it is always an easy (if tedious) matter to reformulate the derivation so that T_1 logically implies some T^*_0 (some approximate version of T_0). In practice, physicists may not bother to transform invalid 'approximate derivations' into valid derivations of approximate laws and theories in this way, not because it is too difficult, but because it is too pedantic. (Experimental results, however, as we have seen, are recorded as approximate laws.) We have every reason, in short, to hold that the above remarks concerning GR, NT, KL, KL*, and G can be generalized to apply to *all* cases where one theory, T_0, can be 'approximately derived', as a limiting case, from another theory, T_1.

It is worth noting just how ubiquitous 'approximate derivations' of the above type are in physics. When empirical predictions are derived from a physical theory approximations are very frequently made during the course of the derivation. Higher-order terms in some expansion are set to zero; complicated expressions reduce to simple ones as a result of the neglect of effects deemed to be sufficiently minute. All such 'approximate derivations', to be found everywhere in physics, are logically invalid in just the same way in which the derivations of KL from NT, and NT from GR, are invalid. It is legitimate to regard such 'derivations' as valid in so far as it is an easy, if pedantic, matter to turn them into valid derivations by replacing the precise conclusion with an approximate one. None of this ought to seem problematic to anyone with any first-hand familiarity with physics.

This concludes my discussion of what it means to say of a series of false, mutually incompatible theories, $T_0 \ldots T_n$, that it constitutes 'theoretical progress' towards T, and 'empirical progress' with respect to T.

I turn now to a consideration of:

(ix) The problem of progress in knowledge about the nature of fundamental physical entities.

This problem arises because the history of physics reveals a number of dramatic changes in ideas about the nature of fundamental physical entities which does not seem to be compatible with steady progress in knowledge. As we have seen, fundamental physical entities have been believed to be, in turn: small, rigid corpuscles that interact only by contact; point-particles that interact at a distance; a rigid, quasi-materialistic stuff spread throughout all of space (the ether); a continuously varying field spread throughout space within which point-particles are embedded; a self-interacting field; curved space-time; probabilistic quantum objects; quantum fields; superstrings. How can these changing ideas be construed to be progress in knowledge?

I have three points to make.

1. At first sight the ideas just indicated about the nature of fundamental physical entities appear to form a random sequence of notions, each idea unrelated to its predecessor or successor. But this is not the case; as we have seen, each idea arises from its predecessor as a result of a process of generalization (Chapter 3, Section 4, and Chapter 4, Section 17).

2. Granted AOE, progress in theoretical physics consists in a more and more complete and accurate delineation of U, the *something* that is implicit in all phenomena and determines the way things change. Progress in theoretical physics is to be assessed in terms of the *unity* and *predictive power* (or empirical content) of the basic theories of physics— granted that increasing theoretical unity specifies, with increasing completeness and precision, the nature of U. Looked at in this AOE way, the history of theoretical physics, as it has actually occurred, can be viewed as an increasingly complete and precise specification of some unified U implicit in all change. The transition from particle to field suggests that U is 'field-like' in character. GR suggests that *space-time* on the one hand, and *energy-density* (roughly *matter*) are unified in U: the reduction of the force of gravity to a geometrical feature of space-time, namely curvature, achieved by GR, suggests that *all* forces can be

reduced in this way to geometrical or topological features of space-time. Quantum field theory (QFT) leads to a further unification of *space-time* and *matter* for, according to QFT, the vacuum seethes with matter, or at least potential matter in the form of virtual particle–antiparticle pairs of every species. In a sense, from the standpoint of QFT, the universe *is* the vacuum, in various states of excitation. In addition to this, QFT can be regarded as ascribing different instanton states to the vacuum when in its lowest energy state; and furthermore, versions of QFT can be regarded as attributing different states to the vacuum in a holistic fashion, as a result of symmetry-breaking associated with the evolution of the cosmos. In these diverse ways, QFT contributes to the progressive unification of *space-time* and *matter* discernible throughout the evolution of theoretical physics since Newton.

More generally, the history of theoretical physics is, above all, the history of increasing theoretical unity throughout an increasing range of diverse phenomena, so much so that (almost) all known phenomena can be brought within the compass of two theories: GR and the standard model (SM). Judged from an AOE standpoint, all this is just what one would expect to find granted that physics is making progress in discovering the nature of U, the unified structure of the universe.

3. The ideas developed above to solve the problem of verisimilitude can be used to make sense of the idea that successive theories of physics, even though mutually incompatible and all false, nevertheless provide an increasingly accurate delineation of the nature of U. Let $T_0 \ldots T_n$ be a series of false, mutually incompatible theories constituting theoretical progress towards the truth T; and let $T^*_0 \ldots T^*_n$ be the associated true, approximate theories constituting empirical progress with respect to T. Granted that $T_0 \ldots T_n$ can be interpreted realistically, as postulating the existence of physical entities $E_1 \ldots E_n$, then $T^*_0 \ldots T^*_n$ can be interpreted as postulating entities approximately characterized as $E^*_1 \ldots E^*_n$. The *truth* of $T^*_1 \ldots T^*_n$ guarantees the *existence* of $E^*_1 \ldots E^*_n$. What exists is U approximately but correctly characterized as $E^*_1 \ldots E^*_n$).

As an example of the distinction, appealed to here, between the entities of a precise and an imprecise theory, consider entities corresponding to the following precise and imprecise versions of NT (NT and NT*).

(NT) Entities are point-particles possessing *precise* Newtonian gravitational charge in the sense that the particles obey precisely $F = ma$, where $F = Gm_1m_2/d^2$.

(NT*) Entities are such that, for states of affairs that satisfy such-and-such restrictions, centres of mass in inertial frames of reference obey $F = ma$, where $F = Gm_1m_2/d^2$, to such-and-such a degree of approximation.

As long as NT* has been made sufficiently restricted and approximate to be true (the truth here being T), then the characteristics that NT* attributes to the entities it postulates will indeed be properties of U.

To give another example, suppose that T_0 is atomic theory with atoms interpreted to be 'corpuscles'—entities that are indestructible and without internal parts; suppose further that T_1 is the Rutherford–Bohr theory of atoms. Here T_0 and T_1 are incompatible. If all that exists is atoms, E_1, in the sense of T_1, then corpuscles, E_0, in the sense of T_0, do not exist. Given T_0 and T_1, we can define T^*_0, compatible with (and indeed derivable from) T_1, where T^*_0 asserts merely that postulated physical entities, E^*_0, are such that they behave *approximately as if* they are corpuscles that are indestructible and without internal parts in such-and-such restricted conditions. Here T^*_0 can be derived from T_1 by restricting the domain of T_1 to systems of atoms that interact at sufficiently low energies for the atoms to remain in the ground states. In this domain, the atoms, E_1, of T_1 do have the features which T^*_0 attributes to E^*_0. If Rutherford–Bohr atoms exist, then so too do E^*_0-type atoms, entities approximately characterized by T^*_0.

All this enables us to interpret a series of theories, $T_0 \ldots T_n$, constituting theoretical progress towards T, as providing increasingly precise, true characterizations of the nature of U, which is precisely characterized by T.

4. A PROBLEM CONCERNING SCIENTIFIC DISCOVERY

According to SE, scientific knowledge and understanding of the nature of the universe extend as far as our best scientific theories, and then abruptly stop. The ultimate nature of the universe is unknown. It is thus, from the standpoint of SE, utterly baffling how theoretical physicists, faced with the total unknown, are nevertheless able to put forward conjectures which, every now and again, turn out to contain a wealth of incredibly accurate predictive content. The mystery deepens when one takes into account the point (much emphasized above) that fundamental theoretical advances almost always seem to involve putting forward theories which *conflict* with existing theories, for this means that existing theories cannot be used straightforwardly as a guide towards new and better theories. And things become even more baffling when one considers those cases where mathematicians, not even thinking about physics, have come up with new mathematical ideas that subsequently turn out to be just what is required to describe theoretically a range of physical phenomena.[4] In some inexplicable way, there seems to be a pre-established harmony between the ultimate nature of the universe and the minds of mathematicians. This would be intelligible if a mathematically inclined God had created both the universe and human beings. Without God, the whole thing becomes a profound mystery. In brief, SE fails to solve:

(x) The problem of scientific discovery.

According to AOE, by contrast, science has already made a substantial discovery about the ultimate nature of reality: the universe is physically comprehensible in some way or other. Furthermore, current theoretical knowledge in physics constitutes partial, approximate glimpses of the kind of unified dynamic structure inherent in the physical universe. The task of creating new, better theories does not proceed in a vacuum. Definite guidelines exist for the creation of new theories. There are level 3 blueprint ideas which amount to embryonic theories: good new theories emerge as a result of modifying slightly one or other of these blueprint ideas, and formulating it more precisely so that it becomes a testable theory. There are definite problems for the theoretical physicist to try to solve, namely clashes between ideas at levels 2, 3, and 4: resolving such clashes leads to the development of new blueprint ideas which, when made more precise, become testable theories. In excluding levels 3, 4, and 5 from science, SE turns the process of discovery into a profound mystery (just as it does for the process of acceptance of theories). Including levels 3, 4, and 5 within the intellectual domain of science enables us to make sense of the process of discovery; it provides a rational, if fallible and non-mechanical, method of discovery. If we restrict scientific knowledge to levels 1 and 2, it is not easy to see how there can be a rational path from Galileo to Newton, and from Newton to Einstein, given that Newton's theory contradicts Galileo's, and Einstein's contradicts Newton's. Include levels 3, 4, and 5, however, and at once it becomes possible to depict knowledge that persists unchanged throughout such revolutionary theoretical developments, namely the level 5 and 4 knowledge that the universe is comprehensible in some way and, more particularly, *physically* comprehensible; and furthermore, within this unchanging, persisting framework of metaphysics and methodology, it becomes possible to depict the progressively *evolving* level 3 blueprint ideas which, when made precise, become new testable theories. In short, AOE provides physicists with a rational, if fallible and non-mechanical, method for the discovery of fundamental new theories in physics.

It is true that most physicists have accepted SE rather than AOE. As I have indicated, this has served to retard the development of good new theories in physics. Fortunately, enough good theoretical physicists have adopted SE in a sufficiently hypocritical fashion to make it possible for them to exploit the rational method of discovery of AOE in scientific practice. Here, as elsewhere, actual science is the outcome of AOE being implemented in scientific practice in a somewhat unsatisfactory manner as a result of the widespread, misplaced conviction that science ought to proceed in accordance with SE.

AOE can also make sense of the apparently amazing fact that pure mathematicians are able, on occasions, to invent mathematical ideas that turn out subsequently to be just what is required to describe a new range of physical phenomena. According to AOE, it is a part of current scientific knowledge that the universe is such that some unified physical theory, T, is the true theory of everything. Furthermore, according to AOE, current physical theories, in so far as they are a part of scientific knowledge, are 'approximately derivable' from T, in the sort of way described above. As a result of letting some combination of variables of T tend to zero, T reduces to an especially simple form, e.g. to GR, QEWD, or QCD, just as GR reduces to the form of NT, and NT, in turn, reduces to KL. It is this process of simplification that must be reversed if theoretical physics is to move closer to T. Some physical feature of things that is presumed not to vary must be depicted as varying, in some fixed way, with the variation of some other feature, if physics is to draw closer to T. The constant acceleration of Galileo's law of free fall needs to be depicted as varying, with the variation of some other feature (such as distance from the centre of gravity of the earth). The constant mass of a body within NT must be depicted as varying with varying velocity, to do justice to phenomena predicted by SR. The fixed, flat character of Euclidean space must be depicted as having curvature that varies, in a fixed way, with variations of energy-density, if justice is to be done to phenomena predicted by GR. And so on.

This process of 'simplification reversal' (as it might be called) almost always requires a profound generalization of mathematical ideas. Thus the move from KL and G to NT required a profound generalization in mathematical ideas available to Kepler and Galileo; it required the invention of coordinate geometry and the differential calculus. The transition from NT to classical electrodynamics required that the mathematical theory of ordinary differential equations be generalized to form the theory of partial differential equations. The transition from NT to GR required that Euclidean geometry be generalized to form Riemannian geometry. It is inherent in the very idea of 'simplification reversal' that mathematical generalization is required. (Sometimes the generalization that is required is, in a sense, mathematically trivial but physically and conceptually profound, as in the case of the transition from Newtonian mechanics to SR.)

If research in theoretical physics were to implement AOE in an explicit and thoroughgoing way, the process of mathematical generalization relevant to physics would be under rational, if fallible, control. It would involve modifying and generalizing existing level 3 blueprint ideas in the direction of new unified blueprints for physics, designed to resolve clashes between existing theories and blueprints. The process of developing new *metaphysical* ideas for physics would involve, at one and the same time, the process of developing new *mathematical* ideas and techniques. There would be no profound *mystery* about how new successful fundamental physical theories are developed; various possible unified dynamical structures would be tried out that modify or generalize pre-existing ideas, until one such possibility leads to a testable theory which correctly predicts a wealth of new phenomena.

All this is rendered obscure by the general acceptance of SE by the scientific community. For, whereas AOE emphasizes the vital role that *metaphysical* ideas and problems play in physics, in both contexts of justification and discovery, SE excludes metaphysical ideas from the public, intellectual domain of scientific knowledge. This means that the activity of articulating, critically assessing, modifying, and developing level 3 blueprint ideas, all vital for the development of new fundamental physical theories, cannot proceed within the public domain of science. It is carried on privately by interested physicists and mathematicians until either new physics or new mathematics emerges. The key unit, the *metaphysical blueprint*, somewhat disappears from view—although it is implicit in conservation and symmetry principles, and in the basic concepts of theoretical physics, having to do with such things as space, time, force, particle, field, energy, momentum, mass, charge.

The result is that the development of new fundamental theories is much more enigmatic a process than it need be. What most needs to be in view to make sense of things—namely level 3 blueprint ideas evolving in response to evolving blueprint problems—is suppressed; interested individuals think about such matters privately and come up either with new mathematics or with new testable physical theories, which may then be further developed by other mathematicians and physicists. On occasions, new mathematical discoveries, developed in this way, turn out to be just what is needed for some subsequent new theory of physics. With the evolving blueprint ideas and problems in view that are associated with the mathematical and physical developments, it would be entirely understandable, in retrospect, how and why the new mathematics led to the new physics. For this would be a case of blueprint ideas evolving in response to problems, giving rise to new mathematics with which to formulate new physical theories in terms of the new blueprint ideas. It is the *suppression* of level 3 blueprint ideas and problems within science, as a result of general acceptance of SE, which obliterates the rational link between mathematics and physics. The task of developing new mathematics relevant for new physics, instead of being under rational (if fallible) AOE guidance, becomes a more spasmodic and arational, even irrational affair, good mathematical and physical ideas emerging inexplicably, the development of mathematics sometimes mysteriously anticipating the course of subsequent physics. Putting AOE into practice changes this part of mathematics and theoretical physics sufficiently to dispel these somewhat spurious, unnecessary mysteries.

This concludes my argument in support of the claim that AOE solves the ten outstanding problems in the philosophy of science which SE fails to solve.

5. IS AIM-ORIENTED EMPIRICISM REQUIRED FOR THE SOLUTION TO THE TEN PROBLEMS?

A loophole remains in the above defence of AOE. It remains possible that a doctrine, stronger than SE but weaker than AOE, solves all ten problems, and is thus to be preferred to AOE. What doctrines are there that might fit this role? What are the grounds for preferring AOE?

I assume in what follows that the arguments so far provide overwhelming grounds for construing science as making a hierarchy of increasingly contentless cosmological assumptions concerning the (partial) knowability of the universe. What is in doubt is that these assumptions need to be as contentful as those of AOE in order to solve our ten problems. We need to consider, in short, generalized AOE, introduced towards the end of Section 6 of Chapter 3. This asserts that science makes some hierarchy of increasingly contentless cosmological assumptions concerning the knowability of the universe, but does *not* commit science to the specific assumptions of AOE.

Generalized AOE may, of course, be rejected. But rivals to AOE which do not exploit generalized AOE are easy to refute. Generalized AOE is too good an option to be neglected by those who oppose AOE.

What potentially viable versions of generalized AOE are there, that might be better options than AOE? The following may be considered.

0. *Instrumentalistic AOE.* At level 4, instead of physicalism, there is the assumption that locally the universe behaves as if comprehensible sufficiently approximately for natural science to continue to meet with apparent empirical success. Appropriate modifications are then made to the assumptions of AOE at levels 5 to 9.

1. *Weak (1) AOE.* At level 4 the universe is assumed to be non-aberrant in sense 1 of Section 5 of Chapter 3, assumptions of AOE at other levels being appropriately weakened.

2 to 7. *Weak (2) AOE to weak (7) AOE.* At level 4 the universe is assumed to be non-aberrant, or weakly unified, in senses 2 to 7 of Section 5 of Chapter 3, assumptions of AOE at other levels being appropriately weakened, as before.

(*a*) to (*t*) *Weak (a) AOE to weak (t) AOE.* At level 4, instead of physicalism, the twenty rivals to physicalism, (*a*) to (*t*), are assumed in turn, listed in Section 3 of Chapter 5, appropriate modifications being made to assumptions of AOE at other levels, as before.

In Section 16 of Chapter 4 I argued that simplicity, in the non-generic sense, forms an important part of what we should mean by 'physical comprehensibility', in addition to unity. All the above may be regarded as building simplicity, in this sense, into their diverse level 4 assumptions. This means that, corresponding to each of the above, there is an even weaker version of weak AOE which makes no assumption about non-generic simplicity at level 4. We have: (*a**) to (*t**). As above, from (*a*) to (*t*), except that in each case the level 4 thesis makes no assumption about (non-generic) simplicity, assumptions at other levels being weakened where appropriate.

Do any of these versions of weak AOE solve our ten problems as successfully as (strong) AOE does? I consider the ten problems in turn, in the order in which they have been tackled, from Chapter 4 onwards.

In Chapter 4 I argued at length that physicalism is implicit in simplicity criteria as these in fact operate in theoretical physics. Some (but by no means all) of the above versions of weak AOE, that incorporate a level 4 thesis weaker than physicalism but which mimics physicalism to some extent, can do justice to the apparent empirical success of physics so far; it may therefore be argued that these versions of weak AOE also contain accounts of what simplicity is, that can do justice to scientific practice. But in each case, the relevant level 4 thesis differs, at some point, from physicalism; it is at this point that the corresponding version of weak AOE fails to do justice to simplicity criteria as these operate in theoretical physics up to the present. It is quite conceivable that non-empirical criteria governing theory choice in physics will change in the future to such an extent that the account of simplicity expounded in Chapter 4 is no longer applicable. Physicalism may be false. But the result would be the abandonment of the present notion of simplicity.

There is one exception to this: asymptotic physicalism (q). But (q) does not, in a sense, deny physicalism; it merely asserts that infinitely many theoretical revolutions are needed before it can be known.

I conclude that, with this reservation, AOE is both sufficient *and* necessary for the solution to problem (iv), the problem of what simplicity is. (This conclusion applies also to problem (iii), the methodological problem of induction.)

In Chapter 5 I gave a number of arguments designed to establish that various rivals to physicalism fail to solve the problems of induction, (i) and (ii). I shall not repeat those arguments here, but confine myself to one point.

In Section 5 of Chapter 5 I put forward seven criteria for assessing the acceptability of theses at levels 3 to 10. Criterion (vii) asserts (in an appropriately qualified way) that, other things being equal, that thesis is to be preferred which has associated with it methods which do not change during the evolution of knowledge. This is a kind of principle of non-maliciousness. Whereas thesis 9 of AOE asserts that there exists something locally that makes local knowledge possible which can be presumed to be extended throughout space and time, criterion (vii) asserts, in effect, that there is a cosmological assumption, at some level, that has associated with it methods that have met with success so far, that can be extended unchanged throughout all future theoretical revolutions. Thesis 9 might be characterized as non-maliciousness in breadth, criterion (vii) as non-maliciousness in depth. As we move out from recent times near the surface of the earth to other times, other places, such as outer space, the centre of the sun, or long ago, milliseconds after the big bang, phenomena become utterly unlike anything occurring here and now; and yet, according to thesis 9, an aspect of things that determines the way events unfold is the same. Somewhat analogously, as we probe deeper into the nature of physical reality, with each theoretical revolution in physics, phenomena appear to change dramatically; and yet, according to criterion (vii), at some level cosmological assumptions persist unchanged throughout the theoretical revolutions. *In seeking to improve knowledge we are justified in assuming that the differences, in both cases, are as minimal and low-level as the facts allow.* In particular, we are justified in rejecting hypotheses that gratuitously exaggerate differences. In the case of non-maliciousness in depth, this means that we should adopt theses which assert no change at as low a level in the hierarchy of cosmological assumptions as possible. We are justified in adopting this edict because, in doing so, we give ourselves the best chance of improving knowledge of factual truth. Physicalism, and AOE, accord with this edict. Most rivals to physicalism, and the corresponding versions of weak AOE that are rivals to AOE, violate the edict, and are justifiably rejected on that account. Both forms of non-maliciousness amount to assuming, at least as a working hypothesis, that the universe is as knowable as experience seems to allow.

On the basis of this consideration, and the arguments of Chapter 5, I conclude that AOE is both sufficient *and* necessary to solve the problems of induction, (i) and (ii). (This conclusion applies also to problem (v), the justificational problem of simplicity.)

In order to solve the two problems concerning evidence, (vi) and (vii), it is not necessary to assume that physicalism is true; it would suffice, I suggest, to assume that the universe is non-aberrant in senses 1, 2, and 3 of Section 5 of Chapter 3. This is just as well. It is clearly desirable that the empirical method is not committed, from the outset, to the truth of physicalism. Some kind of empirical method could survive, indeed, even if senses 1, 2, and 3 were both rejected and false, as long as other cosmological assumptions could be made concerning the (partial) knowability and comprehensibility of the universe. If no such assumptions are made, then any kind of empirical method does indeed collapse, as we saw in Chapter 2.

A somewhat similar point needs to be made concerning problem (viii), the problem of verisimilitude. If physicalism is necessary for the solution to the problem, then it becomes meaningless to assert that physics is progressively improving theoretical knowledge if physicalism happens to be false. It will be impossible to discover, in this way, that physicalism is false (if it is). However, the solution to the problem, set out in Section 3 above, appears to be just as valid if we relax the demand that the true theory of everything, T, is a special case of physicalism and demand, instead, merely that T is a special case of non-aberrance or weak unity, in senses 1 and 2 of Section 5 of Chapter 3. AOE suffices to solve the problem, but is not necessary for the solution.

In a somewhat analogous way, and with some further qualifications, the above solution to problem (ix), the problem of improving knowledge of theoretical entities, may be adapted so that it presupposes weak unity, in senses 1 and 2, but does not presuppose physicalism. (The qualifications arise because, granted merely that the universe is non-aberrant in senses 1 and 2, we may progressively improve our knowledge of the nature of theoretical entities in our locality in complete ignorance of endlessly many kinds of entities that exist elsewhere, an issue that does not arise granted physicalism.)

Finally, the above solution to problem (x), the problem of theoretical discovery, requires that the true theory of everything, T, is such that it is at least as unified as SM + GR, if not more so, but does not require that it exemplifies physicalism.

I conclude that AOE suffices to solve problems (i) to (x), but is necessary only for the solution to problems (i) to (v). Versions of weak AOE suffice to solve (vi) to (x). The case for preferring AOE to any version of weak AOE is very powerful indeed, given especially the astonishing success apparently achieved by natural science in progressively discovering dynamic unity in Nature.

7

Quantum Theory

1. WHY ORTHODOX QUANTUM THEORY POSES A CHALLENGE FOR AIM-ORIENTED EMPIRICISM

There are four ways in which quantum theory (QT) poses a challenge for aim-oriented empiricism (AOE).[1]

QT, given its orthodox interpretation (OQT), dominates modern theoretical physics; apart from general relativity, it pervades the whole of theoretical physics at the fundamental level. It is an astonishingly successful theory empirically. The wealth, diversity, and accuracy of its empirical predictions are unprecedented in the history of physics: and there are no serious experimental refutations. Judged from the standpoint of standard empiricism (SE), it must be deemed to be as firmly established as a theory can be in physics. But viewed from the standpoint of AOE, the following points need to be made.

1. Notoriously, the quantum domain, as depicted by OQT, is bafflingly incomprehensible. The central mystery concerns the nature of quantum entities, electrons, photons, atoms. Any such entity appears to be both spread out in space smoothly in a wave-like way *and* confined to a point in space as a particle (see Appendix). How can one and the same entity be *both* wave *and* particle?[2] And there are other mysteries as well: given an *N*-particle system, the quantum state of the system needs to be specified in a 3*N*-dimensional space—so-called configuration space. And there is the notorious non-local character of the quantum domain (see Appendix).

All this might almost be said to *refute* AOE. The great lesson to be learned from QT, it seems, is that the universe is *not* comprehensible! In order to make progress in acquiring knowledge of the quantum domain, physicists were obliged, it seems, to abandon the attempt to explain and understand, and rest content with a formalism (that of OQT) which predicts the results of experiments with incredible accuracy, but leaves the quantum world incomprehensible. The very title of this book is mocked by the sheer incomprehensibility of the universe, as depicted by OQT!

2. According to AOE, if a theory is to be acceptable, it is not enough that it meets with great empirical success; it must also accord sufficiently well with physicalism. But this in turn means that the theory must meet some minimum standard in rendering the phenomena with which it deals as comprehensible. We have just seen that OQT fails dismally in this respect: AOE must declare OQT to be unacceptable, despite its immense empirical success.

3. There are even stronger grounds for declaring OQT to be unacceptable, granted AOE. OQT is seriously *ad hoc*, even aberrant in the sense discussed in Chapter 2. As a result of failing to solve the wave/particle problem, OQT cannot interpret the ψ-function as specifying the actual physical states of quantum systems such as electrons or atoms; instead the ψ-function must be interpreted as containing probabilistic information about the results of performing measurements on quantum systems. This means, as we shall see below, that OQT consists of two conceptually incoherent parts, quantum postulates (QP), and some part of classical physics (CP), for a description of measurement. QP and CP are incompatible with one another; QP + CP is only rendered consistent by arbitrarily restricting CP to the measurement process, and QP to processes that do not constitute measurement: the result is that OQT is as *ad hoc*, as aberrant, as any of the aberrant theories considered in Chapter 2.[3]

From the standpoint of AOE, then, OQT ought definitely to be rejected, despite its immense empirical success. Indeed, according to the argument of Chapter 2, OQT ought to be rejected whatever methodology one adopts, SE or AOE. Can this be correct?

4. OQT throws down another kind of challenge to AOE. Unlike SE, AOE provides a rational (even though fallible and non-mechanical) method for the discovery of new fundamental theories. This involves developing new blueprint ideas that solve pre-existing blueprint problems, and then giving such ideas more precision until they become precise, testable physical theories. But OQT lacks a coherent blueprint, a coherent quantum ontology, as we have seen; it is this that renders OQT problematic. At once we have the following challenge: if AOE is taken seriously, not only does this mean that OQT is unacceptable (and hence empirically *false* in some as yet undiscovered way), but furthermore, AOE ought to provide the means for developing a better version of QT, based on a comprehensible blueprint, a version that solves the wave/particle dilemma, depicts the quantum domain as comprehensible, and successfully predicts phenomena that OQT fails to predict.

At this point I should perhaps confess that ever since I first thought up AOE around 1970 I have been struggling with the problem of developing a version of QT that accords with AOE.[4] At first I thought that it would be a relatively easy matter to develop a non-aberrant, comprehensible version of QT, with its own (consistent) quantum ontology. Such a theory had not been developed, I thought, not because the task is difficult, but rather because the need to develop such a theory had been overlooked. I am now rather more inclined to suppose that the task is difficult—although the painful slowness of my own efforts over a twenty-five-year period probably owes more to my incompetence as a theoretical physicist than to the inherent difficulty of the problem. Gradually, during this period, I have developed a version of QT which has the merit of being a possible solution to the problem, not obviously wrong, that is simple, testable (in principle), and has its roots in the origins of QT.

When I began work on the task of developing an acceptable version of QT, the subject was taboo; after my first publication I was severely ticked off by two physicists for meddling with a subject I did not understand.[5] Since then, a few physicists have, independently, had ideas somewhat similar to the one I was so laboriously developing;[6] and since the contribution of Ghirardi, Rimini, and Weber (1986), strongly endorsed by John Bell (1987, ch. 22), the general approach has become almost fashionable (but my particular version of the idea has not).

In what follows I put forward my proposal as to how the key wave/particle problem is to be solved. I make this precise to form a new version of QT with its own comprehensible quantum ontology; I indicate that this version is, in a sense, not new in that it can be traced right back to the origins of QT; and I show how this version of QT captures all the empirical success of OQT, but nevertheless yields predictions different from OQT for as yet unperformed experiments. Much of what I have to say is relevant to QT in general, and is not tied to the particular version of QT that I wish to defend; this I make clear in the conclusion.

2. SIX DEFECTS OF ORTHODOX QUANTUM THEORY THAT RESULT FROM THE FAILURE TO SOLVE THE WAVE/PARTICLE PROBLEM

Before I set about solving the wave/particle problem, there is a preliminary issue that must be addressed. Above I argued that, granted SE,

OQT would seem to be eminently acceptable (given the immense empirical success of the theory), but unacceptable granted AOE. OQT and AOE are almost incompatible. Does not this speak against AOE and for SE?

My answer is: No. As a direct result of failing to meet the standards of AOE, OQT is seriously defective in a way which even a proponent of SE ought to recognize. More specifically, as a result of failing to solve the wave/particle problem, and thus of failing to provide a consistent quantum ontology,[7] OQT suffers from the following six defects, not perhaps at once obvious, but which even the most ardent advocate of SE ought to acknowledge as serious.[8] The fact that AOE highlights, and SE obscures, the defective character of OQT speaks in favour of AOE, and against SE.

(i) *OQT is* ad hoc *to an extent that must be unacceptable even to the most ardent proponent of bare SE.* The purely quantum mechanical part of OQT is, perhaps, not *ad hoc;*[9] but, as I indicated above, this part of OQT on its own is devoid of physical content in that it can issue in no physical predictions at all, just because it lacks its own consistent quantum ontology. No combination of initial conditions and dynamic equations, formulated in purely quantum-mechanical terms, can predict any actual physical state of affairs. Quantum postulates (QP) on their own at most only issue in *conditional* or *counterfactual* predictions about what would be the outcome *if* a measurement were to be performed. In order to issue in unconditional predictions, OQT must call upon some additional theory, with its own consistent physical ontology, for a specification of the physical states of preparation and measurement devices. As Bohr (1949) emphasized, only OQT *plus some part of classical physics (CP) for a description of measurement* has genuine physical predictive content. Attempts to dispense with CP by describing measuring instruments quantum-mechanically must fail because such a purely quantum-mechanical description can in turn only issue in predictions about what *would* occur *if* a measurement *were* to be made by some additional measuring instrument which must itself be described in terms of CP. (Such attempts must fail for other reasons as well: the dynamic equations of OQT assert that quantum states evolve deterministically, pure states never being converted into mixed states; measurement, however, is in general a probabilistic interaction, and one which *does* convert pure states into mixed states.[10])

It is thus only the purely quantum-mechanical part of OQT plus (some part of) CP, QP + CP, which has any physical content, and thus constitutes a physical theory. But this hybrid theory, QP + CP, is unacceptably *ad hoc* due to the fact that it is made up of two conceptually incoherent parts.[11] The grounds for holding OQT (i.e. QP + CP) to be false are the same as, and are as good as, the grounds for holding that the grossly aberrant theories considered in Chapter 2 are false. QP + CP is as bad as Newtonian theory (NT) + Kepler's laws of planetary motion (KL), where this latter theory asserts: all objects interacting by means of gravitation move in accordance with NT except for the planets of the solar system, which move in accordance with KL (which conflict with NT). Einstein hit the nail on the head when he remarked: 'This theory [the present quantum theory] reminds me a little of the system of delusions of an exceedingly intelligent paranoic, concocted of incoherent elements of thoughts' (Fine 1986: 1).

Attempts have been made to develop a version of QT applicable to macro-phenomena in a quasi-classical manner, and thus capable of weaning OQT off its conceptual dependence on CP (see e.g. Machida and Namiki 1984). If some such macro quantum theory (MQT) proves to be technically feasible, it would become possible to regard the physical theory of QT as being QP + MQT rather than QP + CP. But freeing OQT of its dependence on CP in this way can do little to reduce the *ad hoc* character of the theory. QP and MQT would be different theories, with different interpretations, arbitrarily restricted in their applications; for these reasons QP + MQT would be just as *ad hoc* as QP + CP.

It is of course true that in order to check the predictions of a classical theory such as NT, we often need to employ additional physical theories, as when optical theory is used to check predictions of NT applied to the solar system. This does not mean, however, that NT is *ad hoc* in the same way in which OQT is. The difference is simply this. Because we can interpret NT as having its own consistent physical ontology (of massive, gravitationally charged particles), NT (plus specification of initial conditions) does issue in quite definite physical predictions about actual physical states of affairs—the positions and velocities of planets at definite times, for example—in the absence of optical or other physical theories, for measurement. NT is a physical theory with physical content in its own right; OQT is not.

(ii) *Despite its immense empirical success, OQT is severely defective as a predictive theory.* Even the most ardent supporter of SE will acknowledge that an acceptable predictive theory should not just presuppose, in its axioms, the phenomena it is intended to predict. But OQT does just this. (*a*) A basic task of QP is to predict complex macro-phenomena in terms of elementary micro-phenomena (so that macro-phenomena can be explained and understood as the outcome of interactions between vast numbers of micro-systems). But this OQT cannot do, because the theory lacks a consistent model for micro-systems, a consistent micro-ontology (point (i) above). OQT can only specify and describe states of micro-systems relative to prior classical descriptions of macro-systems—preparation and measurement devices. Descriptions of micro-states presuppose, as a matter of conceptual necessity, descriptions of macro-states. That which is to be predicted must, to some extent, be presupposed! (*b*) QT has the task of predicting the (approximate) empirical success of CP from purely quantum-mechanical postulates. But this, again, OQT cannot do. In any physical application, OQT must presuppose (some part of) CP for an account of preparation and measurement devices. Once again, just that which is to be predicted must be presupposed.[12]

(iii) *For a fundamental physical theory, OQT is unacceptably imprecise.* We have seen that OQT makes an essential appeal to measurement in its basic postulates (via the notion of observable and the generalized Born postulate which specifies what occurs when observables are measured). But the notion of measurement is inherently imprecise. When does a physical process constitute a measurement? When a physicist calls it a measurement? Specifying measurement in terms of the occurrence of a macro-process, a classical process, an irreversible process, or a conscious observation does not help as these notions are all irredeemably imprecise. Can a mouse make an observation, or must the observer be a conscious person? What about a bacterium? At what precise point does a process become macro, classical, or irreversible as we move up from electron interacting with electron to billions of molecules interacting with one another? Employing some MQT of macro-quantum phenomena, as envisaged by Machida and Namiki, or decoherent theorists,[13] cannot help much either, as any such MQT will be applicable to a great number of quantum systems, and will thus be highly imprecise from an elementary standpoint. QP + CP (or QP + MQT) is thus severely imprecise, in an irredeemable way, and to an unacceptable extent.

(iv) *OQT is a seriously ambiguous theory, in that it is ambiguous as to whether probabilistic events do, or do not, really occur.* Granted that a quantum-mechanically described system *S* (or ensemble of such systems) is measured by a classically described measuring instrument *M*, OQT makes in general a probabilistic prediction about the outcome. One might suppose from this that OQT asserts unambiguously that probabilistic events occur when measuring-type interactions take place.

But this is not correct. In the first place, interpreted as a fundamentally probabilistic theory, postulating the occurrence of probabilistic events in Nature, OQT is a wildly implausible theory. For OQT, given this interpretation, would assert that probabilistic events occur if and only if measurements are made. But if probabilistic events really do occur, objectively, in Nature, this cannot depend on our dubbing some physical process a 'measurement'. It would mean that the occurrence of probabilistic events in Nature depends upon our presence, and our activities as physicists! In the second place, whenever S is measured by M, in principle the *deterministic* dynamic equations of OQT can be applied to the joint system $S + M$, in which case OQT predicts that $S + M$ evolves deterministically until a further measurement is performed by an additional measuring instrument M^*. This has led some to conclude that OQT is fundamentally a *deterministic* theory, probabilistic predictions emerging only because measuring instruments are in different quantum-mechanical states when different particles are measured. Something like this must be assumed by those who try to solve the so-called quantum 'problem of measurement' by trying to show that all measurement interactions evolve in accordance with the deterministic dynamic equations of OQT. A solution to this problem, conceived of in this way, would demonstrate the fundamentally *deterministic* character of OQT. In brief, OQT is only a fundamentally probabilistic theory in a highly *ambiguous* fashion.

(v) *OQT is seriously restricted in scope.* It is standard practice these days to apply QT to states of the cosmos soon after the big bang, in physical conditions which preclude the very possibility of the existence of anything remotely corresponding to preparation and measurement devices. OQT cannot be applied in this way. Only a version of QT which has its own micro-ontology could be thus applied.[14]

Current theorizing about early states of the universe makes it desirable to be able to apply QT to the cosmos as a whole (thus creating the new discipline of quantum cosmology). Once again, OQT cannot be employed in this way, it being conceptually impossible that the cosmos as a whole should be subject to preparation and measurement![15]

(vi) *OQT cannot be generalized to include gravity.* Within the framework of OQT, a physical system only has a quantum state in so far as it is subject to preparation and measurement devices which are external, or additional, to the system in question. In order to quantize general relativity (GR), space-time itself would need to be given quantum states. In order to do this within the framework of OQT, it would be necessary to postulate preparation and measurement devices external to space-time. Such devices cannot exist. Hence GR cannot be quantized within the framework of OQT. The task of unifying QT and GR is obstructed by OQT.

In short, OQT is (i) *ad hoc*, (ii) defectively predictive, (iii) imprecise, (iv) ambiguous, (v) restricted in scope, and (vi) incapable of being unified with GR. Furthermore, these six defects are all consequences of the basic failure of OQT to specify its own consistent, micro-quantum ontology, due to its failure to solve the wave/particle problem.[16] Even a hardline proponent of SE ought to recognize these six defects as being so serious that, taken together, they render OQT unacceptable in its present form. In so far as AOE renders the defective character of OQT obvious, while SE obscures it, this constitutes a success for AOE, and yet another failure for SE.[17]

3. PROBABILISM AS THE KEY TO THE SOLUTION TO THE GREAT QUANTUM MYSTERY

It is clear from the above that in order to develop an acceptable version of QT (acceptable given SE or AOE) it is necessary to solve the great quantum riddle, the wave/particle problem. Can AOE rise to the fourth challenge, discussed above, by solving this problem? Not only does AOE provide a rational (if fallible and non-mechanical) method for the discovery of fundamental new theories in physics; in addition, AOE claims to provide a diagnosis of what went wrong in the development of QT, and what needs to be done to put things right. The development of a new fundamental theory in physics involves the development of a new (level 3) blueprint. If AOE were accepted in scientific practice, physicists would seek to modify existing blueprints in the hope of developing a new blueprint which solves unification problems and which, when made precise, leads to a new, unifying theory. General acceptance of SE, however, discourages sustained explicit exploration of (untestable, metaphysical) blueprint ideas in this way. Theoretical physicists become, as a result, highly innovative as far as equations are concerned, but conservative, resistant to innovation, as far as metaphysical blueprints are concerned. As a result, new fundamental theories tend to be interpreted in terms of old, inappropriate meta-physics; when such (inappropriate) attempts fail, the new theories tend to be judged incomprehensible, the old metaphysics constituting an ideal of comprehensibility.

Thus contemporaries of Newton (and Newton himself, in a way) found his law of gravitation unacceptable if interpreted as postulating a force acting at a distance because it clashed with action-by-contact corpuscularian metaphysics. The false solution to the problem is to cling to the corpuscularian blueprint, or at least to its implications for what is acceptable and intelligible in physics, and abandon physical essentialism and realism, thus adopting an instrumentalist stance: physics predicts observable phenomena but does not describe unobservable physical entities, and thus does not provide genuine physical explanations for observable phenomena. The true solution to the problem (prescribed by AOE) is to recognize that the corpuscular blueprint needs to be generalized to form Boscovich's improved point-atom blueprint: at once, NT becomes entirely intelligible and acceptable.

Again, James Clerk Maxwell and most of his contemporaries and immediate followers found electromagnetic field theory deeply puzzling unless it could be interpreted in terms of a quasi-materialistic ether, which in turn would need to be understood in Newtonian, Boscovichian, or corpuscularian terms. The failure of this (misconceived) programme to interpret and understand electrodynamics in terms of old, inappropriate metaphysics tended to support, once again, instrumentalist views concerning science: physics has the task of predicting observable phenomena but cannot depict the real, essential nature of the electromagnetic field itself. What all this overlooks is that Boscovich's blueprint needs to be generalized to form a field blueprint, to take into account forces that are not rigid in that variations in forces take time to travel through space. Once this more general field blueprint is adopted, classical electrodynamics becomes intelligible when interpreted as field theory; the ether, far from being required for intelligibility, actually undermines it.

This story is, I suggest, repeated as far QT is concerned. The key generalization that needs to be made, in moving from the classical to the quantum domain, is, I conjecture, that deterministic metaphysics needs to become probabilistic metaphysics.[18] According to this conjecture, the quantum domain is made up of entities that evolve and interact with one another probabilistically, the basic dynamic laws being probabilistic, so that probabilistic transitions occur objectively in Nature, entirely independently of measurement. Unfortunately, the creators of QT neglected this possibility, and persistently tried to understand the new theory in terms of physical entities appropriate to the determinism of CP—namely, the classical particle, wave, and field. When the misguided attempt to interpret QT in this way broke down,

physicists abandoned realism and developed QT as a theory which
has instrumentalism built into it, in that OQT is a theory, not about
quantum entities as such, but rather about the results of performing
measurements on quantum systems. The proper way forward is to
recognize the fundamentally probabilistic character of the quantum
domain, this carrying the implication that quantum entities—electrons,
photons, atoms—must be quite different from anything encountered in
classical physics. Once QT is interpreted in terms of a fundamentally
probabilistic blueprint, the nature of quantum entities, combining wave-
like and particle-like properties, ceases to be a mystery. A non-*ad
hoc*, fully realistic version of QT emerges, empirically distinct from
OQT.

All this illustrates the importance of putting AOE into scientific
practice—the importance of attempting to develop good metaphysical
blueprints ahead of the corresponding theories, so that metaphysics
may *aid*, and not *retard*, the discovery, acceptance, interpretation, and
understanding of new fundamental theories in physics.

The thesis that the quantum domain is fundamentally probabilistic is,
of course, a typical level 3 blueprint *conjecture*, which may well turn out
to be false. If QT is interpreted in the way proposed by David Bohm
(1952), it becomes fully *deterministic*. The experimental data do not (at
present at least), decide between determinism and probabilism. Thus,
even though I am here arguing for the probabilistic possibility, I also
wish to maintain that both possibilities need to be explored.

How does the possibility that the quantum domain is fundamentally
probabilistic provide a possible solution to the great wave/particle
riddle?

Granted that the quantum domain is fundamentally probabilistic, and
granted conjectural essentialism (the doctrine expounded and defended
in Chapter 4), it follows at once that quantum entities must differ
radically from those of the classical domain. The nature of physical
entities depends on the nature of the properties these entities possess;
but, according to conjectural essentialism, physical properties, such as
mass and charge, are just what exists physically that makes it necessary
that the entities interact in accordance with the dynamic laws that
govern their interaction. Entities, properties, and dynamic laws are all
intimately interlinked; change the dynamic laws, and you immediately
change the properties, and the entities. Thus, granted that the transition
from the classical to the quantum domain involves a change in dynamic
laws, from deterministic to fundamentally probabilistic, it follows at
once that the probabilistic entities of the quantum domain—photons,

electrons, atoms—must differ radically from all deterministic entities encountered within CP—the particle, the wave, the field.

It follows, immediately, that the *traditional* quantum wave/particle problem is entirely the *wrong* problem to try to solve. If quantum systems, such as photons, electrons, and atoms, are fundamentally probabilistic entities, interacting with one another by means of probabilistic dynamic laws, by means of probabilistic necessitating properties, then they must be quite different from any classical, deterministic particle, wave, or field. Granted that the quantum domain is fundamentally probabilistic, it would be a disaster for the comprehensibility of this domain that quantum objects should turn out to be similar to classical objects. The comprehensibility of the probabilistic quantum domain *demands* that quantum objects seem strange and baffling with respect to our classical, deterministic intuitions.

It may be objected that classical statistical mechanics constitutes a counter-example to this argument, in that it is a *probabilistic* theory, and yet is about entirely classical objects—classical particles (atoms or molecules). In fact this is not a counter-example. Classical statistical mechanics is not a *fundamentally* probabilistic theory: it presupposes that the basic dynamic laws are *deterministic*. Probabilism enters into classical statistical mechanics via probabilistic distributions of initial and boundary conditions in relevant ensembles of physical systems.

Einstein, Bohr, Heisenberg, Schrödinger, and the other creators of QT, despite their differences, in effect agreed on one key point: if quantum objects cannot be understood in terms of the deterministic notions of the classical particle, wave, or field, then this creates a severe problem for the task of developing a fully micro-realistic version of QT. Bohr and Heisenberg concluded that this problem cannot be solved, and as a result developed a version of QT which *evades* the problem— OQT. Einstein and Schrödinger were aware of the damaging consequences of this evasion, and hoped it would be possible to understand quantum objects in classical terms. What Einstein, Bohr, Heisenberg, Schrödinger, and the others all failed to appreciate—and what almost everyone since has failed to appreciate as well—is that (granted probabilism) the problem they all desired to solve (but which most thought insoluble) is entirely the *wrong* problem to try to solve in the first place. Failure to represent probabilistic quantum objects in terms of deterministic classical objects does *not* in itself create any kind of problem for quantum micro-realism at all. Quite the contrary, a severe problem for quantum micro-realism would be created if it did prove possible to represent probabilistic quantum objects in terms of deter-

ministic classical objects. Everyone has tried to do what ought never
have been attempted in the first place. Success would have been a
disaster: long-standing failure ought to be regarded as a promising sign
that the quantum world may well make perfect micro-realistic sense
after all!

Once we appreciate what Einstein, Bohr, Heisenberg, Schrödinger,
et al. failed to appreciate—namely that the wave/particle problem as
traditionally understood is the *wrong* problem—we can move on to
formulate and solve the *right* problem. There are in effect *two* problems
we need to solve in order to develop an acceptable, fully micro-realistic
theory of probabilistic quantum objects. First, we must specify, in general terms, the nature of entirely *unproblematic* probabilistic objects,
wholly irrespective of any considerations taken from QT. Secondly, we
must show that no difficulties lie in the way of holding that quantum
objects are just such entirely unproblematic probabilistic objects (no
doubt of a distinctively quantum type). We have, in short:

> *Problem 1*: What different sorts of unproblematic, fundamentally
> probabilistic entity are there, quite generally (entirely independent
> of quantum-mechanical considerations)?
>
> *Problem 2*: Can quantum objects be construed to be one kind of
> these different sorts of unproblematic, fundamentally probabilistic
> entity?

I take these two problems in turn.

Physical properties which determine how physical objects interact
with one another probabilistically I will call, following Popper (1957),
propensities. And objects that have propensities as fundamental properties I will call *propensitons*. In generalizing classical metaphysical blueprints, from determinism to probabilism, we are engaging in an exercise
similar to that which took us from the corpuscular blueprint to the
point-atom blueprint, and from this in turn to the field blueprint, or
which took Einstein from Newtonian space and time to Minkowskian
space-time in developing special relativity, or from Minkowskian to
Riemannian space-time in developing general relativity (see Chapter 3,
Section 4, and Chapter 4, Section 17). What we need to do is modify
earlier ideas about entities and properties just sufficiently to accommodate the new, more general requirement of *probabilistic* interactions.

Two crucial general points need to be made about classical, deterministic, necessitating properties, as characterized in Chapter 4, to be associated with classical blueprint entities such as the classical corpuscle,
point-atom, or field.

(*a*) Classical, deterministic, necessitating properties have two kinds of change associated with them. First, there is the change which occurs when the property is 'actualized': the inflammable wood burns, the elastic ball bounces, the gravitationally charged objects accelerate towards each other. Secondly, values of the property may themselves change: the inflammable wood may gradually become less inflammable (as it becomes wet), the ball may become less elastic. Newtonian theory postulates that gravitational charge is invariant: and it is of course the task of theoretical physics to discover properties that are invariant through as wide a range of changes as possible, the ultimate ideal being to discover that property which does not change at all throughout space and time, and which determines the way all other properties change.

(*b*) Classical, deterministic, necessitating properties are of two kinds. The first kind are properties which are actualized *discretely* or intermittently in time, when special physical conditions arise, such as when the inflammable object is exposed to a naked flame, or elastic objects collide. The second kind are properties which are actualized *continuously* in time, as in the case of Newtonian gravitational charge, granted that there are at least two gravitationally charged objects in the universe.

These features of classical, deterministic properties and objects, and other features discussed in Chapter 4, carry over to fundamentally probabilistic properties and objects, to propensities and propensitons. The *only* difference is that when a deterministic property is actualized there is just one possible outcome, whereas when a propensity P is actualized there are n possible outcomes (or, conceivably, infinitely many possible outcomes). A specific *value* of a propensity P specifies n probabilities $p_1 \ldots p_n$, and attributes a definite probability p_r to each possible outcome O_r, with:

$$\sum_{r=1}^{n} p_r = 1.$$

Just as classical, deterministic properties determine how things change, so too propensities determine how things change in certain circumstances, but probabilistically and not deterministically. Again, just as there can be necessary causal connections between successive states of affairs, given deterministic properties, so too there can be probabilistic necessary causal connections between successive states of affairs, given that propensities and propensitons exist. Yet again, just as classical deterministic properties have two kinds of change associated with them (point (*a*) above), so too propensities have two kinds of change associated with them: the propensity can be actualized with the occurrence of a probabilistic event, and the value of the propensity itself can change (possibly in a continuous and deterministic fashion, in the absence of probabilistic actualization). And finally, just as classical, deterministic properties are of two kinds (point (*b*) above), so, too, propensities and propensitons are of two kinds. On the one hand, corresponding to such deterministic properties as rigidity and inflammability, there are discrete propensities (and propensitons), actualized probabilistically at intermittent time intervals, when appropriate physical conditions arise, values of propensities evolving deterministically between these intermittent actualizations. On the other hand, corresponding to Newtonian gravitational charge, there are propensities actualized continuously in time.

Corresponding to these two kinds of propensity and propensiton, discrete and continuous, there are two kinds of fundamentally probabilistic dynamic theory, which assert that probabilistic events occur intermittently and continuously (in the intermittent case, physical states of affairs evolving deterministically between intermittent probabilistic events). We need, then, to distinguish *three* kinds of dynamic theory: deterministic, discretely probabilistic, and continuously probabilistic. These ought to be regarded as equally viable a priori, each being considered as a possible framework for QT.

My proposal is that quantum objects are discrete propensitons. Let us, then, consider some simple, unproblematic examples of possible discrete propensitons.

One might try to visualize the evolution and interaction of the discrete propensiton in terms of the flight of a magnetized die tossed into a varying magnetic field. As the die falls the value of its propensity varies continuously and deterministically; when the die hits the table top and comes to rest, the propensity is actualized in a discontinuous, probabilistic way. This is, however, only a very inadequate model for the evolution of the discrete propensiton. The evolution of a real-life die can be conceived of entirely in terms of changing values of *deterministic* properties: the propensity of the die is the outcome of the statistical distribution of different initial conditions of different tosses. In the case of an evolving discrete propensiton, however, there is no evolution of values of *deterministic* properties—only a deterministic evolution of values of *probabilistic properties* or propensities (which is quite different). There is no *deterministic* state; only a *propensity* state. This ensures that all discrete propensitons are utterly unlike familiar objects, such as dice and coins, to which propensities can be attributed but which can be conceived of, more fundamentally, in terms of classical, deterministic properties.

The evolution of a die that is a genuine discrete propensiton would have to be conceived of in something like the following terms. The propensiton die is tossed. As the die flies through the air it is gradually transformed into six potential, virtual, ghostly dice, each with a different face uppermost, each with a different (probability) density (all equal in the case of unbiasedness), which may very well vary with time. When the six virtual dice hit the table top, five vanish and one solid die remains. If the die is tossed repeatedly, the statistical outcomes are determined by the probability densities of the six virtual dice just before contact with the table top.

This, then, is the general character of the unproblematic discrete propensiton. Its state evolves (1) deterministically into a smeared-out range of virtual states; then, when (2) appropriate propensiton conditions arise (3) instantaneously and probabilistically, the virtual states are annihilated except for one which becomes actual. Once discrete probabilism is conceded, this general character of the (unproblematic) discrete propensiton is all but inevitable. As a special case, it is possible to envisage a kind of discrete propensiton which is such that the values of its propensities remain fixed during deterministic evolution. In this case, values of propensities will not spread out during deterministic evolution. In general, however, the propensity state of discrete propensitons *will* spread out during deterministic evolution—whether spatially or in some other way. It is, in other words, not absolutely essential that discrete propensitons exhibit quantum-mechanical-type spatial smearing out, or non-locality: it is, however, entirely natural that discrete propensitons should exhibit such typically quantum-mechanical features.

As a second example of a possible, unproblematic kind of discrete propensiton, consider the following. The propensiton is in the form of a sphere, which expands at a fixed rate. The stuff of the sphere is position probability density, uniformly distributed within the sphere. The condition for probabilistic actualization to occur is for two spheres to touch. The outcome is that the two spheres collapse instantaneously into two small spheres of some minimal size, each localized probabilistically by the position probability density of each sphere. It is vital to appreciate that there is nothing inherently problematic, *ad hoc*, or inexplicable about the instantaneous probabilistic collapse of the propensiton spheres (to re-emphasize a point already made). To demand that any such instantaneous, probabilistic collapse of virtual states must be *explained* in terms of some continuous evolution of states amounts to holding that only deterministic or continuously probabilistic theories are acceptable, discretely probabilistic theories being unacceptable on a priori grounds. Once it is conceded that these three kinds of dynamic theory are equally acceptable a priori (other things being equal), it is thereby conceded that the instantaneous, probabilistic collapses of propensiton states postulated by discrete probabilism are not intrinsically problematic or inexplicable—not especially in need of further explanation in terms of some continuous process.

Discrete propensitons of this rather simple-minded type can easily be made a little more sophisticated by postulating that the position probability density is variable in space—even in a wave-like way. If the conditions for probabilistic events to occur are modified, it would even be possible to create a possible kind of propensiton which is such that an ensemble of such propensitons, passed through a two-slitted screen, creates an interference pattern of the kind created by electrons or photons.

There is nothing *ad hoc* or arbitrary about the discrete propensiton as it has just been characterized. It arises quite naturally as a result of generalizing the classical, deterministic notion of physical entity and property just sufficiently to take into account the case of entities interacting by means of discretely probabilistic dynamic laws.

So much for my solution to problem 1. My solution to problem 2 is that quantum objects can indeed be conceived of as unproblematic discrete propensitons, very roughly of the type just indicated. The two-slit experiment, for example, (see Appendix), which so strikingly reveals both the wave-like and the particle-like aspects of electrons (or photons or atoms) can be understood in the following way. Each individual electron is in the form a wave packet, a spatially smeared-out discrete propensiton. The wave-like character of the electron propensiton is such that the absolute phase is without physical significance: only phase differences which persist through a constant change of phase of the entire wave packet are of physical significance. As a result of this, in many circumstances the wave-like character of the electron is implicit, rather than being explicit in a wave-like variation of position probability density. The propensiton states of individual electrons evolve deterministically, in accordance with the dynamic equation of QT (the time-dependent Schrödinger equation; see Appendix, Section 6): what evolves, however, is the propensity to interact in a probabilistic and quasi particle-like way, should the appropriate physical conditions to do so arise. The deterministic Schrödinger equation does not of course apply to such probabilistic actualizations of propensities. When the electron wave packet encounters the two-slitted screen *either* the electron is absorbed by the screen and there is an instantaneous, probabilistic collapse of the wave packet, *or* the electron wave packet passes through both slits. Granted the latter then, on the other side of the screen, the implicit wave-like character of the propensity state of the electron becomes explicit in an interference-like variation of position probability density. The wave packet then encounters the photographic plate and interacts with all available silver-bromide molecules. The physical condition for a propensiton or wave packet probabilistic collapse is then realized; abruptly, the electron continues to interact in a highly localized way with just one silver-bromide molecule (or crystal) in such a way as to create a developable dot of silver on the photographic plate. The position of the dot is probabilistically determined by the interference pattern of position probability density of the electron propensiton just before the wave packet collapse. As a result, in the case of an ensemble of similarly prepared electrons with the same momenta, and therefore the same wavelengths, the developable dots on the photographic plate fall into the characteristic observed interference pattern—matching the interference pattern in position probability density of each individual electron propensiton just before probabilistic localization occurs.

Above I have conceded that three kinds of dynamic theory are possible and, a priori, equally viable: deterministic, continuously probabilistic, and discretely probabilistic. Why, then, is the third option to be preferred when it comes to QT?

I have two replies to this question.

First, discrete probabilism provides an entirely natural solution to the key quantum wave/particle dilemma. As we have seen, it is entirely natural, though not inevitable, that discrete propensitons should have just the kind of wave-like and particle-like properties apparently possessed by quantum systems.

Secondly, it is important to bear in mind that OQT is an extraordinarily successful theory empirically. OQT has evidently got something very important right, even if it is also seriously defective. In the circumstances, it seems advisable, at least initially, to keep as close to OQT as possible, and modify the theory just sufficiently to remove the basic glaring defect. OQT postulates *deterministic* evolutions of states interrupted by apparently *probabilistic* measuring processes. The structure of OQT is much closer to discrete probabilism than to determinism or continuous probabilism.[19] Discrete probabilism *alone* enables us to retain unchanged the deterministic dynamic equations of OQT, the condition for probabilistic events to occur alone being modified, so that all reference to measurement in the basic postulates disappears; the theory acquires a precise discrete propensiton ontology, and the *scope* (but not the form) of the Schrödinger equation is modified.

Thus, propensiton QT (PQT) retains the dynamic equation of OQT, the Schrödinger equation, but rejects the generalized Born postulate (see Appendix) which interprets the ψ-function as containing probabilistic information about the results of performing measurements on the system. Instead, PQT interprets ψ as specifying the actual physical state of the individual quantum system in physical space and time, even in the absence of preparation and measurement. ψ is interpreted as containing information about the values of various quantum propensities of discrete quantum propensitons, such as position, momentum, and energy probability density, and angular momentum or spin states. In specifying how ψ evolves in time, the time-dependent Schrödinger equation specifies how values of these propensities evolve deterministically, just as long as no probabilistic events occur. Whenever quantum propensities are probabilistically actualized then, at that instant, the deterministic Schrödinger equation does not apply. (It is this restriction of the scope of the Schrödinger equation, basic to the whole propensiton idea, which ensures that any precisely formulated version of PQT must differ experimentally from OQT, at least in principle.) Instead of the generalized Born postulate of OQT we have, within PQT, postulates which specify (1) the precise propensiton conditions for probabilistic events to occur, (2) how the propensiton state at that instant determines possible outcome states, and (3) how the propensiton state assigns probabilities to the outcome states. All quantum measurements will turn out to be no more than special cases of a kind of probabilistic process occurring naturally, throughout the universe. PQT enables us to derive Born's postulate from purely quantum-mechanical postulates, without any assumption being made concerning observables, measurement, or classical physics. Stable macro-objects and macro-phenomena, obeying approximately classical laws, emerge naturally, according to PQT, as the outcome of a vast number of quantum propensitons interacting with one another in a probabilistic manner.[20]

It might seem that the *complex* character of ψ constitutes a serious obstacle to interpreting it as specifying *real* values of propensities of real propensitons. But this is not the case. We may take $|\psi|^2 dV$ to specify the real value of the propensity, position probability density, within each volume element, dV. Analogous remarks hold for momentum and energy probability density, and spin. In this way ψ, a complex function of space and time, is interpreted to attribute real values of quantum propensities to quantum objects in physical space and time.

It might seem that the fact that, for two (or n) interacting systems, we need to resort to a ψ-function in six- (or $3n$-)dimensional configuration space delivers a fatal blow to the propensiton interpretation of QT. How can such a ψ-function be interpreted as specifying the real physical states of two (or n) objects in three-dimensional physical space? In order to carry through such an interpretation, we must first appreciate that n interacting quantum objects do not have independently specifiable propensity states: only the composite object as a whole has a definite propensity state. The propensities of this composite propensiton, in three-dimensional physical space, need to be understood as follows. Consider position probability density. For an n-particle system in a state ψ, this is represented by $|\psi|^2 dr_1 \ldots dr_n$, and is to be understood as determining: the probability of particle 1 being available for a probabilistic interaction in dr_1, particle 2 in dr_2, $\ldots$, and particle n in dr_n (for all possible values of d$r_1 \ldots$ dr_n). Instead of interpreting $|\psi|^2 dr_1 \ldots dr_n$ as assigning a probability to a small region in $3n$-dimensional configuration space, we interpret it as assigning a probability to n small regions d$r_1 \ldots$ dr_n in three-dimensional physical space. The *value* of this propensity cannot be uniquely specified for particle 1 in region dr_1 independently of the other particles: as d$r_2 \ldots$ dr_n are moved through space, the overall probability of particle 1 being available for interaction in the *fixed* region dr_1 (and the other particles being available in d$r_2 \ldots$ dr_n) will *vary* as well. What exists potentially in one small spatial region at an instant depends, in this way, on what exists, potentially, elsewhere—a feature of the quantum world not encountered within classical physics. To say this, however, is just to say that the n interacting particles do not have distinct quantum states, but only have a joint, quantum-entangled state as a whole. In order to specify how the value of the n-fold position probability density of the n-particle system, and the values of other such propensities, evolve in physical space and time, it is convenient to resort to the mathematical fiction of a ψ-function with a unique value at each point in $3n$-dimensional configuration space. This is to be interpreted physically, however, as assigning a unique value to any n points in three-dimensional physical space.

4. WHEN DO PROBABILISTIC JUMPS OCCUR?
AN IDEA AS OLD AS QUANTUM THEORY ITSELF

The key question that must be answered if PQT is to become a viable theory is: When precisely do quantum probabilistic events occur, specified in purely quantum-mechanical terms (without any reference to measurement or its equivalents)?

As I have emphasized above, a number of proposals have been put forward as to how this question is to be answered since I first argued for the need to develop a fundamentally probabilistic version of QT free of any reference to measurement in its basic postulates. In what follows I outline my own attempt at solving the problem.

Probabilistic events occur, I suggest, when and only when, as a result of *inelastic* collisions (or decay processes), new stationary or bound states are created, or new particles are created—all quantum measurements that detect systems invariably involving the creation of such new stationary, bound, or particle states (Maxwell 1982).

A few words about terminology. *Stationary* or *bound* states are created when particles clump together to form composite particles, as in the case of the proton, p^+, and electron, e^-, forming the hydrogen atom, (p^+e^-) or H (or, indeed, the proton itself, in that it is a bound state of quarks and gluons). A bound system behaves as a particle—or rather a propensiton—in its own right as long as interactions with other systems are not sufficiently energetic to disrupt the bound state.

Elastic collisions are such that precisely the same particles (taking bound states as particles) enter into the collision as exit from it. *Inelastic* collisions, on the other hand, create new bound states, or new particles, as in the following interactions:

(1) $(p^+e^-) + e^- \rightarrow (p^+e^-) + e^-$
$$p^+ + e^- + e^-$$

(2) $e^- + e^+ \rightarrow e^- + e^+$
$$2\gamma$$

(3) $(p^+e^-) + e^+ \rightarrow (p^+e^-) + e^+$
$$p^+ + e^- + e^+$$
$$p^+ + (e^-e^+)$$
$$p^+ + 2\gamma$$

Inelastic collisions create distinct interaction 'channels'—each channel with its particular clutch of elementary and bound particles. In each case, the *elastic* outcome is always one possibility. According to OQT, in the absence of measurement, the state of the system persists as a superposition of the different channel states; only on measurement does the state collapse into one or other channel state. According to the version of PQT being advocated here, in the case of an inelastic collision, when the interaction is (almost) at an end, the state of the system collapses probabilistically into one or other channel state.

The basic argument in support of this hypothesis goes like this. Granted discrete probabilism, a condition for probabilistic events to occur has to be found couched in terms of *interactions* between propensitons (and not couched in terms of observables, which would make an implicit appeal to measurement). Elastic interactions do not seem to produce probabilistic interactions. As long as quantum objects interact with macroscopic objects in an *elastic* fashion, as when electrons are diffracted through a crystal or two-slitted screen, no probabilistic localizations seem to occur. It is when quantum objects interact *inelastically* in a highly *localized* fashion, to create new particles or ionized molecules, that probabilistic wave packet collapse seems to occur. All quantum measurements that actually *detect* quantum systems (and do not merely *prepare* quantum states[21]) must involve some such *inelastic* particle-creating (or bound-state-creating) process—usually millions of such processes—simply to produce a permanent record (necessary for measurement to have taken place). Granted that *detection* is (in general) a sufficient condition for a probabilistic event to occur, and granted we seek some elemental quantum condition for the occurrence of probabilistic events, it seems not unreasonable to conjecture that creation and annihilation of particles—whether elementary or composite—is the proper necessary and sufficient quantum condition for the occurrence of probabilistic events (quantum measurements thus exemplifying physical processes that occur in Nature all the time).

There is another point. Other things being equal, we should favour that postulate which is as open to empirical testing as possible. This requires that the condition for probabilistic events to occur is as elementary as possible, involving as few elementary particles as possible. The postulate put forward here satisfies this requirement and is, as we shall see, experimentally testable (in principle at least).

And there is another, historical argument worth taking into account. The postulate that we are considering can be traced back to the origins of QT; it is implicit in Einstein's theory of absorption and emission of light by atoms, put forward in 1916–17[22] (and may even be seen as being implicit in Planck's 1900 theory of black-body radiation, the contribution that gave birth to QT). Einstein's contribution in effect gave a probabilistic interpretation to Bohr's QT of the atom: when atoms jump from one stationary state to another, absorbing or emitting light, the transitions are only *probabilistically* determined. With hindsight, Einstein's contribution may be seen as an early version of the postulate being considered here.

But does not Einstein's probabilistic interpretation of 'old' QT become untenable with the advent of Schrödinger wave mechanics, which predicts that atoms can be in superpositions of stationary states— a prediction that has been amply confirmed experimentally? The answer is No. It remains possible that superpositions of distinct stationary or bound states *exist* but do not *persist*. We may postulate: whenever, as a result of an inelastic interaction, the state of a system evolves into a superposition of distinct stationary, bound, or particle states, and the interaction has almost ceased to influence the creation or annihilation of 'particles' associated with the distinct outcome channels, the state decays, spontaneously and probabilistically, into one or other channel state, one or other stationary, bound, or particle state.

5. THE PRECISE POSTULATE

In order to make this postulate precise we need to specify precisely when an inelastic interaction may be deemed to have ceased. My suggestion, here, is that an interaction has ceased sufficiently for probabilistic collapse to occur *when particles participating in the interaction begin to evolve sufficiently nearly as free particles, with no forces acting between them* (Maxwell 1994a).

Consider, for illustrative purposes, the following toy inelastic interaction, with just two possible outcomes:

$$a + b + c \rightarrow a + b + c \qquad \text{(A)}$$
$$(ab) + c \qquad \text{(B)}$$

Here, a, b, and c are spinless particles and (ab) is the bound state. Let the state of the entire system be $\psi(t)$, and let the asymptotic states of the two channels (A) and (B) be $\psi_A(t)$ and $\psi_B(t)$ respectively.

Asymptotic states associated with an inelastic interaction are fictional states towards which, according to OQT, the real state of the system tends as $t \rightarrow +\infty$. Each outcome channel has its associated asymptotic state, which evolves as if forces between particles are zero, except where forces hold bound systems together.

Thus, according to OQT, for the toy interaction that we are considering, there are states $\phi_A(t)$ and $\phi_B(t)$ such that:

(1) for all t, $\psi(t) = c_A\phi_A(t) + c_B\phi_B(t)$, with $|c_A|^2 + |c_B|^2 = 1$;
(2) as $t \rightarrow +\infty$, $\phi_A(t) \rightarrow \psi_A(t)$, and $\phi_B(t) \rightarrow \psi_B(t)$.

Here, the evolutions of the asymptotic states $\psi_A(t)$ and $\psi_B(t)$ are governed by the respective channel Hamiltonians, H_A and H_B respectively. These differ from the Hamiltonian, H, governing the evolution of $\psi(t)$, $\phi_A(t)$, and $\phi_B(t)$, in that forces between particles that are not in bound states are set to zero. We have:

$$H = -\{T_a + T_b + T_c\} + V_{ab} + V_{ac} + V_{bc}.$$
$$H_A = -\{T_a + T_b + T_c\}.$$
$$H_B = -\{T_a + T_b + T_c\} + V_{ab}.$$

Here, T_a, T_b, T_c represent kinetic energy, so that

$$T_a = \frac{\hbar^2}{2m_a}\nabla_a^2,$$

where m_a is the mass of particle a. V_{ab}, V_{ac}, and V_{bc} are potentials corresponding to the forces between a and b, a and c, and b and c respectively.

The condition for probabilistic collapse can now be stated as follows. Let $\psi^c(t) = c_A\psi_A(t) + c_B\psi_B(t)$. Then:

(P) At the first instant t for which $|\langle\psi^c(t)|\psi(t)\rangle| > 1 - \varepsilon$ holds, the state of the system, $\psi(t)$ jumps probabilistically into either $\phi_A(t)$ with probability $= |c_A|^2$ or into $\phi_B(t)$ with probability $= |c_B|^2$, ε being a universal constant, a positive real number very nearly equal to zero.

It is a straightforward matter to generalize (P) so that it applies to the case of an inelastic interaction with N channel outcomes, with N distinct asymptotic states, $N \geq 2$.

The postulate (P), adjoined to Schrödinger's time-dependent equation (interpreted to apply whenever probabilistic transitions do not occur), provides the basis for a version of (non-relativistic) fundamentally probabilistic QT (PQT) that (a) makes no mention of measurement in its basic postulates at all, and is thus (b) free of the defects of OQT discussed above, but (c) nevertheless recaptures all the empirical success of OQT, and (d) is in principle experimentally distinct from OQT. These are points that I have argued for at length elsewhere (Maxwell 1976a, 1982, 1988a, 1994a); here I will be brief, concentrating on the last two points.

First, all position measurements, that actually detect the system being measured, must leave some kind of semi-permanent trace: atoms must be ionized, molecules dissociated, or new particles created. Position measurements, in other words, realize the conditions for probabilistic transitions to occur, specified by (P).

Secondly, measurement of other observables, such as momentum, energy, or spin, invariably involve (1) a preparation process, which associates distinct spatial locations with eigenstates of the observable in question, and then (2) a detection process, of the type just considered. In these cases, too, the conditions for probabilistic transitions to occur obtain, as specified by the above postulate. The time-dependent Schrödinger equation, for a specification of the deterministic evolution of quantum states, plus (P), for a specification of probabilistic transitions, together suffice to reproduce all the empirical success of OQT. And this is achieved, furthermore, without the need to do, what OQT must do, namely invoke some extra theory, such as some part of classical physics, for a treatment of measurement. The quasi-classical world of macroscopic objects emerges naturally and automatically from the quantum domain, according to PQT, as a result of billions of probabilistic transitions occurring as electrons, protons, atoms, and molecules interact with one another inelastically.

But if PQT yields the same predictions as OQT for all ordinary experiments, under what circumstances do the two versions of QT yield different predictions?

Consider again the interaction between a, b, and c. Whereas OQT predicts that the state continues to be $\psi(t) = c_A \phi_A(t) + c_B \phi_B(t)$ until measurement, PQT predicts that, at some time t_0, in the absence of measurement, the state $\psi(t)$ either becomes $\phi_A(t)$ with probability $|c_A|^2$, or becomes $\phi_B(t)$ with probability $|c_B|^2$. As long as ε is sufficiently small, these distinct predictions will ordinarily be experimentally undetectable. In order to detect the difference, it will be necessary, after t_0, to switch on forces of an experimental apparatus which have the effect of recombining the two channels, $(ab) + c$ and $a + b + c$, so that the $a + b + c$ channel becomes $(ab) + c$, and interference effects can be detected. This requires that the experimental set-up is such that no measurement can determine along which route, $(ab) + c$ or $a + b + c$, the system evolves. In these circumstances, OQT predicts interference effects, since the state of the system is predicted to be the superposition $c_A \phi_A(t) + c_B \phi_B(t)$, whereas PQT predicts no such interference effects as the state of the system is either $\phi_A(t)$ or $\phi_B(t)$.

The possibility, in principle, of performing this crucial experiment establishes that OQT and PQT are empirically distinct theories. The crucial experiment is, however, extremely difficult to do in practice, and has not, as far as I am aware, as yet been performed.[23]

A number of questions arise in connection with the version of PQT just indicated. What is the upper bound placed on ε by current experimental data? How small can ε be before PQT becomes all but indistinguishable from a many-worlds interpretation of QT? What are the prospects for an experimental test of PQT? How can the idea be generalized to take into account relativistic QT, quantum field theory, spontaneous symmetry-breaking as a fundamentally probabilistic cosmic event, and quantum gravity? As long as the idea continues to be ignored by the physics community these questions will, it seems, remain unanswered.

6. WHY HAS THE IDEA BEEN IGNORED?

Given that Einstein's probabilistic interpretation of 'old' QT, when developed in the way indicated above, provides us with a fully micro-realistic version of QT which is free of the problems that plague OQT, and which, though testable, has still not been refuted nearly eighty years after the idea was first indicated, the question arises as to why the idea has not received more attention. Even the new wave of interest in the possibility of developing a fundamentally probabilistic version of QT, stimulated by the contribution of Ghirardi *et al.* (1986), and developed in different directions by Pearle (1989), Penrose (1986), Percival (1994), and others, has failed to awaken interest in an idea that is almost as old as QT itself.

The idea has been neglected, I claim, not for good reasons, but because of the accidents of history, and because of a general failure to put AOE into scientific practice.

First, its author, Einstein, was an ardent determinist; he was in fact disturbed by the probabilistic implications of his 1917 contribution. The idea that I have attributed to Einstein was all but disowned by its author (see Pais 1982: 412). Secondly, those more inclined than Einstein to take fundamental probabilism seriously, at the level of interactions between quanta, may well have abandoned this line of thought with the demise of the Bohr–Kramer–Slater theory, which postulated probabilism at a fundamental level. Thirdly, after the development of the Copenhagen, or orthodox, interpretation of QT, with its emphasis on measurement, discussion of the interpretative problems of QT split into two camps. On the one hand there was Einstein's camp, devoted to upholding both micro-realism and determinism; and on the other there was Bohr's, devoted to abandoning micro-realism and determinism. As a result, the two quite distinct issues of realism versus instrumentalism, and determinism versus probabilism, got fused together into one: realism-plus-determinism versus instrumentalism-plus-probabilism. It became impossible to take seriously the option: micro-realism plus probabilism. This in turn meant that there was no motivation to take seriously Einstein's probabilistic interpretation of old QT, and see how it could be developed in the light of the new QT of Heisenberg and Schrödinger, after 1926. Fifthly, at the time that the new QT was being developed there was a general tendency to believe that introducing statistical or probabilistic considerations into physics meant introducing an element of subjectivity, so that physics ceased to describe systems and became instead a representation of our knowledge of systems. Probabilism, in short, was taken to imply instrumentalism, so that combining prob- abilism and micro-realism did not seem to be an option. That Nature herself might be fundamentally probabilistic did not appear to be a meaningful possibility. Sixthly, there was a failure to appreciate the point made above that probabilism provides a very natural possible solution to the fundamental mystery of the quantum domain: the nature of quantum entities in view of their wave and particle aspects. And finally, no doubt, it was assumed that the new QT of 1926 renders Einstein's 1917 idea obsolete (as a basis, at least, for interpreting QT), an assumption that is incorrect, as we have seen.

At a more general level, I would argue that if physicists during the first three decades of this century had accepted AOE rather than SE, then the kind of AOE reasoning indicated above would have been pursued during this period, and Einstein's idea, even if repudiated by its author, would have been taken up and developed by others.

7. CONCLUSION

In the last three sections I have discussed one approach to developing a fully micro-realistic, comprehensible version of QT, free of the defects which deface OQT. This plausible view, with roots that go back to the origins of QT, would probably not have been ignored if AOE had been generally accepted. It is entirely possible, nevertheless, that this particu- lar version of PQT is false. If so, this must not obscure the general points argued for in this chapter. These are the following.

OQT, despite its immense empirical success, is defective. Its defects result from the failure to solve the wave/particle dilemma, the problem of providing a consistent quantum ontology for the theory. We need a new version of QT that meets the requirements of AOE for an acceptable theory, a version of QT with its own distinctive quantum ontology that depicts the quantum domain as comprehensible (and does not refer to measurement, observables, the environment, or their equivalents in its basic postulates). A probabilistic ontology and blueprint provides a rather natural possible solution to the wave/particle dilemma: quantum entities, whether 'particles' or 'fields', are quantum propensitons. This strongly suggests that QT needs to be developed as a fundamentally probabilistic theory about quantum propensitons, whether discrete or continuous. Any such version of PQT, once precisely formulated, will yield predictions that differ from those of OQT. The version of PQT indicated above is just one of a number of proposals that have recently been made. But, despite all this, determinism remains a possibility.

The all-important point is that theoretical physics should again take seriously the two interrelated fundamental questions about which OQT is so evasive: What is the nature of quantum objects? Is Nature probabilistic or deterministic? Science ought not to abandon the 2,000-year-old attempt to grasp in what way the universe is comprehensible.

MATHEMATICAL AND PHYSICAL APPENDIX

1. Differential Equations

For those not familiar with the notion of a differential equation, here is a very brief explanation. Differential equations are equations that involve derivatives, such as dy/dx, d^2y/dx^2 and so on. Derivatives express the rate at which one quantity, y, changes with respect to another quantity, x. Thus, if s is distance travelled by a body in time t, then ds/dt expresses rate of change of distance, s, with respect to time, t, that is *velocity*, v; and d^2s/dt^2 expresses rate of change of rate of change of distance with time, that is *acceleration*, a. This is also rate of change of velocity with time, dv/dt. We thus have:

$$a = dv/dt = d(ds/dt)/dt = d^2s/dt^2.$$

Given that we plot on a graph distance s against time t to form a curve, then ds/dt, the instantaneous velocity at time t, is, from a geometric standpoint, the slope of the tangent to the curve at time t. If the curve is specified by the function $s = At^n$, where A is a constant and n an integer, then $ds/dt = nAt^{n-1}$.

Examples of differential equations are:

(a) $ds/dt = 0$
(b) $d^2s/dt^2 = a$ (where a is some constant)
(c) $y \cdot dy/dx + x = 0$
(d) $x \cdot d^2y/dx^2 - dy/dx = 0$.

A differential equation, typically, specifies an infinite family of curves or, equivalently, of functions. This is best understood by working backwards, from one such function to the corresponding differential equation. Consider (a) above. Given the above interpretation of s and t, this equation asserts that velocity is zero. This represents infinitely many horizontal straight lines, specified by infinitely many functions of the form $s = s_0$, where s_0 is the distance from the origin at $t = 0$. As the velocity of the body $= 0$, it remains where it is for all time. Given $s = s_0$, if we differentiate with respect to t, we obtain the differential equation (a). From infinitely many functions, $s = s_0$, corresponding to the infinitely many values of s_0, we obtain *one* differential equation, $ds/dt = 0$.

A somewhat more interesting example is obtained if we consider equation (b). This asserts that acceleration is a constant. Given all objects accelerating in the same direction at a constant rate a, these objects may have started from a variety of initial places, s_0, with a variety of initial velocities, v_0, at time $t = 0$. Thus (b) applies to a doubly infinite class of curves, corresponding to the doubly infinite set of values that s_0 and v_0 can have. These curves are represented by the equations $s = (a/2)t^2 + v_0 t + s_0$. Differentiating any of these equations twice we obtain first $ds/dt = at + v_0$, and then $d^2s/dt^2 = a$ (that is, equation (*b*) above). The result of differentiating twice is to lose the two constants, s_0 and v_0. By adding particular values, particular initial conditions, of s_0 and v_0, to the differential equation $d^2s/dt^2 = a$, we pick out the corresponding curve, or path pursued by the object, from the infinitely many possible curves or paths.

Similar points apply to (*c*) and (*d*), and other differential equations.

The essential point, from the standpoint of unity in physics, is that infinitely many diverse functions, each specifying the distinctive way in which some particular physical system evolves in space and time, can be specified by just *one* differential equation. This latter specifies what *all* the different functions have in common: there is a fixed, common, unchanging relationship between the way in which the *rates* of various variable quantities change with respect to one another. *This*, or rather what exists physically which determines this, is what U is. In the case of NT, U is that which exists physically, everywhere at all times, which determines that particles will move in accordance with $F = ma$, $F = Gm_1m_2/d^2$, and $F_{\text{total}} = \Sigma F_i$. These differential equations determine, for any system of particles, with initial positions, velocities, and masses specified, the precise paths that these particles will pursue, the precise functions that determine these paths.

2. Maxwell's Equations of the Electromagnetic Field

Maxwell's equations (actually only given this form by Heaviside and Lorentz) are:

(1) $\nabla \cdot E = 4\pi\varrho$

(2) $\nabla \cdot B = 0$

(3) $\nabla \times E = -\dfrac{1}{c}\dfrac{\partial B}{\partial t}$

(4) $\nabla \times B = \dfrac{1}{c}\dfrac{\partial E}{\partial t} + \dfrac{4\pi}{c}\mathbf{j}$

(5) $F = q\left(E + (v/c) \times B\right)$

Here are a few words of explanation as to what these equations mean (in addition to those given in Chapter 4, Section 11) for those not familiar with vector analysis and classical electrodynamics. *E* and *B* are the electric and magnetic fields of force respectively, each a vector field which assigns a vector to each space-time point, and which varies in a continuous way through space and time. (Vectors are written in bold type thus: *E* and *B*.) A vector field may be thought of as assigning a tiny arrow to each space-time point which varies in length and direction with changes in space and time. The length and direction of the arrow, at any spatial point and instant, represents the strength and direction of the field at that space-time point. A vector field might represent flowing water, in which case the arrow at each space-time point would specify the velocity of the water at that point and instant.

$\nabla \cdot \boldsymbol{E}$ means $\partial E_x/\partial x + \partial E_y/\partial y + \partial E_z/\partial z$, where E_x, E_y, and E_z are the x, y, and z components of the vector $\boldsymbol{E}$. $\boldsymbol{E}$, and its x, y, and z components change, in general, with respect to changing positions at any given time, and with respect to changing time. $\partial E_x/\partial x$, a *partial* derivative, tells us how E_x changes with respect to a change in the direction of the x axis, all other changes being kept constant. $\nabla \cdot \boldsymbol{E}$ thus gives us the sum of the rate of change of $\boldsymbol{E}$ in space with respect to the three spatial directions, x, y, and z. $\nabla \cdot \boldsymbol{E}$ is a measure of the extent to which there is net 'flow' of electric field out of, or into, a region of space (all the arrows pointing away from, or towards, some common point). Postulate (1), $\nabla \cdot \boldsymbol{E} = 4\pi\varrho$, thus tells us that the net 'flow' of electric field out of a region is proportional to the charge density within that region. Postulate (2), $\nabla \cdot \boldsymbol{B} = 0$, tells us that there are no sources (or sinks) for the magnetic field—no isolated magnetic poles. The magnetic field is always the result of the changing electric field and/or the motion of electric charge, in accordance with postulate (4). If $\boldsymbol{B}$ represented the flow of water, then $\nabla \cdot \boldsymbol{B} = 0$ would express the fact that nowhere does water flow into, or flow away from, the given quantity of water (by means of some fixed pipe or drain, for example).

$\nabla \times \boldsymbol{E}$, itself a vector, means:

$$\left(\partial E_z/\partial y - \partial E_y/\partial z\right) \boldsymbol{i} + \left(\partial E_x/\partial z - \partial E_z/\partial x\right) \boldsymbol{j} + \left(\partial E_y/\partial x - \partial E_x/\partial y\right) \boldsymbol{k},$$

where $\boldsymbol{i}, \boldsymbol{j}$, and $\boldsymbol{k}$ are unit vectors that point in the positive directions of the x, y, and z coordinates. $\nabla \times \boldsymbol{E}$ is a measure of the extent to which the 'flow' of $\boldsymbol{E}$ (the spatial array of arrows that represent $\boldsymbol{E}$) has a circular motion or pattern—so that if $\boldsymbol{E}$ represented the flow of water, $\nabla \times \boldsymbol{E} \neq 0$ would express the fact that there are whirlpools. Postulate (3) specifies the manner in which the circular flow of $\boldsymbol{E}$ is related to the change of $\boldsymbol{B}$ with time; and postulate (4) specifies the way in which the circular flow of $\boldsymbol{B}$ is related to the change of $\boldsymbol{E}$ with time and/or the electric current $\boldsymbol{j}$.

3. The Role of Symmetry and Group Theory in Physics

Symmetry, we have seen, is an important ingredient of unity. But what is symmetry? What is its role, in general, in theoretical physics? Symmetry in physics is a vast and complex topic; here I make only a few remarks just sufficient for the purposes of this book.[1]

To say of some object that it exhibits such-and-such a symmetry is to say that if the object is changed in some way, it remains the same. Thus a homogeneous sphere (on whose surface there are no distinguishing marks) can be rotated about its centre through any angle, and it remains the same; a cube, by contrast, can only be rotated through certain multiples of 90° about its centre if it is to remain unchanged. These are examples of continuous and discrete symmetries respectively. Such spatial symmetries, both continuous and discrete, are important in theoretical physics.

The notion of symmetry is not, however, restricted to the spatial; whenever *any* kind of object, however non-spatial or abstract, can be thought of as being changed, as a result of one or other of a number of possible operations, O_1, $O_2, \ldots$, being performed on the object, it becomes possible to speak of the object exhibiting some kind of symmetry (on analogy with the cases of the sphere and cube).

From a mathematical point of view, the object exhibits a symmetry if and only if the set of operations that leave things unchanged, $O_1, O_2, \ldots O_N$, forms a *group*, i.e. satisfies the axioms of group theory. These state: among $O_1 \ldots O_N$ there is the identity operation, I, which does nothing; any two operations, O_p and O_q, can be combined to form a third, O_r, so that $O_q O_p = O_r$; repeated operations are associative, that is such that $O_r(O_q O_p) = (O_r O_q)O_p$; and finally, every operation, O_r, has its inverse, O_r^{-1}, which is such that $O_r^{-1}O_r = I$ (the identity operation). It may, or may not, be the case that $O_r O_s = O_s O_r$. If this does hold, the symmetry (and group) is said to be Abelian, and if it does not hold, non-Abelian. The symmetry of a circle in two dimensions is Abelian, whereas the symmetry of a sphere in three dimensions is non-Abelian. Rotate the circle through angle α (O_α) and then through angle β (O_β), that is, in sum, perform the operation $O_\beta O_\alpha$; the outcome is the same if these operations are done in reverse order, which means: $O_\beta O_\alpha = O_\alpha O_\beta$. This equation does not hold, however, for the sphere; rotating the sphere about one axis X, and then another axis Y (both through the centre of the sphere) in general gives a different outcome if these operations are performed in reverse order. The symmetry of the sphere is non-Abelian. Groups, like the symmetries they represent, may be either continuous or discrete. And just as some symmetries can be thought of as being made up of component symmetries, so some groups possess (proper) subgroups. (For G^* to be a proper subgroup of G, it is necessary and sufficient that both G^* and G satisfy the group axioms, and that G includes G^* in the sense that all operations in G^* are also in G but not vice versa, and G^* consists of more than the identity element.)

Symmetry arises in physics in a number of different ways.

1. Symmetry arises because certain composite physical systems—atoms, molecules, crystals—exhibit spatial symmetries.
2. Symmetry arises because postulated fundamental physical entities exhibit spatial symmetries (for example, the Newtonian point-particle which exhibits spherical symmetry).
3. There are symmetries associated with space and time.
4. There are symmetries of laws and theories (which include symmetries of type 2 and 3).

It is the symmetries of theories that is our concern here. To say that a theory, T, exhibits a symmetry is to say that a characteristic change may be made to any isolated system evolving in accordance with T, and the way the system evolves will be unaffected by the change. Consider, for example, symmetry with respect to rotation. Take any isolated system, evolving in accordance with T, and rotate the entire system about any axis: if the rotated system evolves precisely as before (and this is true of all isolated systems to which T applies), then T exhibits rotational symmetry. In referring to the symmetries of T we are really referring to the symmetries of all possible *evolutions* predicted by T.

Typical symmetries of this type, associated with flat space-time, are invariance with respect to change of (1) initial spatial orientation, (2) initial spatial position, (3) initial time of occurrence, (4) inertial motion.[2] In each case, we take any isolated system, S, and change the initial state with respect *merely* to one or other of (1) to (4). The theory, T, has the associated symmetry if the evolution of any isolated system, S, to which T applies, is unaffected by the change.

What does it mean to say that the evolution of a system S is unaffected by a change in the initial conditions of S? In performing an operation O_t on the state of S at time t (where O_t is a change in orientation, location, or whatever) we are, in effect, creating a new system, S^*. What does it mean to say that the evolution of S and of S^* are the same, when these are two distinct systems in the space of all possible systems to which T applies?

One way of explicating this is to say that it means that the same change performed in reverse at any later time will return one to the original system. In other words, given a system S, and a second possible system S^*, got from S by performing the operation O_t on the state of S at time t_1, we require that the reverse operation, O^-_t, performed on S^* at any later time t_2, will return S^* to S. If we are considering rotational symmetry, we may rotate S through any angle at time t_1 to create S^*, and then at any later time t_2 rotate S^* through the same angle in reverse to re-create S.[3]

There is an obvious sense in which all systems that can be obtained from one system, S, in this way, as a result of the initial state of S being changed by operations $\{O\}$ associated with a symmetry, can be regarded as different versions of the *same* system, the *same* evolution. All systems obtained from S merely by rotations are in effect different versions of the same system. This is a general feature of a symmetry. It has the effect of dividing the space of possible evolutions predicted by the theory, T, into infinitely many equivalence classes,[4] all the evolutions in any one equivalence class being obtainable from any one evolution in that equivalence class by the operations $\{O\}$ associated with the symmetry. In the case of rotational symmetry, one such equivalence class consists of all systems obtained from one system by all possible rotations.

In addition to the symmetries associated with space-time that we have considered so far, there are also so-called 'internal' symmetries. These latter arise when the initial state is changed in some way other than a change with respect to space and time, and the change leaves the evolution of all systems predicted by the theory unaffected (where this is understood as before). The distinction between space-time and 'internal' symmetries corresponds, roughly, to symmetries that arise as a result of the nature of space-time, and those that arise as a result of the nature of 'matter'—the nature of everything physical that exists in addition to space-time (particles, forces, fields).

Examples of internal symmetries are the global and local gauge invariance of MT, QED, QEWD, and QCD, discussed in Chapter 4.

So far we have been considering continuous symmetries, but physical theories also exhibit symmetries that are discrete. Examples are symmetry with respect to time-reversal, charge conjugation, and parity. A theory, T, is time-symmetric if, given any evolving isolated system S to which T applies, the evolution with the direction of time reversed (so that the future is the past, and the past is the future) would also accord with the predictions of T. T exhibits parity symmetry if, given any S to which T applies, a system equivalent to the mirror image of S would also accord with the predictions of T. Finally, T exhibits charge conjugation symmetry if, given any system S (to which T applies) that is made up of fundamental particles, the system that is obtained from S by replacing each particle with its antiparticle also evolves in accordance with T.

At one time it was more or less taken for granted that fundamental physical theories would exhibit all three of these discrete symmetries. Parity symmetry seemed especially obvious and immune to doubt, since it is equivalent to demanding that fundamental physical laws make no distinction between left-handedness and right-handedness. And yet in 1956 it was found to be false. In that year, Yang and Lee proposed that the weak interaction might violate parity symmetry. The conjecture was tested as follows. The nuclei of a radioactive isotope of cobalt were placed in a magnetic field in such a way that the spinning nuclei were aligned by the field. The nuclei decay by means of the weak interaction, and emit electrons. If parity obtains, electrons will be emitted in equal numbers in the direction of the field, and in the opposite direction. In fact electrons were found to be emitted preferentially in the opposite direction to the field. This violates parity symmetry.

It was quickly realized that the experiment does not refute a new discrete symmetry that can be formed by combining charge conjugation, C, and parity, P. According to this new symmetry, CP, a theory, T, is CP-symmetric if, given a system S to which T applies, T also applies to S^*, obtained from S by considering the mirror image of S, and replacing all particles by antiparticles. It was subsequently found, in 1964, that particles called neutral kaons, which decay by means of the weak interaction, do so in a manner which violates CP-symmetry.

We can, however, put parity, P, charge conjugation, C, and time-reversal, T, together to form a new discrete symmetry, CPT. A fundamental theorem (the Luders–Pauli theorem) demands that quantum field theories must comply with CPT-symmetry. Thus, given that the weak force violates CP-symmetry, it can only observe CPT-symmetry if it violates T-symmetry. This is an astonishing result: it means that just *one* of the four basic forces fails to be symmetric with respect to time-reversal.[5]

All this, incidentally, illustrates a basic feature of AOE. Symmetry principles can be regarded as non-empirical methodological principles governing choice of theory in physics; but they can also be regarded as *physical* principles, either true or false, associated with level 3 blueprint ideas. However obviously true such principles may appear to be, they may nevertheless be false; but in discovering such principles to be false, new principles need to be discovered if physics is to continue. Level 4 physicalism is retained, even if more specific level 3 versions of physicalism are rejected.

It is, I hope, quite clear from the above account of symmetry that the symmetry of a theory, T, has everything to do with the content of T, and nothing to do with the form of T, in the first instance at least. This deserves to be emphasized, as symmetry is often characterized in terms of changes which leave the *form* of a theory unchanged.

It is, however, always possible to choose terminology which is such that the symmetries of the physical content of T are reflected in the symmetries of the form of T: all that needs to be done is to formulate T using terminology that satisfies the same symmetry principles as the physical reality which T postulates. Thus, theories that presuppose flat space-time and are invariant with respect to changes of spatial location and orientation become terminologically invariant if formulated in terms of vectors. The result of building the physical symmetries of T into the terminology of T is to create two versions of the symmetry principles, usually called the active and passive. The active version is the one we have been considering above: the evolution of a physical system remains unchanged by a change in initial conditions (such as a change in spatial location). The passive version considers, not a change in the physical system, but a corresponding change in the description of the system: the location of the coordinate system, in terms of which the system is described, is changed. Physical symmetries are fully reflected in terminology if, corresponding to every physical change of initial conditions that leaves the evolution unchanged, there is a change in the description (e.g. a change of coordinate system) which leaves the description of the evolution of the physical system unchanged in the same way. A symmetry given its passive interpretation indicates that certain terminological conventions have been adopted: it is the active, not the passive, version of a symmetry that has real physical content.

I have a final point to make about symmetry concerning the connection between symmetry and conservation principles. According to a famous theorem of Emmy Noether, for every theory that can be given a Hamiltonian or Lagrangian formulation,[6] every continuous symmetry gives rise to a conservation principle. Invariance with respect to spatial location and orientation give rise to conservation of linear and angular momentum respectively; invariance with respect to time of occurrence gives rise to conservation of energy. Gauge invariance of classical electromagnetism (MT) gives rise to conservation of charge.

4. Is Symmetry Necessary for Unity, or is it Just One Possible Ingredient?

The first step in tackling this question is to clear up a possible terminological confusion. Throughout the book I argue that, in order to be a precise version of physicalism a (potential) theory of everything, T, must postulate the existence of a U which is *invariant* throughout all phenomena, and which determines the way in which phenomena occur. It is important to appreciate, however, that to say that T is invariant in this sense of postulating an invariant U is not at all the same as to say that T satisfies certain invariance or symmetry principles, in the way we have just been discussing. A theory, T, might be invariant with respect to position, orientation, time, uniform (inertial) motion, and yet fail miserably to postulate an invariant U: an example would be the aberrant version of Newtonian theory, discussed in Chapter 2, according to which gold spheres, in certain circumstances, attract each other in accordance with an inverse cube law of gravitation.

Nevertheless, that a theory, T, is invariant throughout all phenomena to which it applies is a kind of symmetry of the theory. The group, G, of this symmetry is the group of all one–one mappings of possible evolutions predicted by T into possible evolutions predicted by T. One might think that this means that the idea of T being 'invariant' throughout the possible phenomena to which it applies can be explicated in terms of the notions of symmetry and group theory; but this is not the case. Suppose that T^* is an aberrant version of T; the form of T^* matches that of T throughout the space of all possible evolutions except for a small region R in this space, where T^* is quite different from T. In this case, T^* exhibits a symmetry whose group is $G_T{}^*$. (If points in R according to T^* can be put into one–one correspondence with points in R according to T, then (but only then) will G_T and $G_T{}^*$ be formally the same, even though they are given different physical interpretations.) Appealing to symmetry, and group theory, in this way, does not differentiate between the invariant theory T and the non-invariant, aberrant theory T^*. In order to make the distinction we would need to appeal to the symmetry: 'the theory remains invariant throughout the space of possible evolutions'. If $\{G^l\}$ are all the physically interpreted groups corresponding to this symmetry, for all possible invariant theories $\{T\}$, then G_T is a member of $\{G^l\}$ whereas $G_T{}^*$ is not. But here, in distinguishing between T and T^* we are appealing to the very thing we are trying to explicate, namely 'invariance throughout all phenomena to which the theory applies'.

That a physical theory, T, is invariant (i.e has an invariant content) through-out all phenomena to which it applies is a kind of symmetry of T; but it is not a symmetry of T in the sense in which this notion is used in physics, as explicated above. The two notions of symmetry are, however, related: corresponding to the symmetries of T (as physicists use the term) there is a symmetry group, S, and this is a subgroup of G, where this is defined as above.[7]

What restrictions do we need to place on the one–one mappings that are elements of G to arrive at physical symmetries of the type discussed above?

There appear to be three constraints that must be imposed on the one–one mappings of G to turn this symmetry into physical symmetries in the conventional sense.

1. The one–one mappings must be such that the space of all possible evolutions is divided up into infinitely many equivalent classes, such that any evolution, predicted by T, is only mapped onto evolutions in the same equivalence class.

2. The one–one mappings must constitute some *common, invariant,* operation, O, such as changing the location or orientation of the initial state of the system.

3. This operation must commute with the 'time-evolution operator', $t(t_1 \rightarrow t_2)$, which takes any state, at time t_1, of an isolated system (which evolves in accordance with T) to the state at time t_2. That is, given any state, S, of any isolated system evolving in accordance with T, $O \cdot t(t_1 \rightarrow t_2)(S) = t(t_1 \rightarrow t_2) \cdot O(S)$.

One–one mappings of G which satisfy these three conditions form groups of symmetries of T.

What relevance do the symmetries of T (in this sense) have for the unity of T? Is it possible that T might satisfy minimum requirements for unity, and yet possess no symmetries?[8]

One symmetry does seem to be absolutely necessary for unity, namely symmetry with respect to the passage of time. One could of course imagine that physical laws change with the passage of time, but any such change would need to be uniform, or invariantly related to some factor—such as the size of the universe perhaps—if any semblance of unity of the true theory of everything, T, is to be preserved. Both possibilities would ensure that T has a symmetry with respect to time.

The unity of T does not seem to require that there is symmetry with respect to uniform velocity, spatial orientation, or even spatial position. One could imagine a quasi-Aristotelian universe, W, in which events occur in accordance with a unified theory of everything, T, even though absolute position, orientation, and velocity all exist. We can imagine that this universe has a special position, 0, all objects experiencing a force F_0, directed towards 0, and such that $F_o = -kR_0$, where R_0 is the vector from 0 to the object in question, and k is a constant. As a further Aristotelian law we have: $F = mv$, where v is velocity. Motions are governed by a differential equation, and yet symmetry with respect to location, orientation, and uniform velocity are all violated.

It is also true, however, that a spatial symmetry of a kind does exist in this Aristotelian universe, W: the force on objects has spherical symmetry about the spatial point 0. We could imagine another Aristotelian universe, W^*, in which the force varies in some fixed but arbitrary fashion with distance and direction. Such a non-symmetrical universe would lack unity.

I conclude that symmetries of some kind are a necessary ingredient of unity, although they need not be of the type associated with theoretical physics as we know it.

Symmetry is especially relevant when it comes to unification by synthesis, as we saw in Chapter 4 in connection with the unifying powers of MT, and of QED, QEWD, and QCD (the locally gauge invariant character of these latter theories being essential to their capacity to unify by synthesis). As we have seen, one can even account for the imperfect unity by synthesis of QEWD in terms of the group structure of its locally gauge invariant symmetry. This has the form of a direct product of two distinct groups, one associated with the particles W^+, W^-, and W^0, the other associated with the particle V^0. Unification by synthesis is, I suggest, inherently a matter of discovering symmetries associated with the elements to be unified.

It deserves to be noted, in passing, that symmetry cannot be invoked to overcome Goodmanesque difficulties, of the kind discussed in Section 15 of Chapter 4, not at least if symmetry is invoked in a purely formal sense. Any object (or dynamic structure), however apparently non-symmetrical, could always be construed to exhibit symmetry, if the group of operations associated with the symmetry are sufficiently 'alien' and Goodmanesque in character. Consider an object, O, that is not remotely spherical; suppose, now, by 'rigid rotation' we mean 'rotation that so deforms the object being rotated that the net effect is to leave O unaffected by a rotation in this sense'. With respect to this Goodmanesque interpretation of 'rigid rotation', O has spherical symmetry. In a similar fashion, the quasi-Aristotelian universe, W^*, just considered, which lacks spherical symmetry, could be construed by Goodmanesque aliens to possess spherical symmetry (of a peculiar, alien type). An appeal to symmetry does not of itself overcome Goodmanesque difficulties; these need to be dealt with in the manner indicated in Section 15 of Chapter 4.

5. Groups and Matrices

The continuous groups important in physics are (or have the same group-structure as) groups of matrices.

A matrix is a rectangular (or square) array of numbers, real or complex, such that it can be added to and multiplied by other matrices in specified ways. Thus, if A, B, and C are 3×3 matrices, with $A \times B = C$, the matrix C is defined as follows. Let $A = \begin{pmatrix} a_{11} & a_{12} & a_{13} \\ a_{21} & a_{22} & a_{23} \\ a_{31} & a_{32} & a_{33} \end{pmatrix}$ and let B and C, similarly, have elements b_{ij} and c_{ij}, with i and j running from 1 to 3. Then $A \times B = C$ is defined to be such that, $c_{ij} = \Sigma_k a_{ik} b_{kj}$. The elements of the i-th row of A are multiplied with corresponding elements of the j-th column of B, and the products are then added. Thus $c_{23} = a_{21} \times b_{13} + a_{22} \times b_{23} + a_{23} \times b_{33}$. (In general $A \times B \neq B \times A$.) With this definition of the product of groups, all $N \times N$ matrices form a group, called U(N), as long as the matrices are 'unitary'. A matrix, A, is unitary if its inverse, A^{-1}, is equal to its transpose conjugate. The transpose of a matrix, A, is formed by exchanging off-diagonal elements with each other symmetrically (the diag-

TABLE A1. *Continuous groups and matrices important in physics*

Group name	Matrices in group
U (N)	$N \times N$ unitary matrices
SU (N)	$N \times N$ unitary matrices with determinant = 1
O (N)	$N \times N$ real orthogonal matrices
SO (N)	$N \times N$ real orthogonal matrices with determinant = 1

onal running from the top left-hand corner to the bottom right-hand corner). The conjugate of A is the matrix obtained from A by exchanging each element with its complex conjugate, so that $x + iy$ becomes $x - iy$. Restricting the elements of U(N) to unitary elements ensures that each element has an inverse (which otherwise is not in general the case). The unit member of U(N) is the $N \times N$ matrix consisting of ones on the diagonal, and zeros everywhere else. It is not hard to show that, given these definitions, all $N \times N$ unitary matrices satisfy the axioms of group theory.

If, in addition, it is required that the matrices have determinant equal to 1, the resulting group is called $SU(N)$ ('S' for 'special'). If, on the other hand, the matrices of U(N) are restricted to those that have only real numbers as elements, the resulting group is called $O(N)$; in this case each matrix is such that its inverse is equal to its transpose—such matrices being called 'orthogonal'. If, in addition, the demand is made that the determinant of these matrices equals one, the group is called $SO(N)$. $SO(3)$, in particular, is the symmetry group of the sphere.

All this may be summed up in Table A1.

6. Introduction to Quantum Theory

The central enigma of the quantum domain is vividly apparent in the famous two-slit experiment. Quantum systems—photons, electrons, or even atoms—having a precise momentum are directed at a two-slitted screen. Behind the screen, the systems that go through the slits are detected by a photographic plate (or its equivalent). The intensity of the beam of quantum systems may be so low that on average there is only one system (photon, electron, or atom) in the apparatus at any one time.

In appropriate conditions, interference bands are detected by the photographic plate, a result that can be readily explained if it is assumed that each quantum system is an extended wave-like entity with wavelength $\lambda = h/p$, where h is Planck's constant and p is the momentum of the quantum systems in the direction of flight. The wave-like system passes through both slits. At certain regions on the photographic plate crests from one slit arrive simultaneously with troughs from the other slit; the waves cancel each other out. At other regions, the waves arrive in phase from the two slits, and thus reinforce each other. The outcome is the bands detected by the photographic plate. Essentially the same effect arises when ocean waves enter a harbour with two entrances: at certain places on the beach, the waves interfere destructively, and the water is still; at other places the waves reinforce each other. It is all but impossible to see how this quantum-experimental result (and countless others) can be explained in any other way except by supposing that the quantum systems are extended wave-like entities.

But the very same experiment (and countless others) *also* establishes—so it seems—that individual quantum systems cannot possibly be extended wave-like systems. This is because each quantum system is detected as a minute dot on the photographic plate. The wave-like photon or electron that passes through the two slits, and is spread over the whole of the photographic plate, interacts with just *one* silver-bromide molecule in some minute region on the photographic plate so that the molecule is dissociated and a silver atom is deposited on the plate. (This then becomes a dot of millions of silver atoms when the plate is developed.)

Each individual photon or electron interacts with the photographic plate as if it is a highly localized *particle*, with a definite *trajectory* through space; it is only when millions of such interactions are taken into account that an interference pattern begins to emerge. The *wave-like* aspect of the photon or electron is only detected experimentally via a great number of *particle-like* detections.

Modern QT was first developed by Heisenberg in 1925. From the outset, Heisenberg sought to develop the theory in such a way that it was restricted to predicting the outcome of performing measurements on quantum systems—so that the problem of the paradoxical character of quantum systems could be avoided. Later, in 1926, Schrödinger developed wave mechanics with the idea that the theory would describe the real wave-like character of quantum systems. But Schrödinger's version of QT, so interpreted, could not do justice to the particle-like aspect of quantum systems. In 1927 Born proposed that Schrödinger's wave function should be interpreted as determining the probability of detecting the quantum system in a small region of space *if a position measurement is performed on the system*. Schrödinger proved that his version of QT, and Heisenberg's, are experimentally equivalent. Heisenberg, Born, Bohr, Dirac, and others (but not Einstein or Schrödinger) adopted the view that the new QT had to be interpreted in such a way that it is restricted to making probabilistic predictions about the outcome of performing measurements on quantum systems, it being impossible, and unnecessary, to specify the nature of a quantum system when not being measured.

In short, because the creators of QT did not know how to develop a consistent model of quantum systems capable of doing justice to particle-like and wave-like aspects of quantum systems, they were forced to develop the theory in such a way that it is restricted to predicting the outcome of performing measurements on quantum systems (with unfortunate consequences for the theory: see Section 2 of Chapter 7).

Here, in very briefest outline, is the basic structure of the theory that emerged—'orthodox' quantum theory (OQT). I indicate only the Schrödinger version of the theory.

Corresponding to the wave-like aspect of a quantum system such as an electron, there is a 'wave' function, $\psi(x,y,z,t)$, which assigns a complex number to each point in space (x,y,z) at a given time t. (A complex number c is a number of the form $a + ib$, where a and b are real numbers, and $i = \sqrt{-1}$.)

According to OQT, $\psi(x,y,z,t)$, or ψ for short, changes in *two* quite distinct ways, depending on whether a measurement *does not* or *does* occur.

First, if no measurement is performed, $\psi(x,y,z,t)$ changes with the passage of time in a fully deterministic fashion in accordance with Schrödinger's time-dependent equation:

$$(1) \quad i\hbar \frac{\partial \psi(x,y,z,t)}{\partial t} = -\frac{\hbar^2}{2m} \nabla^2 \psi(x,y,z,t) + V(x,y,z)\psi(x,y,z,t).$$

Here, as before, $i = \sqrt{-1}$. $\hbar = h/2\pi$ where h is Planck's constant, m is the mass of the system, and $V(x,y,z)$ is the potential at each point (x,y,z) which determines the force experienced by the system at (x,y,z). In the one-dimensional case, the force, $F(x)$, at the point x, due to the potential $V(x)$, at that point, is given by $F(x) = -dV(x)/dx$. The more rapidly $V(x)$ changes with x (i.e. the greater the slope of the graph of $V(x)$), so the greater the force on the system, the force always pointing in the direction in which $V(x)$ decreases. $\partial/\partial t$ means differentiate once with respect to time. ∇^2 means $\partial^2/\partial x^2 + \partial^2/\partial y^2 + \partial^2/\partial z^2$; thus $\nabla^2\psi$ means that ψ is to be differentiated twice with respect to position.

The equation tells us that the rate of change of $\psi(x,y,z,t)$ with time is equal to minus the rate of change of rate of change of $\psi(x,y,z,t)$ with respect to space plus the potential at the given spatial point, (x,y,z). That changes in $\psi(x,y,z,t)$ with respect to space and time are interrelated in this way suffices to determine $\psi(x,y,z,t)$ for any t given $\psi(x,y,z,t_0)$ for some initial $t = t_0$.

Secondly, if a measurement is performed, an apparently probabilistic change in general occurs, in that the measurement detects more or less precisely some value of a so-called 'observable', such as position, momentum, energy, or angular momentum. The result is determined probabilistically by the quantum state of the measured system at the moment of measurement. Thus, in the case of position, the probability of detecting the system (an electron, say) in volume element dV is given by $|\psi|^2 dV$.

This postulate, first put forward by Max Born in 1926, can be generalized to include the measurement of other so-called 'observables'—momentum, energy, spin. In general, mathematical operations performed on the ψ-function first determine a range of possible values, a_i, that may be obtained if a measurement of such-and-such an observable, A, is performed, and secondly determine the probabilities, p_i, of obtaining these values. Corresponding to any observable, A, there is a specific mathematical operator, $\hat{A}$, which acts on state functions, ψ, to produce new state functions. Any such operator (corresponding to an observable) is such that there is a set of state functions $\{\phi\}$ such that:

(i) If ϕ_i is a member of $\{\phi\}$, then $\hat{A}\phi_i = a_i\phi_i$, where a_i is a real number.
(ii) Any state function ψ can be represented uniquely in the form: $\psi = \Sigma c_i\phi_i$, where the c_i are complex numbers, and $\Sigma|c_i|^2 = 1$.

In this case, the generalized Born postulate asserts:

(2) Given a system is in a state ψ, if observable A is measured, the value a_i will be obtained with probability $|c_i|^2$, where a_i and c_i are determined as in (i) and (ii).

A geometrical interpretation of all this is available. ψ can be regarded as a vector in an abstract space called Hilbert space; the functions $\{\phi_i\}$ can be regarded as unit vectors pointing along coordinates of a coordinate system in Hilbert space. $c_i\phi_i$ is the projection of ψ onto the i-th coordinate. The Schrödinger equation has the effect of rotating the vector corresponding to ψ in Hilbert space, thus changing the values of the complex numbers $\{c_i\}$, and so changing the probabilities of obtaining one or other of the possible values of the observable A if a measurement of A is made. If $\psi = \phi_i$, then the probability of obtaining the value a_i of $A = 1$.

In the case of a system consisting of two 'particles', 1 and 2, with coordinates (x_1,y_1,z_1), and (x_2,y_2,z_2) respectively, the state function is a function of six-dimensional 'configuration' space, $\psi(x_1,y_1,z_1,x_2,y_2,z_2)$, at any given time t. $|\psi(x_1,y_1,z_1,x_2,y_2,z_2,t)|^2 dv_1 dv_2$ represents the probability of detecting particle 1 in volume element dv_1 and, simultaneously, particle 2 in volume element dv_2, granted that the appropriate position measurement is performed.

In the case of a two-particle system, the potential function $V(x_1,y_1,z_1,x_2,y_2,z_2)$ can be interpreted as representing the force between the two particles when 1 is at (x_1,y_1,z_1) and 2 is at (x_2,y_2,z_2).

One striking feature of the theory is its highly non-local character. Once two particles, 1 and 2, have interacted, they remain 'quantum-entangled' even if widely separated spatially, in such a way that the particles do not have separate states. A measurement performed on particle 1 instantaneously affects the quantum state of 2, even though 1 and 2 are vast distances apart. The manner in which the measurement on 1 instantaneously affects the quantum state of 2 is such, however, that it is not possible to transmit a signal by its means. No local measurement performed on 2 can determine whether or not a measurement has been performed on 1. The change in the quantum state of 2 as a result of the measurement performed on 1 cannot be detected experimentally by means of measurements performed locally on 2.

NOTES

PREFACE

1. It is, however, a transformed metaphysics and philosophy that become central to science—transformed in that philosophical ideas are to be assessed, in part at least, in terms of their scientific *fruitfulness*. That this requires a revolution for philosophy becomes clear when one takes into account that many scientists, with considerable justification, judge philosophy to be irredeemably *sterile* scientifically.
2. For these broader implications, see Maxwell (1976*b*, 1980, 1991, 1992*a,b*, 1997, and esp. 1984*a*).
3. For the text of a revised version of this lecture, see Maxwell (1974).
4. Subsequently, Laudan came to defend a view closer to my 1972 view (see Laudan 1977, 1984), although his anti-realism (Laudan 1980) ensured that his view differed substantially from mine.
5. For favourable assessments, see, however, Kneller (1978: 80–7, 90–1); Longuet-Higgins (1984); Collingridge (1985); Midgley (1986); Easlea (1986); and Hendry (1989).

CHAPTER 1

1. Other factors—economic, technological, cultural, and political—of course contribute to making scientific progress possible; but without the crucial requirement of an appropriate methodology being put into practice, these other factors will be impotent.
2. See Kyburg (1970); Hesse (1974); Watkins (1984); Glymour (1980). The books by Kyburg and Watkins have extensive bibliographies on works concerned with the problem of induction.
3. Some contemporary historians and philosophers of science appear to have abandoned all hope of understanding how scientific *progress* in knowledge is possible. They seek merely to describe and explain, in sociological terms, scientific *change*. See e.g. Barnes and Bloor (1982).
4. For earlier expositions of aim-oriented empiricism, see Maxwell (1974, 1976*b*, 1977, 1979, 1984*a*, 1993*c*).
5. In my view, it is the broader implications of this new conception of scientific method and rationality for the whole of academic inquiry and, above all, for the task of creating a better world, that are really important. In this book, however, there is space only for an exposition and defence of the conception of science itself. For the all-important broader *implications* of

this new view of science, see esp. Maxwell (1984*a*); see also Maxwell (1976*b*, 1980, 1984*b*, 1985*a*, 1986, 1987, 1991, 1992*a,b*, 1993*b,d*, 1994*b*, 1996, 1997).

6. Here, and in what follows, 'simplicity' is taken to include 'explanatoriness', 'unity', and other possible non-empirical considerations governing choice of theory in science, such as 'elegance', 'symmetry', 'beauty', 'comprehensibility'.

7. It deserves to be called 'the fundamental epistemological dilemma of science'. It is more fundamental than the problem of induction, which only arises if the need for science to make some kind of substantial cosmological assumption is denied.

8. It is important to appreciate that even if we try to formulate an assumption that is as much as possible about local observable phenomena only, and thus as far as possible away from being about 'the ultimate nature of the universe', such an assumption will, nevertheless, remorselessly contain some assumption about the ultimate nature of the universe, to the effect that it is such as to permit local, observable phenomena to be as the assumption asserts them to be. However instrumentalistic or phenomenalistic one may seek to be in couching cosmological assumptions of science, such assumptions will carry some implications about the ultimate nature of reality.

9. Even when the assumption that sustains the methodology is a falsifiable theory rather than an unfalsifiable metaphysical thesis, it still may be difficult to reject the theory in the light of empirical difficulties, as Kuhn has shown in his account of the resistance encountered within science to the overthrow of paradigms that have encountered anomalies: see Kuhn (1970, chs. viii–ix and xii).

10. An additional difficulty involved in creating modern science has to do with the nature of the metaphysical conjecture that needs to be adopted for science to succeed, namely that some kind of impersonal unified pattern of physical law determines how events occur. This is an inherently difficult idea to make precise; as we shall see in Ch. 4, it requires, amongst other things, the mathematical theory of differential equations. It has disturbing consequences for the nature and value of human life, having to do especially with consciousness and free will. (How can there be consciousness and free will if everything is physically determined?) And the mode of explanation for natural phenomena that it makes possible is profoundly unintuitive for human beings. Human consciousness evolved within the context of social life, in part as a result of the need to understand others in terms of their desires, intentions, beliefs, feelings. This personalistic mode of understanding, being intimately bound up with our existence as conscious beings, is the 'natural', intuitive way for us to understand things. It is not surprising, then, that humanity should (initially) try to understand the

natural world in the same sort of way, in terms of the desires and intentions of gods. It has been extraordinarily difficult and painful for humanity to discover that the universe is not comprehensible in this personalistic fashion but, on the contrary, is only physically comprehensible in terms of some unified pattern of physical law. In many ways, indeed, the discovery has not yet been made; hence the need for this book.

11. A 'metaphysical' thesis, as understood here, is a general, factual thesis about the world which lacks the *precision* of a physical law or theory, and thus fails to make the precise empirical predictions of a law or theory. In general, given a metaphysical thesis, *B*, it will be possible to make this precise (so that it becomes capable of making precise predictions) in infinitely many different ways. Thus *B* might be atomism: the world is made up of atoms, of some size and mass, which stick together in some way. This vague, metaphysical doctrine becomes a scientific theory as it is given greater precision and becomes, as a result, testable. This notion of 'metaphysical' does not draw a sharp line between the metaphysical and the testably scientific. The 'metaphysical' doctrine that there are only repulsive forces in the world is refuted by the observation that attractive and cohesive forces do exist: the 'metaphysical', as understood here, cannot be equated with the 'unfalsifiable' in a Popperian fashion: see Popper (1959: 40–2, 78–86). On the other hand, most physical theories have an element of imprecision: a constant, such as the constant of gravitation, G, in Newtonian theory, is determined only within a range of values. A theory with an imprecise constant corresponds to an infinity of different precise theories, each with its own distinct, precise value of the constant. Newtonian theory fits the definition of a metaphysical thesis! The distinction between the physical and metaphysical is thus, to some extent, a matter of degree. (Popper's distinction between the scientific and the metaphysical is also, it should be noted, a matter of degree.) As far as Newtonian theory is concerned, if the constant G is fixed as narrowly as possible, within the accuracy of current measurements, the theory is a level 2 *physical* theory; if the constant G is left completely undetermined, the theory becomes a level 3 metaphysical assertion, and further generalizations make it all the more metaphysical in character.

12. The following scheme deliberately ignores vast tracts of scientific knowledge, such as: all of phenomenological physics, including such areas as solid state physics, thermodynamics, and statistical mechanics; observational science carried on for its own sake, in astronomy, geology, and elsewhere, and not in order to test fundamental physical theories; chemistry; biology; all of social science. For a justification of this neglect here, see Ch. 2, Sect. 5. For my views about biology and social inquiry, all that which physics seems to miss out, see Maxwell (1984a) and *How Can there be Life of Value in the Physical Universe?* (Maxwell, forthcoming, *b*).

13. These are in the form of laws appropriately restricted in terms of range of application and accuracy, so as to stand a good chance of being true, and of being derivable, in principle, from appropriate theory.

14. In order to explain, in science, it is not sufficient to predict; it is necessary, in addition, to show that ostensibly diverse phenomena are diverse aspects of *one* phenomenon (or one kind of phenomenon), as when the diverse motions of terrestrial projectiles, the moon round the earth, the earth and other planets round the sun, double stars round each other, and stars round our galaxy are all aspects of the *one* kind of phenomenon of objects moving and interacting in accordance with Newton's laws of motion and law of gravity. The thesis that this is the proper way to understand scientific explanation will be developed throughout the book; but see esp. Ch. 4.

15. The notion of 'rationally discoverable' is problematic. As I am using the phrase, no thesis about the universe is rationally discoverable if it is grossly *ad hoc*, like the theories discussed in Sect. 2 (or the 'aberrant' theories to be discussed in Sect. 7 of Ch. 2), and the *ad hoc* phenomena, postulated by the thesis, lie beyond our experience. Any such thesis is one of infinitely many rivals, all equally arbitrary, there being no rationale to prefer the given thesis.

16. What these terms mean, and how they are interrelated, will be discussed further in Chs. 3 and 5.

17. P_9 is a kind of 'principle of the uniformity of nature'. P_9 is, however, intended to be very much weaker than uniformity principles as these are usually formulated and understood. It does not assert that all phenomena are governed by the same laws everywhere, since the possibility of (some) arbitrary, '*ad hoc*' phenomena is conceded. Instead, P_9 asserts that if such phenomena occur anywhere they occur in our immediate environment. P_9 does not even assert that approximately lawful phenomena occur everywhere, but merely that whatever it is that makes our immediate environment partially knowable extends throughout the universe. We might live in a partially knowable world even though no laws strictly obtain, as the notion of law is understood in natural science.

18. This assumes that T makes B precise everywhere, and not just for selected phenomena. If we relax this requirement, then T might be B-disunified and yet imply B. And, more generally, P_r might be P_s-disunified, with $2 < r < s < 8$, and yet P_r might imply P_s (because what P_s asserts is made more precise by P_r for some restricted range of phenomena only). In general, however, if P_r only exemplifies P_s in a disunified or imperfect way then P_r will be incompatible with P_s.

19. Persistently rejecting empirically successful *ad hoc* theories involves making a persistent, substantial assumption about the world, which contradicts the basic tenet of standard empiricism. We shall return to this point in Ch. 2.

20. For a discussion of scientific research programmes, see Lakatos (1970). Lakatos brings out clearly how competing research programmes can be assessed in terms of their empirical fruitfulness and progressiveness, but is quite unable to consider the possibility that they can be assessed in terms of how well their basic metaphysical assumption, or 'hard core', accords with the thesis that the universe is comprehensible in some way or other. As I explain in the text in a moment, Lakatos, being wedded to standard empiricism, cannot conceive of all of science as being one gigantic research programme with the one fixed metaphysical assumption that the universe is comprehensible in some way or other.

21. Possibilities of this type will be considered in Chs. 3 and 5.

22. It is possible, of course, that the order that we find in the world around us so far may abruptly and inexplicably change at some time in the future. This would not provide grounds for rejecting the assumption at level 9, although it certainly would provide grounds for changing our ideas about the nature of our 'local' world. The solution to the problem of induction that I offer in Ch. 5 does not guarantee that the order we find in the world around us will not abruptly change; no such guarantee is possible. What it does do is justify adopting the conjecture that this will not occur (until such time as it does!).

23. From the standpoint of aim-oriented empiricism, we are justified in holding that we possess some knowledge of the nature of ultimate reality, and justified in holding that we can improve this knowledge. The traditional view that God is ultimately unknowable is, in part at least, designed to defuse objections to the existence of God on the grounds that an all-knowing, all-powerful, all-loving God is refuted by all the suffering and death that such a God would knowingly inflict on people via natural processes. How can God be so cruel? We cannot know; the ways of God are inherently inscrutable! One sees here, incidentally, how anti-rational *ex cathedra* pronouncements are on inherent limits to knowledge: such pronouncements, arrogant under a cloak of humility, protect dogma from criticism.

24. Standard empiricism demands that *no* persistent assumption can be made about the universe independently of empirical considerations; but in persistently accepting explanatory theories independently of, or even against, unbiased empirical considerations, science *does* make a persistent, substantial assumption, along the lines that the universe exhibits sufficient comprehensibility for the search for explanations to meet with empirical success, however much this may be denied out of misguided ideas about scientific propriety.

25. What has made it so extraordinarily difficult for humanity to develop science has been the difficulty of making the right (level 4 or 3) choice as to the kind of way in which the universe is comprehensible, or 'nearly' comprehensible (this task being made all the more difficult by the grim

implications of the thesis that needs to be accepted, it seems, for science to be successful, discussed in n. 10). As I have indicated, a bad choice that fails to promote the growth of knowledge will contain its own inbuilt explanations why failure is to be expected: there will be no spur to look for something better. All this demonstrates how important aim-oriented empiricism is for the long-term growth of knowledge. Its adoption spurs one to develop more fruitful rivals to existing level 3 or 4 ideas. If the idea had been available to the ancient Greeks they might well have created modern science 2,000 years ago. As it was, modern science was created and developed without aim-oriented empiricism being explicitly understood and adopted; on the whole, explicitly accepted philosophical, epistemological, metaphysical, and methodological ideas (as opposed to those implicit in scientific practice) have been more or less hostile to the advance of science, and science has had to struggle against them.

26. It is perhaps more correct to say that Newton's followers in the 18th century and subsequently understood Newton to have espoused a version of standard empiricism. Newton himself may be interpreted as having defended an early version of aim-oriented empiricism. This is apparent in Newton's First Rule of Reasoning, which asserts: '*We are to admit no more causes of natural things than such as are both true and sufficient to explain their appearances*. To this purpose the philosophers say that Nature does nothing in vain, and more is in vain when less will serve; for Nature is pleased with simplicity, and affects not the pomp of superfluous causes' (Newton 1962: 398).

27. For a discussion of the way in which standard and aim-oriented empiricism influence, and are, in a sense, a part of the intellectual–institutional structure of science, see Maxwell (1984*a*).

28. There is insufficient space to include this part of the argument here; instead, see Maxwell (1993*c*: III).

29. As long as scientists believe that, ultimately, evidence alone decides what is accepted in science, they will continue to believe, with some justification, that the rest of culture (apart from mathematics) has no rational role to play within science.

30. For my views as to how our human world, imbued with colours, sounds, meaning and value, consciousness, and free will can be accommodated within the universe, presumed to be physically comprehensible, see Maxwell (1966, 1968*a,b*, 1976*b*, 1984*a*, ch. 10, 1995*b*, forthcoming, *b*).

31. The level 5 thesis of comprehensibility in effect implies the more and more attenuated theses at levels 6 to 9, represented in Fig. 1.

32. '. . . *it must be possible for an empirical scientific system to be refuted by experience*' (Popper 1959: 41).

33. Metaphysical propositions tend to be empirically untestable, and therefore cannot, as a rule, be 'empirically fruitful' in the sense of 'successfully predicting phenomena'. What is meant, rather, by an 'empirically fruitful'

metaphysical assumption is an assumption which supports an empirically progressive research programme, so that successive testable theories, progressively making precise the metaphysical assumption more and more extensively and satisfactorily, are *also* increasingly successful *empirically*. An 'empirically fruitful' metaphysical idea is thus one which generates scientific theories of increasing empirical success. This important idea will be discussed in more detail in Ch. 5.

34. Newton's attitude towards his law of gravitation, as expressed in his *Principia*, is that the law describes the way objects in fact move, *as if* there is a force of gravitation acting at a distance across empty space. Newton vehemently rejected the idea, however, that there really is such a force. On one occasion he declared: 'That gravity should be innate, inherent, and essential to matter, so that one body may act upon another, at a distance through a vacuum, without the mediation of anything else . . . is to me so great an absurdity, that I believe no man who has in philosophical matters a competent faculty of thinking can ever fall into it' (Burtt 1932: 265–6).

35. Since 1972 I have not only *argued* for aim-oriented empiricism; I have also tried to put the view into scientific practice in connection, in particular, with quantum theory: see Ch. 7.

36. These somewhat technical features of theoretical physics, referred to briefly in this paragraph, will be explained and discussed in more detail in Ch. 4.

37. For a magnificent introductory account of the Presocratics as precursors of what is best in modern science, see Popper (1963, ch. 5).

38. See e.g. Ziman (1968: 31); Weinberg (1993, ch. vii).

39. In arguing for standard empiricism, philosophers of science help bring about the very opposite of what they intend: in seeking to defend the rationality of science they help sabotage it by defending a view which suppresses scientific discussion of problematic implicit metaphysical assumptions.

40. See works referred to in n. 30.

CHAPTER 2

1. For a good, non-technical account of modern theoretical physics, see Adair (1987). For an excellent, but much briefer account, see Squires (1985). See also Penrose (1990, chs. 5 and 6); Carrigan and Trower (1989). For more technical accounts, see Dodd (1984); Okun (1985); Kenyon (1987); Griffiths (1987); Friedman (1983); Schutz (1989). The best introductory textbook on physics known to me is Feynman *et al.* (1965).

2. For a popular account of the power of Darwinianism to account for evolution, see Dawkins (1986). See also Smith (1993); Cronin (1991); Moore (1994).

3. See Frank-Kamenetskii (1993); Brown (1992).

4. Weinberg (1977); Silk (1989).
5. For an attempt at a non-technical survey of the whole of science, physical and biological, see Asimov (1987).
6. For references, see nn. 13 and 20.
7. I first introduced this terminology in a lecture given to the Bloomsbury Particle Group (the joint seminar of the Physics Departments of University College London and Birkbeck College) in 1993. Physicists distinguish between the 'bare' and 'dressed' electron in connection with quantum electrodynamics.
8. It should perhaps be said that Popper *intends* to defend a version of bare SE: as we shall see in Sect. 8 of the present chapter, Popper's demand that theories be 'strictly universal' violates bare SE.
9. See Fig. 1.
10. For example, Steven Weinberg (1993: 185), who writes, 'If history is any guide at all, it seems to me to suggest that there *is* a final theory.'
11. For the distinction between the contexts of justification and discovery, see Reichenbach (1938: 6–7), Popper (1959: 31).
12. Lakatos makes the point explicitly when he asserts: 'Even science as a whole can be regarded as a huge research programme with Popper's supreme heuristic rule: "devise conjectures which have more empirical content than their predecessors"' (Lakatos 1970: 132). Kuhn's and Lakatos's allegiance to SE is, however, inherent in their whole account of science. For both, paradigms (or hard cores) have a quasi-metaphysical character, and are thus not straightforwardly verifiable or falsifiable empirically. They can only be assessed by considering the extent to which research programmes based on them achieve, or fail to achieve, empirical success. It is the lack of any other means of assessment which renders the assessment of paradigms at best a long-term business, and which makes instantaneous rational choice of paradigm, during a revolution, a non-rational affair. For further discussion of this point, see Maxwell (1974: 149–52).
13. Bloor (1976); Barnes (1985); Shapin and Schaffer (1985); Shapin (1994).
14. That SE is entirely compatible with the view that science, reason, and knowledge are all inherently social in character is explicitly acknowledged in Maxwell (1984*a*); see e.g. p. 40.
15. See his objection to the idea of a non-social, 'Robinson Crusoe' science (Popper 1962: 217–20); see also Popper (1961: 154–7).
16. Strictly speaking, there are *three* positions: (1) radical empiricism, or SE (which holds that all factual knowledge is based exclusively on experience); (2) radical rationalism (which holds that all factual knowledge is based exclusively on reason); and (3) empirico-rationalism (which holds that factual knowledge is based on an admixture of experience and reason). In practice, no one holds (2), and 'rationalism' means 'empirico-rationalism'. Popper, with some justice, has suggested that 'rationalism' really ought to be called 'intellectualism', since otherwise the unfortunate impression is

created that empiricism is opposed to the rationalist creed, when actually it is a version of it. I have decided, however, to go along with traditional usage; I hope no one will be bamboozled into thinking that there is intended to be something anti-rationalist in traditional empiricism.

17. This is a generalization of Einstein's remark, which was restricted to *mathematical* propositions: see Einstein (1954: 233).

18. For a discussion of the influence of SE on scientific practice, and of the way SE prohibits discussion of itself within the context of science, see Maxwell (1984*a*: 122–55).

19. Something of this attitude of scientists towards contemporary philosophy of science can be found in Weinberg (1993, ch. 7).

20. Shapin (1994); Bloor (1976); Barnes (1985); Shapin and Schaffer (1985).

21. Theoretical physics is intellectually fundamental within natural science granted that the basic aim of science is to improve knowledge and understanding of Nature; theoretical physics is not intellectually fundamental, however, within rational inquiry as a whole granted that the basic aim of inquiry is to improve *wisdom*: see Maxwell (1984*a*).

22. A true law of nature is such that nothing could be done to refute it; a true accidental generalization, such as (perhaps) 'All lumps of gold are less than 1 million tons', is such that endless things could be done to refute it; it just so happens that none of these things *is* done. For further discussion, see Ch. 4, Sect. 14.

23. For a detailed critical examination of Bayesianism, see Earman (1992).

24. For the idea of formulating the problem of induction in terms of empirically successful aberrant theories, see Maxwell (1974: I). This generalizes and improves upon Goodman's (1954) way of formulating the problem, in terms of 'aberrant' predicates 'bleen' and 'grue'.

25. Versions of instrumentalism or conventionalism have been defended by Duhem (1954) and Poincaré (1952).

26. For expositions of 'induction-to-the-best-explanation', see Jeffreys (1957); Barker (1957); Popper (1963: 241); G. Harman (1965, 1968); Lycan (1988); Lipton (1991).

27. I am appealing here to the Stone–Weierstrass theorem, which tells us that any continuous function can be approximated arbitrarily closely throughout a finite interval by analytic functions: see Dieudonné (1960: 131–4).

28. For other criticisms of Friedman's proposal, see Kitcher (1976); Salmon (1989: 94–101).

29. For other criticisms of Watkin's proposal, see Oddie (1989); for Watkins's reply, see Watkins (1991).

30. This was discovered independently by Miller (1974) and Tichý (1974).

31. For discussion of the problem, see Niiniluoto (1987).

32. The case against progress in knowledge about theoretical entities has been presented by Laudan (1980).

CHAPTER 3

1. See Ch. 1, Sect. 4, for a preliminary indication of what the comprehensibility thesis means.

2. How does one distinguish a physically comprehensible universe from one which is comprehensible in some non-physical way? I would wish to argue that, at a fundamental level, there are just *two* distinct kinds of explanation and understanding: (1) physical, and (2) personalistic: see Maxwell (1984*a*, ch. 10). There are purposive explanations in addition, it is true; but they are a diminished form of personalistic explanation (purposive explanations lacking the empathic, anthropomorphic dimension of personalistic explanations—that dimension which enables one to be, in imagination, the other person that is being explained and understood). There are historical explanations in addition; but these are parasitic on those already mentioned. In response to this, the question may still be asked: But what is a specifically physical explanation? What is a physically comprehensible universe? One can attempt to give a general characterization that does not beg the question: physical explanations are impersonal, non-experiential, causal, couched in terms of interpreted mathematics, predictive, unifying. A better response is to produce examples, both of legitimate physical explanations, and of explanations that are not physical. This, in effect, is what I do in the text.

3. See Chapter 4, Sect. 14.

4. See the discussion of Maxwell's equations in empty space without charge in Ch. 4, Sect. 11, together with Sect. 14 for an exposition and defence of interpreting such equations essentialistically.

5. For a detailed, scholarly account of the Presocratics, see Guthrie (1978). For a magnificent, much shorter and much more controversial account—one which casts the Presocratics in the role of creating rational inquiry as Popper envisaged it—see Popper (1963, ch. 5).

6. He said that the atomic hypothesis contained the most information in the fewest words: see Feynman *et al.* (1965: i. 1–2).

7. It may be thought anachronistic to interpret the Presocratics as putting forward theories that are precursors of those of modern physics. I do not wish to deny that the thought processes, the motivations, of a Thales, Anaximander, or Pythagoras differ radically from those of Faraday, Boltzmann, or Einstein. One vital point must, however, be emphasized. The Presocratic philosophers were, without doubt, tackling *the fundamental problem* of modern physical science and cosmology, especially when understood in AOE terms. They sought to understand the nature of the one kind of stuff that persists throughout diversity and change, and in terms of which diversity and change can be understood. And they did this in a way which does not just appeal to gods, or God. Thales may have asserted that the world is full of gods, but Democritus, by contrast, put forward a thoroughly

impersonal view of the world. What makes comparisons with modern science legitimate, however, is the undoubted fact that the Presocratics struggled with *the* fundamental problem of natural philosophy: to understand unity-throughout-diversity-determining-change.

8. For an account of the emergence of the corpuscular hypothesis from the views of ancient Greece, see Dijksterhuis (1969).

9. Just as velocity may be thought of either as an absolute, intrinsic property of an object, or as a relational property between two objects, so too length and time intervals may be thought of as absolute or relational. We ordinarily think of length and time intervals as absolute; SR demands that they be construed as relational, so that one and the same rod or clock can have different lengths or rates relative to different frames, just as they can have different velocities relative to different frames.

10. I assume that tachyons (hypothetical particles that only travel faster than light) do not exist.

11. For lucid non-technical accounts of SR, see Einstein (1920); d'Abro (1950: pt. II).

12. For a further development of this point see Maxwell (1993c: III).

13. The superstring blueprint might be regarded as a special case of the blueprint that I am about to put forward as the best available for current physics, namely Lagrangianism. And given this, it may be argued, the superstring research programme needs to meet with some empirical success before its blueprint deserves to be regarded as better than Lagrangianism.

14. For accounts of Lagrangian formulations of classical and quantum mechanical theories, see Feynman *et al.* (1965, vol. ii, ch. 19); Mandl and Shaw (1984, ch. 2); Goldstein (1980).

15. Even the thesis that the universe is non-aberrant may be judged to be too substantial. It may be argued that, in order to make theoretical knowledge possible, it suffices to assume that local phenomena, accessible to us, occur sufficiently approximately *as if* the universe is non-aberrant for physics to continue to make (ostensible) theoretical and empirical progress. I will argue against this minimalist, instrumentalist position in Chs. 5 and 6.

16. In this chapter no attempt is made to solve the problem of induction, since the argument assumes (and does not try to justify) that theoretical knowledge exists (in some appropriate sense of 'knowledge').

17. If there is no universal force, then for some regions in the space of possible phenomena (or possible universes) there will be non-interacting parts.

18. Counting entities is rendered a little less ambiguous if a system of M particles is counted as a (somewhat peculiar) field. This means that M particles all of the same kind (i.e. with the same dynamic properties) is counted as *one* entity. In the text I continue to adopt the convention that M particles all the same dynamically represents one *kind* of entity, rather than one entity. Type 4 and 5 unity/disunity distinctions in effect reformulate Jeffreys's and Wrinch's idea (see Ch. 2, Sect. 8) that simplicity has to do

with paucity of constants, as an idea about, not the *form* of a theory, but rather its *content*. It is not the number of constants that matters, but rather the number of different kinds of physical entity with different dynamic properties. As we shall see in Ch. 4, this difference is decisive when it comes to solving the problem of what the simplicity, or unity, of a theory *is*.

19. For a discussion of symmetry and group theory, see the Appendix, and Sects. 11 to 13 of Ch. 4.

20. An informal sketch of these matters is given in Ch. 4, Sects. 11 to 13, and the Appendix. For rather more detailed accounts of the locally gauge invariant structure of quantum field theories see: Moriyasu (1983); Aitchison and Hey (1982); and Griffiths (1987, ch. 11). For introductory accounts of group theory as it arises in physics, see Isham (1989), Joshi (1982), or Jones (1990).

21. For accounts of spontaneous symmetry-breaking, see Moriyasu (1983) or Mandl and Shaw (1984).

22. One of the difficulties that has to be overcome in explicating what 'unity' means in theoretical physics is to appreciate the point that the *concept* of unity is itself, in a sense, disunified, in that there are eight or more distinct facets to the distinction between unity and disunity, eight or more ways in which theoretical unity may, in thought, become theoretical disunity. If this seems surprising at first, it ought not to do so, perhaps, after a moment's thought, in that it reflects no more than the inevitable diversity of disunity, the inevitable diversity of ways of transforming unity, in imagination, into disunity.

23. In the next chapter I argue that we need to add simplicity (in the non-generic sense) to the list.

24. The task is not to establish that the thesis of unity in senses 1 to 8 is *true*, but merely that we are justified in holding it to be a part of (conjectural) scientific knowledge *if* we are justified in holding that the thesis that the universe is unified in senses 1 and 2 is a part of scientific knowledge.

25. (C2) is likely to clash with (C4) in that potential fruitfulness is likely to be inversely related to content. (C4) is, despite this, a desideratum because the lower the content, the more likely a thesis is to be true.

CHAPTER 4

1. Tradition has forced me, in the present chapter, to use the word 'simplicity' in two different senses. On the one hand, in discussing 'the problems of simplicity' (as it is traditionally called), I use the word as the generic term, to stand for all the terms that may be used in the present context: 'unity', 'explanatoriness', etc. On the other hand, in Section 16, I use 'simplicity' to refer to just one (hypothetical) aspect of theories in addition to the other aspects, such as unity, explanatoriness, etc. In this second sense, 'simplicity'

really does mean simplicity. I hope this ambiguity of usage is not too confusing.

2. See Ch. 2, Sect. 8.

3. 'Theory', throughout this discussion, means the conjunction of fundamental dynamical theories required to cover, in principle, all known phenomena, or the conjunction of laws of some domain of phenomena if no theory of the domain exists.

4. The case of wooden objects, $O_1 \ldots O_N$, and corresponding descriptions, $D_1 \ldots D_N$, differs from the case of possible physical universes, $U_1 \ldots U_N$, and corresponding theories, $T_1 \ldots T_N$, in the following important respect. Whereas each O_r picks out one specific possible object, each U_r picks out infinitely many possible universes—all those that evolve everywhere in accordance with T_r. Put another way, each U_r picks out, not an object, but a specific 'necessitating property' (see Section 14 of the present chapter) that determines the way events unfold. This disanalogy between the case of wooden objects and universes does not affect the point of the analogy: to emphasize that the simplicity or complexity of *objects* (of whatever kind) need have no connection with the simplicity or complexity of *descriptions* of these objects.

5. I have assumed that the distinction between form and content is absolute and unproblematic. In practice, this is not always the case. A given formalism may be given two different physical interpretations; in this case there is identity of form but two distinct theories. On the other hand, two very different formalisms, physically interpreted, may appear to state quite different theories (i.e. have very different physical content), which subsequently turn out, controversially perhaps, to amount to the same content, the same theory. Thus, Heisenberg's quantum matrix mechanics, proposed in 1925, appeared to have a quite different form from Schrödinger's quantum wave theory, proposed in 1926; the two formalisms were initially believed to constitute two distinct, rival theories until Schrödinger showed that they were, in some sense, equivalent. Both were subsequently subsumed into the so-called transformation theory developed by Dirac and others. It remains a controversial question, however, whether Heisenberg's and Schrödinger's theories are the same. But such uncertainties concerning form and content only arise because of uncertainty about how a given formalism should be interpreted physically, what the physical content should be taken to be. The point that content and form are utterly distinct is not affected. The content of a physical theory is the possible physical states of affairs that the theory specifies and asserts to exist; the form applies to what we write down on paper.

6. The point that persistent favouring of explanatory theories in science carries metaphysical implications has been defended by Railton (1989).

7. We see here, clearly, why SE cannot conceivably solve the problem of what simplicity is. (The point is so fundamental to the argument of the book that

I feel compelled to restate it.) Any epistemologically and methodologically significant conception of simplicity that has a bearing on whether or not a theory is true must be concerned with the content of the theory, not its form. But if, in physics, we persistently favour theories that are simple in the sense that what these assert to be the case is simple, it is entirely obvious that we are thereby making a persistent assumption about Nature, to the effect that Nature herself is simple. This blatantly violates SE. In order to avoid bringing this contradiction out into the open, those who defend (dressed) SE are forced to obscure the issue by interpreting the simplicity of theories in such a way that it has to do with form and not content. But then there can be no way of avoiding the devastating objection that such a notion of simplicity cannot conceivably be epistemologically significant, since one and the same theoretical assertion can be formulated in as simple or complex a way as we please. SE is inherently incapable of doing justice to the point that simplicity, in an epistemologically significant sense, must be concerned with content and not form.

8. When physical symmetries are reflected in the language used to describe the phenomena, symmetry transformations are of two kinds: 'active', involving a real physical change (such as a change of position or orientation in space) and 'passive', involving a change of description (a change of the position or orientation of the coordinate system in terms of which the phenomena are described).

9. For a lucid discussion of the simplicity of classical electromagnetism when formulated in such a Minkowski-appropriate language, see Feynman *et al.* (1965: ii. 25. 8–11).

10. For earlier expositions of this account of simplicity, see Maxwell (1974: II, 1979).

11. Strictly speaking, two non-empirical requirements are involved in the explanatory character of a theory. The explanatory character of a theory becomes all the greater (1) the more unified it is, and (2) the greater its empirical content. This second requirement is related to the goal of theoretical physics of discovering unity throughout *all* the diverse physical phenomena that there are; the goal of theoretical physics, we might say, is to discover dynamic unity running through all possible diversity.

12. I use the term 'simplicity', here, in its non-generic sense. 'Simplicity', here, really does mean simplicity.

13. GR yields ten equations, but the Bianchi identities reduce this to six: see Schutz (1989: 200) for details.

14. It is possible, however, that physicalism, as I have formulated it, is false, even though the universe is physically comprehensible in a broader sense. Physicalism, as I have characterized it, embodies the classical distinction between theory, on the one hand, and initial conditions on the other—so that, in order to pick out our universe, initial conditions (those of the big bang) need to be added to the true fundamental theory, T. But it could be

that T contains an inherently cosmological dimension to it, so that T alone determines what the initial conditions of the universe are. Future developments in physics may require us to revise our ideas at level 4, and not just at level 3.

15. For accounts of blueprints proposed by Wheeler, Penrose, and Schwartz and Green, see Wheeler (1968); Penrose (1975); Davies and Brown (1988).

16. Those unfamiliar with the idea of differential equations should consult the Appendix for a brief exposition.

17. In Ch. 3, Sect. 5 I distinguished eight facets of unity. The first five of these are involved in Newton's unification of Kepler and Galileo.

18. It would not be possible to formulate the true, unified theory of everything in the form of differential equations if space-time is discontinuous.

19. Maxwell's theory, as understood by Maxwell himself, and by his followers, Fitzgerald, Lodge, Heaviside, Larmor, and even Lorentz, presupposed the existence of the ether; given that standpoint, real unification would only be achieved by a theory of the ether. A long process of development was required before Maxwell's theory acquired the post-Einsteinian form that I am considering, the theory being interpreted as a fundamental theory about the electromagnetic field rather than a phenomenological theory about an aspect of the ether, assumed to be an entity about which little was known. For an account of the development of Maxwellian theory, see Hunt (1991); and, at a somewhat more technical level, Buchwald (1985).

20. In terms of the eight facets of unity listed in Ch. 3, Sect. 5, MT appeals to facets 4 or 5 in unifying light and electromagnetism by annihilation, but appeals to facet 6 in unifying the electric and magnetic forces by synthesis.

21. Strictly speaking, it is not accurate to refer to the magnetic field as a field of *force*, because the force exerted by the magnetic field on a charged particle depends, not just on the position, but also on the velocity of the particle in question.

22. Those unfamiliar with the idea of partial differential equations should consult Sect. 2 of the Appendix before reading on.

23. In terms of the eight facets of unity listed in Ch. 3, Sect. 5, the Maxwellian unification by synthesis of electricity and magnetism is, as I have already mentioned, an example of type 6 unity.

24. It is sometimes argued that quantum field theory unifies particle and field, in that particles are, according to the theory, nothing more than excitations of the field. Quantum field theory goes some way towards a resolution of the problem, but ultimately fails to solve the problem for reasons to be discussed in Ch. 7.

25. For two excellent non-technical accounts of the theories of modern physics (covering the ground of the present section in much more detail), see Squires (1985); Adair (1987). For two somewhat more technical accounts, see Okun (1985); Dodd (1984). For two histories of the two main branches

of 20th-century theoretical physics, relativity theory and theory of matter, see Pais (1982, 1986). See also Schweber (1994); Marshak (1993).

26. This is a step towards unification by annihilation (in that it involves an immense reduction in the number of distinct fundamental substances). In terms of the eight facets of unity listed in Ch. 3, Sect. 5, this step is a type 5 unification.

27. One might perhaps regard this as the discovery of a broken symmetry— type 7 of the eight facets of unity listed in Ch. 3, Sect. 5.

28. Unifying in a type 5 way in terms of the eight facets of unity of Ch. 3, Sect. 5.

29. For an account of 19th-century physics, see P. M. Harman (1982).

30. Type 6 unification.

31. For good informal expositions of SR and GR, see Einstein (1920); d'Abro (1950); Thorne (1994).

32. Wheeler (1968), in particular, has argued that the universe might consist of nothing more than a topologically complicated but otherwise empty space-time.

33. Type 8 unification.

34. Type 5 unification.

35. As I have already indicated, and as I shall argue at greater length in Ch. 7, the astonishing unifying power of QT is marred by the failure of the ortho-dox version of the theory to stand on its own feet, independently of some part of classical physics, required for a treatment of measurement. For lucid, non-technical expositions of QT, see Squires (1994); Rae (1986); Penrose (1990, ch. 6). For excellent textbook introductions, see Gillespie (1973); Feynman *et al.* (1965: iii); French and Taylor (1979).

36. For a non-technical account of QED, see Feynman (1985). For a not too technical exposition of the elements of QED plus discussion of some of the conceptual problems, see Auyang (1995). For an excellent history of the development of QED, see Schweber (1994). For textbook introductions, see Mandl and Shaw (1984); Aitchison and Hey (1982); or Griffiths (1987).

37. QED thus exhibits type 6 unity. For more detailed, if rather more technical, accounts of the gauge invariance of MT and QED, see Moriyasu (1983); Aitchison and Hey (1982, ch. 8); Griffiths (1987, ch. 11).

38. The positron was detected in 1931, the neutron in 1932; the neutrino, whose existence was first conjectured by Pauli in 1930, was first detected in 1956.

39. QEWD unifies in type 6 and 7 ways.

40. For non-technical accounts of QEWD, see: Adair (1987, ch. 15); 't Hooft (1989). For somewhat more technical accounts, see Kenyon (1987, chs. 2, 4, 5, 7, 8); Dodd (1984, pt. 5); Aitchison and Hey (1982, chs. 8–11); Moriyasu (1983).

41. For accounts of QCD, from the non-technical to the somewhat more tech-nical, see Adair (1987, ch. 14); 't Hooft (1989); Kenyon (1987, chs. 2, 4–6); Dodd (1984, pts. 2, 7); Aitchison and Hey (1982, chs. 8–10); Moriyasu (1983).

42. The gauge group of the Weinberg–Salam theory is $SU(2) \times U(1)$; this is a direct product of subgroups, which means that the theory lacks full unity; see Appendix and account of sixth type of unity in Ch. 3, Sect. 5.

43. QCD unifies in type 5 and 6 ways.

44. In other words, whereas the Boscovichian blueprint demands type 4 or 5 unity, what might be termed the Yang–Mills blueprint of locally gauge invariant quantum field theories demands type 6 unity (although type 5 unity may still be relevant, as it is in connection with QCD).

45. A part of the reason for the lack of unity of SM is that the local gauge group of the theory is a direct product. (A group G is a direct product of subgroups, A and B, written $G = A \times B$ if: (*a*) For any element a in A and any element b in B, $ab = ba$; (*b*) Every element g in G can be written in a unique way as $g = ab$.) The gauge group of QEWD (partially unifying the electromagnetic and weak forces) has the form $U(1) \times SU(2)$, and the gauge group of SM, consisting of QEWD plus QCD, has the form $U(1) \times SU(2) \times SU(3)$. In attempting to unify the disunity of the standard model, physicists have proposed so-called 'grand unified theories' (GUTs) which have gauge groups that are *not* direct products of subgroups: the simplest of these, proposed by Georgi and Glashow, takes the group $SU(5)$ as its gauge group. (For a non-technical account of this GUT, see Georgi 1989. Original papers introducing this and other candidate unifying theories are reproduced in Zee 1982.) Georgi and Glashow's theory postulates twelve new bosons in addition to the twelve associated with the strong and electroweak forces of SM; despite doubling the number of particles associated with interactions, the theory has greater unity because the gauge group, $SU(5)$, is not a direct product of subgroups, unlike the gauge group of SM. GUTs, it should be noted, exploit type 6 unification in the same kind of way as QED, QEWD, and QCD do.

46. For a fascinating, non-technical discussion of string theory, some of it highly critical, with contributions from Schwartz, Witten, Green, Salam, Glashow, Feynman, Weinberg, and others, see Davies and Brown (1988).

47. For a discussion of this notion of a probabilistic necessitating property, or 'propensity', its relevance to interpreting probabilistic quantum theory, and how it differs from Popper's closely related propensity notion, see Ch. 7, and Maxwell (1976*a*, 1985*b*, 1988*a*).

48. See Maxwell (1966, 1968*a*, 1968*b*, forthcoming, *b*, and esp. 1984*a*, ch. 10).

49. Essentialism is necessary for physical comprehensibility, but it is not sufficient. We can imagine a universe which is such that there is a physical theory of everything, *T*, which is true even when interpreted essentialistically (so that there are necessary connections between successive events); but if *T* lacks unity or is aberrant, the universe is not physically comprehensible.

50. This is an amended version of Goodman's argument concerning 'grue' and 'bleen': see Goodman (1954).

51. In order to solve Goodman's paradox, it is essential to distinguish two ways of interpreting his argument. Modifying Goodman's notions slightly, let us say that an object is grue if it is green before time *t*, blue after *t*; and that it is bleen if it is blue before *t*, green after *t*. The two interpretations are as follows. (1) The aliens have the same notion of 'invariance' as we do, and hold that objects that are grue and bleen do not change at *t* (with respect to our common notion of 'do not change') because *terminology*, 'grue' and 'bleen', does not change. (2) The aliens have a different notion of 'invariance' from ours, so that, for them, objects that are grue and bleen do not change at time *t*, i.e. the *content* of 'grue' and 'bleen' do not change, though in this case the *terminology* does change for them, in that for us the terminology remains constant at *t*. The nub of the solution to Goodman's paradox is as follows (taking the two interpretations in turn). (1) It is just false that invariance of terminology implies invariance of content: 'grue' and 'bleen' are counter-examples. As far as science and induction are concerned, what matters is *content* and not, in the first instance, terminology or form. (2) As far as science and induction are concerned, it is *our* notion of invariance that matters, not some crazy alien notion.

52. I am assuming, here, that *G* is a continuous group. The order of *G* is the number of continuously varying parameters needed to specify the members of *G*. I assume, further, that the elements of *G* can be put into one-to-one correspondence with the points of a subset of an *n*-dimensional space, where *n* is the order of *G*. *G* is simply connected if this subset is simply connected. A space is connected if a continuous curve joins any two points in the space; it is simply connected if any closed curve in the space can be contracted continuously to a point.

53. For the genesis of field theories, see Hesse (1965, ch. VIII) and Berkson (1974).

54. This in itself requires that the new ideas can be related to pre-existing ideas—so that some pre-existing mathematical structure can stand as a model for the new structure.

CHAPTER 5

1. In effect problems (i) + (ii) = problem (v), just as problem (iii) = problem (iv), even though this does not always seem to be appreciated in the philosophical literature.

2. For earlier expositions of this approach to the problem of induction, see Maxwell (1972*a*, 1974, 1976*b*, 1977, 1979, 1984*a*, ch. 9, 1993*c*). My proposed solution to the problem of induction has some features in common with Mill (1973–4, book 3, ch. 3); Keynes (1921); Russell (1948, pt. VI); Popper (1959); Reichenbach (1938); Lakatos (1970). The basic difference between any of these views and the one I argue for here is that, as AOE requires, I stress

the need to consider a hierarchy of increasingly attenuated cosmological conjectures implicit in the methods of science, low-level conjectures requiring revision as knowledge advances which in turn leads to revision of associated methods. This difference is decisive from the standpoint of solving the problem of induction. I might add that, in recent years, an approach to inductive learning, along Reichenbach lines, has been developed which does not assume fixed methods, namely *formal learning theory*; see Osherson *et al.* (1986). This is however, in other respects, thoroughly standard empiricist in conception, and its highly restrictive assumptions concerning computability render it inapplicable to physics. For critical assessments of the theory, see Earman (1992); Howson and Urbach (1993: 434–7).

3. See Mill (1973–4, book 3, ch. 3); Keynes (1921); Russell (1948, pt. VI); Clifford (1886). For an excellent critical discussion of these views, see Watkins (1984: 92–8). The approach can be traced back further to the so-called rationalism of philosophers such as Descartes and Leibniz, and the qualified rationalism of Kant.

4. Russell (1948: 506) argues that *five* postulates are 'required to validate scientific method'. These postulates are not, however, ordered with respect to content and implication in the way specified by AOE: they are all on the same level and may, therefore, be treated as five components of one composite postulate.

5. The important notion of 'empirical fruitfulness' will be defined below.

6. A cosmological thesis, P_a may very well be fruitful if not too false, that is if some other, vaguer cosmological thesis, P_b, is true. In other words, given the truth of P_b, P_a is fruitful even though false. (The truth of P_b ensures, as it were, that P_a is not too false.)

7. In what follows in the text, the distinction between 'apparent' and 'real' empirical success will be important, and so I indicate here what the distinction is. By an 'apparently' empirically successful research programme I mean one which has led to *real* empirical success at level 1 even though empirical success at level 2 (the level of laws and theories) is only apparent because endlessly many aberrant research programmes with associated aberrant theories could be regarded as being equally successful empirically. (A *theory* is apparently empirically successful if it successfully predicts phenomena (including surprising phenomena etc.); a *research programme* is apparently empirically successful if it produces a succession of theories that exemplify increasingly well the basic idea of the programme, at some level between 3 and 7 inclusive, *and at the same time* are increasingly apparently successful empirically. It is much more demanding for a programme to be apparently empirically successful than a theory.)

It might be thought that the distinction between real and apparent empirical success is artificial because empirical knowledge, as far as physics is concerned at least, is itself lawlike; the distinction between level 1 and 2 dissolves. But descriptions of experimental results can always be couched in terms of dispositional properties of things, and this need not be regarded as being equivalent to asserting universal laws. Asserting that a bit of apparatus is a copper wire involves attributing dispositional properties to the thing in question (such as having the disposition to melt at such-and-such a temperature, conduct electricity in such-and-such a way, and so on); such an assertion need not imply that the thing in question would have the same dispositional properties everywhere, at all times and places, and throughout all conditions; much less need it imply that *all* pieces of copper-like material have these dispositional properties everywhere. There is a real distinction between level 1 and level 2 knowledge; it is not merely a matter of degree: and, leading on from that, there is a real distinction between apparent and real empirical success (of theories and research programmes).

8. As evidence changes so too what we are justified in accepting at any level from 1 to 7 at least may change as well. In practice, of course, arguments for accepting P_r, given P_{r+1} and P_1, for some r, may depend on how fertile our imagination is in thinking up good rivals to P_r. This is the case even in connection with proofs in mathematics; see Lakatos (1976). In this context I use the word 'proof' in the Lakatosian sense, as a spur to thinking up fruitful counter-examples rather than as a soporific to stop further thought.

9. The following is a slightly amplified version of the criteria for choosing cosmological assumptions formulated in Sect. 6 of Ch. 3.

10. It is in connection with these notions that the solution to the justificational problem of induction being proposed here calls upon the solution to the problem of simplicity put forward in the last chapter.

11. The more nearly a theory, T, can be formulated in terms of *one* Lagrangian, with *one* physical interpretation and *one* set of symmetries with an appropriate group structure, so the greater is its degree of Lagrangian-simplicity. SM + GR, with its three distinct Lagrangians, corresponding to QEWD, QCD, and GR, fails to exemplify the Lagrangian blueprint as well as a hypothetical string theory which has just *one* Lagrangian; SM + GR does not, in other words, have as high a degree of Lagrangian-simplicity.

12. In addition, as I have already indicated, recent developments in theoretical physics having to do with duality suggest that the Lagrangian approach needs to be superseded; see Isham (1997: 194–7).

13. It is above all to Lakatos (1970) that we owe the idea of construing science in terms of competing research programmes, those that are empirically progressive triumphing over those less progressive in character. There are, however, major differences between Lakatos's conception and use of research programmes and mine. (Lakatos was defending a version of SE.) We may, nevertheless, construe Fig. 1, and the 'proof' of the induction theorem, as displaying science as a number of nested research programmes, the 'hard cores' of these programmes becoming increasingly contentless

and epistemologically secure as we ascend from level 3 to level 10 ('hard core' here having a meaning different from Lakatos's).

14. 'Empirical adequacy' has here a meaning quite different from that given to it in van Fraassen (1980).

15. However, the discussion of blueprint development, from the corpuscular hypothesis to Einstein, in Sect. 4 of Ch. 3, casts doubt on this conclusion.

16. This is not quite correct: abrupt, catastrophic changes in our environment might occur because of the arrival in our vicinity of hitherto undetected physical entities, such as small black holes, for example: this could be compatible with P_4, compatible, indeed, with current level 2 theories.

17. Generalized AOE was defined in Sect. 6 of Ch. 3.

18. How could we discover that the universe is meta-knowable (if it is)? One way would be to assess the relative merits of rival existing methods or research programmes for the acquisition of knowledge, from the standpoints of both productivity and reliability. Another would be to vary existing methods in an attempt to develop better methods. Another would be to attempt to make explicit, and to develop, methods for improving knowledge that have up to then been only implicit in the way of life and culture. Yet another would be to put forward some hypothesis about the ultimate nature of the universe which depicts the universe as meta-knowable in some way, and then attempt to discover whether the methods (or research programme), that the hypothesis predicts should be successful, do in practice yield reliable new knowledge. All this is possible because of the assumption that there already exists some knowledge, and some capacity to improve knowledge. The reliability of new methods, and the relative merits of different methods, can be determined by comparing them with pre-existing knowledge and methods.

   All this requires, of course, considerably more intellectual maturity than humanity has, on the whole, managed to exhibit so far. It requires the capacity to doubt the efficacy of existing methods for acquiring knowledge, the ability to entertain the possibility that new methods can be discovered or invented, and the ability to assess the relative merits of rival methods.

19. See n. 7.

20. This is one way (amongst others) in which I part company with Kant, who held that ultimate reality, the noumenal world, is unknowable.

21. Two such cosmological theses are the following. *Patchwork physicalism*: The universe is such that different theories apply in different space-time regions. *Local physicalism*: The universe behaves as if physicalism is true in the particular space-time region we have lived in and interacted with so far; elsewhere, the universe behaves differently.

22. See n. 7 for a definition of 'apparent empirical success'.

23. 'Real' empirical success means success at level 2, at the level of laws and theories, and not just success at level 1, the level of evidence, which is all that 'apparent' success involves.

24. There is positive feedback between new knowledge, and new knowledge-about-how-to-acquire-new-knowledge. As knowledge improves, know-ledge-about-how-to-improve-knowledge improves as well.

25. Further details can be added so that the result is nearer to the actual course taken by the development of human knowledge and modern science. Research programmes can be added which, after some apparent initial empirical success, meet with lack of success. Prejudice against acknowledg-ing the cosmological and metaphysical dimensions of science can be added; religious views can be added that are upheld, not for their empirical pro-gressiveness but out of a desire for reassurance. And so on.

26. See n. 7 for this crucial distinction between *apparent* and *real* empirical success.

27. For further discussion of dispositional or 'necessitating' properties, see Maxwell (1968a, 1993c: ii) and Sect. 14 of the previous chapter.

28. It is important to appreciate that *content* and *unity* (or explanatoriness) are, in general, almost bound to be at odds with one another. Granted a mass of disunified information, we can always increase unity by throwing away information (i.e. by decreasing content); and granted that we possess some unified nugget of information, this unity can easily be destroyed by adding on a mass of disparate information (i.e. by increasing content). The miracle of science is that, as science has developed, the *content* and the *unity* of knowledge have *both increased*, to an astonishing extent. It is this extraor-dinary feature of science which tempts one most strongly to conclude: what science is trying to tell us about the nature of the universe is that it is fundamentally unified, i.e. comprehensible. More precisely, it is this feature of science which makes strong unity such an empirically fruitful conjecture.

29. This is not to deny the validity of the rather different argument, spelled out during the proof of the induction theorem, that strong unity has greater empirical fruitfulness than weak unity, and is to be preferred on that account. I return to this point in my reply to objection 6 of Sect. 9.

30. In Ch. 4 nothing was said about different branches of science having some-what different methods. But that this is to be expected follows immediately from the basic tenet of AOE that *methods* are liable to vary with varying *aims*. In so far as the proper aims of chemistry, molecular biology, ethology, or psychoneurology differ from one another, and differ from theoretical physics, it is to be expected that *methods* will differ as well. There are other factors that can influence what methods are adopted in a given scientific discipline. Experiments, vital within physics, have a more limited role to play within astronomy and cosmology, for practical reasons, and within human psychoneurology, for moral reasons. Experiments are not so important within historical or geographical sciences such as geology, or aspects of observational astronomy.

31. Some contemporary philosophers, of course, reject this argument, and hold that physicalism, narrowly interpreted, can do justice to everything it seems

to leave out (sensory qualities, consciousness, etc.); see e.g. J. J. C. Smart (1963).

32. See Maxwell (1984*a*, ch. 10, 1966, 1968*b*, forthcoming, *b*).

33. Asymptotic physicalism was defined in Sect. 3 above to assert: The universe is such that infinitely many theoretical revolutions are required before its ultimate structure can be correctly and completely captured by means of a true, unified 'theory of everything'.

34. This is an improved version of Goodman's argument concerning 'grue' and 'bleen'; see Goodman (1954).

35. Objections 4 and 5, directed against arguments 2 and 3 of step $r = 9$ of the proof of the induction theorem, justifying acceptance of non-maliciousness, can be reformulated so as to be directed against the argument of step $r = 4$ and criterion (vii) of that step. (vii) asserts that cosmological conjectures which lead to methods that remain invariant through theoretical revolutions are to be preferred, other things being equal. However, my replies, 4 and 5, can also be reformulated to counter these objections.

36. But it does not satisfy criterion (vii): reasons for rejecting the more general conjecture that the universe is comprehensible in some non-physicalist way, spelled out in step $r = 4$ of the proof of the induction theorem, apply also to the special case that the universe is comprehensible because God exists.

CHAPTER 6

1. See Ch. 2, Sect. 10 for a discussion of the problem.

2. Given NT, precisely the right initial conditions, and nothing external to the system disturbing its evolution, the two spheres move in circular orbits with uniform speeds about the point midway between them. Interestingly enough, given GR, this is no longer the case: the rotating spheres radiate gravitational waves, and thus, very gradually lose energy. The spheres slowly spiral inwards—something that has been observed in the case of a double star system.

3. And on the other hand if it is precisely true when applied to all physically possible systems that differ slightly from the symmetric systems then, granted physicalism, it will be readily extendable to become T.

4. Some examples were indicated in Sect. 10 of Ch. 2.

CHAPTER 7

1. Those unfamiliar with quantum theory should consult the Appendix before reading further.

2. It is sometimes claimed that orthodox quantum field theory (QFT) solves the wave/particle problem, in that, according to orthodox QFT, 'particles' are no more than excitations of the quantum field. But if orthodox QFT solved the problem, it would provide a consistent model of the quantum field, with no need to call upon measurement to give physical content to the theory. In fact orthodox QFT is just as dependent on measurement in this respect as non-relativistic OQT is. Orthodox QFT does not solve the problem.

3. Many hold that the fundamental problem posed by OQT is the so-called problem of measurement. (Some, absurdly, have even interpreted this as the problem of showing that measurement evolves in accordance with the Schrödinger time-dependent equation!) But, as we shall see in Sect. 2, the wave/particle problem is the *fundamental* problem posed by OQT; the solution to this problem would supply QT with its own quantum ontology, and would eliminate measurement from the postulates of QT altogether. The problem of measurement is the misbegotten child of the failure to solve the wave/particle problem.

4. See Maxwell (1972*b*, 1973*a,b*, 1976*a*, 1982, 1985*b*, 1988*b*, 1993*a,f*, 1995*a*, and esp. 1988*a*, 1994*a*).

5. See Band and Park (1973); for my reply, see Maxwell (1973*b*).

6. See Bedford and Wang (1975, 1977); Bussey (1984).

7. It ought perhaps to be admitted that there is a sense in which OQT can be interpreted realistically, even essentialistically: the ψ-function can be interpreted as attributing what may be called micro–*macro* essentialistic (or dispositional) properties to quantum systems, properties which determine the probabilistic way in which quantum systems interact with macro measuring instruments. However, such a micro–macro interpretation of OQT does not free OQT of its dependence on some additional theory for a treatment of measurement, and thus does not cure OQT of the five defects to be discussed. In order to do this it is necessary to interpret QT in such a way that the theory attributes what may be called micro–micro properties to quantum entities, properties which determine (perhaps probabilistically) how micro-entity interacts with micro-entity. It is the lack of this kind of *micro-realistic* interpretation which is the root cause of the six defects of OQT to be discussed.

8. For earlier expositions of these arguments, see my publications referred to in n. 4.

9. It is perhaps not quite clear what this would consist of, given that 'observables' are an essential part of the purely quantal aspect of OQT, and observables contain, implicitly, a reference to measurement and hence to whatever additional theory is invoked to deal with measurement.

10. See Wigner (1970, ch. 12); Fine (1970); Maxwell (1972*b*).

11. The severely *ad hoc* character of OQT means, in addition, that OQT is seriously non-explanatory (despite its predictive power), in that the more

ad hoc a theory is, the less is its explanatory power. A single-minded proponent of bare SE, however, might not recognize explanation as a proper goal for science. At the moment I am considering only those defects of OQT which even the most hardline proponent of bare SE ought to recognize.

12. Defects (*a*) and (*b*) can also be regarded as indicating that OQT is defective as an explanatory theory: but I am here considering only those defects that any proponent of SE would recognize.

13. For a discussion of decoherence, see Omnès (1994).

14. The 'consistent histories' approach to QT attempts to get round this problem, but fails in that it is obliged to presuppose measurement in the present, if not in the past.

15. Decoherence, and consistent history, approaches to QT attempt to get round this defect of OQT; these approaches do not succeed, for reasons already indicated.

16. How right Einstein was when he remarked: 'one simply cannot get around the assumption of reality—if only one is honest. Most . . . [physicists] simply do not see what sort of risky game they are playing with reality—reality as something independent of what is experimentally established'. (Letter to Schrödinger, 22 Dec. 1950, in Przibram 1967: 39.)

17. Elsewhere I have argued (Maxwell 1993*a*) that the above points, (i) to (vi), tell not just against the instrumentalistic theory OQT; they tell also against instrumentalism itself.

18. The idea that interpretative problems of QT can be solved, and realism be upheld, by means of a probabilistic or propensity interpretation of the theory we owe primarily to Popper (1957, 1967, 1982), even though, as Popper himself has pointed out, Born, Heisenberg, Dirac, Eddington, Jeans, and Landé have on occasions made remarks in this direction (Popper 1982: 130–5), and Margenau's *latency* view may be held to amount to a propensity interpretation of QT (Margenau 1950). Popper's approach is, however, in crucial respects different from the one put forward here; as a result it fails to solve the wave/particle problem, and does not, in the end, issue in a realist interpretation of QT (see Maxwell 1976*a*: 285–6, 1985*b*: 41–2).

19. In opposition to this it may be argued that Bohmian quantum theory reproduces the predictions of OQT precisely, and hence QT itself cannot be said to favour either probabilism or determinism. Nevertheless, OQT (as opposed to QT as such) has the character of a theory that postulates two kinds of change: deterministic evolutions of state in the absence of measurement, and probabilistic transitions when measurements are made.

20. For further details concerning PQT, see Maxwell (1976*a*, 1982, 1988*a*, 1994*a*).

21. For the distinction between preparation and measurement, see Margenau (1954).

22. See Jammer (1966: 112–14); Pais (1982: 405–12).
23. For further details concerning this version of PQT, see Maxwell (1988*a*, 1994*a*).

APPENDIX

1. For a marvellous, entirely non-technical account of the role of symmetry and group theory in theoretical physics, see Zee (1986). For more technical expositions of the elements of group theory relevant to physics, in increasing difficulty, see Rosen (1983); Joshi (1982); Isham (1989); Jones (1990). See also Moriyasu (1983).
2. Inertial motion is uniform motion in a straight line with respect to any one of infinitely many privileged reference frames—so-called 'inertial' reference frames—all moving with uniform velocity with respect to each other, and in terms of which the (relevant) laws of physics (such as Newton's law of gravitation) are valid. This last clause rules out a set of reference frames all accelerating off at the same constant rate in some direction, or a set of rotating reference frames.
3. Physicists usually characterize a symmetry of a theory, T, as corresponding to a type of physical transformation performed on isolated systems to which T applies that leave the Hamiltonian unchanged. (The Hamiltonian is an expression for the total energy of the system.) It is not hard to show, however, that the requirement that the Hamiltonian is invariant under such transformations is equivalent to the demand that the transformations commute with the time evolution operator, that is, leave the evolutions of the systems unaffected. This latter way of characterizing a symmetry seems, however, closer to the intuitive idea of what a symmetry of a theory is.
4. Equivalence classes are defined as follows. Given a set of objects (such as all possible systems to which a theory, T, applies), then a binary relation, R, between the objects (such as '. . . can be rotated into . . .') divides the set into mutually exclusive subsets called equivalence classes if and only if the following holds. Given any objects (systems), s_1, s_2, and s_3, in any one subset, then: (1) s_1Rs_1; (2) s_1Rs_2 implies s_2Rs_1; and (3) s_1Rs_2 and s_2Rs_3 imply s_1Rs_3.
5. For a more detailed account of the downfall of the discrete symmetries, P, CP, and T, see Pais (1986; ch. 20).
6. For a discussion and proof of Noether's theorem, see Goldstein (1980: 588–96).
7. This point is made by Houtappel *et al.* (1965). See also Redhead (1975).
8. A quick answer is that if T is devoid of symmetry, then it will fail to satisfy many, if not all, of the facets of unity discussed in Sect. 5 and 6 of Ch. 3. These eight facets of unity do not, however, define 'unity': it is certainly the

case that some of these possible facets of unity will turn out to be irrelevant to the particular way in which the universe is unified. The question is: Could they all be irrelevant? Could there be a meaningful notion of unity devoid of symmetry?

REFERENCES

ADAIR, R. K. (1987), *The Great Design: Particles, Fields and Creation* (Oxford University Press, Oxford).

AITCHISON, I. J. R. (1985), 'Nothing's Plenty: The Vacuum in Modern Quantum Field Theory', *Contemporary Physics*, 26: 333–91.

——and HEY, A. J. G. (1982), *Gauge Theories in Particle Physics* (Adam Hilger, Bristol), pt. III.

ARMSTRONG, D. (1978), *A Theory of Universals* (Cambridge University Press, Cambridge).

——(1983), *What is a Law of Nature?* (Cambridge University Press, Cambridge).

ASIMOV, I. (1987), *Asimov's New Guide to Science* (Penguin, Harmondsworth).

ATKINS, P. W. (1983), *Molecular Quantum Mechanics* (Oxford University Press, Oxford).

AUYANG, S. Y. (1995), *How is Quantum Field Theory Possible?* (Oxford University Press, Oxford).

AYER, A. J. (1956) *The Problem of Knowledge* (Penguin, Harmondsworth).

BAND, W., and PARK, J. L. (1973), 'Comments Concerning "A New Look at the Quantum Mechanical Problem of Measurement"', *American Journal of Physics*, 41: 1021–2.

BARKER, S. F. (1957), *Induction and Hypothesis* (Cornell University Press, Ithaca, NY).

BARNES, B. (1985), *About Science* (Blackwell, Oxford).

——and BLOOR, D. (1982), 'Relativism, Rationalism, Sociology of Knowledge', in M. Hollis and S. Lukes (eds.), *Rationality and Relativism* (Blackwell, Oxford), 21–47.

BEDFORD, D., and WANG, D. (1975), 'Towards an Objective Interpretation of Quantum Mechanics', *Nuovo Cimento*, 26B: 313–25.

————(1977), 'A Criterion for Spontaneous State Reduction', *Nuovo Cimento*, B37: 55–62.

BELL, J. S. (1987), *Speakable and Unspeakable in Quantum Mechanics* (Cambridge University Press, Cambridge).

BERKELEY, G. (1957), *A New Theory of Vision [1709] and Other Writings* (J. M. Dent, London).

BERKSON, W. (1974), *Fields of Force* (Routledge & Kegan Paul, London).

BLOOR, D. (1976), *Knowledge and Social Imagery* (Routledge & Kegan Paul, London).

BOHM, D. (1952), 'A Suggested Interpretation of the Quantum Theory in Terms of "Hidden" Variables', I and II, *Physical Review*, 85: 166–79, 180–93.

BOHR, N. (1949), 'Discussion with Einstein on Epistemological Problems of Atomic Physics', in P. A. Schilpp (ed.), *Albert Einstein: Philosopher-Scientist* (Open Court, La Salle, Ill.), 199–241.

BOSCOVICH, R. J. (1966), *A Theory of Natural Philosophy*, trans. J. M. Child (first pub. 1763; MIT Press, Cambridge, Mass.).

BROWN, T. A. (1992), *Genetics: A Molecular Approach* (Chapman & Hall, London).

BUCHWALD, J. (1985), *From Maxwell to Microphysics* (Chicago University Press, Chicago).

BURTT, E. A. (1932), *The Metaphysical Foundations of Modern Physical Science* (Routledge & Kegan Paul, London).

BUSSEY, P. J. (1984), 'When Does the Wavefunction Collapse?', *Physics Letters*, 106A: 407–9.

CARNAP, R. (1950), *Logical Foundations of Probability* (Routledge & Kegan Paul, London).

CARRIGAN, R., and TROWER, W. P. (eds.) (1989), *Particle Physics in the Cosmos: Readings from Scientific American* (W. H. Freeman, New York).

CLIFFORD, W. K. (1886), *Lectures and Essays*, ed. L. Stephens and R. Pollock (Macmillan, London).

COLLINGRIDGE, D. (1985), 'Reforming Science', *Social Studies of Science*, 15: 763–9.

CRONIN, H. (1991), *The Ant and the Peacock* (Cambridge University Press, Cambridge).

D'ABRO, A. (1950), *The Evolution of Scientific Thought* (Dover, New York).

DAVIES, P. C. W., and BROWN, J. (eds.) (1988), *Superstrings: A Theory of Everything?* (Cambridge University Press, Cambridge).

DAWKINS, R. (1986), *The Blind Watchmaker* (Longman, Harlow).

DESCARTES, R. (1949), *A Discourse on Method etc.* (first pub. 1637; J. M. Dent, London).

DIEUDONNÉ, J. (1960), *Foundations of Modern Analysis* (Academic Press, London).

DIJKSTERHUIS, E. J. (1969), *The Mechanization of the World Picture* (Oxford University Press, Oxford).

DODD, J. E. (1984), *The Ideas of Particle Physics: An Introduction for Scientists* (Cambridge University Press, Cambridge).

DRETSKE, F. (1977), 'Laws of Nature', *Philosophy of Science*, 44: 248–68.

DUHEM, P. (1954), *The Aim and Structure of Physical Theory* (Princeton University Press, Princeton).

EARMAN, J. (1992), *Bayes or Bust? A Critical Examination of Bayesian Confirmation Theory* (MIT Press, Cambridge, Mass.).

EASLEA, B. (1986), *Journal of Applied Philosophy*, 3: 139–40.

EINSTEIN, A. (1920), *Relativity, the Special and General Theory* (Methuen, London).

—— (1949), 'Autobiographical Notes', in P. A. Schilpp (ed.), *Albert Einstein: Philosopher-Scientist* (Open Court, La Salle, Ill.), 1–94.

—— (1954), *Ideas and Opinions* (Souvenir Press, London).

FEYERABEND, P. (1978), *Against Method* (Verso, London).

—— (1982), *Science in a Free Society* (Verso, London).

—— (1987), *Farewell to Reason* (Verso, London).

FEYNMAN, R. P. (1985), *QED* (Princeton University Press, Princeton).

——LEIGHTON, R., and SANDS, M. (1965), *The Feynman Lectures on Physics*, i, ii, and iii (Addison-Wesley, Reading, Mass.).

FINE, A. (1970), 'Insolubility of the Quantum Measurement Problem', *Physical Review*, D2: 2783–7.

—— (1986), *The Shaky Game* (Chicago University Press, Chicago).

FRANK-KAMENETSKII, M. D. (1993), *Unravelling DNA* (VCH Publications, New York).

FRENCH, A. P., and TAYLOR, E. F. (1979), *An Introduction to Quantum Physics* (Thomas Nelson, Walton-on-Thames).

FRIEDMAN, M. (1974), 'Explanation and Scientific Understanding', *Journal of Philosophy*, 71: 5–19.

—— (1983), *Foundations of Space-Time Theories: Relativistic Physics and Philosophy of Science* (Princeton University Press, Princeton).

GEORGI, H. (1989), 'A Unified Theory of Elementary Particles and Forces', in Carrigan and Trower (1989: 53–77).

GHIRARDI, G. C., RIMINI, A., and WEBER, T. (1986), 'Unified Dynamics for Microscopic and Macroscopic Systems', *Physical Review*, D34: 470–91.

GILLESPIE, D. T. (1973), *A Quantum Mechanical Primer* (International Textbook Company, Aylesbury).

GLYMOUR, C. (1980), *Theory and Evidence* (Princeton University Press, Princeton).

GOLDSTEIN, H. (1980), *Classical Mechanics* (John Wiley, New York).

GOODMAN, N. (1954), *Fact, Fiction and Forecast* (Athlone Press, London).

—— (1972), *Problems and Projects* (Bobbs-Merrill, New York).

GRIFFITHS, D. (1987), *Introduction to Elementary Particles* (John Wiley, New York).

GUTHRIE, W. K. C. (1978), *A History of Greek Philosophy*, i and ii (Cambridge University Press, Cambridge).

HARMAN, G. (1965), 'The Inference to the Best Explanation', *Philosophical Review*, 74: 88–95.

—— (1968), 'Enumerative Induction as Inference to the Best Explanation', *Journal of Philosophy*, 64: 529–33.

HARMAN, P. M. (1982), *Energy, Force and Matter: The Conceptual Development of Nineteenth-Century Physics* (Cambridge University Press, Cambridge).

HEMPEL, C. G. (1965), *Aspects of Scientific Explanation* (Free Press, New York).

HENDRY, J. (1989), *British Journal for the History of Science*, 22: 246–7.

HESSE, M. (1965), *Forces and Fields* (Littlefield, Adams, Totowa, NJ).

——(1974), *The Structure of Scientific Inference* (Macmillan, London).

HOLTON, G. (1978), *The Scientific Imagination* (Cambridge University Press, Cambridge).

HOOKYAS, R. (1973), *Religion and the Rise of Modern Science* (Scottish Academic Press, Edinburgh).

HOUTAPPEL, R., VAN DAM, H., and WIGNER, E. P. (1965), 'The Conceptual Basis of Use of the Geometric Invariance Principles', *Reviews of Modern Physics*, 37: 595–632.

HOWSON, C., and URBACH, P. (1993), *Scientific Reasoning: The Bayesian Approach* (Open Court, La Salle, Ill.).

HUME, D. (1959), *A Treatise of Human Nature*, book 1 (first pub. 1739; J. M. Dent, London).

HUNT, B. J. (1991), *The Maxwellians* (Cornell University Press, New York).

ISHAM, C. J. (1989), *Lectures on Groups and Vector Spaces for Physicists* (World Scientific, London).

——(1993), 'Canonical Quantum Gravity and the Problem of Time', in L. A. Ibort and M. A. Rodriguez (eds.), *Integrable Systems, Quantum Groups, and Quantum Field Theories* (Kluwer Academic, London), 157–288.

——(1997), 'Structural Issues in Quantum Gravity', in *General Relativity and Gravitation: GR 14* (World Scientific, Singapore), 167–209.

JAMMER, M. (1966), *The Conceptual Development of Quantum Mechanics* (McGraw-Hill, New York).

JEFFREYS, H. (1957), *Scientific Inference* (Cambridge University Press, Cambridge).

——and WRINCH, D. (1921), 'On Certain Fundamental Principles of Scientific Enquiry', *Philosophical Magazine*, 42: 269–98.

JONES, H. F. (1990), *Groups, Representations and Physics* (Adam Hilger, Bristol).

JOSHI, A. W. (1982), *Elements of Group Theory for Physicists* (Wiley Eastern, New Delhi).

KAKU, M. (1993), *Quantum Field Theory* (Oxford University Press, Oxford).

KANT, I. (1961), *Critique of Pure Reason* (first pub. 1781; Macmillan, London).

KENYON, I. R. (1987), *Elementary Particle Physics* (Routledge & Kegan Paul, London).

KEYNES, J. M. (1921), *A Treatise on Probability* (Macmillan, London).

KITCHER, P. (1976), 'Explanation, Conjunction and Unification', *Journal of Philosophy*, 73: 207–12.

——(1981), 'Explanatory Unification', *Philosophy of Science*, 48: 507–31.

——(1989), 'Explanatory Unification and Causal Structure', in P. Kitcher and W. C. Salmon (eds.), *Scientific Explanation, Minnesota Studies in the Philosophy of Science*, xiii (University of Minnesota Press, Minneapolis), 428–48.

KNELLER, G. F. (1978), *Science as a Human Endeavor* (Columbia University Press, New York).

KOYRÉ, A. (1958), *From the Closed World to the Open Universe* (Harper & Brothers, New York).

——(1968), *Metaphysics and Measurement* (Chapman & Hall, London).

KUHN, T. S. (1970), *The Structure of Scientific Revolutions* (Chicago University Press, Chicago).

KYBURG, H. E. (1970), *Probability and Inductive Logic* (Collier Macmillan, London).

LAKATOS, I. (1970), 'Falsification and the Methodology of Scientific Research Programmes', in I. Lakatos and A. Musgrave (eds.), *Criticism and the Growth of Knowledge* (Cambridge University Press, Cambridge), 91–196.

——(1976), *Proofs and Refutations* (Cambridge University Press, Cambridge).

LANCZOS, C. (1970), *Space through the Ages* (Academic Press, London).

LAUDAN, L. (1977), *Progress and its Problems* (University of California Press, Berkeley).

——(1980), 'A Confutation of Convergent Realism', *Philosophy of Science*, 48: 19–48.

——(1984), *Science and Values* (University of California Press, Berkeley).

LEIBNIZ, G. W. (1956), *Philosophical Writings* (J. M. Dent, London).

LIPTON, P. (1991), *Inference to the Best Explanation* (Routledge, London).

LOCKE, J. (1961), *An Essay Concerning Human Understanding* (first pub. 1690; J. M. Dent, London).

LONGUET-HIGGINS, C. (1984), 'For Goodness' Sake', *Nature*, 312: 204.

LUCAS, J. (1985), *Space, Time and Causality* (Oxford University Press, Oxford).

LYCAN, W. (1988), *Judgement and Justification* (Cambridge University Press, Cambridge).

MACHIDA, S., and NAMIKI, M. (1984), 'Macroscopic Nature of Detecting Apparatus and Reduction of Wave Packet', in S. Kamefuchi *et al.* (eds.), *Foundations of Quantum Mechanics* (Physical Society of Japan, Tokyo).

MANDL, F., and SHAW, G. (1984), *Quantum Field Theory* (John Wiley, New York).

MARGENAU, H. (1950), *The Nature of Physical Reality* (McGraw-Hill, New York).

——(1954), 'Advantages and Disadvantages of Various Interpretations of the Quantum Theory', *Physics Today*, 7–10: 6–13.

MARSHAK, R. E. (1993), *Conceptual Foundations of Modern Particle Physics* (World Scientific, London).

MAXWELL, N. (1966), 'Physics and Common Sense', *British Journal for the Philosophy of Science*, 16: 295–311.

——(1968a), 'Can there be Necessary Connections between Successive Events?', *British Journal for the Philosophy of Science*, 19: 1–25; repr. in Swinburne (1974: 149–74).

MAXWELL, N. (1968*b*), 'Understanding Sensations', *Australasian Journal of Philosophy*, 46: 127–46.

—— (1972*a*), 'A Critique of Popper's Views on Scientific Method', *Philosophy of Science*, 39: 131–52.

—— (1972*b*), 'A New Look at the Quantum Mechanical Problem of Measurement', *American Journal of Physics*, 40: 1431–5.

—— (1973*a*), 'Alpha Particle Emission and the Orthodox Interpretation of Quantum Mechanics', *Physics Letters*, 43A: 29–30.

—— (1973*b*), 'The Problem of Measurement—Real or Imaginary?', *American Journal of Physics*, 41: 1022–5.

—— (1974), 'The Rationality of Scientific Discovery', I and II, *Philosophy of Science*, 41: 123–53, 247–95.

—— (1975), 'Does the Minimal Statistical Interpretation of Quantum Mechanics Resolve the Measurement Problem?', *Methodology and Science*, 8: 84–101.

—— (1976*a*), 'Towards a Micro Realistic Version of Quantum Mechanics', I and II, *Foundations of Physics*, 6: 275–92, 661–76.

—— (1976*b*), *What's Wrong with Science? Towards a People's Rational Science of Delight and Compassion* (Bran's Head Books, Frome).

—— (1977), 'Articulating the Aims of Science', *Nature*, 265: 2.

—— (1979), 'Induction, Simplicity and Scientific Progress', *Scientia*, 114: 629–53; Italian trans. 655–74.

—— (1980), 'Science, Reason, Knowledge and Wisdom: A Critique of Specialism', *Inquiry*, 23: 19–81.

—— (1982), 'Instead of Particles and Fields: A Micro Realistic Quantum "Smearon" Theory', *Foundations of Physics*, 12: 607–31.

—— (1984*a*), *From Knowledge to Wisdom: A Revolution in the Aims and Methods of Science* (Blackwell, Oxford).

—— (1984*b*), 'From Knowledge to Wisdom: Guiding Choices in Scientific Research', *Bulletin of Science, Technology and Society*, 4: 316–34.

—— (1985*a*), 'From Knowledge to Wisdom: The Need for an Intellectual Revolution', *Science, Technology and Society Newsletter*, 21: 55–63.

—— (1985*b*), 'Are Probabilism and Special Relativity Incompatible?', *Philosophy of Science*, 52: 23–44.

—— (1986), 'The Fate of the Enlightenment: Reply to Kekes', *Inquiry*, 29: 79–82.

—— (1987), 'Wanted: A New Way of Thinking', *New Scientist*, 14 May, 63.

—— (1988*a*), 'Quantum Propensiton Theory: A Testable Resolution of the Wave/Particle Dilemma', *British Journal for the Philosophy of Science*, 39: 1–50.

—— (1988*b*), 'Are Probabilism and Special Relativity Compatible?', *Philosophy of Science*, 55: 640–5.

—— (1991), 'How Can we Build a Better World?', in J. Mittelstrass (ed.), *Einheit der Wissenschaften. Internationales Kolloquium der Akademie der Wissenschaften zu Berlin* (Walter de Gruyter, Berlin), 388–427.

—— (1992*a*), 'What Kind of Inquiry Can Best Help us Create a Good World?', *Science, Technology and Human Values*, 17: 205–27.

—— (1992*b*), 'What the Task of Creating Civilization Has to Learn from the Success of Modern Science: Towards a New Enlightenment', *Reflections on Higher Education*, 4: 47–69.

—— (1993*a*), 'Does Orthodox Quantum Theory Undermine, or Support, Scientific Realism?', *Philosophical Quarterly,* 43: 139–57.

—— (1993*b*), 'Can Academic Inquiry Help Humanity Become Civilized?', *Philosophy Today*, 13: (May), 1–3.

—— (1993*c*), 'Induction and Scientific Realism: Einstein versus van Fraassen', I, II, and III, *British Journal for the Philosophy of Science*, 44: 61–79, 81–101, 275–305.

—— (1993*d*), 'Science for Civilization', *Ethical Record*, 98: 12–17.

—— (1993*e*), 'On Relativity Theory and Openness of the Future: A Reply', *Philosophy of Science*, 60: 341–8.

—— (1993*f*), 'Beyond Fapp: Three Approaches to Improving Orthodox Quantum Theory and an Experimental Test', in A. van der Merwe, F. Selleri, and G. Tarozzi (eds.), *Bell's Theorem and the Foundations of Modern Physics* (World Scientific, London), 362–70.

—— (1994*a*), 'Particle Creation as the Quantum Condition for Probabilistic Events to Occur', *Physics Letters*, A187: 351–5.

—— (1994*b*), 'Towards a New Enlightenment: What the Task of Creating Civilization Has to Learn from the Success of Modern Science', in R. Barnett (ed.), *Academic Community: Discourse or Discord?* (Jessica Kingsley, London), 86–105.

—— (1995*a*), 'A Philosopher Struggles to Understand Quantum Theory: Particle Creation and Wavepacket Reduction', in M. Ferrero and A. van der Merwe (eds.), *Fundamental Problems in Quantum Physics* (Kluwer Academic, London), 205–14.

—— (1995*b*), 'The Evolution of Consciousness', *Ethical Record*, 100/4: 16–19.

—— (1996), 'Are there Objective Values?', *Ethical Record*, 101/4 (Apr.), 3–6.

—— (1997), 'Science and the Environment: A New Enlightenment', *Science and Public Affairs* (Spring), 50–6.

—— (forthcoming, *a*), *The Odd Couple*.

—— (forthcoming, *b*), *How Can there be Life of Value in the Physical Universe?*

MIDGLEY, M. (1986), 'Is Wisdom Forgotten?', *University Quarterly*, 40: 425–7.

MILL, J. S. (1973–4), *A System of Logic*, in *Collected Works of John Stuart Mill*, ed. J. M. Robson, vii, viii (University Press, Toronto).

MILLER, D. (1974), 'Popper's Qualitative Theory of Verisimilitude', *British Journal for the Philosophy of Science*, 25: 166–77.

MOORE, J. (1994), *Science as a Way of Knowing: The Foundations of Modern Biology* (Harvard University Press, Cambridge, Mass.).

MORIYASU, K. (1983), *An Elementary Primer for Gauge Theory* (World Scientific, Singapore).

NEWTON, I. (1962), *Principia*, ii, trans. in 1729 by A. Motte and F. Cajori (first pub. 1687; University of California Press, California).

NEWTON-SMITH, W. H. (1981), *The Rationality of Science* (Routledge & Kegan Paul, London).

NIINILUOTO, I. (1987), *Truthlikeness* (Reidel, Boston).

ODDIE, G. (1989), 'The Unity of Theories', in F. D'Agostino and I. Jarvie (eds.), *Freedom and Rationality: Essays in Honor of John Watkins* (Kluwer, Dordrecht), 343–68.

OKUN, L. B. (1985), *Particle Physics: The Quest for the Substance of Substance* (Harwood Academic, London).

OMNÈS, R. (1994), *The Interpretation of Quantum Mechanics* (Princeton University Press, Princeton).

OSHERSON, D. N., STOB, M., and WEINSTEIN, S. (1986), *Systems that Learn* (MIT Press, Cambridge, Mass.).

PAIS, A. (1982), *'Subtle is the Lord...': The Science and the Life of Albert Einstein* (Oxford University Press, Oxford).

——(1986), *Inward Bound: Of Matter and Forces in the Physical World* (Oxford University Press, Oxford).

PEARLE, P. (1989), 'Combining Stochastic Dynamical State-Vector Reduction with Spontaneous Localization', *Physics Review*, A39: 2277–89.

PEIRCE, C. S. (1934), 'The Fixation of Belief', in *Collected Papers of Charles Sanders Peirce*, ed. C. Hartshorne and P. Weiss (Harvard University Press, Cambridge), v, 223–47.

PENROSE, R. (1975), 'Twistor Theory, its Aims and Achievements', in C. J. Isham, R. Penrose, and D. W. Sciama (eds.), *Quantum Gravity* (Clarendon Press, Oxford), 268–407.

——(1986), 'Gravity and State Vector Reduction', in C. J. Isham and R. Penrose (eds.), *Quantum Concepts in Space and Time* (Oxford University Press, Oxford), 129–46.

——(1990), *The Emperor's New Mind* (Vintage, London).

PERCIVAL, I. C. (1994), 'Primary State Diffusion', *Proceedings of the Royal Society of London*, 447: 189–209.

POINCARÉ, H. (1952), *Science and Hypothesis* (Dover, New York).

POPPER, K. R. (1957), 'The Propensity Interpretation of the Calculus of Probability and the Quantum Theory', in S. Körner (ed.), *Observation and Interpretation* (Butterworth, London), 65–70.

——(1959), *The Logic of Scientific Discovery* (first pub. 1934; Hutchinson, London).

——(1961), *The Poverty of Historicism* (Routledge & Kegan Paul, London).

——(1962), *The Open Society and its Enemies* (Routledge & Kegan Paul, London).

——(1963), *Conjectures and Refutations* (Routledge & Kegan Paul, London).

——(1967), 'Quantum Mechanics without "The Observer"', in M. Bunge (ed.), *Quantum Theory and Reality* (Springer, Berlin), 7–44.

——(1972), *Objective Knowledge* (Oxford University Press, Oxford).

——(1982), *Quantum Theory and the Schism in Physics* (Hutchinson, London).

PRZIBRAM, K. (1967) (ed.), *Letters on Wave Mechanics* (Philosophical Library Inc., New York).

RAE, A. (1986), *Quantum Physics: Illusion or Reality?* (Cambridge University Press, Cambridge).

RAILTON, P. (1989), 'Explanation and Metaphysical Controversy', in P. Kitcher and W. C. Salmon (eds.), *Scientific Explanation, Minnesota Studies in the Philosophy of Science*, xiii (University of Minnesota Press, Minneapolis), 220–52.

REDHEAD, M. (1975), 'Symmetry in Intertheory Relations', *Synthese*, 32: 77–112.

REICHENBACH, H. (1938), *Experience and Prediction* (Chicago University Press, Chicago).

RESCHER, N. (1992), *A System of Pragmatic Idealism*, i: *Human Knowledge in Idealistic Perspective* (Princeton University Press, Princeton).

ROHRLICH, F. (1989), 'The Logic of Reduction: The Case of Gravitation', *Foundations of Physics*, 19: 1151–70.

ROSEN, J. (1983), *A Symmetry Primer for Scientists* (John Wiley, New York).

RUSSELL, B. (1948), *Human Knowledge: Its Scope and Limits* (Allen & Unwin, London).

SALMON, W. (1989), *Four Decades of Scientific Explanation* (University of Minnesota Press, Minneapolis).

SCHUTZ, B. F. (1989), *A First Course in General Relativity* (Cambridge University Press, Cambridge).

SCHWEBER, S. (1994), *QED and the Men who Made It* (Princeton University Press, Princeton).

SHAPIN, S. (1994), *A Social History of Truth* (University of Chicago Press, Chicago).

——and SCHAFFER, S. (1985), *Leviathan and the Air-Pump* (Princeton University Press, Princeton).

SILK, J. (1989), *The Big Bang: The Creation and Evolution of the Universe* (Freeman, New York).

SINCLAIR, W. A. (1945), *An Introduction to Philosophy* (Oxford University Press, London).

SMART, J. J. C. (1963), *Philosophy and Scientific Realism* (Routledge & Kegan Paul, London).

SMART, W. M. (1953), *Celestial Mechanics* (Longmans, Green, London).

SMITH, J. M. (1993), *The Theory of Evolution* (Cambridge University Press, Cambridge).

SOBER, E. (1975), *Simplicity* (Oxford University Press, Oxford).

SPINOZA, B. (1955), *Works of Spinoza*, ii (Dover, New York).

SQUIRES, E. (1985), *To Acknowledge the Wonder* (Adam Hilger, Bristol).

SQUIRES, E. (1994), *The Mystery of the Quantum World* (Institute of Physics, Bristol).

SWINBURNE, R. (ed.) (1974), *The Justification of Induction* (Oxford University Press, Oxford).

'T HOOFT, G. (1989), 'Gauge Theories of the Forces between Elementary Particles', in Carrigan and Trower (1989: 78–105).

THORNE, K. (1994), *Black Holes and Time Warps: Einstein's Outrageous Legacy* (Picador, London).

TICHÝ, P. (1974), 'On Popper's Definition of Verisimilitude', *British Journal for the Philosophy of Science*, 25: 155–60.

TOOLEY, M. (1977), 'The Nature of Law', *Canadian Journal of Philosophy*, 7: 667–98.

TRIGG, R. (1993), *Rationality and Science* (Blackwell, Oxford).

VAN FRAASSEN, B. (1980), *The Scientific Image* (Clarendon Press, Oxford).

——(1985), 'Empiricism in the Philosophy of Science', in P. M. Churchland and C. A. Hooker (eds.), *Images of Science* (University of Chicago Press, Chicago), 259–60.

——(1989), *Laws and Symmetry* (Clarendon Press, Oxford).

WATKINS, J. W. N. (1984), *Science and Scepticism* (Princeton University Press, Princeton).

——(1991), 'Scientific Rationality and the Problem of Induction: Responses to Criticisms', *British Journal for the Philosophy of Science*, 42: 343–68.

WEINBERG, S. (1977), *The First Three Minutes* (André Deutsch, London).

——(1993), *Dreams of a Final Theory* (Hutchinson, London).

WHEELER, J. A. (1968), 'Superspace and the Nature of Quantum Geometrodynamics', in C. M. DeWitt and J. A. Wheeler (eds.), *Battelle Rencontres* (Benjamin, New York), 242–307.

WHEWELL, W. (1989), *Theory of Scientific Method*, ed. with introd. by R. E. Butts (Hackett, Indianapolis).

WIGNER, E. P. (1970), *Symmetries and Reflections* (MIT Press, Cambridge, Mass.).

ZEE, A. (ed.) (1982), *Unity of Forces in the Universe*, i (World Scientific, Singapore).

——(1986), *Fearful Symmetry* (Macmillan, New York).

ZIMAN, J. (1968), *Public Knowledge* (Cambridge University Press, Cambridge).

INDEX